California Studies in Food and Culture

DARRA GOLDSTEIN, EDITOR

The publisher gratefully acknowledges the generous support
of the Humanities Endowment Fund of the University
of California Press Foundation.

————————

The publisher also gratefully acknowledges the generous
support of the Director's Circle of the University of California
Press Foundation, whose members are:

Clarence & Jacqueline Avant
Nancy & Roger Boas
Janelle Cavanagh & Dominic Walshe
Earl & June Cheit
Charles R. & Mary Anne Cooper
Lloyd Cotsen
John & Jo De Luca
Carol & John Field
Walter S. Gibson
Prof. Mary-Jo DelVecchio Good & Prof. Byron Good
Mrs. Charles Hine
Edmund & Jeannie Kaufman
Patricia & Robin Klaus
Carole & Ted Krumland
Diane Leslie
David Littlejohn
Thomas & Barbara Metcalf
Margaret L. Pillsbury
Ramsay Family Foundation
Lucinda Reinold
Tommi & Roger Robinson
Barclay & Sharon Simpson
Marc & Rowena Singer
Peter J. & Chinami S. Stern

THE COOKBOOK LIBRARY

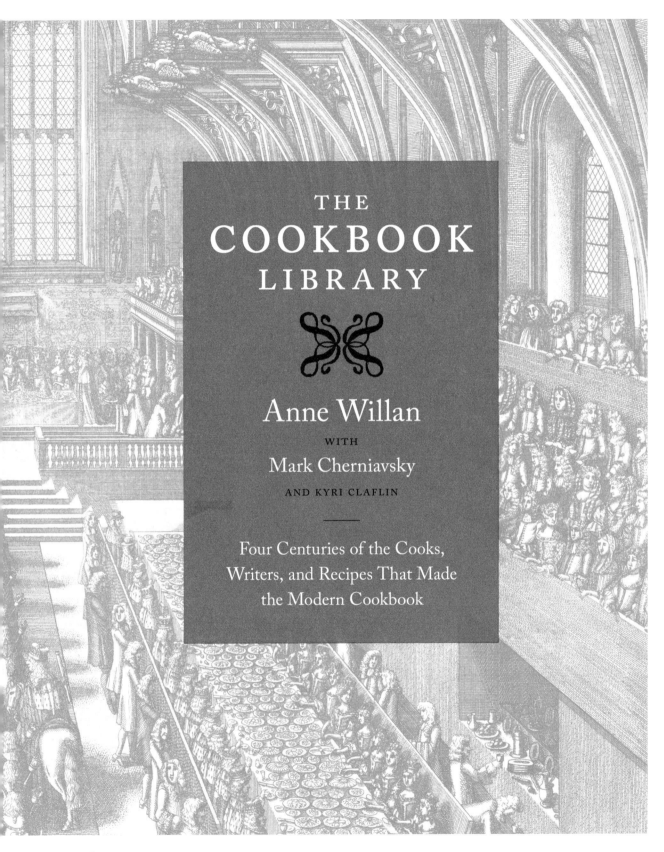

THE
COOKBOOK
LIBRARY

Anne Willan

WITH

Mark Cherniavsky

AND KYRI CLAFLIN

Four Centuries of the Cooks,
Writers, and Recipes That Made
the Modern Cookbook

University of California Press   *Berkeley Los Angeles London*

To Mark Cherniavsky
Sine Quo Non
Without Whom Nothing

CONTENTS

OUR LIBRARY

THIS BOOK BEGAN IN 1966, when Mark and I were first married and I worked at *Gourmet* magazine. Mark was already a collector of used books, mainly on travel, but nothing antiquarian nor even scarce. At *Gourmet* I had become familiar with the magazine's small but select cookbook collection, using it every day to pursue my humble task of answering readers' letters. I knew which books were most useful, and during the following months, we pursued all of them in used bookstores wherever we went. The partnership has continued: Mark collects our books, I put them to use.

The experience of gathering what is now a distinguished collection of antiquarian cookbooks and associated texts fired me with a passion for discovery. Trying out old recipes intensified my curiosity about where they came from. Who wrote them, and cooked them, and ate the finished dishes? How do they fit into their time? Regardless of the cookbook author's primary purpose, for Mark and myself what has mattered most is what a book says about cooking. If we found a book that discusses an important aspect of the subject in some depth and contains recipes, we tried to add it to our collection.

No library is ever complete. Mark and I have concentrated on English and French books, as these are the languages in which we are at ease. Over the years we have focused on the older (and more valuable) sixteenth- and seventeenth-century books, sometimes in Latin. The pride of our collection is Scappi's *Opera*, a treasury that displays Renaissance printing and illustration at its finest. Our smattering of Italian is helpful here, as it is with our other half dozen early Italian books. As collectors, we rarely go for works in Spanish or German, as we are comfortable in neither language, but we rely on translations where they exist. Early American cookbooks hardly enter the time span we cover in this book (1474–1830), though we do have the first (and only) edition of *New-England Cookery* by Lucy Emerson (1808). As for the oldest book in our collection, *De institutis coenobiorum* (On the Management of Monastic Communities, 1491), neither of us can make sense of Latin despite several years of studying it in school. But we turn the book's sturdy five-hundred-year-old pages with pleasure, in awe of their longevity.

Every collector has a personal relationship with his or her books. Mark can close his eyes and picture the size and color of the spine of every one of our antiquarian books, needing no catalog to find them on the shelves. The feel in the hand, the density of type, the condition, robust or frail, pristine or battered, allow us to know each book as we would know an old friend. We find that facsimiles—photo reproductions—of old books and reprints in which the text is reproduced in a different layout and typeface do not evoke the same empathy, though they are extraordinarily useful working tools, standing in for the very old or rare cookbooks to be found only in national libraries or museums. The most famous such understudy in our collection is Samuel Pegge's *The Forme of Cury* of 1780, which is a rendering of the original recipe manuscript commissioned by King Richard II of England around 1390. Perhaps 15 percent of our antiquarian cookbooks are facsimiles or reprints, the production of which has become a cottage industry in several countries.

Books about cooking are far more varied than those that are simply cookbooks with recipes. For us, a great strength has been Mark's more general interest in seventeenth- and eighteenth-century history, biography, and travel journals—the last being particularly enticing when the author enjoyed eating on the road. I have an abiding vision of Mark squashed in an airplane seat on a flight from Los Angeles to San Francisco reading Erasmus on the inferior food in German inns in the early sixteenth century. At the most unexpected times, he offers me eighteenth-century quotes from Dr. Johnson on women cookbook writers (derogatory) or a sixteenth-century traveler's tale of drinking sorbet in Turkey (ecstatic). Years ago Mark introduced me to the gossiping Reverend Richard Warner, whose anecdotes of Elizabethan banquets are scurrilous but whose record of medieval feasting menus in *Antiquitates culinariae* (1791) is definitive. So between the two of us, Mark and I view old cookbooks in a wider context than as simple compendiums of recipes or guides to the work of the kitchen.

We have enjoyed an international life, and so have met many cookbook authors, whether in practice or by proxy in their books. Together we have lived in four countries, and I have taught cooking classes in nearly a dozen. For his work with the World Bank, Mark must have visited at least double that number, and all along the way, he has looked for, and often found, old cookbooks in several languages. Even Taillevent in the 1390s gave recipes for a *brouet d'ailmegne* (Germany) and a *brouet d'engleterre* (England) in *Le viandier* (The Victualler). From the sixteenth century on, cooks enjoyed international careers and dubbed recipes *à la parisienne* or *alla bolognese* according to their provenance. The more worldly ones scattered references to a dozen or more places throughout their texts. Many cookbooks themselves have had an international outreach. The vestiges of the fifteenth-century library of the dukes of Burgundy now reside in the Bibliothèque Nationale in Brussels, once part of the Burgundian domains. Our copy of Domenico Romoli's *La singolare dottrina* (The Exceptional Doctrine, 1560) once belonged to an anonymous Bolognese buyer of 1590, as well as to a certain

Christopher Rechlinger of Augsburg, who inscribed his name on the flyleaf. Catherine de' Medici possessed a copy of Scappi's *Opera* in her personal library.

Every time we open an old cookbook, we find something new. One of my discoveries was that the four earliest European printed cookbooks were written by working cooks in four different countries and four separate languages. The facts were already known, but no one seems to have put them together. For his part, Mark solved a mystery in the fourth edition (1751) of *The Art of Cookery Made Plain and Easy* (1747), written "By A Lady." He knew from his reading of bibliographies, but the book dealer did not, that this very rare edition holds the vital clue to the identity of the mysterious author. How proud he was to have outwitted an expert! Smaller pleasures include little anecdotes that hint at an author's love of cinnamon, or wild game, or strong drink. The books of Carême, artworks in their own right, lead directly to Escoffier and the master chefs of today. These treasures are just a start. Please join us on this enthralling journey through old cookbooks.

ACKNOWLEDGMENTS

We wish to thank:

Darra Goldstein, commissioning editor, who brought us all together.

Sheila Levine, University of California Press associate director and publisher, whose vision kept us on the right path.

Dore Brown, Adrienne Harris, and Sharon Silva, editors who have made outstanding contributions to the finished book.

Nola Burger, whose design and visual talent bring history alive.

Photographer John Kiffe, an image maker of distinction.

Kyri Claflin, whose contribution was so instrumental in laying the foundations of this book.

Todd Schulkin and Lisa Ekus, advisers and friends on so many fronts.

Randall Price, recipe tester and taster extraordinaire.

Assistant editors Angelika Lintner, Christine Matsuda, Claire Parker, Anna Watson, and Elizabeth Weinstein.

Consultants Laura Calder, Elizabeth Evans, Varena Forcione, Jenn Garbee, Carl Schulkin, Timothy Shaw, George Wanklyn, and Carolin C. Young.

And the many trainees at La Varenne Cooking School who have helped shape this book over the years.

Working with all of you has been a pleasure.

Anne Willan and Mark Cherniavsky

THE WORLD IN A COOKBOOK

O LD COOKBOOKS ARE CAPTIVATING, and important too, leading us into the
world beyond the hearth. Without them, we could not have tasted our way
down the centuries to the dishes we embrace with such affection today. This
book began as a personal account of Mark's and my collection of cookbooks and
culinary images. It has gradually expanded to be a more general history of European
and early American cookbooks, though always seen from a personal viewpoint. We've
made some surprising, illuminating connections between the way people lived and
the books they used.

What is a cookbook? First, it is a collection of recipes—blueprints for a cook to re-
create a dish. More specifically, according to cookbook bibliographer Henry Notaker,
"A cookbook is a book with about two-thirds cookery instruction and . . . at least
40–50 percent in recipe form."[1] Surprisingly early, right from the start of the age of
printing, a number of published books fit this description. The recipes in them may be
embryonic, expressed in just a few lines, but their purpose of instruction is clear. Early
books with recipes covered far wider topics as well. Some sought to preserve the wisdom
of the ancients, others offered advice on how to live a healthy life, and still others were
preoccupied with glorifying the banquets and feasts of a wealthy patron. In later
centuries, the voices of the authors come through more clearly and, indeed, a few such
books seem designed to showcase a personality rather than to instruct their readers.

In writing about the evolution of cookbooks, I have separated chapters by century
(rarely does an author overlap from one century to the next). The first chapter gives
an outline of manuscript cookbooks before printing began. The opening date for the
main text, that of the first printed cookbook in 1474, was easy to determine. The close-
out of 1830 allows a little leeway for the geopolitical map drawn at the Congress of
Vienna in 1815 to become firmly established, opening avenues for cookbooks to develop
that were to remain clearly defined for almost a century.

The first four printed cookbooks are known as incunabula, from the Latin word for
"swaddling clothes," which came to be used figuratively in nineteenth-century England
for the "childhood" of books, denoting those printed with moveable type before 1501.
These early books were intended for the small audience of professionals who already

knew how to cook, serving more as an exchange of ideas among the initiated than as instruction manuals for the novice. Each was published in a different country and compiled in a different language—Latin, French, German, or English. From these books' roots grew many genres. The sixteenth century brought cookbooks intended for the maître d'hôtel, or steward responsible for managing the household of a wealthy nobleman or a prince of the church. Their authors gave space to organizing elaborate banquets and planning menus; recipes were numerous but sometimes played a secondary role. Many aimed to enhance the reputation of their patrons or employers. A famous early example is *Banchetti composizioni di vivande e apparecchio generale* (Banquets, Composition of Dishes and General Presentation, 1549), by Cristoforo di Messisbugo, steward at the famous court of Alfonso d'Este, duke of Ferrara. Around the same time, a new prototype author appeared, the gentleman dilettante who enjoyed spending time in his kitchen, which he sometimes described as his laboratory. He discussed cooking, but within the broader context of distillation and other scientific or medical experiments. Some cookbook writers were also medical doctors, one example being Nostradamus, famous for his astrological predictions.

Later books often explored cooking in combination with gardening. For example, Nicolas de Bonnefons's *Les delices de la campagne* (The Pleasures of the Countryside, 1654) includes excellent advice on how to cook garden produce. This book, together with François Pierre de la Varenne's *Le cuisinier françois* (The French Cook, 1651), strongly influenced the evolution of French classical cuisine. (As a good luck talisman, I kept a copy of *Le cuisinier françois* in my desk drawer when I opened La Varenne Cooking School in Paris in 1975.) In England at the same time, books containing household advice began to appear regularly. Many, such as Gervase Markham's *The English Hous-wife* (1615), were primarily recipe books that provided extensive instructions for preparing food and drink, whereas others, such as Hannah Woolley's *The Gentlewomans Companion* (1673), emphasized domestic conduct side by side with the practicalities of cooking. In England from the seventeenth century on, many books about cooking were written *by* women for a readership *of* women. These books were the seminal influence in the kitchens of the new nation of America.

The words on the pages of old cookbooks reveal the cooks themselves. An almost messianic fervor is characteristic of many great cooks, no matter what their nationality. In his *Opera*, Scappi addresses the young man who is his chosen successor: "I [took] you on as an apprentice and instruct[ed] you to the fullest of my ability in all that makes up the very best of my profession . . . making you a knowledgeable and astute expert in the art, so that . . . all my work and practical experience . . . should remain in you."[2] This ideal of passing knowledge and practical expertise from generation to generation likely stemmed from the apprenticeship structure common in many kitchens. In large establishments, cooks were ranked in a formal hierarchy, almost military in its precision—an organizational structure that was already developed in medieval times and remains firmly entrenched in today's French professional kitchen. Such a

Nature. f. in fine pnm g̃. b̃. in ĩ p g̃ .melioꝛ eꞇ eis .camoſa ſbꞇilis coꝛꞇi
as.Jnuaniꞇuꝛ· conſeruꞇ ſꞇomaco flegmaꞇico pleno ſupfluiꞇaꞇib꜡ noꝛu
mentum taꝛde deſcenduꞇ a ſꞇomaco ꝛemoꞇio noꝛumenꞇ .
aieuimis ſupꞇa

ABOVE *Tacuinum sanitatis* was a treatise on health and hygiene written in Arabic in the eleventh century by Ibn Butlân, a Christian physician born in Baghdad. When the book was first printed in Latin and then highly illustrated in the mid-1470s, it had immediate and long-lasting success. Ibn Butlân recommended a healthy life in harmony with nature, and the more than two hundred images illuminate everyday life in medieval Italy. He talks of the seasons, food and drink, sleep, and the humors of body and mind. The original *Tacuinum sanitatis* was republished by fascist dictator Benito Mussolini in the twentieth century as part of a celebration of Italian heritage.

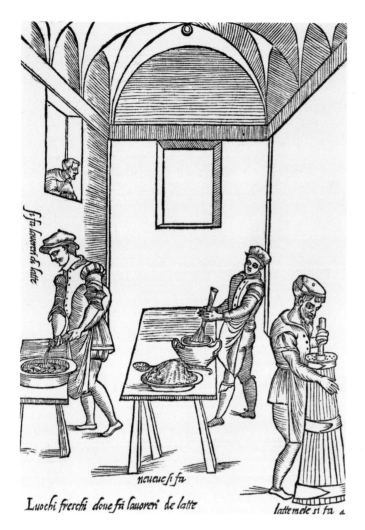

Luochi freschi doue fu lauoreri de latte

pattern was rarely found in England, and then usually in kitchens headed by a French-trained chef.

English cooks took a different path, opting to write household books on cooking at home for the family. The importance of a well-ordered home kitchen became a central topic in sixteenth-century England, first promoted by male authors and then by women writers, who supplemented their recipes with earnest advice for the novice and the poorly educated about menus and marketing, diet and medicine, brewing and preserving, the management of staff, and, inevitably, financial economy. The first books were lively, venturing into a new world of exciting ingredients and semiscientific discoveries. Later household works became more evangelical, useful no doubt but less warmhearted.

Until the eighteenth century, writing cookbooks was a sideline. Then as now, few authors could expect to earn a living from books about cooking (hence Hannah Glasse's second career as a dressmaker). Promotional ideas began as early as the sixteenth century, when an author's portrait might be used as a frontispiece or titles might allude to a famous personage, as in *The Queen's Closet Opened* (W.M., 1655). The acknowledgment of a patron, which had customarily appeared at the opening of a cookbook, gradually gave way to a first-person preface with declamatory statements about the superiority of the author above all rivals. Publishers began to piggyback on the reputation of a known author; for example, several texts were attributed to La Varenne but almost certainly not written by him. Yet another approach was to solicit subscribers as a guarantee of revenue before publication.

If cookbooks did not enrich their authors' purses, they did enhance their reputations. Chef François Menon wrote eight cookbooks in twenty years, not just to record his knowledge but also to ensure his professional success in the competitive environ-

ABOVE This early 1596 edition of Bartolomeo Scappi's *Opera*, one of the most authoritative cookbooks of any century, was printed in Venice and contains nearly thirty woodcuts chronicling life in the kitchens of the time. Here in the "cold room for working with milk," cooks are pouring milk from a bag, whisking cream, and churning milk, probably to make butter. For cleanliness, all three are wearing hats and aprons. Scappi is one of the first cooks to give complete cooking instructions and include little asides on what to do in tricky moments and how to avoid disaster.

ment of mid-eighteenth-century Paris. With the establishment of restaurants and gentlemen's clubs with fine dining rooms toward the end of the century, the chefs at these elite venues began writing cookbooks for their patrons to take home, thus making the general public aware of what delicacies they might be missing. As a further twist, in the free and easy atmosphere of the early Napoleonic era, Grimod de la Reynière actually made a business of selling his personal journal, the *Almanach des gourmands* (perhaps benefiting from free dinners in the many restaurants he reviewed).

In the four centuries after the first four printed cookbooks appeared, they moved far beyond the role of simply documenting what happened in the kitchen. As we'll see, they became textbooks, memoirs, dietary guides, gardening manuals, scientific treatises, restaurant guides, and even political tracts, as well as leaders of fashion into the future.

About This Book

One of my roles has been testing and tasting recipes from each century for inclusion in this book. I've embarked with excitement on the pungent spiced sauces of medieval times, moving through the massive roasts and *ragoûts* of Louis XIV's court to the elegance of eighteenth-century chilled and molded desserts. All the recipes are from books in our collection, and for each, I note the edition in which it appears—often a first and usually an early edition. Within each chapter, recipes appear in the order of their date of printing. The style of the text is a whole other subject, as I explore in "The Writing of a Recipe." I have chosen the recipes both to represent their century and to be accessible to today's home cooks. Most are easy to prepare: Carême's apple soufflé (1815), for example, calls for just three ingredients. A few are more challenging: Hannah Glasse's Yorkshire Christmas Pie (1747) calls for five different birds, all boned and reshaped one inside another to bake inside a robust, freestanding wall of pastry crust. The modern recipes follow the old as closely as possible, though the early authors can be difficult to interpret, their mind-set and methods of cooking being inevitably so far from our own. In all of these dishes, I've looked for that little element of surprise, the opportunity to try an odd combination of ingredients or a new way of doing things.

Each chapter in this book has two parts: text interspersed with boxes and a separate section of recipes (translated into English as needed) with notes and renderings for the modern kitchen. Boxes supplement the text and add a contemporary slant, covering subjects such as women in the kitchen and changes in the use of sugar. Spelling was not standardized in Europe or the United States until recently. For this reason, the spellings of book titles and authors' names in the text may not match what appears in the images. Unless otherwise stated, the English translations in the text and recipes are by me or Mark. Where a published English translation is cited, quotations in the text have come from this version. All images are from our cookbook and print collection, unless otherwise stated. Bon appétit!

THE WRITING
OF A RECIPE

When I set out to explore the style and content of recipe texts, I had certain expectations. I assumed that at the dawn of printing, culinary recipes would be just a few lines, with rare measurement of ingredients and minimal directions. The details that we look for today—precise quantities, with comprehensive, step-by-step instructions for the finished dish—would be lacking. I also believed that as time advanced, recipes would become longer and more precise, with authors providing more background details and flourishes. The reality is far more complex.

The word *recipe* in all the Latinate languages shares the root *recipere*, meaning "to receive," which when conjugated in the imperative becomes *recipe*. Sources agree that "recipe" (or "receipt") originally meant a medicinal formula, with the first English usage of the term appearing in the late fourteenth century. Recipes were a valuable tool, giving readers access to expert advice on how to achieve consistent results when making remedies for gout or headache, curative wines and herbal infusions, hair dye and skin cream, as well as tasty dishes. Doctors, alchemists, apothecaries, and cooks came to depend on these formulas. One eleventh- or twelfth-century poem addressed to Robert of Normandy, son of William the Conqueror, sums up the benefits: "Every man may be a Graduate, and proceed [as] Doctor in the ordering of his owne body."[1]

Though rare, cooking instructions existed long before cooks developed the notion of a "recipe"; they appear in manuscripts at least as far back as the fourth century—for example, in Apicius's *De re coquinaria* (On Cooking). By the fourteenth century, cooking instructions were still uncommon, though in his manuscript cookbook *Forme of Cury*, King Richard II's master cook precisely describes the ingredients of dishes and explains how to cook and serve them.[2] Printing brought books of recipes into the kitchen, until at last in the late sixteenth century, the term *recipe* appeared in print to describe a specifically culinary preparation.[3]

In investigating the progress of printed recipes, I decided to follow the dish called "white eating," famous throughout Europe from medieval times to the present day under such names as *blancmange* in English, *blancmanger* in French, *bianco mangiare* in Italian, and *manjar blanco* in Spanish. Chaucer mentions "Blankmanger" in the prologue to his *Canterbury Tales* at the end of the fourteenth century. The dish itself changed radically over the centuries, but here I'm interested in the style and coherence of the recipe explanation and its value as an instructional sheet on the page.

The recipe for *cibaria alba* (white food) in *De honesta voluptate et valetudine*, the first printed cookbook, already had most of the key elements of a successful recipe.[4] Every recipe has two basic components: a description of the required ingredients, preferably in order of use, and a clear explanation of how to put them together. Other details—ingredient measurements, information on equipment, cooking times, serving suggestions—are secondary to the essentials. The style in which these elements are presented varies markedly over time and from

Cibaria alba.

CIbarium album, quod aptius leucophagū dicetur, hoc modo pro.xij.conuiuis cōdies Amygdalarū libras.ij.per noctem aqua maceratas, ac depilatas in mortario bene tundes, inspergendo modicum aquę, ne oleum faciant. Deinde capi pectus ex ossatum in eodem mortario conteres, indesq̨ excauatum panem, agresta prius aut iure macro remollitum. Gingiberis praeterea vnciam, ac saccari selibram addes, miscebisq̨ hęc oīa simul, mixtáq̨ per excretorium farinaceum in ollam mundam trāsmittes. Efferueat deinde in carbonibus lento igne facies, cochlearíq̨ saepe agitabis, ne seriæ adhęreat. Coctum vbi fuerit, aquę ro

In this recipe for *cibaria alba* (white food) from the first printed cookbook, *De honesta voluptate et valetudine*, 1520 edition, Bartolomeo Sacchi (Platina) acknowledges his debt to his friend, the "immortal" cook Martino of Como. The advice to add a little water to emulsify the oil when grinding almonds, along with many other such tips, most certainly came from Martino rather than from Platina. The recipes also include quantities for many ingredients, though little in the way of cooking instruction.

country to country. One author often echoes another, and recipes may include sections of text, and indeed whole recipes, from other authors, though usually with some rewording. We might call such borrowing plagiarism (a comparatively recent term), but in the early development of culinary recipes, cooks considered it a duty to pass on key knowledge to readers.

As the centuries pass, a structure emerges in the organization of recipes within cookbooks. The apparently random order of medieval dishes is gradually codified, first by arranging recipes in the order of serving—whether at the start, middle, or end of the meal. Grouping by ingredient rapidly follows, with particular attention to separating the foods permitted on fast days from those for feast days. Seventeenth-century authors further subdivide recipes according to cooking technique, with clear divisions for confectionery and pastry work. At this time, only a few little books of recipes focus on a single subject, such as preserving.

RECIPE TITLES & INTRODUCTIONS

Cookbook authors from Apicius onward give recipes titles to make them easy to identify on the page. Always, the goal has been to convey the maximum information as succinctly as possible. Titles in Platina, for example, range from Edible Birds to How to Cook a Peacock to simply Boiled Meats. At the same time, specialized descriptions appear such as *torta* (tart), *marzapanem* (almond paste), and *frictellae* (fritters). A few scattered national attributions are made, such as *Catellonica* (Catalonian) and *Florentinorum* (Florentine), reflecting the increasingly cosmopolitan outlook in Europe. During the next century, more technical terms creep in, such

BLANC-MANGER.

On sert du Blanc-manger dans l'Entremets, ou pour plat, ou pour hors-d'œuvres. Pour le faire, prenez des pieds de Veau, & une Poule qui ne soit pas tout-à-fait grasse. Il faut faire cuire tout cela sans sel, & le passer quand il est bien cuit, prenant garde qu'il ne soit ni trop fort, ni trop délicat. Si vous avez trop de gelée, ôtez-en : ensuite mettez-y du sucre, de la canelle, & de l'écorce de citron; & faites boüil-

In Blanc-manger (White Food), from *Le cuisinier roial et bourgeois* (1693) by François Massialot, the author intensifies the flavor of his meaty blancmange by adding a few bitter almonds, with hints on removing any fat that might sully the pristine white surface. He instructs that the dish may be served as an hors d'oeuvre, an entremet, or a main course.

as *fricassée* and *ragoût*, both familiar to us today. In the sixteenth century, Cristoforo di Messisbugo helpfully includes the number of servings in his titles, though the habit did not catch on. As time progressed, authors began to employ shorthand for familiar culinary terms.

The French were particularly adept at codifying terminology, until by the eighteenth century, an insiders' shorthand of French culinary terms had taken root. Recipe titles frequently invoke royalty, as in *à la reine* ("in the manner of the queen") to describe a mushroom wine sauce. Proper names are popular, such as *à la Béchamel* (after a modish marquis of the time) for a cream sauce. Regional names become associated with certain sources of key ingredients, such as *Germiny* (now a suburb of Paris), referring to sorrel in a dish, and *bourguignonne* for a gar-

nish of bacon, baby onions, mushrooms, and red wine.

Despite the increasing sophistication of recipe titles, they could be misleading. Authors, or even a single author, might use the same name to describe a variety of preparations. Early blancmange, for example, referred variously to a spiced purée of almonds and water, a dish that included fish, or white meats such as veal and chicken; the purée was thickened with bread or rice, and later with flour. Despite the literal meaning of the title "white eating," variations of blancmange were sometimes colored with saffron or red berries. Cooks also added more and more sugar over the years until blancmange gradually became a dessert. A familiar preparation might also hide under other names. In the seventeenth century, the title "blancmange" ▸

7

seems to have gone out of fashion in England, prompting Hannah Woolley to call the dish "blanched manchet" (a type of bread)—in other words, bread pudding. The "Whitpot" of Amelia Simmons, author of the first American cookbook, was a baked version of blancmange, yet another kind of bread pudding under a pastry cover.

Eventually, many recipe titles shared their position at the top of a recipe with headers, short introductions in which authors offered their personal takes on a dish. Even well before the advent of headers, the style of a recipe reflected the author—brusque or cursive, didactic or beguiling. For example, Guillaume Tirel, called Taillevent, author of *Le viandier* (The Victualler, c. 1486) wrote in a forthright manner that ensured that his book would remain in print for more than two hundred years. His instructions for *blanc mengier* are typical: "cook [capon] in water, pound almonds, and [add] pourable broth, so it is thickened."[5]

In early cookbooks, comments that would appear in headers today were often buried in the text, when they were made at all, so readers might need to do some detective work to find them. For example, hidden at the close of the recipe for *cibaria alba*, Platina reveals the source of many of his recipes: "What a cook, oh immortal gods, you bestowed in my friend Martino of Como, from whom I have received, in great part, the things of which I am writing."[6]

The familiar sales pitch that almost invariably precedes instructions today did not show up until toward the end of the nineteenth century, when the practice of presenting a separate ingredient list at the head of a recipe also began. Perhaps authors decided to include the header to offset the naked appearance of the new list of ingredients and their measurements.

Per fare mineſtra di bianco magnare   Cap. CLXII.

PIGLINOSI libre dodici, che ſon due boccali Romaneſchi, di latte di capra, ò di vacca freſco & graſſo, & paſſiſi per lo ſetaccio con ventidua oncia di farina di riſo nuouo di Salerno ò di Milano fatto nel modo che ſi dice nel Cap. 154. & come ſarà paſſata ogni coſa per lo ſetaccio, pōgaſi in vna baſtardella, ò cazzuola ſtagnata, & habbiaſi auuertenza, che eſſo vaſo ſia liſcio, perciocche molte volte le battiture del martello che ſon nel vaſo, ſon cagione che la viuanda ſi attachi, pongaſi eſſo vaſo con il latte al fuoco, cioè ſul trepiedi, ò ſul focone, & vengaſi a meſcolar cō la ſpatola, e come comincierà a ſcaldarſi, pōgauiſi un poco di ſale, & il petto d'vna gallina aleſſata morta in quel giorno, e ſfilato ſottile come il capello, lequali ſfilature prima che ſi pongano nel vaſo, ſi potranno ſbattare in vn'altro vaſo, con un bicchiero d'altro latte, & ſe ui ſi uorranno dare due, ò tre botte cō il piſtone nel mortaro di marmo, ſara in arbitrio, & dapoi un'altra uolta ſi ſbatteranno col latte, di modo che ſi uengano a ſeparare una dall'altra, & mettanoſi in eſſa baſtardella con tre libre di zuccaro fino, non mancando di meſcolarlo continuamente fin'a tanto che ſia

In Per Fare Minestra di Bianco Magnare (To Make Soup of White Food) from *Opera,* 1570, Bartolomeo Scappi sets a standard for future recipe writers. He includes precise quantities, specifying what equipment to use and presenting instructions in a logical order; when ingredients are lacking or of poor quality, he offers alternatives. As for the appearance of his *bianco magnare,* it should be "a lustrous white."

COOKING INSTRUCTIONS

Most early recipes plunge straight into the action. "Take" is a common opening instruction, followed by a string of ingredients. Even in the earliest cookbooks, well-organized cooks start with a mise en place by preparing and chopping ingredients before they begin cooking. A few authors convey a sense of order and timing. Taillevent, for instance, often uses "then" to signal a new preparation, but most cooks simply start with the lead ingredients and jog along from there. Until the appearance of household cookbooks in the late seventeenth century, cooks typically led a team of trained subordinates, so their instructions assumed that many steps, such as the boning and chopping of fish and simmering of rice for blancmange, would be performed in parallel rather than in sequence.

The first printed cookbooks used instructions such as "pound" and "temper" without explanation, though authors offered an occasional caution about the dangers of curdling or the likelihood of food sticking to the pan. Very soon, however, cookbook writers felt the need to explain technical terms in a systematic way, adding details within every recipe. Here's Bartolomeo Scappi in Per Fare Minestra di Bianco Magnare (*Opera,* 1570): "To tell when it is done, lift the spoon and if the bianco mangiare sticks to it and makes a thread and is transparent, then it is ready."[7]

From the first printed books, cooks have wanted to control the appearance of their creations on the table. "Present as you like it," says *Küchenmeisterei* in 1485. However, less than a century later, Scappi is far more specific: "And when the *bianco magnare* is as its name says it should be, a lustrous white, the taste matching its fine appearance, you can serve it hot or cold as you wish, with sugar over it."[8] He paves the way for the great buffet displays of the eighteenth and early nineteenth centuries that have led to today's elaborate presentations, now on single plates.

Recipe instructions also reflect the equipment that was available to the cooks of the time. By the late 1600s, merchants and country gentry, particularly in England and Germany, could afford help in the kitchen. Recipes were now being written for more modest households and a less knowledgeable audience than in previous centuries. Texts expand, adding more basic, meticulous instructions for novice cooks and housewives, together with hints about ingredients and serving instructions. As Europeans grew more prosperous (though at very different rates in different places), their kitchens became better and more copiously equipped, particularly with small-scale tools. For example, Blanc-manger in *L'Escole parfaite des officiers de bouche* (The Ideal School for Household Officers, 1662) calls for "a saucepan or terrine" and instructs cooks to "strain it [the mixture] three times . . . through a very clean tamis sieve."[9]

Two large-scale pieces of equipment were of even more importance: the purpose-built kitchen oven and the raised stove. A wood-fired oven inside the kitchen was a quantum leap from ad hoc baking arrangements in the embers of an open hearth. The greater control of oven heat is reflected from the seventeenth century onward in recipes for larger and more complex cakes and baked puddings such as whitepot. The introduction of the raised stove, starting in sixteenth-century Italy, made delicate operations far more feasible, such as the gentle cooking and constant stirring described in *Para Hacer Platos de Manjar Blanco* (To Make Dishes of White Food) by Diego Granado Maldonado in 1614.[10]

Cooking times begin appearing in recipes much later than might be expected. Timing had been quite arbitrary when the speed depended on the cook's ability to control the embers in a hearth, which in turn varied with the wood available, even with the direction of the wind. The introduction of the raised stove and the availability of a greater variety of pots and pans made a difference. However, not until the nineteenth century, with the arrival of the cast-iron closed stove, did a cooking surface with constant, even heat become available, bringing with it the possibility of estimating cooking time. As for the wood-fired oven, every cook knew that quick-cooked pastries should go in first, followed by loaves of bread, and then finally stews, to simmer in the declining warmth of the oven bricks. Cooks tested the temperature of the oven with the hand or with a bit of paper set inside to see how long it took to scorch. The infamous instruction "cook until done" (a phrase that is meaningless to any inexperienced cook) lingered until the late nineteenth century. Precise oven temperatures, and times, are a product of the technology of the twentieth century.

INGREDIENTS
& MEASUREMENTS

Until quite recent times, a cook had to design meals around the contents of the larder or the garden. This constraint is reflected in early recipes that call vaguely for "sweet spices" or "greenery for color." If a pig had just been killed, a cook would substitute pork for the veal or chicken specified in a recipe. In winter, dried bay leaves took the place of the fresh herbs of summer, and dried fruits replaced fresh. Cookbooks often devoted a good deal of space to choosing and preparing ingredients, skills that were at least as essential in the kitchen as the ability to cook them. At a given time, a chicken was a chicken more or ▸

A White-Pot.

TAKE two Quarts of new Milk, eight Eggs, and half the Whites beat up, with a little Rosewater, a Nutmeg, a quarter of a Pound of Sugar, cut a Pennyworth in very thin Slices, and pour your Milk and Eggs over ; put a little Bit of sweet Butter on the Top ; bake it in a flow Oven half an Hour.

A Rice White-Pot.

BOIL a Pound of Rice in two Quarts of new Milk, till it is tender and thick, beat it in a Mortar with a quarter of a Pound of Sweet Almonds blanched ; then boil two Quarts of Cream, with a few Crumbs of white Bread, and two or three Blades of Mace ; mix all together with eight Eggs, a little Rose-water, and sweeten to your Taste ; cut some candied Orange and Citrons-peels thin, and lay it in, when it is in the Oven. It must be put into a flow Oven.

By the mid-eighteenth century, in *The Art of Cookery Made Plain and Easy*, 1747, Hannah Glasse is giving precise quantities for the ingredients in A White-Pot and A Rice White-Pot. However, her instructions are sparse, particularly as this dish can curdle or brown in the oven, thus losing the right to its name.

** La Magnonaise de volaille à la gelée,

* Le pâté chaud de pigeons à l'ancienne,

La noix de veau glacée en surprise.

La carpe à la Chambord.

Les poulets à la Reine, au vin de Madère;

* Les filets de soles à la Orly,

** L'aspic de cervelles d'agneaux,

Les petits canetons à la purée de champignons.

———

Les escalopes de saumon à la maître d'hôtel,

** Le salmis de perdreaux à la gelée,

* Le fritot de poulets à la Maringo,

Les attereaux de palais de bœufs au gratin.

La dinde braisée aux marrons glacés.

Les côtelettes de mouton à la minute,

* Les petites croustades à la Béchamel,

** La salade de filets de brochet à la Provençale,

Les ailes de poulardes à la Chevalier.

Quatre grosses pièces d'entremets pour les contre-flancs.

La brioche à la crème,

Le buisson de grosses écrevisses,

Le flan de pommes méringuées,

Le buisson de truffes.

Quatre plats de rôts.

Les cailles bardées,

Les gougeons de Seine en aiguillettes,

Les merlans panés à l'Anglaise,

Les poulets gras au cresson.

Seize entremets.

** Le blanc manger renversé,

Les pieds de céleri à l'Espagnole.

La brioche à la crème.

Les choux de Bruxelles à l'Anglaise,

* Les pains à la Duchesse.

Like many good cookbook writers, Antonin Carême excites the imagination by putting recipes in context. In *Le maître d'hôtel français*, 1822, he states the number of dishes, such as *relevés*, hors d'oeuvre, and entremets, for each stage of service. In some cases he mentions the guest of honor, as for the historical supper given for Louis XV at La Muette on the outskirts of Paris on Saturday, February 28, 1749. The page shown here is just part of the menu of more than fifty dishes for only thirty to thirty-six people. *Le blanc manger* is featured among the entremets, appearing here with a definite article that denotes its new character and status.

less throughout Europe, but "salad greens" could vary dramatically. For many early cooks, a description in a cookbook might be the first time they encountered a new ingredient or a new way of using a familiar one.

Recipes give clues to fashions in food and the availability of new ingredients. The influx of novelties from the New World in the seventeenth century brought new challenges to authors, who responded by adding information on how to tackle a turkey or what to do with those mysterious beans of coffee and chocolate. Sugar had long been familiar, but it became an ever-increasing inspiration when prices declined during the seventeenth century. Sugar work is tricky, and cookbook writers had to provide detailed and accurate instructions to help their readers master the craft. By the late seventeenth century, similar precision was spreading into books on pastries and even savory dishes.

QUANTITIES

The appearance of exact quantities in recipes cannot be pinned down to a particular century. Medical doctors, who were keenly aware of the importance of accuracy in their prescriptions, tended to be more precise in their instructions than cooks did, though the line between culinary and medicinal recipes was blurred. As late as the nineteenth century, many cookbooks continue to include medical remedies. In the late fifteenth century, Platina gives precise measurements for a few ingredients in certain recipes. In 1552, Nostradamus provides measurements in all the recipes in his little book on preserving, *Excellent et moult utile opuscule à touts nécessaire qui désirent avoir cognoissance de plusieurs exquises recettes* (An Excellent and Most Useful Little Work Essential to All Who Wish to

Become Acquainted with Some Exquisite Recipes), because as a scientist and physician he insisted on precision.

As time passed, the matter of measurement continued to vary from author to author. Practical cooks would add the details they felt a professional would need, giving weights of primary ingredients such as meats and fish but leaving aromatics and spices to the taste of the reader. In a tricky recipe, or a personal favorite, exactitude might creep in, as in a recipe from 1596 for "blewmanger" that calls for "a pinte of creame, twelve or sixteene yolkes of eggs" to make the custard base.[11]

Le pastissier françois (The French Pastry Cook, 1653) is a landmark in recipe writing, as the anonymous author was happy to point out: "until now no Author has given the least instruction in this [pastry] art." Here a professional pastry cook defines the essentials of his trade, from how to weigh ingredients and prepare basics such as pastry cream to how to store and serve the cakes and pastries in his recipes. His explanation of weights specifies how many ounces to the pound (sixteen) and what a pint is (the measure of wine in Paris, weighing two pounds minus one ounce), and he declares that his recipes use the standards of the city of Troyes (troy weight is still the jewelers' measure). His remarks reveal that early cookbook writers had to deal with major variations in measurements from region to region, not to mention from country to country. This lack of standardization is yet another reason for the frequent absence of exact measures, which continues into the nineteenth century. Confusion reigns to this day when translating U.S. volume measures into the French metric or English imperial system.

As with the definition of weights, specification of serving quantities was rare and seemingly random in early recipes. Before the nineteenth century, the universal practice of serving multiple dishes in a single course, buffet style, made irrelevant the estimation of how many diners a recipe might feed. In any case, most cooks were aware that a plump hen or a grown rabbit would serve four to six people. Food that was left over did not go to waste; it would migrate to another meal or might appear on the servants' table, if they were lucky. Only in the nineteenth century, with its emphasis on domestic economy, did cookbook authors make an effort to list how many servings a recipe would yield. Even then, few of them systematically followed the early example of Messisbugo by indicating portions.

THE KEY TO SUCCESS

The fine line between brilliance and banality in individual recipes has varied from century to century. Certainly, fashion has played a part: woe betide the author who does not switch to the modish title "whitepot" when the name "blancmange" is passé. A sharp eye on new ingredients, perhaps calling for vanilla rather than the old-fashioned rose water, gives the reader a sense of immediacy. Some writers prefer a free-form style; others feel the need to note down every detail. Cooks writing for their peers can use shorthand; those who want to educate the novice give more detail on ingredients and method. Some writers take a very personal approach, adding helpful hints; others adopt a more rigid structure, particularly in more recent times.

Above all, the text of a successful recipe keeps moving with a clear narrative thread, though the occasional tangential comment is permissible. Clarity is vital. After reading a recipe, the cook must have an instant picture of the process to come, from the ingredients to the necessary equipment and the required commitment of work and time. Ideally, the recipe also creates a verbal image of how the finished dish will look on the plate. At the final count, the writing of a winning recipe comes back to the author. Among my personal favorites are Bartolomeo Scappi, master cook of the Renaissance, for his skill in breaking new ground; the chatty Hannah Glasse, eighteenth-century cookbook author, for her down-to-earth English common sense; and Antonin Carême, celebrity chef in the nineteenth century, for his worldview on cuisine and pastry during a revolutionary time in France. One theme unites them all: their recipes are clear, accurate, and designed to succeed in the real world of the kitchen. ♦

1 Alexander Croke, trans., *Regimen Sanitatis Salernitanum, a Poem on the Preservation of Health in Rhyming Latin Verse* (Oxford: D. A. Talboys, 1830).

2 See Constance Heiatt and Sharon Butler, eds., *Curye on Inglysch* (London: Early English Text Society, 1985).

3 *Widowes Treasure* (1595): "A notable receite to make Ipocras." Quoted in *The Oxford English Dictionary*.

4 Bartolomeo Sacchi, called Platina, *De honesta voluptate et valetudine* (Of Honest Indulgence and Good Health), c. 1474.

5 Taillevent, *Le viandier* (Houilles, France: Editions Manucius, 2001), 65.

6 *Platina's On Right Pleasure and Good Health*, trans. Mary Ella Millham (Ashville, NC: Pegasus Press, 1999), 118.

7 *Opera di M. Bartolomeo Scappi* (Venice: Ad instantia de Giorgio Ferarij, 1596), 48.

8 Ibid., 223.

9 *L'Escole parfaite des officiers de bouche* (Paris: la Veuve de Pierre Ribou, 1729), 418.

10 Diego Granado Maldonado, *Libro del arte de cozina* (Lleida: Pagès Editors, 1991), 81.

11 Thomas Dawson, *The Good Huswifes Jewell* (Amsterdam: Theatrum Orbis Terrarum, 1977), 29.

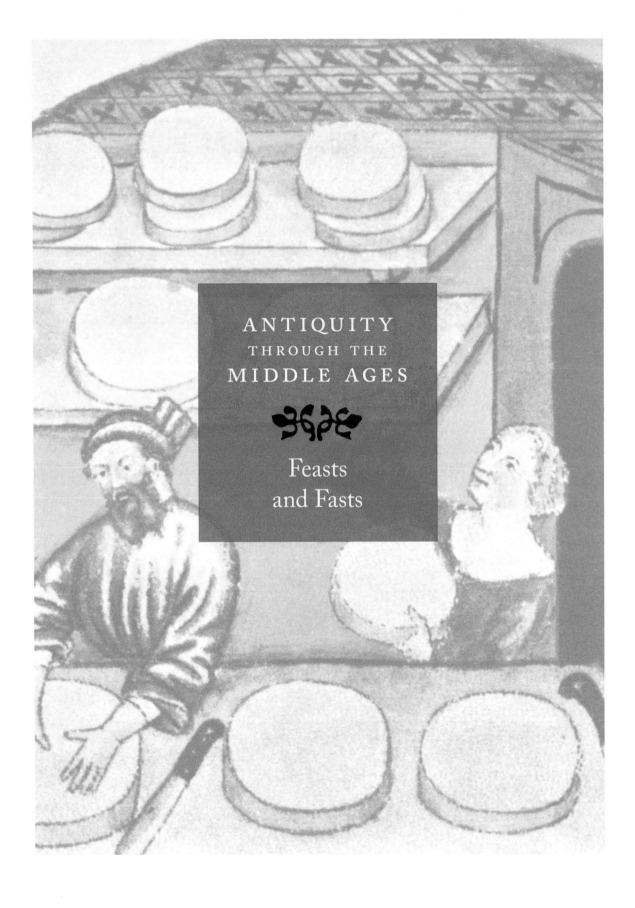

ANTIQUITY
THROUGH THE
MIDDLE AGES

Feasts
and Fasts

I N THE HISTORY OF PRINTING, cookbooks were right there in the first legendary group of printed books that included the Gutenberg Bible and Homer's *Odyssey*. Four cookbooks are among them, published in four different countries and four different languages—one in Latin, the language of learning; one in French, the widespread language of culture; one in German; and the last in English. All four are practical cookbooks, compiled by working cooks who had spent their careers in the kitchen. These cookbooks are simple collections of recipes, without the explanations or personal comments of today. None have more than two hundred recipes. They are pioneers, a part of the advance guard of seven hundred or so printed books whose influence on the development of Western cooking has been profound.

But long before these pioneers found their way into print, cooks were driven to pass on their expertise to their peers, even if they wrote to a much more select audience than their descendants would reach in print. Early European cookbooks were manuscripts, painstakingly written by hand, almost all in Latin, and limited to scholars and the wealthy, created for the nobility and princes of the church who could afford them. Cookbooks served a private world, mainly documenting the feasts enjoyed in noble houses and reflecting the lifestyle of the rich and powerful. Often, early cookery manuscripts were commissioned by rulers to record their authority and thus influence posterity. They were copied and became seminal documents for printed cookbooks, which in their turn were often directly copied. The study of the hundred or so medieval culinary manuscripts that have survived is a field unto itself, and only a few have made it into print, even with today's technology.

To find the roots of the earliest manuscript cookbooks, we must go back more than two thousand years to classical times. The Greeks and Romans were keen to celebrate with wine and feasting, but few records have survived. The earliest account of food in Europe is a poem in *Athenaei dipnosophistarum* (The Sophists' Banquet) written by Athenaeus, a literary figure of the second century C.E., who, to judge from his verses, relished his dinner. Athenaeus was a scholar, born in Egypt, and *Dipnosophistarum* is not a cookbook in the sense of a practical manual, but it is the first serious consideration

OPPOSITE Detail of cheese merchant from *Tacuinum sanitatis*. Full image on page 26.

of dining and drinking as an art form. It draws from a much earlier text by the Greek Archestratus from the fourth century B.C. Athenaeus clearly considered gustatory pleasure a sophisticated accomplishment, and his manuscript scatters culinary observations throughout fifteen books (chapters), culminating in a lyrical, gutsy account of a great Thessalonian feast. The table, he declares,

> Is full of fish fresh from the sea, besides,
> Here's tender veal, and dainty dishes of goose,
> Tartlets, and cheesecakes steeped most thoroughly
> In the rich honey of the golden bee.[1]

Manuscripts from Roman times abound with descriptions of lavish meals from Lucullus (c. 60 B.C.) onward, but only a single cookbook with recipes survives, *De re coquinaria* (On Cooking). The source is a mysterious gourmet called Apicius. His identity is unclear, though by repute he was M. Gabius Apicius, a prosperous Roman gourmet during the reigns of the emperors Augustus and Tiberius early in the first century C.E.[2] *De re coquinaria* is an astonishingly polished and sophisticated work, divided in the classic tradition into ten books. Book one, "The Careful, Experienced Cook," starts cheerily with some refreshing drinks; continues with advice on the storage of meat, fish, and fruits; and ends, just in case, with a digestive remedy. Like many a modern cookbook author, Apicius divided the rest of his material by ingredients—meats, poultry, fish and shellfish—adding some elegant fish sauces and making a happy digression into "fancies" that include sow's womb, fig-fed pork, braised truffles, milk-fed snails, and half a dozen sweetmeats flavored with honey.

The book is substantial, with over four hundred recipes, some running to a dozen lines or more. The array of foods is wide, with particularly broad use of herbs and many sweet-sour-salty combinations of dried fruits and honey with vinegar or verjuice, *garum* (fish sauce), or olives. Apicius is careful to specify ingredients, though without quantities and often in random order. He leaves culinary instructions to the cook but offers helpful comments here and there. "Immerse the cooked meat in this sauce to penetrate and soften," he instructs in a recipe for venison sauce. To judge by the following caution, he must have had an unfortunate experience: "Leave plenty of room for expansion [of a pig's paunch] lest it bursts while being cooked. Put it in a pot with boiling water, retire, and prick with a needle so that it does not burst."[3]

His culinary observations take us on a trip to a slightly exotic gourmet restaurant, but how can we know what Roman food tasted like? The ingredients bear the same names as those in today's cookbooks, but domesticated animals would have been scrawnier than those we know, the goats and pigs half-wild, the chickens far smaller than ours. Spices were stale: the journey from Asia could take over a year. Flour varied enormously from harvest to harvest, as did the bread made from it. Fruits were pungent, closer to our crab apples or hedgerow berries. Even greens would have lacked the tender fleshy leaves we are used to. As for flavors on the plate, how can we imagine them? An occasional whiff wafts from the past—the reek of an aged Muenster cheese, the punch of raw garlic and anchovy still found in some Catalonian dishes, the crunch of a live Australian witchetty grub. Nearly a millennium was to pass between Apicius and the next surviving manuscripts that contained recipes, and the same disconnect lingers into the Renaissance. Apicius set a literary example for posterity; records show

ABOVE When a medieval German prince sat down to dinner, an elaborate ballet choreographed the service of his meal to the tiniest gesture. Ritual ensured that every participant had a place and stayed in it according to his status. He would sit above or below the salt, displayed in this 1491 woodcut as a tower in front of the prince. Religious symbolism was central: a square trencher of bread is on the table, and wine is cooling at the lord's feet. He sits at a high table in full view of the guests and household members, who are seated at right angles on benches (*banquets* in French, hence the term), a table placement that is still followed today at formal gatherings. In this scene, titled *A Princely Banquet,* the artist has reversed the prince so we can see his face.

that his work was studied at the court of Charlemagne, proving that *De re coquinaria* was more than a passing fad.[4]

As the Roman Empire declined, asceticism took over. Feasting lost favor and with it any intellectual investigation of gastronomy. Curbed by Christianity, good eating was permissible to maintain health, but only when punctuated by fast days. Here entered Joannes Cassianus, or John the Hermit, who was the first to set the scene for clean living at the start of the fifth century C.E. His writings inspired Dante and Thomas Aquinas, and his *De institutis coenobiorum et de octo principalium viliorum remediis* (On the Management of Monastic Communities, and on Eight Ways of Curing Their Main Defects) established principles for community life that strongly influenced the monastic orders established in later centuries. Christians were preoccupied, not to say obsessed, with right and wrong, with sin and sanctity. And one of the deadly sins was gluttony. Since ecclesiastical institutions often took the lead in educating the surrounding population, and also offered open hospitality to travelers, Cassianus's rules have had immense influence down the centuries.

Cassianus's manuscript opens with four books on the appropriate garb for the secluded life, then launches into an analysis of eight principal vices, of which gourmandise is the first. The book has no recipes but plenty of very modern advice. Cassianus identifies three dangers: eating earlier than the customary time (in effect, snacking), eating too much of any food, and overenjoyment of rare and succulent dishes. Following the ascetic principle, he recommends periods of fasting, but like a modern diet guru, he recognizes that one's diet should be varied to suit the human body and the willpower of the spirit.

ABOVE In the early sixteenth century, the austerity of the Reformation had not yet reached monastic communities like that of these Benedictine monks, pictured in a fresco by Sodoma from 1505–8 at the Monastery of Monte Oliveto Maggiore. Members of religious orders often lived as comfortably as their secular counterparts did.

OPPOSITE The oldest book in our collection is Cassianus's *De institutis coenobiorum et de octo principalium viliorum remediis*, printed in Venice in 1491 and therefore one of the coveted band of incunabula that appeared before 1501. The book, of almost quarto size, is bound in vellum that probably dates from the sixteenth century. It lacks a title page; indeed, like many books of the period, it may never have had one. Early printed books looked very much like manuscripts, with wide margins for the insertion of comments. Gaps at the heads of chapters or paragraphs invited the addition of brightly colored capital letters or illuminations, though none have been inserted here. The crisp black Gothic type of *De institutis coenobiorum* is eminently legible, in keeping with the author's down-to-earth, albeit pious, style. No one, admonishes Cassianus, should eat to satiety lest heaviness of body and spirit kindle the fires of vice. The author, trained in the hard monastic life of lower Egypt as well as the more pliant approach of Palestine, Constantinople, and Rome, founded the celebrated monastic Abbey of Saint-Victor (which still exists) as well as a convent for nuns.

De octo
Principalibus viciis.

Erman⁹. Quó igit octo sunt vicia q̄ nos
ipugnát. cū p moysen septē dinūerate sint
gētes q̄ aduersant populo israel. vl̄ q̄mad
modū terras vicioꝛ cōmodū nobis é possidere.
℣ Responsio quó ⁱm octo vicia octo gentiū nume
rus impleatur. Cap.xviij.
Erapion. Octo esse pꝛicipalia vicia q̄ im
pugnát mōachū:cūctoꝛ absoluta sn̄ia est.
Que figuralit sub gētiū vocabulo nomia
ta.idcirco nūc oı̄a nō ponunt:eo ꝙ egressis ı̄a ō egy
pto ꞇ liberati ab vna gēte validissima.i.egyptioꝛum
moises vl̄ p ipm dn̄s ı̄ deuteronomio loq̄bat. Que
figura ı̄ nobis quoꝗ rectissime stare dephendit:q̄ ō
seculi laq̄is expediti castrimargie.i.vētris vel gule
vicio caruisse cognoscimur:ꞇ habem⁹ ı̄aꝗ cōtra bas
residuas septē gētes simili rōne cōflictū:pꝛima .s. q̄
ı̄a deuicta é minime cōputata. Cn̄t ét terra ı̄ posses
sione israeli nō dat:s̄ꝗ vt deserat eā ꝑpetuo. ꞇ egredi
atur ab ea.dn̄i ꝑceptiōe sancit. C idcirco ita sūt mo
derāda ieiunia:vt nō necesse sit p̄ imoderatiōe ꝓti
nētie.q̄ ōsectōe carnis vel ı̄firmitate ꝓtracta é.reuer
ti rursus ad egyptioꝛ terrā.i.pꝛistinā gule ꞇ carnis
cōcupiscētia.quā cū mūdo huic abꝛenūciaremus⁹ ab
iecim⁹.Qó figuralit illi pꝑessi sūt.q̄ egressi ı̄ solitu
dine vtūtū.rursus desiderauerūt ollas carniuꝫ sup
quas sedebāt in egypto.
℣ Cur vna gens qdem deseri:septem vero iuben
tur extingui. Cap.xix.
Quod aut illa gēs ı̄ qua nati sūt filij israel
nō penit⁹ extingui.s̄ꝗ ı̄mmó deseri eī terra
ꝑcipit.he vo septē vsꝗ ad ı̄ternitiōe iube
tur extingui hec rō é:ꝗ q̄tūlibet ardoꝛe spūs succēsi
beremū virtutū fuerim⁹ igressi.in ciuitate ac miste
rio castrimargie ꞇ quodāmō quotidiano eī cōmer
tio nequaꝗ carere poterim⁹.Semp.n.i nobis edu
lij ꞇ escaꝛ vt ingenit⁹ ac naturalis viuit affect⁹.licꝫ
amputare supfluos eī appetit⁹ ac desideria festine
mus:q̄ sicut p oı̄a deleri nō possut.ita debet quadaꝫ
declinatiōe vitari. De hac.n.dicit.Et carnis cura
ne feceritis ī desiderijs.Dū hui⁹ ergo cure quā pꝛeci
pimur nō p oı̄a abscidere.s̄ꝗ absꝗ desiderijs exhibe
re retinem⁹ affectū:euident egypti ōnatiōne nō exti
guim⁹.s̄ꝗ ab ipsa quadā discretōe separamur. non ō
supfluis seu lautioꝛib⁹ epulis cogitātes.s̄ꝗ ⁱm apo
stolū.victu quotidiano indumētoꝗ ꝓtēti.Qó figu
ralit ét ī lege mādat non abbominaberis egyptiuꝫ:
qꝛ fuisti icola ī terra ei⁹.Necessariū.n.vict⁹ coꝛpoꝛi.n̄
sine vel ipsi⁹ pnicie vel aı̄e scelere ōnegat. Illaꝝ vo
septē pturbationū velut oı̄modis noxiaꝝ.ō recessi
b⁹ aı̄e n̄re penit⁹ exterminādi sūt mot⁹.De his eni
ita ōt.Dis amaritudo ira ꞇ indignatio.ꞇ clamoꝛ ꞇ
blasphēia.tollat a vobis cū oı̄ malitia. Et iteꝝ.Foꝛ
nicatio aut ꞇ ois imudicia ꞇ auaritia nec noı̄et⁹ ī vo
bis.aut turpitudo.aut stultiloqm.aut scurrilitas.
Possum⁹ ergo boꝛ q̄ nature supiducta sunt radi
ces abscidere vicioꝛ:vsu vo castrimargie nequaꝗ
valebim⁹ āputare.Nō.n.possum⁹ quātūlibꝫ pfece

rim⁹.id nō eē ꝙ nascimur.Qó ita eē tā n̄ra.ꝗ sum⁹
exigui.ꝙ oı̄m pfectoꝛ vita ꞇ ꝓuersatiōe mōstrat:q̄
cū reliquaꝝ passionū reciderint stimulos.atꝗ here
mū toto mēs feruoꝛe ꞇ coꝛpoꝛis expetant nuditate.
nihilomin⁹ quotidiāi vict⁹.pudētia ꞇ annui panis
ꝑparatiōe nequnt liberari.
℣ De natura Castrimargie ad similitudinē agie
comparande. Cap.xx.
Al⁹ passiōis figura qua necesse é q̄uis spi
ritalē sūmuꝗ mōachū coartari.ꝓpꝛie sat
agle similitudie ōsignat.Que cū excelsis
simo volatu vltra nubiū fuerit altitudinē sublimata
seseꝗ ab ocnl cūctoꝛ moꝛtaliū.ac a facie terre toti⁹
absconderit:rursⁱ ad valliū ima submitti.ꞇ ad terre
na ōscédet.ac moꝛticinis cadauerib⁹ iplicari vētris
necessitate cōpellit.Quib⁹ manifestissime cōpꝛobat
cāstriargie spiritū nequaꝗ posse vt cetera vicia re
secari.vl̄ p oı̄a similⁱ extigui:s̄ꝗ aculeos ei⁹ ac supflu
os appetit⁹ virtute animi refudi tm̄ atꝗ cohiberi. ꝫ
℣ De ꝑseuerātia castrimargie aduersus philo
sophos disputata: Capi.xxi.
Am bui⁹ vicij naturā qdā senū cū philoso
phis disputās q eū p simplicitate christia
na velut rusticū crederēt fatigādū.sub b p
bleumatⁱ figurās coloꝛe elegant expssit.Multi iꝗt
creditoꝛib⁹ pf me⁹ me ōreliqt obnoxiū:ceteris ad ī
tegrū solues.ab oı̄ ꝗuetiōis coꝛ molestia liberat⁹:sū
vni satisfacere quotidie soluēdo n̄ possit.Cunꝗ illi
ignoꝛātes vi ꝓposite q̄stiōis absolutiōeꝫ ei⁹ pcario
postularēt:multi ait vicⁱis sol naturali ꝓditiōe ꝓstri
ct⁹.s̄ꝗ ispirāte dn̄o ōsideriū libertat⁹.cūcꝗ illis tanꝗ
molestissimis creditoꝛib⁹ ꝛnūciās buic mūdo.ꞇ oēꝫ
sbam q̄ mihi successiōe pꝛiis obuenerat a me pariter
abⁱiciēs satisfeci.atꝗ ab eis sū oı̄modis absolut⁹:ca
strimargie vo stimul nullo mō carere pualui. Hec
n.q̄uis eā ī paruū modū vilissimaꝗ redigere q̄ptita
rē.vi quotidiane cōpulsiōis euado:s̄ꝗ necesse é me ꝑ
petuis ei⁹ ꝗuetiōib⁹ purgeri.ꞇ iterminabile quādaꝫ
solutiōne ı̄ugi sictiōe depēdere.atꝗ iexplebile in di
ctiōib⁹ ei⁹ iserre vectigal Tū illi buc quē velut idio
tā acrusticū ante ōspexerāt.pnūciauerūt pꝛias phi
losophie ptes.i.ethicā disciplinā appꝛime cōpꝛehēdis
se:mirati admodū potuisse eū naturalⁱ asseq̄.ꝙ nul
la ei secularis eruditio ꝑtulisset.cū ipi sudoꝛe multo
lōgaꝗ doctria hec attigere nequisset.Hec spālⁱt.de
castriargia ōixisse sufficiat.Nunc reuertamur ad di
sputatōeꝫ quā ō generali vicioꝛ cognitione cepera
mus exponere.
℣ Cur abꝛahe pꝛedixerit de⁹ decem gentes expu
gnādas a populo israel. Cap.xxij.
Um ad abꝛabā dn̄s de futuris loq̄ret qd
vos minie reqsit.nō septē gentes legit ōi
numerasse s̄ꝗ decē:quaꝝ terra semini ei⁹ dā
dā ꝓmittit.Qui numer⁹ adiecta idolatria atꝗ bla
sphemia euident iplet:qb⁹ ante noticiā ōi ꞇ gꝛaꝫ ba
ptismi vel ipsa gētiliū vel blasphema iudeoꝛ ı̄stitu
do subiecta é.ōōec ī itellectuali egypto cōmoꝛatur.

FOODS FOR
FAST DAYS

From the very earliest cookbooks, authors made a distinction between fast days and feast days (also called meat days), often dividing recipes accordingly. The recipes marked many occasions, from holy festivals such as Christmas to agricultural high points of the year like Michaelmas (near the autumn equinox). At its simplest, fasting meant the absence of cherished foods such as meats and butter, whereas feasting referred to meals with delicacies added, though through history the distinction between the two could be very complicated indeed. A shocking number of fast days could be mandated by law—up to 150 per year in early modern Europe.[1]

Typically, fasting did not mean less eating; it meant the avoidance of meat (and at times products such as butter and eggs as well). Three days in any given week were fast days (nonmeat days), along with a number of "holy days" during which the faithful were allowed only one meal during twenty-four hours. Human nature must have rebelled against such restrictions, because a kind of relay eventually developed, with fasting and feasting playing off each other throughout the calendar year. The greatest Christian feasts were Christmas and Easter, so by implication the most important (and longest) fasts were Advent (four weeks long) and Lent (six weeks). Carnival (also called Fat Tuesday or Mardi Gras) may have its origins in the Latin tag *carne vale* (farewell to meat).

What kept people going on fast days was fish. This option was manageable for those who lived by the sea or who were rich enough to raise fish inland. In his sixteenth-century book, *A Hundredth Good Pointes of Husbandrie,* Thomas Tusser recommended stocking the stew pond for Lent in September: "Thy ponds renew / put eeles in stew / to leeve til Lent / and then be spent."[2] Not everyone had the luxury of a pond, of course, so the poor had to subsist on smoked or dried fish. The words of a young school boy suggest how trying this diet must have been: "Thou wyll not beleve how wery I am off fysshe, and how moch I desir that flesch wer com in ageyn."[3] No wonder people drank a lot of wine during Lent on the principle that fish *must* swim.

Because long fasts were so monotonous, believers, at least those in upper-class households, found ingenious ways to circumvent the rules on forbidden foods. Almond milk replaced cow's milk, and yeast dough substituted for egg-bound pastry. An ingenious invention was the "mock egg," which was created by boiling and puréeing almonds with sugar; then dividing the mixture in two and dyeing one part yellow with saffron, ginger, and cinna-

Hunters kill a boar for a feast day [above] in this Mussolini-era reprint of miniatures from *Tacuinum sanitatis,* c. 1475. Fishermen haul in the catch for a fast day [opposite].

mon; and finally blowing out the contents of a real egg, washing the shell, and stuffing the almond mixture inside. The whole was roasted in ashes and, triumphantly, served as a hard-boiled egg! Another ruse was to buy a dispensation from church authorities. One of the splendid fifteenth-century towers of the gothic cathedral in Rouen is known as the "Butter Tower" because it was paid for with butter dispensations during Lent. Those who could not afford butter had to eat oil—of such poor quality, complained Martin Luther, that "people in Rome would not use [it] to grease their shoes."[4]

With the Reformation in the sixteenth century, fasting took another turn. People were fed up with the corruption of the Catholic Church, which had found ways to turn fasting into profit. Reformer John Calvin remarked, "It would be much more satisfactory if fasting were not practiced at all, than diligently observed and at the same time corrupted with false and pernicious habits."[5] The practice remained strongest in Catholic countries, reflected in cookbooks such as *Le cuisinier français* (1651), which still divided recipes according to fast days and meat days, with specific sections for Lent. But even in France, fasting was increasingly questioned. Voltaire attacked it in the eighteenth century, asking, "Why does the Roman church consider it a crime to eat terrestrial animals during the days of abstinence, and a good action to be served soles and salmon? The rich papist who has five hundred francs' worth of fish on his table will be saved; and the poor man dying of hunger who ate four sous' worth of pork, will be damned."[6]

By the nineteenth century, the observance of fast days was just a memory for all but the dedicated few. In America, the tradition of

fasts and feasts never became established. Yet with the decline of fasting, something has been lost: feasting without fasting lacks the sybaritic edge. Eggs were beloved at Easter precisely because they had been forbidden during Lent. Feasting is far more fun to contemplate than fasting, but one reason that any banquet is such a treat is the abstinence that precedes it. ♦

1 Ken Albala, *Food in Early Modern Europe* (Westport, CT: Greenwood Press, 2003), 196.

2 Thomas Tusser, *His Good Points of Husbandry*, ed. Dorothy Hartley (London: Country Life Limited, 1931), 29.

3 William Nelson, *A Fifteenth Century Schoolbook* (Oxford: Clarendon Press, 1956), 8.

4 Albala, *Food in Early Modern Europe*, 200.

5 *Calvin: Institutes of the Christian Religion*, ed. John T. McNeill, trans. Ford Lewis Battles (Philadelphia: Westminster, 1960), 2:1245.

6 Voltaire, quoted in Albala, *Food in Early Modern Europe*, 207.

"The blandness of grain soaked in water does not suit everyone, and some cannot be content with a few raw vegetables or the austerity of dry bread."[5] So timeless was *De institutis coenobiorum* that more than a thousand years later, in 1491, a revised version was printed in Venice, one of the influential incunabula printed before 1501.

The Manuscript Tradition

The gulf of the Dark Ages stretches between Apicius's cookbook and the hundred or so medieval recipe manuscripts that have come down to us. They portray the feasts of the noble houses of Europe in an overwhelming panorama of meat, game, fowl, and fish. The menus resemble an inventory of the inhabitants of a game park. Stuffed peacocks are reconstituted in their feathers, giant pies burst with live birds, castles of pastry or sugar icing loom so large that they have to be moved by horse and cart—all

designed as jokes, part of the entertainment and not intended to be eaten. The huge quantities of spice that perfumed fashionable dishes were not so much culinary refinements as expressions of wealth and power, like the coatings of gold and silver leaf used today in Indian cuisine. To us it seems another world.

One of the earliest manuscript cookbooks in this period was compiled by Taillevent, master cook to the court of Charles V of France in the 1370s and author of *Le viandier* (The Victualler). At this time, cooking was considered a manual trade, although a master cook could achieve a powerful position in an important

LEFT An engraving of Taillevent's sarcophagus in the Museum of St.-Germain-en-Laye near Paris shows the master cook flanked by his two wives, with his coat of arms and its three cooking pots emblazoned on the shield at his side.

OPPOSITE This menu from *Antiquitates Culinariae* by Richard Warner (1791) records one of the great feasts held in the fifteenth century for the "intronization of the reverende father in God George Nevell, Archbishop of York, and Chauncelour of Englande in the VI. yere of the raigne of kyng Edwarde the fourth." Warner comments on the astonishing amount of "goodly provision" that went into the celebrations, including 300 tons (*tonneaus*) of ale, 100 tons of wine, 104 oxen, 6 wild bulls, 1,000 sheep, and 400 swans. Significantly, lists of provisions mention only meats, game and birds (or fish on fast days), with dainties such as custards, fritters, wafers, and fruit pies; vegetables are not considered worthy of note. The author provides lively commentary on the medieval entertainments between courses and the personalities involved in them. "I would observe too," he remarks tartly, "that from the profusion of dishes served up, and from the formal ceremonial with which the most esteemed ones were placed upon the table, the repasts of those days were necessarily continued to a most tedious length."

THE INTHRONIZATION OF ARCHBISHOP NEVILL. 99

Here foloweth the fervyng of Fyfhe in order.

The firft courfe.

First potage.

Almonde Butter.

Red Herrynges.

Salt fyfch.

Luce falt.

Salt Ele.

Kelyng, Codlyng, and Hadocke boyled.

Thirlepoole roft.

Pyke in Harblet.

Eeles baked.

Samon chynes broyled.

Turbut baked.

And Fritters fryed.   13

The feconde courfe.

Frefhe Samon jowles.

Salt Sturgion.

Whytynges.

Pylchers.

Eeles.

Makerels.

Places fryed.

Barbelles.

Conger roft.

Troute.

Lamprey roft.

Bret.

Turbut.

Roches.

Salmon baked.

Lynge in gelly.

Breame baked.

Tenche in gelly.

Crabbes.   19.

The thirde courfe.

Jowles of frefhe Sturgion.

Great Geles.

Broyled Conger.

Cheuens.

Breames.

Rudes.

Lamprones.

Small Perches fryed.

Smeltes roft.

Shrympes

Small Menewes.

Thirlepoole baked.

And Lopfter.   13.

Hereafter foloweth the fervice to the Baron-bifhop within the clofe of Yorke.

Firft the Ufher muft fee that the Hall be trymmed in every poynt, and that the Cloth of eftate § be hanged in the Hall, and that foure Quyfhions of eftate be fet in order upon the Benche, beyng of fine Silke, or cloth of Gold, and that the hygh Table be fet, with all other Boordes, and Cubberdes ‖, Stooles and Chayres requifite within the Hall, and that a good fire be made.

Item,

§ " Cloth of eftate." A pallium, pall, or canopy which was fufpended over the high table, or at leaft over that part of it, where the moft honorable and exalted perfonages were feated.

‖ " Cubberdes." Thefe cup-boards were different from thofe repofitories of plate, china, &c. which we call by that name in the prefent age; being nothing more than moveable boards, or tables, on which were placed the bread, falt, knives, fpoons, drinking veffels, &c. They fo far refembled our fide-boards, that on them, as with us, was difplayed the gold and filver plate belonging to the houfe; and where there was not a fufficient number of utenfils compofed of thefe *valuable* materials, the deficiency was fupplied by plated or gilt veffels, which were denominated by our anceftors, " counterfoot veffel." Vide fupra, and North. Houfe. book.

WHEN IS DINNER?

The times at which people take their meals have long depended not only on social status but also on nationality and lifestyle—whether they lived in the town or in the countryside. Over the centuries, mealtimes have changed, sometimes dramatically, but the trend has been consistent, with the timing of the day's main meal gradually moving from before noon to early evening. In England, for example, the main meal of every day is called dinner, and in medieval times, it took place as early as ten o'clock in the morning (giving weight to the French *déjeuner* [dinner], which also means to end a fast). Breakfast in early times was reserved for children, invalids, and workmen; supper (related to the word *soup*) was no more than a simple meal before bed. In a modest household, daylight was a determining factor—people cooked and ate when they could see to do so—and supper time followed the seasons.

In sixteenth-century England, the "correct" time to eat meals became a subject of debate, and books argued whether digestion was best served by eating the main meal at midday or in the evening. Many authors insisted that dinner was best at ten or eleven in the morning, leaving the rest of the daytime hours for the sun's warmth and the diner's movements to ease the body's job of processing the meal. Others declared that a hearty supper around six in the evening was the better choice, because it would allow more hours for digestion before the next meal. The English doctor Andrewe Boorde, who wrote extensively on health and diet in the 1500s, declared, "One meal should be digested before the next be taken, for there is nothing more hurtful for man's body than to eat meat upon meat."[1]

The main meal of the English day gradually inched later and later. Whereas King Henry VIII dined around eleven in the morning, by the 1600s, dinner had moved one or two hours later and, as described by diarist Samuel Pepys, involved substantial amounts of drink as well as food. The eighteenth century saw dinner move later again and breakfast move up to the time at which the previous generation had enjoyed the main meal. Again, light came into play. By the 1700s, increasingly affluent urban dwellers could afford artificial light to illuminate the grand dinners that were in full swing once the sun went down. In a parallel development, new factories kept workers far from home at midday, so dinner had to wait until they returned home in the evening.

By the early 1800s, eating patterns began to resemble those that are familiar to us today. In towns, dinner had moved to six or seven in the evening, opening long stretches of time between breakfast and the main meal. At this point, "luncheon" entered the scene. The word comes from *nuncheon* or *nuntion,* which in earlier times was no more than a snack taken generally around noon, especially by laborers. Jane Austen mentioned "noonshine" in a letter of 1808, a fashion created by ladies to fill the gap between the morning and evening meals. Men at first eschewed this habit as effeminate and did not take up lunching until the Victorian era.

The meals called breakfast, lunch, dinner, and supper continue to evolve (brunch is a rare example of two meals coalescing into one). Mealtimes still vary across countries and cultures. Differing dinnertimes over the centuries have indicated occupation, social status, health, lifestyle, even nationality, and they continue to do so. When we eat indicates who we are. ♦

1 Andrewe Boorde, quoted in P. W. Hammond, *Food and Feast in Medieval England* (Phoenix: History Press, 1993), 104–5.

A couple is enjoying an outdoor feast of crayfish in this Mussolini-era reprint of an image from *Tacuinum sanitatis,* c. 1475.

household. Taillevent is unusual in that his career at the French royal court was documented. He began as a humble *happelapin* (kitchen boy) in the household of Queen Jeanne of France. By 1346 he had risen to *keu* (cook) to King Philip VI and in that year was granted a house "in consideration of the good and pleasant service the king has received."[6] Soon after, he was granted the rank of *écuyer* (squire), one down from that of knight and an extraordinary honor. Taillevent did a great deal more than simply supervise the cooking at the French court. Much like a modern quartermaster, he was also in charge of provisions—hence, the name of his book. His full name was Guillaume Tirel, but his nickname—*taille vent,* "to tame the wind"—gives a clue to the force of his character.

France at that time was just one of the leaders of European fashion. England, too, had some claim to culinary vision. *Forme of Cury* (Model of Cooking), which dates from around 1390 but did not appear in print until the late eighteenth century, records the recipes of the master cook (whose name is unknown) at the court of the flamboyant, ill-fated English king Richard II.[7] The text outlines a jumble of meat, fish, poultry, and game dishes in a primitive script that is hard to decipher. Recipes range from Spynoches Yfryed (fried spinach) to Vyannd Ryal (royal meat), a multipurpose sauce of Greek or Rhenish wine thickened with rice flour and flavored with honey, ginger, pepper, cinnamon, cloves, saffron, Cypress sugar, and mulberries. It describes how to build chastletes (little castles) from pastry dough that are embellished with battlements, baked with stuffings of pork, almonds, apples, or pears, and surrounded with fritters colored variously with saffron, sandalwood, and green herbs. King Richard dearly loved display, but surely the contemporary chronicler Holinshed exaggerated in saying, "In his kitchen there were two thousand cooks and three hundred servitors" employed in feeding a crowd of up to ten thousand.[8]

These two manuscripts by royal cooks were enormously influential in northern Europe, while farther south another seminal text had appeared even earlier, in the first half of the fourteenth century. *Libre de Sent Soví* (the untranslatable title possibly refers to Saint Silvain) is the first record of a Catalan culinary tradition.[9] It reflects a Mediterranean palate, featuring eggplant, goat, chickpeas, pine nuts, semolina, and arugula. The author suggests using coriander seed rather than mustard as a condiment. Recipes include a dizzying number of sauces for meats, fish, and fowl, offering a solution to the problem of what to do with an unfamiliar ingredient. (Most of us have gazed in bewilderment at the display of fish at the market in a new place.) Like all well-known cookbook manuscripts, *Libre de Sent Soví* was much copied and had wide circulation, though it did not appear in print until 1979. Plagiarized versions of the recipes often turned up in later cookbooks such as *Libre del coch* (The Cook's Book, 1520) by Mestre Robert (Ruberto de Nola), the first printed cookbook in Spanish. Yet another important culinary manuscript, compiled by Amiczo Chiquart, master cook to Duke Amadeus of Savoy, was only discovered and printed recently. *Du fait de cuisine*

(On Cookery, 1420), as recorded by the scribe Johannes Doudens, prefigured the lighter, healthy picture of cooking painted by Platina, author of the first published cookbook (1474), but the manuscript could not have had much contemporary influence as it was not printed at the time.

The Medieval Table

The food depicted in medieval manuscript cookbooks was strikingly similar across Europe. The aim was to create a single, unique flavor from many ingredients—the antithesis of today's ideal of highlighting a single, prime ingredient by cooking it to perfection. Cookbooks of the time offered many of the same dishes, and recipes for cryspels (crêpes), darioles (custards), hastletes (skewers), galyntyne (a stew flavored with galingale root), and macaroons were available from England to Italy and west into Spain. Disguise was a preoccupation, so ingredients were hacked, boiled, pounded, and sieved out of all recognition. Color was prized when so many objects and surfaces were grey or brown, and broths and purées were brightened with saffron (golden yellow), sandalwood (red), herbs (green), or mulberries (blue). A popular early dish that survives to this day was blancmange (literally "white eating"), which could use any puréed white meat, including veal, chicken, and capon, or simply blanched almonds.

Meat was the mainstay of the wealthy, and banquet menus often consisted of lists of domestic and game animals. Affluent medieval diners ate a wide assortment of birds, including swan, capon, partridge, heron, cormorant, and wild duck. Baby animals and immature meats such as veal were favored over older, tougher beasts. Beef, from cattle that had worked their lives in the fields, mainly appeared in the stockpot.[10] However, fast days mandated by the church took up nearly half the year, during which the imaginative fish recipes proposed by Taillevent and his peers must have made an agreeable change. In the cookbooks of the time, salted salmon, simmered in wine and chives, competed with eel, cod, haddock, and oysters. Lobster might have been roasted in an oven or by the fire, then coated with bread crumbs and served with vinegar. Whole fish were coated in a spiced, wine-laden aspic or served to invalids in a spiced, sugared broth. Exotica included porpoise, dolphin, and lamprey, a type of eel.

The Roman palate carried through to medieval tables, with the same love of spices such as pepper, ginger, turmeric, cumin, and saffron, and sweet-sour flavorings of vinegar and honey or figs with wine and mustard. Sugar was used as a seasoning like salt, and both were scarce and expensive. Illuminated manuscripts show towering gothic salt cellars at table in front of the lord, a display of his power; anyone not seated near him was thus "below the salt." Sauces remained in favor, though the focus changed from the sweet-sour of honey and vinegar and the pungency of fermented and salted fish (which came from the Greeks) to the milder, thicker medieval sauces such as cameline (mixed spices thickened with bread soaked in vinegar) and jance (pounded almonds with verjuice, white wine, ginger, and saffron. Spices showed up again at the end of the meal with *épices de chambre*—parlor spices, we might call them—such as candied coriander seed, cardamom comfits, and ginger root, which diners chewed to sweeten the breath.

Other scattered sources of medieval cooking came from the Moorish occupation of Spain, southwestern France, and southern Italy, influences that lingered well into the fourteenth century. An Arabic manuscript from the tenth century called *Kitāb al-tabīkh* (The Book of Cookery) may be the earliest to survive from the medieval period.[11] The book describes a sophisticated, multilayered cuisine that perhaps inspired the medieval habit of double and triple cooking foods. Certainly the Arab tradition shows in the intensive use of so-called sweet spices such as cassia (often confused with cinnamon and with a similar flavor), nutmeg, mace, and cloves—all common in European recipes. The Arabs helped spread the cultivation of sugarcane and use of sugar, as well as introducing the first, bitter orange trees to the Mediterranean. The descendants of these trees still grow in Seville's old town. Layered pastries, too, date from this time, popping up unexpectedly in regions such as southwestern France, with its *galette landaise* of strudel-like dough brushed with goose fat and layered with dried fruits and Armagnac.

A fool rides a crayfish in this woodcut from *Das Narrenschiff*, or *The Ship of Fools*, a well-known work of religious satire written by Sebastian Brant in 1494 and believed to be illustrated by Albrecht Dürer. The fool above, one of 112 follies, illustrates "predestynacion." Crayfish and its look-alike, the lobster—mainstays on church-mandated fast days—both represent the water sign Cancer in the zodiac.

Just one early cookbook manuscript is an odd man out, reaching beyond the rarefied world of the rich and powerful. *Le ménagier de Paris* (The Householder of Paris), dating from the late fourteenth century, is an anonymous book of instruction for a small but newly expanding group of prosperous tradesmen or administrators. In this endearing collection of household hints and recipes from northern France, an elderly man gives—at considerable length—guidelines for the comportment of the perfect wife. This model of wifeliness should not only love God and her husband but also oversee the garden, choose and manage indoor servants, and most importantly, manage the family table (good eating occupies by far the most space in the book). The author discourses fluently on how to talk to the butcher and where to find green branches to adorn a room; he proposes some remarkably lavish menus of over 30 dishes (duly noting their cost) for service in six courses. As so often happens in early cookbooks, a sizable chunk of the 350 recipes can be traced to Taillevent, emphasizing his influence on the cooking of the time.[12] They follow the familiar medieval repertoire of soups, stews, egg dishes, meats, fish, and sauces, rounding out prudently with a couple of chapters on cookery for invalids.

These images from *Tacuinum sanitatis* show a cheese merchant with his wares and a man plucking seeds from fennel plants.

First printed in the late nineteenth century and much discussed since then, *Le ménagier* is a curiosity and a rich source of period domestic details, remarkable for the background text rather than the recipes.[13] Speculation about the identity of its author has ranged from the romantic hypothesis of a rich elderly man living in Paris with a new young wife to the more plausible one of an officer in a noble household, possibly Guy de Montigny, who was in the service of the first duc de Berry, father of King Charles VI. Whoever he was, the author emerges as "sensible, yet full of sensibility, deeply religious, yet a man of the world, gravely dignified, yet modest at heart."[14]

THE VAST MAJORITY of ordinary people lived at a far lower level than that represented in the period's cookbooks, experiencing episodic hunger with little or no festivity. Bread was the staple in every European country. Since contemporary cookbooks did not record the diet of the rank and file, our knowledge is limited to reports of events such as Charles IX of France's 1567 order to build city granaries large enough to hold a three-month supply.[15] The harvest was crucial, and in bad years most people had to rely on hardy grains such as oats and barley that yielded a poor yeast bread, since they contain no gluten. They also ate beans, lentils, and other legumes, hedgerow fruits, and such vegetables as they could grow themselves. Depending on the climate, their kitchen gardens might have included cabbages, leeks, onions, garlic, fennel, fava beans, greens like spinach and asparagus, a type of squash, and roots such as carrots, parsnips, turnips, and parsley. Herbs—a wide range that included borage, dittany, hyssop, rue, caraway, lovage, burnet, bergamot, and woodruff as well as our common herbs—added zip to bland dishes. Homegrown mustard and horseradish could replace expensive imported spices. Dairy milk, cheese, and butter were relative luxuries, as was a bit of bacon from a pig. Soups (*potages*), porridges, and gruel (*bouilli*) were the mainstays. Piers Plowman, writing in England in the latter half of the fourteenth century, lamented:

> I have no peny, pullets [young hens] for to buy
> Nor neither geese nor piglets, but two green cheeses,
> A few curds and cream and an oaten cake
> And two loaves of beans and bran for to bake for my little ones.
> And beside I say by my soul, I have no salt bacon,
> Nor no little eggs, by Christ, collops [meat sliced in scallops] for to make
> But I have parsley and leeks and many cabbages.[16]

The rural poverty outlined in these few lines was universal throughout Europe, though details of diet varied from country to country. Famine could strike in time of war or when harvests were poor. A prosperous class of artisans, merchants, and professional doctors and lawyers was only starting to emerge, mainly in Germany and England. At the dawn of printing, the market of buyers who could both afford and read a cookbook was tiny, but soon to be transformed.

BREAD, THE STAFF OF LIFE

Early cookbooks make much mention of bread, which was an integral part of any medieval meal. Bread was set flat on the table as a "trencher," a thick slice of dark or white bread, usually cut square to take the place of a dinner plate, so it became soaked with meat juices and sauce. At the end of dinner, a trencher might be eaten by the guest or, more often, given to the poor. Bread was the thickener of choice for sauces and stews: "toast bread, then soften it with your broth," says the French cook Taillevent. Several cookbooks offer recipes for French toast made with leftovers, or *pain perdu* (lost bread). In Italy, Martino of Como described how to make a savory little *brodetto* with bread crumbs, eggs, and cheese, a thickened version of modern *stracciatella* soup, colored with saffron. He uses bread crumbs to bind several sauces, including an ancestor of aioli mayonnaise and a verjuice sauce to serve with squash.

By contrast, early cookbooks say almost nothing about how to make the bread itself, showing that bread baking was already an art entrusted to specialist professionals. French bakers had already been dubbed *boulangers* because of the round loaves (*boules*) that they baked. In England, the equivalent everyday loaf was called a manchet. The size and shape of the standard loaf varied from place to place, and much depended on the type of flour and its composition. In the countryside, bakers had to rely on whatever grain was grown locally, but city dwellers had more choice. From medieval times onward, rivalry was keen in Paris and other wealthy cities between the light, white breads favored by the affluent and the cheaper, unbolted (unsifted) flours full of bran that yielded heavier but more nutritious breads. Parisian bakers were renowned for fine fantasy breads with names like *à la reine* and *à la mode* and had to be restrained by royal decree from making too many of them.[1] In Germany, stuffed yeast breads like *Krapffen* have survived to the present day. In Italy, the taste for white bread began in ancient Rome, where women reputedly powdered their faces with fine white flour.[2]

Bakers in every country have always agreed that wheat is the most desirable grain—for bread raised with yeast, that is. "White flour is always the best," declared Louis Liger in *Oeconomie générale de la campagne, ou La nouvelle maison rustique* (General Management for the Countryside, or The Country House, 1700); "then comes *méteil* [a mixture of wheat and rye grown together], then rye, barley, and finally oats."[3] Wheat contains generous amounts of the

Bakers are hard at work in *Description et détails des arts du meunier, du vermicelier et du boulanger* by Paul-Jacques Malouin, 1767.

gluten proteins needed to hold the bubbles of carbon dioxide formed by yeast as the dough rises. A few grains such as rye and barley also contain gluten, but the resulting bread is heavy unless these flours are mixed with wheat flour. Other common grains—notably corn, oats, millet, and buckwheat—have little gluten and so are suited only for porridge or heavy cakes such as American hoecakes or the French *gaudes.* Flat Brittany crêpes evolved to make the best of the buckwheat plant that grows well in the area's thin soil.

Recipes for bread are conspicuously lacking in early cookbooks. Even the late fourteenth century *Le ménagier,* which gives exhaustive advice on selecting meats and fish, does not mention how to buy bread or how to bake it at home. Only in the sixteenth century was much written about bread, and the subject was given full play in agricultural books. Charles Estienne, for example, devotes two chapters of *L'agriculture et maison rustique* (Agriculture and the Country House, 1564) to *la boulangerie* (the art of baking), with information on various grains, flours, types of bread, and ways to use them in the kitchen for bread crumbs, toasts, croustades, and soup thickeners. He then launches into pâtisserie—the distinction between the two métiers was clear by this time. Books on pastry began a century later with the anonymous *Le pastissier françois* (The French Pastry Cook, 1653), which includes a single bread recipe for *pain bénit,* an egg bread that was distributed to the poor on Sundays. To this day, such luxury breads continue to be a pastry cook's rather than a baker's specialty.

Where wheat flourished, so did the art of baking yeast bread. Southern England, with its soft climate and fertile soil, was lucky on both counts

and was a bread basket from Roman times, though Scotland and parts of Germany were forced to plant hardier grains such as rye and oats. However, disaster could strike at any time—war, pestilence, or simply the wrong weather for planting and harvest. In Italy, agriculture, and with it the growing of wheat and baking of all but the simplest breads, was badly hit by the Black Death in the 1400s and took centuries to recover.[4]

In the nineteenth century, when small ovens began to appear in household kitchens, a purpose-built oven for breads and pastry was a luxury restricted to grand houses, so bread was almost always baked in a communal oven on a large scale. The reasons are simple: dough is more rapidly worked, shaped, and risen in large quantities; a large oven is more economical and easier to control than a small one; and the baked bread just tastes better. Not only did professional bakers use the communal ovens, but household cooks would prepare dishes in their home kitchens and then bring the loaves for baking for a small fee. Even after World War II, the inhabitants of villages like Plouhinec in Brittany would bring their *fars bretons* (a prune batter pudding) to bake in the baker's oven for the Feast of the Virgin on August 15, enjoying a good gossip while they waited. Dogs were on the watch for a treat when the unwary talked too much.

A few individual loaves were, of course, baked at home, often in an open hearth in a Dutch oven with embers above and below. One of the earliest recipes for baking bread, given by Gervase Markham in *The English Hous-wife* (1615), calls for sixty pounds of flour, clearly envisaging a large household, possibly with a communal oven. Markham recommends using a brake, a me-

chanical device to help with kneading, and instructs the baker to "fold it in a cloth, and with your feet tread it a good space together, then letting it lie an hour or thereabouts to swell, take it forth and mould it into manchets, round and flat, scorcht [slashed] about the waste to give it leave to rise."[5]

Grain is heavy and expensive to transport, so all but the very wealthy made do with whatever grew close by. The catchment area of a mill was limited by the range of a horse or mule unless waterways were near. The cozy, rural picture of growing grain locally, milling it, and baking the flour into bread lasted almost unchanged until the early nineteenth century. In towns, the process was simply more commercial and competitive. Everywhere cooks kneaded the dough by hand and left it to rise in coffin-shaped wooden tubs, raised on legs to a convenient height. They shaped loaves on floured tables and set them to rise again on sturdy, unbleached woolen or linen cloths before sliding them into the beehive oven with long-handled wooden peels (from the French *pelle,* meaning "shovel"). The beehive ovens, some round (called "apples"), some oval ("pears"), had no chimney and were fed with slender logs through the mouth at one side. Such ovens are easy to control once you know how, and the baked bread is superb, crisp-crusted and slightly chewy within. ♦

1 Alfred Gottschalk, *Histoire de l'alimentation et de la gastronomie* (Paris: Hippocrate, 1948), 2:18–19.

2 Carole Field, *The Italian Baker* (New York: Harper Collins, 1985), 28.

3 Louis Liger, *La nouvelle maison rustique* (Paris: Durand, 1775), 1:811.

4 Field, *The Italian Baker,* 29.

5 G. M. [Gervase Markham], *The English Hous-wife* (London: W. Wilson, 1664), 186.

RECIPES FROM ANTIQUITY
THROUGH THE MIDDLE AGES

THE ROOTS OF TODAY'S RECIPES begin in manuscript cookbooks and the medieval kitchen. The oldest recipe in this book, for a spicy roast pork called Cormarye, dates back to the late 1300s and the height of medieval feasting. It comes from *Forme of Cury,* a fourteenth-century manuscript that belonged to Richard II but did not appear in print until the late 1700s. The script of the time can seem almost a code, but this is clearly a recipe for the cook to follow in the kitchen. "Prick it well with a knife and lay it in the sauce," say the instructions for Cormarye, and "serve it [the sauce] with the roast immediately." What actually ends up on the plate is difficult to imagine, and recipes were written mainly for the record. The manuscript itself would have been a treasured item, stored with care in the master's library, rather than thumbed through in the kitchen by the cook, who almost certainly could not read. Advice on serving seems of prime importance so as to please the master (who after all had commissioned the book in the first place).

I've included two other early manuscript recipes, as between them they illustrate the medieval tradition that was still dominant in the first printed cookbooks of the next century. Already, cooks are exploring complex sauces and the layers of flavor created by multiple cooking processes. Brouet de Verjus et de Poulaille comes from the late fourteenth century and *Le ménagier de Paris,* a book of advice and recipes compiled for a prosperous French housewife. The term *brouet* is the equivalent of our word *broth,* which can refer to a thin soup or to a stock used as a basis for more complex dishes, such as this colorful spiced chicken broth. The recipe includes a spice mix called *poudre fine,* rather like today's curry powder. Combinations varied from cook to cook, and this one calls for cinnamon sticks, whole cloves and nutmeg, dried ginger and galangal (a rhizome not unlike ginger), grains of paradise (a peppery relative of cardamom), and black peppercorns.

The full panoply of medieval dishes is laid out in Taillevent's *Le viandier,* a book that existed as a manuscript a century before it was printed in 1486. By now, cooks had developed a sophisticated culinary vocabulary, including terms familiar to us. *Coulis* or *couliez* is a flowing sauce of puréed white fish or chicken and almonds thinned with a little white wine and sweetened with sugar. Taillevent simmers *friquassées* of chicken and a dark *civet* of hare with instructions to thoroughly toast the bread for thickening to add color to the sauce. He loves stews and sauces, including the wine-laced jance. Heady seasoning sauces are universal in medieval cookbooks, an accompaniment to the roasted meats that anchored the menus. Jance is based on almonds bright with ginger and often colored with saffron, three of the most common ingredients of the time. Every cookbook includes at least one jance, and consistency would have been thick, like hummus, as fluid sauces were a problem in the days before the dinner plate. *Saupiquet* is equally classic, a sauce colored with saffron and piquant with black pepper and grains of paradise. The recipe in this chapter comes from *Du fait de cuisine*, a manuscript dating from 1420 and inscribed for Duke Amadeus of Savoy. Together these five recipes provide a brief glimpse of the complexities of medieval cooking, set against the backdrop of the demanding world of the kitchen with its smoky open fires and hard, muscular work.

Cormarye

From the master cook to Richard II of England, *Forme of Cury* (England, 1390; recipe from 1780 edition): *Take Colyandre [coriander], Caraway, smale groñden, Powdõ of Pep, and garlic ygroñde ī rede wyne, medle [mingle] alle þise [this] togyd, and salt it, take loyne of pork rawe and fle [free] of the skyn, and pryk it wel with a knyf, and lay it in the sawse, roost þof [thereof] what þ [thou] wilt, & keep þat, þ [that that] fallith þfrom [therefrom] ī the rosting, and seeþ [seethe] it in a poffynet [pipkin] with faire broth, & serve it forþ [forth] with þ [the] roost anoon [immediately].*

THIS SUCCULENT PORK RECIPE is easier to decipher than most. The meat is seasoned with a lively mixture of spices (all native to Europe except for black pepper), crushed garlic, and red wine, then cooked twice, first roasted on a spit to caramelize some of the juices for flavor, and then simmered in broth until meltingly tender. I've modified the method slightly so one pot serves for both stages of cooking. The peppery sauce marries perfectly with a side dish of roasted root vegetables.

Spicy Roast Pork   *Serves 4*

2 teaspoons coriander seeds
2 teaspoons caraway seeds
2 teaspoons pepper
1 teaspoon salt
10 to 12 garlic cloves, cut into pieces
2 to 3 tablespoons red wine
One 2-pound (900-g) boneless pork loin roast
2 cups (500 ml) veal broth

Kitchen string

Heat the oven to 400°F (200°C). Finely grind together the spices and salt in a mortar with a pestle. Add the garlic and crush it also. Work in enough wine to form a paste.

Slash deep, lengthwise cuts in the meat, about 1 inch (2.5 cm) apart, and insert some of the spiced garlic paste. Roll and tie the roast with the string. Put the meat in a flameproof casserole and spread the remaining garlic paste on top. Roast the pork, uncovered, for 1 hour. The coating will have browned and the meat will be partially cooked.

Remove the pork from the oven. Reduce the oven temperature to 350°F (180°C). Add the broth to the casserole and stir to dissolve the pan juices. Bring the broth to a boil on the stove top, cover, and return to the oven. Continue cooking the pork until very tender and a skewer inserted in the center is hot to the touch when withdrawn, 1¼ to 1½ hours longer.

Transfer the roast to a platter, cover loosely with aluminum foil, and let rest for at least 10 minutes before carving. If the pan juices taste thin, boil to reduce and concentrate them, then taste and adjust the seasoning. Carve the roast and serve the juices as a gravy on the side.

Brouet de Verjus et de Poulaille

Chicken Broth with Verjuice

From *Le ménagier de Paris* (Paris, 1393; recipe from 1846 edition): *(For summer.) Take a quartered chicken, or veal, or baby chickens and cook in broth or other liquid with bacon, wine, and verjuice, so that the flavor of verjuice mellows: then fry your meat in good lard, and have egg yolks and Poudre Fine beaten together and work them through a tamis sieve; then trickle your eggs into your pot of broth very slowly, and stir rapidly with a spoon while the pot is on low heat: then have parsley sprigs and juice from boiled meat or meat broth, stirred with the spoon into the pot on low heat, or alternatively cooked in another small pot in fresh water to extract the first green; then present your meat, and coat it with your cooking broth, then with your green parsley.*

THIS RECIPE MUST HAVE HAD a novice in mind. The cooking instructions include advice on not boiling egg yolks to avoid curdling them, as well as how to preserve the bright green of the parsley by blanching in boiling water. The writer does not say whether the end result should be a soup or a stew, however. Since *brouet* implies a broth, I'm assuming the former, so we have pieces of chicken in a broth of striking golden color, garnished with brilliant green parsley leaves.

The chicken is cooked twice, first simmered, then fried before serving. Double cooking was a medieval habit, perhaps a health precaution, or else a way of precooking ingredients so they would keep longer. In any case, the chicken ends up well done and falling from the bone—easily pulled apart with a spoon. *Poudre fine* spices the broth, and the bacon provides salt, so more may not be needed. A side dish of boiled rice (rice was grown in Italy during the fourteenth century) would be appropriate to absorb the fragrant broth.

ANTIQUITY THROUGH THE MIDDLE AGES \ RECIPES

Chicken in a Spiced Broth   *Serves 4*

> 5 ounces (140 g) slab bacon, cut into lardons
> 2 cups (500 ml) chicken broth, more if needed
> 1 cup (250 ml) medium-dry white wine
> 1 cup (250 ml) verjuice
> 1 chicken (3 to 4 pounds or 1.35 to 1.5 kg), quartered
> 1 medium bunch parsley (about 2 ounces or 60 g)
> 1 tablespoon (15 g) lard
> 4 egg yolks
> 2 tablespoons (15 g) Fragrant Spice Powder (below)
> Salt, if needed

In a shallow saucepan, combine the bacon, broth, wine, and verjuice and bring to a boil. Add the chicken pieces, pushing them below the surface of the liquid. Add more broth if needed to immerse them. Cover and simmer, skimming away any foam from time to time, until the chicken is very tender, about 1 hour. The meat should be almost falling from the bone. Using a wire skimmer, remove the chicken pieces to a plate, cover tightly, and set aside.

Bring the broth in the pan to a boil, and boil until reduced to about 1 quart (1 liter), 10 to 15 minutes. Turn off the heat and return the chicken pieces to the warm broth. Let them cool to room temperature.

Meanwhile, strip off the parsley leaves, put them in a heatproof bowl, and discard the stems. Bring a saucepan filled with water to a boil, pour it over the leaves, and let stand until the leaves turn bright green, 1 to 2 minutes. Drain the parsley, rinse with cold water, and then drain again thoroughly and set aside.

To finish: In a frying pan, heat the lard over medium-high heat. Remove the chicken pieces from the broth and pat them dry with a paper towel so they won't sputter when you put them in the pan. Add them to the hot pan and fry, turning them once, until brown on both sides, 3 to 4 minutes total. Transfer to a plate, cover, and put aside.

To make the spiced broth, in a small bowl, whisk together the egg yolks and Fragrant Spice Powder. Put the saucepan of broth back on the stove, and turn the heat on very low. While whisking vigorously, dribble the spiced egg yolks into the warm broth, then continue to whisk until the eggs are cooked and the broth has thickened slightly. Do not let the broth boil or the yolks will curdle. Taste and adjust the seasoning with salt, though it may not be needed as the bacon is salty.

Put the chicken pieces in 4 warmed shallow bowls, ladle the broth over the top, and sprinkle the chicken with the parsley. Serve very warm with a spoon and fork. The chicken should be tender enough to cut with a spoon, but you may also want to have knives at table.

33

Poudre Fine
———
Excellent Powder

🌿 From Estienne Servain for Jean Antoine Huguetan, *Le thresor de santé* (Lyon, 1607): *Ginger, one ounce; cinnamon, three and a half ounces; peppercorns, one ounce; long pepper, one ounce; nutmeg, two ounces; whole cloves, one ounce; grains of paradise, galangal, an ounce of each.*

POUDRE FINE IS ONE of several medieval spice mixes often referred to in cookbooks of the time. Cooks tended to be vague on proportions, so this recipe comes from an early-sixteenth-century medical book. Because even a little of the mix goes a long way, after we tested this recipe, ideas for using up the spice mix became commonplace in our small household. I urge you to try it with fish, chicken, veal, and vegetables, as well as for seasoning cookies. Indeed, we've become quite addicted! If you prefer to use ready-ground spices, allow 4 tablespoons per ounce (30 g). The mix keeps well in an airtight container. "Powders keep their strength for a month, even forty days," remarks the author. "They should be kept in leather pouches so they stay fresh." Here I make half the original quantity. Long pepper is the fruit of a flowering vine in the same genus as black pepper. Both long pepper and grains of paradise can be found in specialty stores and online.

Fragrant Spice Powder   *Makes about 1¾ cups (200 g)*

2 oz (60 g) cinnamon sticks
1 oz (30 g) whole nutmeg
½ oz (15 g) dried ginger
½ oz (15 g) peppercorns
½ oz (15 g) long pepper
½ oz (15 g) whole cloves
½ oz (15 g) grains of paradise
½ oz (15 g) dried galangal

Grind the spices together to a fine powder in a spice grinder or in a mortar with a pestle, then transfer them to a small bowl. (If using ready-ground spices, stir them together.) The spice mix can be stored in an airtight jar in a cool place for up to 6 months.

Jance
———

🌿 From Taillevent, *Le viandier* (Paris, 1392; recipe from 1892 edition): *To make jance, hull almonds and pound them in a mortar, then strain them with verjuice and white wine and then take an ounce of ginger for a pint, strain and restrain the sauce through a tamis sieve; let it simmer in a pan for a very short time and, at once, put in a crock, otherwise it will taste of tin, and do not boil it in an iron pan because it will discolor.*

JANCE IS ONE OF THOSE ANCIENT NAMES like hot pot and salamagundy that can cover a huge range of dishes. The name is related to *jaune,* or "yellow," so it is surprising that Taillevent does not use saffron to color his recipe. His version I take to be a sauce that would have been served with roast meats or poultry. Also surprising, Taillevent mentions a couple of measurements—an ounce and a pint—but they mean little as no other quantities are given. In any case, in early times weights varied from region to region and even town to town.

Taillevent likes to include bits of advice, and here he's concerned about the risks of contamination from his unlined iron pans. He warns against leaving this white sauce (the color is a spectacular pale cream), which is acid with wine and verjuice, to linger in the cooking pan as it will discolor; transfer it to a ceramic pot at once. He also calls for sieving the finished sauce, though I find the modern food processor makes this step unnecessary. In Taillevent's time, ginger, the key flavoring, had to make the long trip from Asia, so it would have been available to him only dried, either in chunks, slices, or powdered. When made with today's ground ginger, his sauce packs a notable punch, tempered by wine and verjuice. For a quick glimpse of medieval flavors, try it with roast chicken or a pork or veal chop. I particularly enjoy it as a dip for raw vegetables.

Sauce Jance   *Makes 2¹/₂ cups (625 ml) sauce to serve 6 to 8*

    8 ounces (225 g) blanched almonds
    1 cup (250 ml) verjuice
    1 cup (250 ml) full-bodied white wine
    2 tablespoons (15 g) ground ginger

    Tamis strainer or food mill (optional)

Put the almonds in a food processor and pulse until they are finely ground and starting to clump (evidence that the oil has been drawn out of them), 3 to 5 minutes. Add half the verjuice and continue working until well combined, about 30 seconds. Add the remaining verjuice, the wine, and the ginger and pulse until well mixed.

Transfer the mixture to a saucepan and heat gently, stirring constantly with a wooden spoon, until the sauce thickens but still falls easily from the spoon, 2 to 3 minutes. Take the sauce from the heat and let cool to tepid.

If you like, work the sauce, a little at a time, through a tamis strainer or food mill. It should be thick enough to hold a shape. The sauce keeps well, tightly covered, in the refrigerator for up to 3 days, and the flavor will mellow. The sauce may separate on standing, so stir well before serving at room temperature.

Saupiquet

꿈꿈꿈 From Amiczo Chiquart, *Du fait de cuisine* (Savoy, 1420): *To instruct the person who will be doing the Saupiquet, he should take onions and prepare them well, slice and chop them up very small; then he should get well-clarified oil and sauté his onions properly in it, then drain away the oil so that none is left. Then he should get a good clean kettle and very good wine, and put in enough for the amount of fish he has already fried; then he takes his spices—ginger, grains of paradise, saffron, and pepper—all in appropriate amounts for the quantity of fish that is to be eaten with the saupiquet. He should flavor it well but lightly with vinegar, and with salt too.*

DUKE AMADEUS OF SAVOY was yet another medieval ruler who wished to underline the importance of feasting in power politics. The introduction to *Du fait de cuisine* (On the Matter of Cookery, c. 1420) makes clear that the work had been commissioned by the duke himself from his head cook, Amiczo Chiquart, and phrases are dropped here and there pointing out Chiquart's skill and the importance of his role in the ducal household. His style is colloquial, dictated to a clerk. Few, if any, cooks of the time would have been able to write. The manuscript did not make it into print, however, and only recently came to light in the archives of the Swiss canton of the Valais.

Here is another classic medieval seasoning sauce, colored with saffron and piquant with black pepper and with grains of paradise (black pepper can be substituted). *Saupiquet* is still popular with game and pork in northern Burgundy, traditionally made with the dry white wine of Chablis. I'm taking the easy way out in suggesting you use ready-ground spices, but if you grind them fresh, they will have an even stronger burst of flavor. Follow the weights given in the recipe and use a mortar and pestle or small coffee grinder (your coffee will have a pleasing aroma for several batches afterward!). Either way, medieval sauces were thick, intended to cling to food, rather than flowing, as they are today. Chiquart destines this slowly cooked sauce for fried fish, and I'd suggest it also for roasted vegetables or chicken.

Sour and Spicy Sauce for Fish   *Makes 1 cup (250 ml) sauce to serve 4*

3 tablespoons (45 g) lard
3 medium onions (about 1 pound or 450 g total), very finely chopped
1 teaspoon ground ginger
1 teaspoon ground grains of paradise
1 teaspoon ground pepper
Pinch of ground saffron
2 tablespoons white wine
2 tablespoons red or white wine vinegar
Salt

Heat the lard in a medium saucepan over very low heat. Fry the onions uncovered, stirring often, until meltingly soft and golden brown. This will take quite a long time, 1¼ to 1½ hours.

Stir the ground spices into the onions and cook, stirring constantly, until very fragrant, 2 to 3 minutes. Stir in the wine and simmer the sauce, stirring steadily, until it is thick and clings to the spoon, 1 to 2 minutes. Take the sauce from the heat, and stir in the vinegar and the salt to taste. Taste and adjust with more vinegar or salt, if you wish. Serve at room temperature.

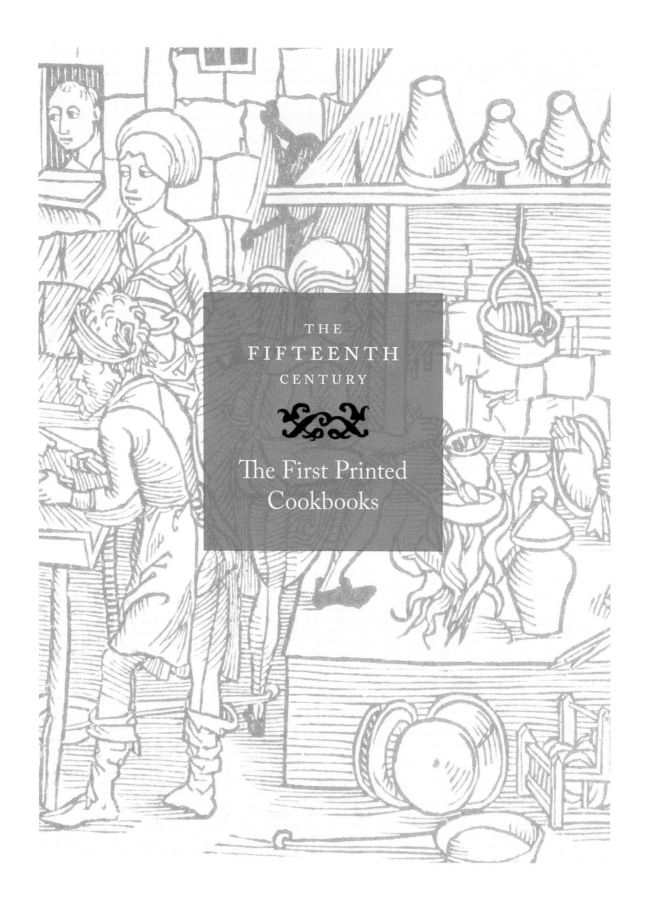

THE
FIFTEENTH
CENTURY

The First Printed
Cookbooks

THE FIRST FOUR COOKBOOKS to be printed were written by working cooks who had spent their careers in the kitchen. These books are more modest than many of their peers, without the illustrations or hand-painted illuminations that adorn the first print versions of literary classics and religious works. Simple compendiums of recipes, only one has fewer than two hundred recipes and three were written in the vernacular, although even the one Latin cookbook among the four was based on a book written in Tuscan Italian. The everyday, working language of these cookbooks permitted them to serve as household records and as manuals that stewards could take to the kitchen to give verbal instructions to the cooks.

The first printed cookbook, *De honesta voluptate et valetudine* (Of Honest Indulgence and Good Health), became a best seller after it was published in 1474. The author, Bartolomeo Sacchi, often called Platina, combined his philosophical manual on how to maintain good health with practical recipes from the Italian manuscript *Libro de arte coquinaria* (Book of the Art of Cooking, c. 1465) by a master cook called Martino. Next came the anonymous German *Küchenmeisterei* (Mastery of the Kitchen, 1485). Taillevent's *Le viandier* (The Victualler) was the oldest of the early printed cookbooks, compiled as a manuscript by the French royal cook in the 1370s and printed about 1486. Last of this prestigious group was the English *Boke of Cokery* of 1500. All are incunabula, meaning that they were printed before 1501.

Printing followed the beginning of humanism, reviving classical learning and adding a more secular orientation to medieval culture. With its emphasis on human values and worldly pursuits, humanism had far-reaching practical implications that included a recognition of artisan trades such as cooking, which in turn inspired practitioners to write down their lore and techniques. The arrival of printing technology transformed books from a luxury for the rich elite who could afford access to a rare manuscript to a commodity that was available to the merely wealthy. At this time (and for many years to come), prosperous groups outside the aristocracy were most numerous in England, less so in France and the Germanic states, with Burgundy and the Italian

OPPOSITE Detail from the frontispiece of *Küchenmeisterei*, 1490. Full image on page 51.

city-states in between. In the 1460s, printing presses were already established in a handful of countries, and by the end of the sixteenth century, printing had made it possible for every well-to-do household to possess a cookbook.[1]

Printers were primarily craftsmen operating small family businesses. The printed book was created by packing together tiny blocks of metal cast into single letters, punctuation marks, and spaces to spell out words and then sentences; finally the printer inked the blocks and pressed them onto a page. Books were typically sold as unbound sheets for the buyer to commission his own binding, simple or elaborate according to taste or pocket.

German printers, trained under the efficient apprenticeship system that was already in place in many Germanic cities, were at the forefront. By the late 1450s, Pope Paul II had brought German printers to a monastery in Italy, where they published church literature before moving to Rome in 1467 to found an independent press. In the 1460s, Duke Philip III of Burgundy had both scribes and printers working side by side creating books for his renowned library in Dijon.

German printers in Italy developed their connections with the church and were probably responsible for the printing of Platina's *De honesta voluptate et valetudine* in Rome in 1474. In Venice, an early edition of Cassianus's *De institutis coenobiorum* (On the Management of Monastic Communities) appeared in 1491. In England, Wynkyn de Worde was partner and successor to the first English printer, William Caxton, who seems to have been a cross between a banker and a philanthropist. Their partnership saw the creation of some of the most famous early books, including *Boke of Kervynge* (1508) and an edition of Chaucer's *Canterbury Tales* (1483).

When *De honesta voluptate* first appeared, the political map of Europe was very different than in the centuries that followed. In the city-states of Italy, the Renaissance was in full artistic and philosophical flower, while the prosperous Germanic states were developing the new printing technology at home as well as throughout Europe. The Catalonian region maintained a strong cultural presence along the northwestern Mediterranean, at this time including Sardinia and Sicily, while Spain kept a low profile behind the barrier of the Pyrenees. The Kingdom of France, covering rather less than today's territory, was at an impasse, harried by English invaders. In contrast, for a brief, brilliant span, the Dukedom of Burgundy was paramount, a sprawling territory with a budget almost equaling that of France.[2]

On the Fifteenth-Century Table

The first printed cookbooks were plain in appearance, but the lifestyle they described was anything but modest. Any pretense of gastronomy—and a great deal of pretense was going on—was limited to the very wealthy: royalty, nobles such as the dukes of Burgundy and Savoy, and the princes of the church. Almost all early cookbooks assume dozens, if not hundreds, of servants and a complex household hierarchy in the kitchen and dining hall. Indeed, a military-style organization typically prevailed in these large households, likely designed to reflect the family's similar control in the outside world. When hosts invited guests to dine, the feast that followed was not just for pleasure; it was a visible, inescapable symbol of power. As in summit meetings today, the lineup of guests at high table made the top players visible, and recognizable, to all.

In this period of flamboyance, the court of the duke of Burgundy set the standard by which all others were judged. Duke Charles the Bold, who ruled Burgundy from 1467 to 1477, was as powerful as the contemporary kings of France and England and fancied himself grander than both. His territory stretched from the North Sea, through what was known as the Low Countries to Mâcon in the south, bordered by the Loire river to the west, and Alsace, Luxembourg, and the Rhine to the east. His might was documented by his chief pantler, or master of ceremonies, Olivier de la Marche, whose

In the illuminated manuscript *Chroniques du Hainault* from 1448, Jean Wauquelin presents a book to Duke Philip the Good of Burgundy, who had the foresight to install experts in the new craft of printing beside the traditional scribes in his library in Dijon.

ABOVE The richly illuminated manuscript of *Très riches heures du duc de Bérri* by the Limbourg brothers (Flanders, c. 1412) records the events of the year for Jean, duc de Berry, a renowned connoisseur of the arts and brother to King Charles V of France (who had commissioned the cookbook *Le viandier*). Here guests line up to present New Year's gifts. At left are key members of the ducal household, the *échansonnier* in charge of wine and the *panetier* for bread, whose offerings are given precedence for their sacred connotations. Eating utensils were minimal, and bread was useful, either for dipping in sauces and stews or in the thick platelike form of a trencher (from the French *tranche,* or slice). A napkin was commonly draped over the shoulder for wiping the fingers. In front of the seated duke is the carver, whose technical brilliance showcased the most valuable foods, including whole birds, animals, and fruits, while beside him the boat-shaped *nef,* or salt cellar, marks his importance. On the table, two little dogs eagerly share the feast.

ENTERTAINING ENTREMETS

Over the centuries, an integral part of a first-class feast has always been the entertainment. Medieval banquets would have seemed interminable, daunting the most ardent epicure, if the courses had not been interspersed with entremets, or side shows. At the court of Burgundy, the acknowledged leader of fifteenth-century fashion, guests were entertained with *pièces montées* involving complicated and novel contrivances, mimes or acrobatic displays, castles manned by soldiers, and fantastic or symbolical animals. At one banquet, a colossal pie was brought in holding an orchestra of twelve musicians.

Some entremets were in principle edible, like those for a 1343 reception that Cardinal Annibale de Ceccano gave for Pope Clement VI in Avignon (the seat of the papacy at the time). One set piece featured a castle as a backdrop for a full-grown stag, a boar, some roebucks, and hares and rabbits; history does not disclose if the animals were live, stuffed, or cooked and ready for eating. The grand finale, between the seventh and eighth courses of this lengthy feast, featured two trees, one of silver hung with golden apples, pears, figs, and plums; the other was green and spangled with multicolored candied fruits (still a specialty of the region). This gathering of sweets at the end of the meal is an early example of dessert.[1]

Other entremets were outright stage performances with little or no food connection. Gamboling horses, live lions, mock battles, and sundry saints and dragons vied with fountains spouting wine and frogs escaping from pies "which make the ladies to skip and shreek."[2] In England during the reign of Elizabeth I, an athletic display known as the Alamain leap was popular: a jester would run into the room, leap over the heads of seated guests, and plunge into an outsize custard pie "to the unspeakable amusement of those who were far enough off from the tumbler not to be bespattered by this active gambol."[3] The English were particularly literal minded with their "subtleties," elaborate architectural constructions often made in sugar or marzipan to be edible, draped with poems and messages for all to read. The tradition continues to this day in tiered wedding cakes that offer good wishes to the bride and groom in white icing.

Only so much can be done to amuse a static audience, and by the end of the fifteenth century, guests were going with the flow, moving from dining hall to buffet tables set in another room or possibly outdoors. In the benign Italian climate, the buffet itself became the entertainment, with the room in which it was served, and the table on which it was spread out, becoming known as a *credenza*. Cristoforo di Messisbugo talks in *Banchetti* (1549) of a credenza course of cold dishes featuring pies, sausages, boiled shellfish, vegetables, salads, and other typical *antipasti,* as well as fruits, sweet cakes, and candies. Display was half the attraction, with fine Venetian glass and precious gold and silver plate, wrought by masters such as Benvenuto Cellini, standing cheek by jowl with sugar statues and gelatin molds. The credenza spread of food was the forerunner of the French cold buffet. Over time, the entremet as an entertainment almost disappeared in continental Europe, and we are left with a lone reminder of such diversions with this English nursery rhyme:

Sing a song of sixpence, a pocket
 full of rye,
Four and twenty blackbirds baked
 in a pie.
When the pie was opened, the birds
 began to sing,
Oh, wasn't that a dainty dish to set
 before a king! ♦

The successful entremet had amusement value but was also symbolic. The whole stuffed peacock in full plumage in this medieval manuscript from *Antiquitates Culinariae* compiled by Richard Warner, 1791, was a ritual part of a medieval feast, symbolizing pride, protection, and nobility. A suitable virgin lady, her hair unbound to signal her status, was selected to carry the sculpture in procession to the high table. With a bit of ingenuity and judicious use of camphor, the bird would seem to breathe fire during its progress.

1 Roy C. Strong, *Feast: A History of Grand Eating* (Orlando, FL: Harcourt Publishing, 2002), 118.

2 Robert May, *The Accomplisht Cook* (London, 1660).

3 See Richard Warner, *Antiquitates Culinariae or Curious Tracts Relating to the Culinary Affairs of the Old English* (London: R. Blamire, 1791), 130.

Dogs as well as ladies are invited to this fifteenth-century feast in the splendid vaulted palace of the dukes of Burgundy in Dijon. Across the courtyard from the main hall, the kitchen with its five chimneys still stands today as witness to the lavish entertainments offered six centuries ago.

Memoires de Messire Olivier de la Marche (a late fifteenth-century manuscript) is a unique source about life at the most luxurious and sophisticated court in Europe.[3] Power brokering was taken for granted, and the extravagant entertainment of allies was the stuff of politics. In the world described by La Marche, all the elements of entertaining—the order of service, the ranking of guests, the performance of carving, and the conventions of hospitality—were convoluted in the extreme.

One banquet orchestrated by La Marche in Dijon, the capital of Burgundy, featured five *mestz* (courses arrayed buffet style on the table) dotted with rare ingredients, including eagle, cygnet, and peacock. Technical terms already in use include *cretonnée,* a white stew of meat or poultry thickened with egg yolks and cream; *brouet* (or pot-au-feu), flavored with cinnamon; and *saupiquet,* a sauce piquant with wine and vinegar, in this case served with rabbit. Capons were stuffed with cream, pigeons came in pies, custards were gilded, possibly with real gold, and pears were simmered in the already famous local red wine (one recipe in Taillevent calls for "the best wine of Beaune"). The splendid banquet ended with walnuts, hazelnuts, and pears arranged at random on the table along with a dish called white cream, probably a version of blancmange made of pounded almonds, milk, and often a white meat such as chicken or veal.

No one was more convinced than La Marche that a splendid court and lavish entertainment were of vital importance to the prestige of the house of Burgundy. He oversaw an enormous staff to ensure that all went well—at the head, five gentlemen of the bedchamber, each with nine pantlers. Under the pantlers were scores of *écuyers,* or squire-assistants—La Marche, as chief pantler, had fifty of them. When the duke dined, the ceremonial requirements were precise:

> The butler of the pantry hands him [the pantler] a napkin and kisses it as a sign of service. The pantler places the napkin on his left shoulder, one end hanging in front, the other behind. The butler then hands him the covered salt-cellar which the afore-mentioned pantler has to carry with his fingers, holding the base and center of the dish, unlike the goblet which is held by the stem. The pantler, bare-headed, follows the usher.
>
> The pantler places the meat on the table, tastes it [poison was a common threat], then hands it to the others, one after the other. Then the pantler takes up his position at the end of the table in front of the dish and gives the duke two helpings, and each time he helps him to twelve or thirteen dishes. The meal is served in one sitting. And the pantler has to take one of the knives and put salt from the large dish into the small dish, taste it, and place it in front of the duke.[4]

All this pomp was to fade with astonishing rapidity. In 1477, at the height of his power, Charles was killed on the battlefield—not for nothing was he nicknamed Charles the Rash—and by the end of the century, the medieval lifestyle represented by Burgundy was already being engulfed by the humanist tide from across the Alps.

The First Printed Cookbook

After the stuffy rituals described by Olivier de la Marche, the innovations of *De honesta voluptate et valetudine,* the very first printed cookbook, are like a burst of sunlight. Here we see the gale wind of humanism in full, brilliant force, with Platina making a fundamental break with the medieval cookbook tradition. Gone is the religious focus, yielding to the well-being and pleasure of humanity. The book became an instant and long-standing success thanks to Platina's excellent advice on diet and health. In his dedication, Platina hastens to explain, "I have written for the citizen who wishes good health and a clean life rather than debauchery." Indeed, bits of his advice could have been written by a modern health counselor. For example, on the matter of sex, he asserts, "It is not so satisfactory in summer and autumn, and more suitable in winter and spring, and safer at night than during the day, if one does not stay up late or work immediately afterward."[5]

Platina's decision to include recipes was experimental, as was much of the humanist writing circulating in his day. Organized like Pliny's *Natural History, De honesta voluptate* meanders through myriad (to us) incongruous styles, sprinkling poetry, fictional anecdotes, and dialogue amid the prose. In keeping with his times, Platina was writing for a new audience, the literate gentleman of eclectic interests and humanist leanings. (He himself was the Vatican librarian.) The recipes he included were not his own but mainly those of the pope's cook, Maestro Martino, with a few from Apicius.[6] Platina

The Sanguine Man

The Phlegmatic Man

The sanguine man, the phlegmatic man, the choleric man, and their counterpart the melancholy man illustrate the four humors in the 1830 Oxford edition of the medieval *Regimen sanitatis salernitatum*.

MAINTAINING A GOOD HUMOR

In the fifteenth century, people took for granted that what they ate determined how they felt. Food and medicine were sometimes indistinguishable; doctors were interested in cooking, and cooks were to some extent physicians, called on to fine-tune the appetites of their masters. People believed in the theory of humors propounded by the second-century Greek physician Galen, who defined the four fluids that governed the body: blood, phlegm, yellow bile, and black bile. For good health, Galen writes, these humors have to be in balance, and people should adjust their diets with this in mind. He states that all people are inclined to one of four types: those dominated by blood are sunny tempered and optimistic (sanguine); those with too much moisture are inclined to sloth and idleness (phlegmatic); those with too much yellow bile lean toward bad temper, even violence (choler); and those dominated by black bile are subject to gloom and depression (melancholy).[1] Eating the right foods, correctly cooked, would counteract these tendencies.

Reading early recipes according to this diet principle reveals a structured world of hidden meanings. A person of choleric temper, considered hot and dry, should look for foods of opposite characteristics, like green salads, cucumber, or fish (which are moist and swim in water). Laziness can be treated with hot spices to counteract an excess of cold, moist humor. Those of sanguine temperament, hot and moist, should take care not to eat too many red meats. Foods themselves were also allotted characteristics, so that the moist, warming properties of onion and ginger were good for boosting the cold, dry tendencies of the habitual pessimist. Fruits and leafy vegetables, by nature cold and moist, were appropriate for the hot tempered and for everybody in hot weather. Bread was essential for all because it bound disparate foods.[2]

To add to the complexity, fifteenth-century proponents of Galen's theory specified cooking methods as well. For example, they advocated simmering beef or lamb to tenderize it (and as a hygiene precaution), then roasting or sautéing the meat to reduce its natural moistness; this instruction provided another justification for the medieval habit of double cooking. Cold and moist foods could be corrected with hot, dry spices; vinegar, lemon juice, and other tart condiments were considered cold and dry and therefore helpful with vegetables and fish. Sauces were a quick fix for many main ingredients. For instance, the popular *sauce jance* provided verjuice and wine (cold and dry) and ginger (hot) to complement the moist heat of meats, and *sauce cameline* gave cold, moist fish a similar lift with cinnamon, ginger, cardamom, cloves, and mace (all hot and dry) and vinegar (cold and dry). The chopping, pounding, and puréeing found in so many recipes of the period can be seen as an effort to unite several conflicting characteristics in a final whole.

The theory of the humors was not swept away by humanism. On the contrary, with modifications, it underpinned medical, and to some extent culinary, practice until the eighteenth century. And its influence in the kitchen, almost imperceptible to us, has shaped our traditional dishes and flavorings—mint jelly with lamb, lemon with fried fish, bacon with baked beans, ginger in butter cookies—for all time. ♦

1 Roy C. Strong, *Feast: A History of Grand Eating* (Orlando, FL: Harcourt Publishing, 2002), 11.

2 Ken Albala, *Food in Early Modern Europe* (Westport, CT: Greenwood Press, 2003). 214–19.

The Choleric Man.

The Melancholy Man.

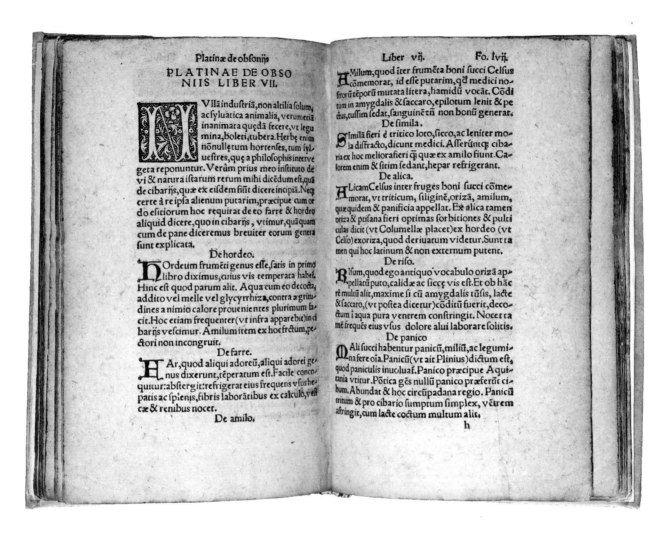

ABOVE Given the small print runs of early editions such as this 1530 copy of *De honesta voluptate. De ratione victus, & modo viuendi. De natura rerum & arte coquendi libri* by Bartolomeo Sacchi (Platina), it is encouraging how many have survived for four centuries or more. But when you handle them, it is less surprising. They are tough and durable, printed on rag paper, then sturdily bound to resist changes in temperature and humidity and general wear and tear. The finest of them are artworks of great beauty, but even simple, stubby little volumes such as this have the serviceable appeal of objects that were made to use, and to last.

OPPOSITE The airy, italic writing on this first page of *Libro de arte coquinaria* by Maestro Martino (1465) seems to echo the dishes he describes. His recipes are light and refreshing, with the many side dishes and vegetables epitomizing our vision of Mediterranean cooking. What a contrast to the traditional dense Gothic script that was used in contemporary Germany and France to describe these nations' earthier, more robust cuisine.

freely admitted the practical origins of his recipes in his glowing acknowledgment: "What a cook, O immortal gods, you bestowed in my friend Martino of Como, from whom I have received, in great part, the things of which I am writing."[7] Platina's text illustrates the clear link between practical cookery and the medical theory of the humors propounded by the Greek physician Galen, which was enormously influential at this time.

The recipes in *De honesta voluptate* have an artisanal rather than an intellectual bent, reflecting the new scientific philosophy of the humanist era, which so keenly sought the advancement of learning from all sources. As a cook, Martino adopted a recipe style very different from that of his medieval forerunners. He ordered his recipes under headings like "Meats for Boiling and Meats for Roasting," "Sauces," "Tarts," "Fritters," "Eggs," and "Fish." Just a glance at his chapter titled "Prepared Dishes" reveals more than a dozen vegetable dishes, including fried squash, cooked lettuce, fava bean fritters, and, in a return to classical tradition, cabbage with bacon or pork fat "in the Roman way." Many more ideas are scattered among the nearly two hundred recipes; he favors little amusements such as stuffed fava beans and trout eggs disguised as peas.

He recognizes regional Italian styles of cooking, with the sausages of Bologna, crayfish of Venice and Rome, the rice of Lombardy, and a bow to Catalonia in roast partridges flavored with orange juice, and squash *"al modo catalano,"* baked with sweet spices, sugar, and verjuice.

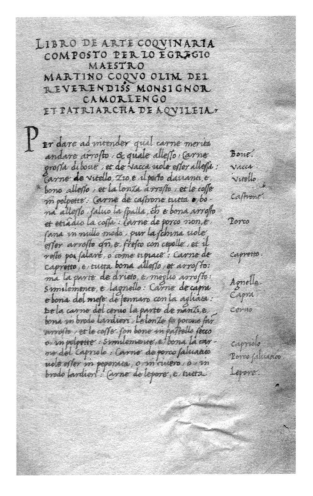

The recipes are clearly those of an experienced cook. Martino carefully explains the reasoning behind his instructions, such as his suggestion that the cook cover the soup pot with a damp cloth to prevent the contents from acquiring a smoky taste (a persistent problem when cooking over an open fire). His approach to ingredients reflects our own appreciation of local products, particularly fruits and vegetables. He veered away from the medieval reliance on imported spices, preferring a few lighter favorites such as cinnamon, ginger, and home-grown saffron. He clearly loved the aromatic herbs that remain Italian favorites: sage, rosemary, mint, marjoram, fennel, and bay leaf. His dishes throughout the meal use sugar both as a condiment and as a main ingredient, though the recipes give no quantities, so we cannot be sure how the sugar was used. "Make your tart sweet or sharp according to your taste, or how your lord and master likes it," Martino instructs in his recipe for pigeon tart. His *bianco magnare*, which calls for pounded cooked capon breast, rice simmered in milk, and a pound of sugar, is definitively sweet, a forerunner of today's blancmange dessert.

Mastery in the German Kitchen

Germany was the birthplace of so many early printed books that it seems natural that one should be a cookbook. *Küchenmeisterei* (Mastery of the Kitchen, 1485), printed in Nuremberg by Peter Wagner (in an unusual turnabout, we know the name of the printer but not the author), reflects the entrepreneurial, forward-looking spirit of the time. The original manuscript dates back to earlier in the century, and the southern German language includes a few dialect words that indicate that the unknown author almost certainly came from the Nuremberg region of Bavaria. Given his wide culinary experience and the sophistication of his recipes, he was probably master cook to a local aristocrat.[8] The author states he is writing for a wide audience: "for princely households, for prosperous city-dwellers, for wealthy cloisters, and for master chefs in the taverns and inns of the nobility and their families."[9] However, the expansive style and generous overview of the recipes suggest a wider audience than the restricted court circles of rich clerics and nobility. Another possible source for *Küchenmeisterei* is monastic, because the ingredients are typical: "the complete absence of hare despite other game recipes (hare was regarded as unchaste). . . . the lack of sugar, which was very much in fashion at the time for the rich, and its substitution by honey (for whose production monasteries were famous); and the use of home-grown herbs rather than an abundance of expensive spices."[10]

Küchenmeisterei was not just a book for the wealthy; the title Mastery of the Kitchen hints at a German tradition that was to develop in later centuries—the trade book. Guilds were strong in medieval Germany and nowhere more than in Nuremberg, which was ruled by a town council that included trade-guild representatives. Printing made possible simple, inexpensive leaflets and books of instruction that were to flourish in following centuries. At a more affluent level, *Küchenmeisterei* reflects the preoc-

Drinking is surely a penance rather than a pleasure for Beughkan and Braskan, depicted in this woodcut by an unknown German or Flemish artist, possibly in the fifteenth century. "Braskan is pouring you this beer / Don't you want wine, are you sure about beer?"/"Oh Beughkan, this beer is very bad, / Give me more wine, and don't take long," runs their dour exchange.

cupation with scientific and artistic "secrets" that was to in-trigue Europeans in the following century.

In the late fifteenth century, the city of Nuremberg was a buzzing center of commerce, an independent city within the Holy Roman Empire, a German ministate subject only to the emperor's personal authority and placed on an equal footing with principalities such as Strasbourg and Mainz. Preceding centuries had seen an explosion in the number of Catholic religious orders in the city, from the Teutonic knights to the Franciscans, Dominicans, Carthusians, and the Order of the Poor Clares, culminating in the 1330s with the Hospital of the Holy Ghost. Prosperity brought with it culture: Nuremberg was the birthplace of Albrecht Dürer in 1471, and during the fifteenth century, the city's manufacturers were so well known that they were recognized in an adage, "Nuremberg's hand goes through every land." Its citizens lived in such luxury that Pope Pius II noted, "A simple burgher of Nuremberg was better lodged than the King of Scotland."[11] The people of Nuremberg formed an increasingly prosperous class that had been brought up to seek cultural improvement. *Küchenmeisterei* was their guide to the invigorating world of gastronomy.

The book is remarkably comprehensive within its scanty thirty-two pages. An overview of the contents in order of importance shows fasting-day dishes first, with some vegetable soups and fruit pre-serves among the all-important fish; beaver is mentioned, and crayfish were so abun-dant that a city ordinance forbade households from feeding them to staff more than once a week. Next come meats, chicken, and game, including the jellied meats that were so admired at the time. A third section lists a few side dishes such as soups and eggs (much appreciated in medieval times) and baked goods, with tips on how to color breads with cornflowers and saffron, of which the author is very proud. Instructions for making sauces and remedies for the sick—a common household duty—occupy the end of the book, together with hints on how to use vinegar and wine. The style is practical and, as in almost all fifteenth-century cookbooks, assumes that the reader is a professional cook with no need of detailed instruction. "Make a dough" and "prepare the insides as they're supposed to be" are typical directions. Already among the 170 recipes the reader finds local specialties, such as *Krapffen* (honey and wine pastries) and *Leberwürst* (liver sausage).

The Nuremberg readership for *Küchenmeisterei* must have been more egalitarian than that for Taillevent at the royal court of France and for Martino at the papal court in Rome, but it was nonetheless influential. The city maintained a strong military presence to defend its commercial interests, and the dining halls of the central castle

The raised hearth seen in the frontispiece of the 1490 edition of *Küchenmeisterei* makes stirring a pot much easer for the cook.

The frontispiece of *Tacuinum sanitatis* in this Italian edition from around 1475 shows a scholar teaching from one of the most famous books of the time on health and well-being. Even better known than the text were the illustrations: nearly fifty full-page depictions of animals, birds, fish, and edible vegetables, fruits, and herbs. The text is from an eleventh-century Arab treatise by Ibn Butlân of Baghdad; the fifteenth-century version illustrated here was reproduced in the Mussolini era of the last century.

LITERACY IN THE KITCHEN

For us in the Western world, to open a cookbook and look through it for a recipe for the next meal is common-place, but such inspiration is really quite recent. In earlier centuries, literacy was not to be taken for granted. So when looking at old cookbooks, says bibliographer Henry Notaker, "It is important to distinguish between those who bought the books, those who read the books, those who cooked the food described in the books, and those who were eating this food."[1] In the fifteenth century, at the dawn of printing, only a tiny minority of those who did the cooking at home or worked in other people's kitchens could read and write; fewer still could do the arithmetic to deter-mine, for example, how many pints of water would be necessary to cook three pounds of turnips if two pints were required for each pound. Lit-eracy, including numeracy, in the kitchen was a rarity before the eigh-teenth century, restricted largely to stewards or maîtres d'hôtel who oversaw large kitchen staffs in es-tablishments of the nobility or the church.

The few cookbooks by working cooks were almost certainly dictated to scribes of the master of the household. Not until several hun-dred years after the invention of printing could authors assume that kitchen workers would be able to read their books. Books were expen-sive: in the mid-fourteenth century, an average manuscript in England cost almost ten times as much as the yearly wage of a kitchen servant.[2] Printing changed all that; book prices dropped slowly until by 1798, an English apprentice could afford as many as twenty-seven texts in a single year.[3] In the interim, a book about cooking was more likely to adorn the shelves of a stately home, or act as the key reference work for the steward or mistress of a prosperous household, or serve as amusement for an idle lady or gentleman. Not until the late nineteenth century did printed cookbooks commonly become practical manuals in the kitchen.

Surprisingly little is known about the nature or extent of early literacy, and no reliable estimates are available of the number of people who could read and write at any time between 1500 and 1800. In general, those of high income and elevated social status were literate, whereas almost all peasants and ordinary laborers were not. A few talented boys might be educated by the church (the word *clerk* derives from *cleric*). Historians also know that males far outnumbered females in the ability to read, write, or sign their names. Finally, the small minority of the population that lived in towns was more likely to be literate than was the overwhelming majority that lived in the countryside.

Apart from the small number of people in the privileged social groups—the ones most likely to be educated during these three centuries—we can be sure that very few were literate. As late as 1700, according to estimates, more than 85 percent of the population of Europe did not get adequate nutrition, clothing, or shelter. Thus, those with high incomes and social status probably were no more than 10 to 15 percent of the population. As late as 1800, about 10 percent of the population of France and the German states lived in cities of ten thousand or more, where people were most likely to learn to read or write. Only in England and the Low Countries

was that figure significantly higher, but even there, it barely surpassed 20 percent. The widespread literacy that we take for granted today in the Western world simply did not exist, even among males, until the latter half of the nineteenth century.

As for the specific issue of literacy in the kitchen, the picture is even less clear. Recent scholarship on education and literacy makes not a single reference to cooking, cookbooks, or kitchens.[4] The promising genre of instructional cookbooks—as they developed from small beginnings in the fifteenth and sixteenth centuries—seems never to have been sufficiently popular to justify making enough copies of a book to ensure wide circulation. The works most people were reading and writing had little to do with food preparation. With the outstanding exception of medical treatises, most books devoted to religious or secular subjects touched only occasionally on recipes or cooking.

If so few people who cooked or worked in early kitchens could read or write, why would anyone want to write or print and sell a book about cooking? One answer is that until the nineteenth century, not many people did. Those who undertook the task certainly were not writing for the kind of mass audience that cookbook authors take for granted today. Authors who wrote books about cooking before the mid-eighteenth century tended to be more interested in paying homage to a patron, as did Platina in acknowledging his superior, Cardinal Roverella, in the late fourteenth century, or in calling attention to their own accomplishments, as did François Menon in the mid-1700s. However, their books would have found their way into the kitchen in the hands of the steward or mis-

tress of the household, who would use them to give verbal instruction to the cooks. Sensing this audience as time passed, a growing number of cookbook authors were eager to instruct an audience of novice cooks. They explored how to select and store ingredients, plan menus, and prepare a wide variety of dishes. And as literacy gradually increased in the nineteenth century, the information these printed books conveyed was no longer locked inside the covers. ◆

1 Henry Notaker, *Printed Cookbooks in Europe, 1470–1700: A Bibliography of Early Modern Culinary Literature* (New Castle, DE: Oak Knoll Press, 2010), 14.

2 Joanne Filippone Overty, "The Cost of Doing Scribal Business: Prices of Manuscript Books in England, 1300–1483," *Book History* 11 (2008): 32.

3 Stephen M. Colclough, "Procuring Books and Consuming Texts: The Reading Experience of a Sheffield Apprentice, 1798," *Book History* 3 (2000): 21–44.

4 R. A. Houston, *Literacy in Early Modern Europe* (New York: Longman, 2002).

could seat six hundred guests. A huge courtyard hinted at the size of the market held within it, and the city's well was an engineering marvel, one of the deepest in Europe. Given this backdrop of prosperity, *Küchenmeisterei* was bound for success. First printed in 1485, the earliest surviving copy dates from 1490 and is one of thirteen incunabula editions. Over sixty more were to come from printers all over Germany during the next two centuries.[12] The titles of these editions vary, one being *Neu wolzugerichtes Kochbüchlein* (New Little Cookbook of Well-Prepared Meals) and another, *Koch und Kellermeisterei* (Mastery of Cooking and Winemaking), taking an independent line. Even so, the book did not enjoy the international exposure of Taillevent's and Platina's books. It seems to never have been translated, perhaps reflecting a lack of interest in German culture in Europe west of the Rhine.

Taillevent, the Traditionalist

Taillevent's *Le viandier* is the storehouse of the medieval cooking tradition. As a cookbook author, Taillevent is unique, and his book was widely read throughout Europe for more than three centuries. First printed in Paris in 1486, *Le viandier* remained in print for over two centuries, a remarkable feat even by the standards of today. The manuscript originated at the French court, probably around 1375 during the reign of King Charles V. Until 1505, it was the only French cookbook in print, so popular that at least twenty-four editions followed the first, ending in Lyon in 1615. The book was even reincarnated in a nineteenth-century reprint of three early manuscript versions, compared and annotated by Baron Jérôme Pichon.[13]

The printed book that appeared in 1486 is in two parts, one containing recipes that can be traced back to Taillevent himself and the other offering recipes that reflect more contemporary, fifteenth-century ideas. It makes no distinction between sweet and savory offerings; all the dishes would have been served on the table at once, the number depending on the simplicity or grandeur of the meal. The recipes reflect the fact that table implements were sparse—including only spoons, knives, and a few bowls, and certainly not one per person. Purées and porridges appear frequently, and most meats are "hew'd," "smitten," or "ground to doust," with a "gobbet" the size of a finger being the largest permissible morsel. Sauces had to be thick so as not to spill over from the trencher, the hefty slice of bread that was set in front of each diner instead of a plate. Taillevent lists a range of thickeners based on eggs, bread, blood, almonds and other nuts, and a variety of vegetable purées, though flour was not used as a liaison until the seventeenth century.

The popular picture that centers the medieval feast around a whole roast ox is inaccurate, for the days of selective breeding were long in the future. Large beasts must have been too tough to be roasted, and Taillevent mentions only young animals—calves, kids, and suckling pigs—as well as flocks of birds. In winter, even these were in short supply, and almost the only meat available was salted. Just a few medieval dishes have survived to the present day. *Hochepot* is very like a modern hot pot, and *froumentée* is still known in some parts of England as frumenty, a wheaten porridge that is traditionally served on Christmas Eve. *Galantine* and *couliez* are familiar words in Taillevent's book, but their modern equivalents are different. Taillevent's *galantine* was any dish flavored with the aromatic galingale root, and *couliez* was a stew rather than our soft, pourable purée.

Taillevent portrays the late medieval love of spice in full bloom: the text of *Le viandier* does after all date back a century before its first printing. In all the editions, early and late, recipes abound for explosive mixtures such as lamprey in hot sauce spiced with ginger, cinnamon, clove, grains of paradise (resembling black pepper), and nutmeg, all bound with blood and bread crumbs soaked in wine and vinegar. Taillevent makes much use of *poudre fine*, one of several spice mixes that are referred to in early cookbooks, sold by spice merchants as proprietary brands. One recipe from *Le ménagier de Paris* calls for a mixture of white ginger ("the best kind"), cinnamon, peppercorns, long pepper, nutmeg, cloves, grains of paradise, and galingale.[14] After pounding, the powder should be kept in leather bags, says the anonymous author, where it will stay fresh a month or more. However, the spices could not have been fresh in the sense that we think of today. Almost all had to come overland from Asia or, after 1498 and the navigation of the Cape of Good Hope, via the sea route around Africa; in either case, the journey would have taken a year or more. Such was the power of the spice trade that wealthy merchants were nicknamed "pepper-sacks."

Taillevent's recipes largely follow the French style of tempering spice mixes, using verjuice or wine more often than sugar. Packing a double punch, they often suggest cooking with the spiced red wine called *ypocras* or the white version, *clairet*, both of them steeped with honey or sugar and spices for flavor and longevity in these days before corked bottles. In Taillevent's lexicon, quantity of spice rather than refinement seems to have been the aim, and astonishingly potent combinations emerge, added in two, even three layers. Both *ypocras* and *clairet* found use in cooking—for example, for poaching pears. In England, sugar was already a favorite condiment to balance the spice in savory dishes, while in Italy, pasta was sprinkled with cinnamon and sugar, a practice of Arab origin that continued into later centuries.

Why so much spice? Several theories have been advanced, one suggesting that spices would help preserve meats, even though salting, drying, or smoking was far cheaper. Another explanation is that spices would distract from the gamy taste of stale meats, but many gourmets of the time would have enjoyed aged meats. Far more important is the flamboyance of spices as a conspicuous display of wealth, a means of exerting influence over friends and allies in the complex politics of the feudal structure. In addition, spices were a convenient investment, easy to buy and sell, not as durable as gold or silver but lighter and more portable. They could be bartered, and people could even pay their taxes with them. The counts of Provence levied taxes in the form of pepper, ginger, cubebs, cloves, saffron, and cumin from the towns in their domain.[15]

In the fifteenth century, at the height of the spice craze, spices were enormously valuable; at times, a pound of nutmeg seeds could cost as much as seven fat oxen. One of the most popular imports was dried ginger, either in the piece or powdered, which together with peppercorns provided a kick of heat before chiles arrived from the New World. Mustard, which we associate with Burgundy and Dijon, was grown throughout Europe, along with fennel, celery, and coriander seed, but it is rarely mentioned in

The fifteenth-century French manuscript *Régime des princes* depicts shops on a Parisian street, including a furrier, a tailor, a barber, and an apothecary who is selling *ypocras*, the spiced wine that was considered beneficial as a medicine as well as good for cooking and drinking at the table.

cookbooks, perhaps because it was so common and therefore less prestigious. Ironically, the most valuable European spice was grown at home. Saffron, the threadlike stigmas of the autumn crocus (three per bloom), flourished north from the Mediterranean, especially in Spain, and into England (hence the town of Saffron Walden in Essex). The stigmas must still be picked by hand, and saffron remains the most expensive spice of all. Despite its cost, saffron appears in many early recipes, prized for its intense golden color and elusive fragrance. Taillevent was well aware that saffron loses its musky perfume if cooked too long, and his recipes often add it toward the end of cooking.

Given this overload of spices, their abandonment in European cooking scarcely a century later is hard to imagine. However, during the great seventeenth-century expansion of world trade, the volume of spices increased, and prices dropped steadily. The prestige factor no longer held. At the same time, titillating new ingredients were coming from the New World: turkeys, pineapples, corn, root artichokes, and the many members of the chili family. Fashion in the kitchen moved on, and the habit of spicing diminished. The first breath of this radical change can be seen in Platina's *De honesta voluptate*, and both the German *Küchenmeisterei* and the English *Boke of Cokery* are far less dramatic than Taillevent in the use of spice.

The Boke of Cokery

Treasures turn up all the time, and a pristine copy of the very rare first English collection of recipes, *Boke of Cokery*, has recently been discovered in the archives of Longleat House near Bath, England. The text is based on a fifteenth-century manuscript, which in turn draws on at least two fourteenth-century handwritten books. First published in London in 1500 by the pioneer printer Richard Pynson, *Boke of Cokery* just makes the cutoff date as an incunabulum. On the one hand, the book is firmly rooted in the medieval past, with classics such as frumenty, daryolites (custard tarts), and moumbles, a stew of entrails for lesser guests that led to the expression "to eat humble pie." *Brouets* abound, including one from Germany (a spicy, sugarless broth) and one from Spain (also sugarless). The filling for chicken pie is not only spiced but sweetened with dried dates and the little black raisins of Corinth that we call currants, already demonstrating the English penchant for balancing pungency with sweetness that was to mark their dishes in the next century and beyond. On the other hand, the future direction of English cookery can be discerned, with its love of pure flavors and lack of pretension, so suited to the merchants and gentry who were forming an increasingly prosperous middle class.

In an early example of self-promotion, the anonymous author attempts to enlarge his market with some promotional hype on the title page: "Here begynneth a noble boke of festes ryalle and Cokery, a boke for a pryncis housholde or any other estates; and the makynge therof accordynge as ye shall fynde more playnly within this boke."[16]

SMITE, HACK, & SEETHE: LIFE IN THE MEDIEVAL KITCHEN

Early cookbooks and manuscript pictures—often cartoonlike representations of contemporary scenes—give us a sense of the layout and workings of medieval kitchens, depicting a world of varied and vigorous activity. The kitchens of the dukes of Burgundy set the example: their dimensions were heroic, with seven gigantic chimneys that still anchor a corner of the ducal palace in Dijon. In more modest households, a single chimney in a room dedicated to cooking still implied wealth.

As a smelly, dirty, noisy, even dangerous place, the medieval kitchen was set well away from the lord's quarters whenever possible, and often a distance from the dining hall. Servitors to carry dishes to and fro were a necessity. Smaller rooms abutted the kitchen, a garde manger for cold food, a larder (from the French *lard*, or bacon) for meats, a well-guarded spicery, an acatery (the storeroom for the *acheteur*, or caterer), a bouteillery for bottled drinks, later corrupted to "buttery" in English, and a pantry for storing bread (*pain* in French). Whenever possible, water would be piped in from a nearby stream.

Illustrations depict the kitchen as a bustling yet ordered world, ruled by fire and equipped with rugged, jumbo-size implements. Cooking on an open hearth was an all-embracing way of life, far more intimate than the closed-stove kitchens of today. The flickering flames warmed and illuminated the room, and the action within the hearth was constant. Whether flipping the contents of long-handled frying pans, swinging and stirring the pots that hung on a crane above the fire, or basting fragrant meats as they turned on the spit, cooks worked in close relationship to the food they prepared.

Kitchens were likely to have more than one fireplace to serve different cooking needs. (The baker's oven, however, was already separate from the main kitchen.) The direction of the prevailing wind dictated which chimneys would draw well. One fireplace would be kept burning at a low steady heat around the clock for the gentle simmering of broths and stews and for routine tasks like boiling water. A couple more might glow with the fierce, radiant embers that are ideal for grilling on a spit. Rabbits and whole small birds would turn nearest the heat to cook fast, with suckling pig and larger pieces of meat set higher to cook more gradually. The first responsibility of a *happelloppin* (young apprentice) was to turn the spit.

Records also reveal an innovation at the Hospice de Beaune, the great charitable hospital founded in the

An active life in the medieval kitchen leads to a formal table at dinner, at right, shown in the *Luttrell Psalter*, c.1340. © The British Library Board.

early 1430s: an early example of an automatic spit driven by a weight hanging from the ceiling. Not only did the hospice have a state-of-the-art kitchen, but its pharmacy adjoined the great hall for the treatment of the sick and featured a large *potager*, a raised stove for concocting medicines. This enabled the cooks to keep a close watch on the potions as they bubbled and to forge a close relationship with the physicians in the spirit of the time.

Contemporary drawings of cooking tools depict an almost martial-looking kitchen arsenal. Huge cleavers sit on butcher-block tables with the pestle and mortar standing by, elevated to working height on a stout column of stone. These implements were essential for the chopping and pounding of ingredients in preparation for putting them through multiple cooking processes—perhaps simmering and then roasting shoulder of veal or sautéing and then baking pieces of chicken. Other cookware was designed for the needs of open-fire cooking. Pots had to be raised on feet or set on a trivet to rest among the embers. To equalize top and bottom heat, cooks would spread embers on the lids, which preferably were concave to keep the ashes in place. Cookbooks of the time call for wrapping foods in oiled paper (good for meats and fish), large leaves (for doughs and cakes), or clay (for whole birds) in order to bake them directly in the ashes.[1]

For broiling, cooks used a flat iron or shovel, heating it until red hot and then holding it an inch or two from the surface of the food or occasionally pressing the sizzling iron directly on the food to toast it or caramelize it. Tools and frying pans had long handles so that the cook could retreat a little from the heat. Some pans were dimpled to hold batter for cooking little cakes; oth-

ers had holes for roasting chestnuts or root vegetables. One enemy was smoke (except when smoking hams and sausages), and contemporary cookbooks warned cooks to cover pots tightly to avoid spills and sudden flares.

Given the high level of activity and risk in the kitchen of a great household, a rigid, stylized environment prevailed in which each player had his place. The *écuyer de cuisine* (kitchen steward) came first, followed by the master cook; the roasting cook; the *potagier*, cooking soups and vegetables; the *gardemanger* (a name still used today), in charge of the larder and cold foods; and finally the sauce cook and the fruiterer. Olivier de la Marche, Duke Philip's steward in the 1480s, described a typical scene: "The [master] cook was seated between the fireplace and the sideboard on a high chair, so he could survey the whole room. In his hand he held a huge wooden ladle which served a double purpose: with it he tasted the soups and the sauces, and chased the scullions back to work, beating them if necessary."[2]

The appointment of the master cook was a major event, an early example of practical democracy. The maître d'hôtel would call in the kitchen squires and all others employed in the kitchen, one by one. Each would solemnly give his vote, attested by an oath. In his memoirs, La Marche even asks rhetorically, Who takes the master cook's place when he is absent? The spit master? The soup master? "Neither," he answers, "the substitute will be designated by election."[3]

The stations of kitchen service and their specialized staff, called *parties*, or teams, have changed little over the years. The classic Escoffier kitchen of the twentieth century follows the same hierarchy as in medieval times, with only the fish cook missing. (In the early kitchen, fish alternated with meat on fast days and feast days, so both were cooked by the same team.) In other respects, however, the predecessors of today's cooks, accustomed to the hard labor of the medieval kitchen, would scarcely recognize today's air-conditioned kitchens, packed as they are with electric appliances and small, specialized tools for every preparation. ♦

1 William Rubel, *The Magic of Fire: Hearth Cooking: One Hundred Recipes for the Fireplace or Campfire* (New York: Ten Speed Press, 2002), 14.

2 Olivier de la Marche, *Les memoires de Messire Olivier de la Marche* (Ghent: Gerard de Salenson, 1567).

3 Ibid.

The book opens with menus for two- and three-course suppers and dinners, composed simply of the names of a dozen or more meats (or fish on fast days). Just such a meal must the fourteenth-century romantic hero Sir Gawain have enjoyed on Christmas Eve, a fast day:

Several fine soups, seasoned lavishly
Twice-fold, as is fitting, and fish of all kinds –
Some baked in bread, some browned on the coals,
Some seethed, some stewed and savored with spices
But also subtly sauced.[17]

The recipes in this last of the four incunabula cookbooks seem in many ways the most ancient. *Boke of Cokery* is hard to read, the language is archaic (a knowledge of Chaucerian English might help), and the arrangement of the nearly two hundred recipes is chaotic. However, close attention reveals a wide range of dishes and ingredients, with surprisingly detailed instructions for putting them together. An experienced cook would find valuable hints on how to flavor, how to adjust dishes for young or old meats, and how to alter recipes for Lent. The author simply lists meats, suggesting sauces for each one, so presumably all would have been roasted or boiled. The sauces include *sauce madame* (spices) and *sauce galentyne* (vinegar), both echoing Taillevent and, above all, *Forme of Cury*, the 1390 manuscript by the master cook to Richard II.

Like other fifteenth-century cookbooks, the printed edition of *Boke of Cokery* is based on earlier texts. A manuscript version in the library of Corpus Christi College, at Cambridge University, has been dated to the late 1460s because of its inclusion of the menu for the installation of the archbishop of York in 1465, and, as we have seen, some of the recipes date further back to *Forme of Cury*. A royal provenance for the book is implied by menus ranging from "the ffeste of kynge henry the iiijth [fourth] to the herawldes and frenche men when they had justef in Smytheffelde" (Smithfield is a district of London) to a banquet for "the crownance of kyng henry the ffifte." *Boke of Cokery* closes with the acknowledgment "Her endethe the fest ryalle and the servys to a kyng or a prince," suggesting again that the anonymous author must have been in royal service. However, the style of the book is modest, belying its future influence as the foundation for almost all the English cookbooks that were to follow in the sixteenth century.

ALL FOUR OF THE INCUNABULA COOKBOOKS printed before 1501 have roots in earlier texts. *Boke of Cokery* is a classic example of the "tree" that is created when one book (or manuscript scroll) is copied by others, branching out from the original. These books were integral to the spread of culinary learning that began before the invention of printing and continued long afterward. For example, some of Taillevent's recipes were picked up by sixteenth-century cookbooks, and he himself borrowed from a manuscript of the early 1300s, written before he was born.[18] Part of Martino's text of 1460

derives from an earlier manuscript.[19] The practice was to flourish in the next century and continues (with or without acknowledgment) to this day.

Not only were the four earliest printed cookbooks much copied by later authors, but there was a substantial delay before new ones appeared. In France, for example, no fresh, indigenous French cookbooks emerged to compete with *Le viandier* for nearly sixty years, at which point *Le grand cuisinier de toute cuisine* (The Great Master of All Cooking, 1543) appeared, initiating in its turn a series of similar cookbooks.[20] In England, the gap between *Boke of Cokery* (1500) and its descendants was about fifty years. In Italy, Platina was not rivaled for more than seventy years, until a steward called Messisbugo published *Banchetti composizioni di vivande e apparechhio generale* (Banquets, Composition of Dishes and General Presentation) in 1549, while Germans took sixty years to rival *Küchenmeisterei* with Walther Ryff's *Wahrhaftige Unterweisung Confect zu bereiten* (Reliable Instructions for Preparing Confections, 1540).

The cookbooks of the fifteenth century provided signposts to the future, though perhaps this was not obvious to their contemporary readers. Taillevent exemplified the firm medieval foundation, reflecting the culinary training and discipline essential to a leading kitchen. Many features of his style, particularly the complex spicing and use of sugar as a condiment, were to linger far into the sixteenth century. The same was true in England, where expanding prosperity brought with it conservatism; *Boke of Cokery* set the precedent for almost a century of unassuming, useful cookbooks written for cooks with the urge to copy existing ways. In the German states, the increasing number of prosperous town dwellers could indulge in cooking from a book.

Platina stands out from the pack with his inclusion of artisan recipes in a book of philosophy, thus raising the intellectual status of cooking from artisan to art. He opened the way for the groundbreaking volumes of the next century in Italy and France that were at once intellectually sophisticated treatises and splendid visual works in their own right. They formed part of the humanist renaissance scholarship that, sometimes sooner, sometimes later, would in different ways transform the concept of good eating throughout Europe from the sixteenth century on.

The Bayeux Tapestry was embroidered by the ladies of Queen Mathilde, wife of William the Conqueror, to celebrate his victory at the Battle of Hastings in 1066. The tapestry, with its hundreds of images, survives to this day in the town of Bayeux in Normandy. In this scene, cooks roast outsize kebabs over open fires, then rush them piping hot to a table of guests. Four centuries later, the anonymous *Boke of Cokery* (1500) demonstrated that the English had maintained their devotion to roast meats.

COOKBOOKS, COPYING, & COPYRIGHT

Right from the start, printing was a sophisticated trade, employing skilled and literate craftsmen who had to be kept busy. Chances to cheat were rife as the technical process of printing a book made it easy to remove both authors' texts and entire runs of printed pages to sell illicitly. Furthermore, once a text had entered the press, the printer and the compositor who set up the type had surprising latitude in interpreting the author's work: indeed, the original text might never be faithfully reproduced. Printers could make up alternative, cheaper versions of popular books and sell them through different outlets.[1] As a result, any author who could do so was wise to monitor the printing of his book on the spot.

In these early days, the uniformity we associate with printing was far from the reality; books varied, even within a single edition.[2] Most printers had only enough letters and tools to set up about two dozen pages at a time, and proofreading was concurrent with the printing. Since paper was expensive, already-printed pages were retained, and mistakes were corrected on the next run. Printed sheets from different books, wet with ink, hung around

A printing shop bustles with artisans in *Impressio librorum* (Printing Press) from *Encyclopédie raisonné des sciences, des arts et des métiers,* by Diderot and Alembert. On the left, lines of type are locked into a frame called a forme, following the page of text pinned to the wall; in the background, a man applies ink using inking balls, while the pressman screws down a forme onto a damp sheet of paper, which will be passed to the bespectacled proofreader at center left. Damp sheets hang all over the shop, and after they dry, the apprentice in the front stacks them under the eye of his master.

the shop to dry for however long the weather dictated. Unbound galleys were stored flat until a buyer asked for a copy of the book, which would then be custom-bound either in cheap paper or more costly vellum or leather. As publishing became more competitive, counterfeit and unauthorized copies of works migrated out of shops and surfaced all over Europe. Tracking a characteristic recipe such as syllabub from one edition to another, even from one "author" to another, can make a fascinating study all its own.

From its beginnings, the business of printing and selling books was fraught with worries about the potential theft of authors' words, which were rapidly becoming commodities that could be bought and sold (the word *plagiarism* did not find use until the early seventeenth century). However, the issue was not clear-cut. On the one hand, the copying of revered texts (the manuscript tradition) spread knowledge and furthered education. Books, and with them cookbooks, that drew heavily on previous writings provided a service in building on existing expertise and passing it on to the reader. Even today no one questions the right of a grandchild to copy grandma's cookie recipe so that it can be treasured by future generations. On the other hand, printed books brought with them the new concept of intellectual property, the right of an author to protect—to copyright—his original (potentially valuable) work within a legal framework. Several countries early on recognized unauthorized reproduction as a serious offense, yet such activities were endemic and unstoppable. In 1517, while Martin Luther's translation of the Scriptures was still in the pressroom, pirated copies of his work were already circulating in the streets of London. Every genre of book, every text that entered the printing house, was at risk of being stolen, in part or in whole.[3]

Culinary historians and cooks often assume that recipes are particularly tempting to copy, and it is true that short bursts of instructional text that are independent of surrounding paragraphs can easily be transposed. The movable metal type of early printing (groups of letters that could be slid from place to place like a fillet of fish in the frying pan) and the international nature of the book trade did enable recipes to get around Europe. Evidence is easy to find. The recipes of Martino of Como, published (and acknowledged) in *De honesta voluptate* by Platina (1474) were republished in Italian in 1516 as *Epulario* (The Italian Banquet) in a tiny three-by-six-inch format with a certain Giovanni de Rosselli claiming authorship. Much translated, *Epulario* appeared in English as well and was still being printed in the mid-1600s. As another example, several Dutch cookbooks borrowed freely from Bartolomeo Scappi, though without his name attached.[4] The Spanish cook Diego Granado Maldonado published a cookbook at the very end of the sixteenth century that lifted liberally from both Ruberto de Nola's and Scappi's books.[5] Dr. William Kitchiner summed up the problem in 1821 when he remarked of contemporary cookbooks, "The Books vary very little from each other. . . . Cutting and pasting seem to have been much oftener employed than the Pen and Ink."[6] Henry Notaker has observed that before 1700, only about one hundred cookbook titles were published throughout Europe in more than a dozen countries.[7] Many contained overlapping information.

However, despite the common theft of material, complacency toward plagiarism was hardly the case. By 1500, major publishing nations were trying to prevent authors and printers from using the work of others without authorization. Contractual bonds and lawsuits of the era testify to an early grasp of intellectual ownership. Where this effort fell short was in reaching across borders. None of the local and national protections were internationally enforceable, and money was a strong motive. Communities of printers and booksellers buzzed with accusations of improprieties. Over the centuries, a sense has developed that culinary creation is an artistic property. But where to draw the line between honorable inspiration by a previous writer and outright plagiarism, particularly of recipes, is just as controversial a topic now as it was five hundred years ago. ♦

1 Adrian Johns, *The Nature of the Book: Print and Knowledge in the Making* (Chicago: University of Chicago Press, 1998), 166.

2 Ibid., 91.

3 Henry Notaker has done interesting work on the subject of plagiarism and cookbooks. See his "Comments on the Interpretation of Plagiarism," *Petits Propos Culinaires* 70 (2002); and Mary and Philip Hyman, "La Chapelle and Massialot: An 18th Century Feud," *Petits Propos Culinaires* 2 (1979): 44–54.

4 Jozef Schildermnas and Hilde Sels, "A Dutch Translation of Bartolomeo Scappi's *Opera*," *Petit Propos Culinaires* 74 (2003): 59–70.

5 Jeanne Allard, "Diego Granado Maldonado," *Petits Propos Culinaires* 25 (1987): 35–41.

6 William Kitchiner, *The Cook's Oracle* (London: A. Constable / Edinburgh: Hurst, Robinson, 1821), 24.

7 Notaker, "Comments on the Interpretation of Plagiarism," 3.

RECIPES

FROM THE FIFTEENTH CENTURY

WITH A FEW NOTABLE EXCEPTIONS, fifteenth-century recipes remain typically medieval, pungent with spices, tart with verjuice and vinegar, and invariably cooked in at least two stages: roasted and then simmered in broth, for example, or fried in lard and then simmered in broth. The aim may have been partly hygienic, but the effect was the creation of layers of flavor that can be astonishingly complex.

Throughout Europe, spices in impressive variety and generous quantity continue to be the mark of the sophisticated, affluent table. By the end of the century, glimpses of a new style appear in the very first printed cookbook, *De honesta voluptate et valetudine* (Rome, 1474), which contains recipes by Maestro Martino, a leading cook from Como, in the Italian Alps. Martino refers to *peperata* (a peppery sauce) and to *soffrito* (a zesty chopped meat dish, today a mix of diced vegetables used for flavoring). With recipes like sage leaves dipped in batter, he heralds the simpler, lighter cooking that began in Italy and was to sweep Europe in the next century and a half. He emphasizes more modest ingredients available to a wider audience in dishes such as a salsa of grape leaves, or *herbe con latte damandole* (greens in almond milk).

National characteristics are beginning to emerge as well. Italian cooks feature vegetables such as *zucca* (squash), fennel, and lettuce. The German book *Küchenmeisterei* (1485) has a surprising proportion of the baked pastries and tortes that were to become the national specialty. The taste for *Krapffen*, a type of stuffed beignet, continues to this day. I've also chosen a festive recipe from Germany that sums up the medieval love of jokes. A whole salmon is divided in three, cooked three ways, then reassembled and blanketed with chopped parsley to mimic the original fish. What a surprise when the "fish" is opened!

Eating habits change slowly, and the familiar medieval fare depicted by Taillevent in *Le viandier* (printed in 1486) remains the norm outside centers of fashion for at least another century. The book clings to tradition—after all, it harks back to a manuscript that is at least a century old, with roots still farther back. Meanwhile, *The Boke of Cokery*, printed in 1500, brings a very English view to the cooking scene. Suggested menus list a formidable parade of plainly cooked meats, such as the "bolde [boiled] meate or stewed meate, chekins [chickens] and bacon, powdred beyfe, pyes, goose, pygge, roosted beyfe, and roosted veal" that form a single first course that also includes a "custarde." Perhaps this might have been the fresh cheese mold called *mon amy* (my good friend), which is resolutely English despite its French name. *Mon amy* looks forward to the national love of possets and frothy syllabubs. Remember Little Miss Muffet sitting on a tuffet, eating her curds and whey?

From Platina, *De honesta voluptate et valetudine* (Rome, c. 1474; recipe from 1520 Paris edition): *Soak flour meal with eggs, sugar, cinnamon, and saffron, and blend. Put in whole leaves of sage, as broad as you want, and, when they have been coated, fry with liqmine or a little oil in a pan. This is nourishing and helps the nerves, even if it is slowly digested and induces blockages.*

THE DISHES OF MARTINO OF COMO have come down to us as part of the first printed cookbook, the influential and long-lived *De honesta voluptate et valetudine* (Of Honest Indulgence and Good Health, 1474). The author, Bartolomeo Sacchi, also known as Platina, acknowledges that his recipes come from Maestro Martino, cook to the Duke of Savoy. Martino must have been a leader of culinary style, and he likes fritters, savory extras on the side that lift a dish from the mundane to the memorable. His temptations include batter-coated elder flowers, sliced apples and parsnips, and these attractive little sage fritters, as well as more substantial offerings such as rice cakes, stuffed figs, and pounded almond paste shaped to resemble ravioli or turnovers, all sautéed for serving. In *De honesta voluptate,* Platina adds his own dietary comment that sage fritters are nourishing and help the nerves, although they can cause constipation.

Sage-leaf fritters are delicious with a glass of Prosecco, or they make a tasty garnish for chicken or veal. The batter is unexpectedly cakelike and slightly sweet, holding up for an hour or two, though it never gets crisp after frying. *Liqmine,* or liquamen, was a saucelike condiment made from fermented fish.

Sage Fritters with Saffron   *Serves 4 to 6*

1 medium bunch sage (about 1½ ounces or 45 g)
Vegetable oil for frying

BATTER
¼ cup (30 g) flour
½ teaspoon ground cinnamon
Pinch of ground saffron
2 eggs
2 tablespoons (30 g) sugar

Pull the sage leaves from the stems, discard the stems, and set the leaves aside.

To make the batter: Sift together the flour, cinnamon, and saffron into a small bowl, and make a well in the center. In a separate bowl, whisk the eggs with the sugar until lightly colored and slightly thickened, 3 to 4 minutes. Pour the egg mixture into the well and stir, gradually pulling in the flour to make a smooth batter.

To fry the leaves: Pour oil to a depth of ¾ inch (2 cm) into a frying pan over medium heat, and heat until a dab of batter dropped into the oil sizzles on contact. Dip a sage leaf into the batter, drain the excess on the side of the bowl, and at once lower the leaf into the hot oil. Add several more leaves to the pan, being careful not

Frictella
Ex Salvia
———
Fritters of Sage

to crowd them, and fry until lightly golden, about 1 minute. Keep a close eye on them, as the sugar in the batter scorches easily. Lift out the leaves with a wire skimmer and drain them on paper towels. Fry the remaining leaves the same way. Serve within an hour or two.

Dreyerley Essen von Einē Visch

Three Dishes from One Fish

From *Küchenmeisterei* (Nuremberg, 1485; recipe from 1490 edition): *You want to make three varieties of food from one fish, but the fish stays whole in appearance. Cut a pike or otherwise another prepared fish in three or in four parts. Lay the first part on an iron and roast it. Cover another part in wine and spice. The third is salted. The fourth the tail is baked and the fish should be laid together each piece after another as if it was whole. The head first. After that the middle piece. After that the tail straight one on another and with much chopped parsley well sprinkled and set there. There should be set good salt or vinegar in many small bowls; a guest eats one piece then another as a surprise.*

FIFTEENTH-CENTURY COOKS LOVED A JOKE, particularly when the food became an edible work of art. One favorite was a "cockentrice," made by sewing together the front half of a chicken and the back half of a suckling pig, stuffing and roasting the creation, and then glazing it with saffron and decorating it with herbs. In this flight of fancy, the anonymous German author of *Küchenmeisterei* cooks a giant fish in several parts. Other versions of this three-way fish appear elsewhere, including in Italy with Maestro Martino. "You want to make three kinds of food from one fish so it still looks whole," explains *Küchenmeisterei*. The head and tail are set aside and the body is cut into three parts to be fried, salted, and braised with wine and spice. Finally, the fish is reassembled, sprinkled generously with parsley to conceal the joins, and served with individual bowls of salt or vinegar for dipping.

The recipe was probably created for pike or salmon, both abundant in the rivers of Germany (Nuremberg is on a major tributary of the Danube). Whole salmon is readily available today on special order, and you should ask for it to be cleaned and scaled, with head and tail left on. You'll save a lot of work if your fish vendor will also fillet and bone the fish for you, though I've included instructions if you want to start from scratch.

Traditionally, a whole fish is always presented on the plate with the head to the left and the belly toward the carver. When cooking, you need to keep the shape of the salmon in mind so that the upper side of the fillets (which look more attractive) will re-create a left-facing fish. Removing the backbone before cooking makes serving easier, and you'll need a very large, long platter or tray to reassemble the fish.

Such a culinary fantasy invites creative presentation: you might want your fish to swim on a sea of jelly, set with gelatin and dyed green with parsley juice. Waving branches of herbs could suggest a riverbank. At the very least, the parsley-coated fish deserves a bright eye of carrot or orange zest. This is a lengthy recipe, taking a day to marinate and salt, and then another to cook the fish, but it can be prepared several hours ahead to serve at room temperature. And the joke of a fish in disguise, flavored in three parts, is just as theatrical today as it was more than five hundred years ago.

Salmon in Disguise   *Serves 10 to 12*

- 1 whole salmon (10 to 11 pounds or 4.5 to 5 kg), cleaned and scaled, with head and tail attached
- Small round piece of carrot or orange zest, for garnish
- 5 or 6 lemons, halved, for garnish
- Cider vinegar or white wine vinegar, for dipping
- Sea salt, for dipping

ROASTING
- 1 medium bunch thyme
- Salt and pepper
- ¼ cup (60 ml) vegetable oil, more for the pan

BRAISING
- 2 teaspoons ground ginger
- 1 teaspoon ground mace or freshly grated nutmeg
- 1 teaspoon ground cinnamon
- 3 cups (750 ml) Spiced Red Wine (recipe follows)
- 1 onion, diced
- 1 carrot, diced

SALTING
- 3 tablespoons (45 g) coarse sea salt
- 2 bay leaves
- 2 large bunches parsley (about 4 ounces or 110 g total)

Kitchen string

To fillet and divide the fish: Wash the salmon thoroughly and pat dry with paper towels. With a large chef's knife, cut off the head, including the gills, on a slight diagonal. Cut off the tail. Set the head and tail aside. Next, remove the fillets of salmon from the backbone with a flexible knife by cutting along the upper back of the fish on one side and lifting off the fillet. Work from the head to the tail and keep the knife close to the backbone as you slice the flesh from the bone. Repeat on the other side of the backbone. Pull out the fine bones running down the center of each fillet with a pair of pliers or strong tweezers. Reshape the body of the fish, discarding the backbone.

Arrange the salmon on a large cutting board with the head at your left and the belly facing you. Cut the body of the fish crosswise into 3 pieces of about equal weight (the tail piece will be longer than the head piece). Work from head to tail, being careful to keep the rearranged body sections right side up.

To ready the body portion nearest the head for roasting: Put it on a tray and arrange the thyme between the two fillets. Tie the fillets together in 3 or 4 places with the kitchen string and refrigerate.

To marinate the central body portion for braising: In a small bowl, mix together the ginger, mace, and cinnamon. Sprinkle the spice mixture on both sides of the top and bottom fillets, then replace the top fillet on the bottom fillet. Tie the fillets together in 3 or 4 places with the kitchen string and put into a large zip-top bag. Pour in the Ypocras, seal the bag closed, and refrigerate.

To salt the body portion nearest the tail: Put the bottom piece, skin side down, on a tray. Sprinkle it with 1 tablespoon (15 g) of the salt and top with the other fillet, skin side up. Sprinkle the top fillet with ½ tablespoon of the salt, then tie the fillets together in 3 or 4 places with the kitchen string and refrigerate.

Store all the fish portions, including the head and tail, tightly covered in the refrigerator for 12 to 18 hours.

The next day, braise the central piece of salmon: Heat the oven to 350°F (180°C). Spread the onion and carrot in a deep, flameproof casserole just large enough to hold the fish. Remove the fish from the bag, set it on top of the vegetables, and pour the Spiced Red Wine in the bag over the top. Cover and bring to a boil on the stove top. Transfer to the oven and braise, covered, until a metal skewer inserted into the center of the fish is very warm to the touch when withdrawn, 45 to 55 minutes. Remove from the oven and let cool in the braising liquid.

Meanwhile, cook the salted salmon, head, and tail: Transfer the tail portion of the fish to a flameproof casserole, and reserve the head and tail. Pour enough water over the tail portion to eventually cover the head and tail as well, and sprinkle the remaining 1½ tablespoons (22 g) salt over the water. Add the bay leaves. Pull the parsley leaves from the stems, set the leaves aside, and add the stems to the pot. Cover and bring to a boil on the stove top, stirring to dissolve the salt. Transfer to the oven and cook, covered, alongside the braised salmon for 10 minutes. Add the head and tail to the salted salmon pot and continue cooking until a metal skewer inserted in the center of the salmon is very warm to the touch when withdrawn, 20 to 25 minutes longer. Remove from the oven and let cool in the liquid. Meanwhile, chop the parsley leaves.

To roast the head portion of the fish: When the braised and salted fish portions have been removed from the oven, raise the oven heat to 400°F (200°C). Oil a roasting pan just large enough to accommodate the head portion of the fish and add the fish. Sprinkle it with salt and pepper, turn, and season the other side. Drizzle the fish with the oil. Roast until a skewer inserted in the center of the fish is very warm to the touch when withdrawn, 30 to 35 minutes. Remove from the oven and let cool completely.

To present the salmon: Drain the braised salmon, discarding the braising liquid. Pat the fish dry with paper towels and remove the string. Set it, belly toward you, in the center of the platter (it will be a spectacular deep purple). Drain the salted fish and dry it with paper towels. Remove the string and set it to the right of the braised fish. Trim any protruding stems of thyme at the center of the roast fish, and arrange the trimmed stems to the left of the braised fish. Add the head and tail at each end. To hide the joins, sprinkle the chopped parsley all over the fish, leaving only the head and tail uncovered. Replace the fish eye with a round of carrot, and set the lemon halves around the edge of the platter.

Serve the salmon at room temperature, with bowls of vinegar and salt for dipping. Each diner should receive a small portion of each type of fish.

Ypocras

From Taillevent, *Le viandier* (Paris, 1392; recipe from 1892 edition): *For a pint of ypocras, you need three tréseaux [about a teaspoon] of the best stick cinnamon, a tréseau of mace, or two if you wish, a half tréseau of clove and grains of paradise, and six ounces of the best sugar; and pound them to powder, and put all in a strainer with the wine, with the crock below, and strain until it has run through, and the more often it is strained the better, but it must not be weakened.*

THE SPICED WINE CALLED *ypocras* or *hypocras* was used in cooking, or drunk on its own as a favorite remedy for illnesses caused by cold humors. The name harks back to the great Greek physician Hippocrates. This recipe for spiced red wine comes from Taillevent, who instructs that the wine be strained several times to ensure it is properly clarified. If you wish to grind your own spices, allow a quarter ounce or seven grams per tablespoon. Grains of paradise resemble flowery, mild black peppercorns and are available online. *Ypocras* is heady stuff, so you'll need to consume just a little!

Spiced Red Wine   *Makes 3 cups (750 ml)*

1 cup (200 g) brown sugar
1 tablespoon ground cinnamon
1 tablespoon ground mace
1½ teaspoons ground cloves
1½ teaspoons ground grains of paradise
1 bottle (750 ml) fruity red wine such as Merlot

Cheesecloth

In a medium nonmetallic bowl, stir together the sugar, cinnamon, mace, cloves, and grains of paradise. Add the wine and stir well. Leave for 10 minutes, then stir again to dissolve the sugar fully. Cover tightly and leave at room temperature for 1 to 2 days.

Strain the wine mixture through a strainer lined with a double layer of cheesecloth into a bowl. A brown deposit will be left on the cheesecloth. Rinse it off and strain the wine at least once more through the cheesecloth to clarify it as well as possible.

Store the wine in an airtight container (if you like, use the original bottle) at room temperature. It will keep for up to 1 month.

Zu Maché ein Krapffen Teig

———

To Make a Krapffen Dough

From *Küchenmeisterei* (Nuremberg, 1485; recipe from 1490 edition): *To make a Krapffen dough. Heat as much honey in wine as you want and also take a shallow bowl and whisk the wine with white flour to make a batter. crack an orange egg yolk in another bowl and also a little saffron and mix very well into the prepared honey wine and add it to the whisked batter mix it well and sprinkle flour into the bowl until you have made a firm dough. then prepare a clean towel and pull the dough over it with a wooden rolling pin to make it thin. and cut shapes large or small as you want the Krapffen, depending on the filling that suits you. or you can make the dough with yeast or beer or hops water; all of these you must let rise and afterward knead; make them with lukewarm water or with a cooked honey wine to suit your own taste.*

Pigeon Filling: Perhaps you want a smaller filling. then you prepare it like this with fried chicken and pigeon, or what meat you have. you must have good herbs also fennel seed with juniper berry or caraway, ground and cooked with the filling. with raw eggs mixed already together and filled in and fried well.

Apple Filling: So you want to bake good Krapffen from apples or pears. Take care that they are fried well before putting them in a mortar crack an egg or two therein and a little salt and spice then pound well and fill it in the Krapffen.

AS DESCRIBED IN *KÜCHENMEISTEREI*, *Krapffen* are large or small dumplings wrapped in a yeast dough, then cooked. The word used for the cooking technique in the recipe is *backen*, which can mean "to bake" or "to fry," so I've chosen deep-frying to produce robust pastries, large as a fist, still found today all over Germany. Think of a luscious New Orleans beignet enclosing a savory filling, freshly fried, and you get the idea. Even in the fifteenth century, *Krapffen* must have been well established in southern Germany, as the author of *Küchenmeisterei* assumes that the cook knows how to shape and fill the dough. He deep-fries the dumplings in lard or beef fat, or in butter in one recipe. The dough itself is sweetened with wine and honey, but the fillings seem to have been savory because no sweetener is included, even for apples and pears. Birds such as chicken, dove, pigeon, and other "forest-birds" are a favorite filling, with lung and liver also mentioned. In present day Germany, "*Krapfen*" are enjoyed for breakfast or as a snack throughout the day.

Pigeon or Apple Dumplings   *Makes 12 dumplings to serve 6*

Pigeon Filling or Apple Filling (below)

Lard or vegetable oil for deep-frying and oiling the bowl

YEAST DOUGH

1½ cups (300 ml) medium-dry white wine

1 heaping tablespoon honey

1 tablespoon (7 g) active dry yeast

¼ cup (60 ml) warm water

Large pinch of ground saffron

1 egg yolk

4 cups (500 g) flour, more for kneading

1 teaspoon salt

3-inch (7.5-cm) round cookie cutter

Deep-fat thermometer

To mix the dough: In a small saucepan, heat the wine and honey until the honey melts. Set aside to cool. Sprinkle the yeast over the warm water in a cup, stir, and leave until foamy, about 5 minutes. In a small bowl, stir the saffron into the egg yolk.

Sift the flour with salt onto a work surface, and sweep a well in the center with the back of your hand. Add the wine mixture, dissolved yeast, and egg yolk to the well and mix with the tips of your fingers. Using a pastry scraper, gradually draw in the flour, working with your hand to make a smooth dough. It should be soft but not sticky, so work in more flour if needed.

To knead and raise the dough: Flour the work surface and transfer the dough to it. Knead the dough, pushing it away from you with one hand, then peeling it back to form a loose ball. Give the ball a quarter turn. Repeat this kneading action, adding more flour if needed, until the dough is smooth and elastic, 4 to 5 minutes.

Transfer the dough to an oiled bowl, flip it so the surface of the dough is oiled, and cover the bowl with plastic wrap. Leave the dough to rise in a warm place until doubled in bulk, 45 to 60 minutes. (The dough can also be mixed and kneaded in an electric mixer fitted with the dough hook.) Meanwhile, make the filling and leave at room temperature.

To shape the dumplings: When the dough has risen, once again turn it out onto a floured work surface and knead lightly to knock out the air. Then roll it out ⅜ inch (1 cm) thick. Stamp out 24 rounds with the cookie cutter. Transfer 12 rounds to a baking sheet lined with parchment paper. (If the dough is soft and hard to handle, chill the rounds in the refrigerator until firm.) Spoon the filling onto the rounds, leaving a ½-inch (1.25-cm) border of dough uncovered. Brush the border with water. Set a second round of dough over each filling-topped round, and pinch the edges together with your fingers to seal. If they are not already risen, leave the dumplings in a warm place until puffy, about 15 minutes.

To fry the dumplings: In a deep, heavy pot, heat lard or oil about three inches deep to 360°F (185°C) on the deep-fat thermometer. Using a wire skimmer or slotted spoon, lower 2 or 3 dumplings into the hot fat and fry until one side is browned, 2 to 3 minutes. Turn them with the skimmer and brown the other side, 1 to 2 minutes longer. Transfer them to paper towels to drain and keep them warm in an oven with the door open. Fry the remaining dumplings in the same way. The dumplings are best eaten warm, but like a doughnut, they can be kept an hour or two.

Pigeon Filling   *Makes ¾ cup (200 g) filling, enough for 12 dumplings*

This and the apple filling provides a burst of flavor to the bland background of dough. Both fillings are exuberantly spiced, so a tablespoon or two goes a long way. One little pigeon (squab) makes enough for 12 puffy dumplings, or you can substitute 2 boned quail.

Carve the meat from 1 cooked pigeon (about 6 oz or 170 g), cut the meat into pieces, and put them in a food processor. Crush together 1 teaspoon fennel seeds and 1 teaspoon juniper berries or caraway seeds, and add the mixture to the processor. Pulse until the meat is coarsely chopped. Transfer to a bowl and stir in 2 teaspoons chopped fresh parsley, 1 teaspoon chopped fresh thyme, and ½ teaspoon salt. In a small frying pan, heat 2 teaspoons vegetable oil over low heat. Add the pigeon mixture and fry, stirring constantly, until hot and fragrant, about 2 minutes. Taste and adjust the seasoning. Let the mixture cool, then stir in 1 egg, lightly beaten.

Apple Filling   *Makes 1 cup (200 g) filling, enough for 12 dumplings*

For the apple filling, reminiscent of our apple pies, a sweet dessert apple is best.

Peel, core, and dice 2 dessert apples (about ¾ pound or 330 g total). In a frying pan, melt 1 tablespoon butter over high heat. Add the apples and fry until very soft, about 10 minutes. They should be very dry. Let the apples cool, then smash them with a fork. Stir in 1 teaspoon each ground cinnamon and ginger, a large pinch of freshly grated nutmeg, and 1 egg, lightly beaten.

Hericoq de Mouton

Haricot of Lamb

From Taillevent, *Le viandier* (Paris, 1392; recipe from 1892 edition): *Take your lamb and put it raw to deep-fry in lard, and divide it in small pieces, put onions chopped small with it, and moisten with beef broth, and add some wine, and verjuice, and mace, hyssop, and sage, and simmer well together.*

HERICOQ OR *HARICOT* OF MUTTON appears in almost all the medieval French cookbooks, but at that time the term had nothing to do with beans (also called *haricots* in French). Possibly it was related to an old verb, *harigoter*, meaning "to chop up." At least three versions of *hericoq* appear in the various manuscripts of *Le viandier*, and this is the simplest: mutton and onions cut into small pieces and simmered with a little bit of everything, including wine, verjuice, herbs, and mace. A dark, fragrant stew is the result, which some historians link to Arab cuisine.

A lean cut of meat is best for stewing, so I use a leg of lamb here, but a less-expensive shoulder would work just as well. Hyssop is a narrow-leaved herb, aromatic but tinged with bitterness. You could substitute rosemary or apple or pineapple mint. Mace, preferably ready ground, and verjuice, the juice of unripe grapes or sometimes of apples, are available in good supermarkets or on the Internet. Taillevent does from time to time instruct, "and be sure that the salt be reasonable," so I've followed the modern practice of adding salt at the start of cooking. Note that *hericoq* should be simmered for several hours until the lamb falls apart and binds the stew to the texture of beef chili, thick enough to scoop up with the fingers or a chunk of bread. As a play on the recipe title, you could serve the *hericoq* with braised white kidney beans on the side, together with a flat bread such as pita.

Spiced Lamb Stew   *Serves 4 to 6*

> 1 medium boneless lamb leg (about 3 pounds or 1.35 kg), in one piece
> Salt
> ¼ cup (60 g) lard
> 4 onions (about 1½ pounds or 675 g total), finely chopped
> 3 cups (750 ml) beef broth, more if needed
> 1 cup (250 ml) fruity red or white wine
> ½ cup (125 ml) verjuice
> 2 teaspoons ground mace
> 3 or 4 sprigs hyssop or rosemary, finely chopped
> 3 or 4 sprigs sage, finely chopped

Divide the leg into 4 or 5 convenient pieces. Trim the meat of connective tissue and fat and discard. Sprinkle the pieces with salt. Heat the lard in a sauté pan or frying pan over high heat until very hot. Add the meat pieces, standing back as they will sputter. Fry until browned on the first side, 4 to 5 minutes. Turn them and brown the other side, about 5 minutes longer. Remove the meat, let it cool to tepid, then cut into ½-inch (1.25-cm) cubes.

Discard all but about 2 tablespoons of the fat from the pan. Replace the meat and stir in the onions. Stir in the broth, wine, verjuice, mace, and chopped herbs. Cover the pan and bring to a simmer over low heat. Cook, stirring occasionally, until the meat is tender, about 1 hour. Remove the lid and continue simmering, stirring often, until the mixture is thick, about 1 hour longer. Be sure to keep cooking the mixture longer than you think you should. When the stew is ready, it should be rich and deeply colored and fall easily from a spoon. Taste and adjust the seasoning.

The stew can be made ahead and the flavor will mellow on reheating.

Mon Amy

My Good Friend

From *Boke of Cokery* (London, 1500; recipe from 1882 edition): *To make mon amy / take and boyle cows creme and whan it is boyled sette it asyde and lette it kele than take cow cruddes [curds] & press oute the whey and braye them in a mortar and cast them into the potte to the creme and boyle all togider [together] put therto suger or hony [honey] & may butter and colour it up with saffron and in the settynge downe put in yolkes of egges, wel bett [beat] and do away the streyne [strain] & lette thy potage be standynge than lesk [lift] it in dyshes and plant there in floures of vyolettes and serve it.*

THE FRENCH TITLE OF THIS RECIPE is misleading, as this delicate curd pudding is a forerunner of such homey English desserts as curd tart, custard tart, and syllabub. It is a luxurious creation sweetened with honey, colored with saffron, and rich with butter and eggs. Fresh curd cheese is not generally available, so I suggest you use Greek-style yogurt, which is close in taste to the curds from nonpasteurized milk. The yogurt should be warmed gently so as not to kill the enzymes that will thicken the mixture to pudding consistency. This temperature and the stages of mixing and letting the pudding stand are key to success. You can omit the original step of pounding the yogurt in a mortar, as it is already smooth. Fresh violets are the decoration, suggesting this is a dish for spring that uses the new season's milk, which would also go to make the "May butter." The floral, slightly sour flavor of the mousse is perfect with berries.

Fresh Cheese Mold *Serves 4 to 6*

1 quart (1 liter) Greek-style yogurt
¼ cup (60 ml) heavy cream
½ cup (100 g) brown sugar
¼ cup (100 g) honey
¼ cup (60 g) butter, cut into pieces, softened
Large pinch of saffron threads
4 egg yolks
1 bunch violets, for decoration

Cheesecloth

Line a colander with the cheesecloth, set it over a bowl, spoon in the yogurt, and leave to drain, at least 3 hours or overnight in the refrigerator. Bring the cream just to a boil in a saucepan and then leave it to cool.

Transfer the drained yogurt to the saucepan of cooled cream, and add the brown sugar, honey, butter, and saffron. Heat very gently, whisking until the sugar is melted and the mixture is smooth, 3 to 4 minutes, then remove from the heat. Do not let the mixture get above hand-warm, or it will not thicken. In a small bowl, whisk the egg yolks until lightly thickened, then whisk them into the cream mixture. Leave the mixture to stand and thicken for about 1 hour.

Line the colander with fresh cheesecloth, set it on a tray to catch drips, and transfer the honey-saffron mixture to it. Cover and leave to drain in the refrigerator so that it thickens, at least 4 hours or up to 12 hours. It will thicken enough to hold a shape.

To serve, spoon the firmed mixture into bowls and tuck a violet or two into each serving.

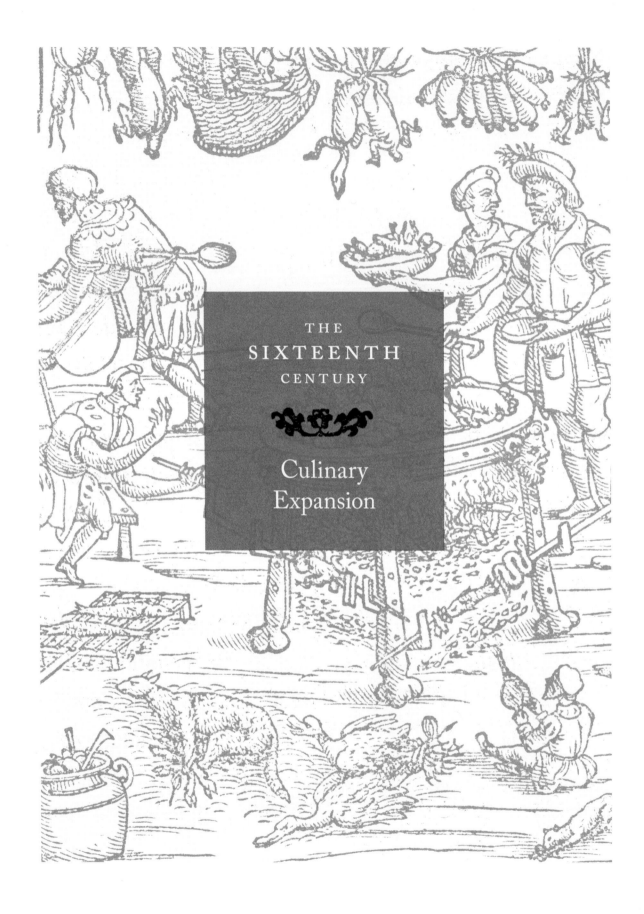

THE
SIXTEENTH
CENTURY

Culinary
Expansion

B Y THE BEGINNING of the sixteenth century, the printing press had shrunk the world of late Renaissance Europe. Book publishing flourished in many cities, and one by one, significant new cookbooks began to appear in print. Under humanist influence, ideas passed from one kitchen to another faster than ever before, sometimes via printed recipes and published cookbooks but also in poems, works of natural philosophy, and medical treatises on diet. People were hungry for knowledge, and writers were eager to reveal the "secrets" of new medical, astrological, agricultural, scientific, and culinary expertise. Books embraced multiple genres—encyclopedias contained fables and poems, natural histories included travelogues—so cooking instructions and advice on good eating could be hidden in many places. Books on agriculture explained how to grow foods and, by implication, how to bring them to the table. Cookbooks with recipes as we know them today were still few, but printing had already launched a range of culinary information that was to widen throughout the century.

More and more people were traveling at this time, tasting new foods and indulging in strange habits (using forks!). Not only royal entourages but also clergy, ambassadors, naturalists, merchants, and adventurers traveled and wrote books for the waves of wanderers that followed. The "Grand Tour" for the education of elite young gentlemen made its debut, while the less well heeled also found ways to travel for self-improvement and adventure. These travelers detailed what they ate and drank in the royal courts of England, the inns of Flanders, the streets of Constantinople, and the Vatican in Rome.

Cooks and household stewards followed their masters' example in traveling from country to country, taking with them their practical information and expertise on cooking. The last illustration in *Opera di M. Bartolomeo Scappi* (The Work by Master Bartolomeo Scappi, 1570), the leading cookbook of the century, displays hampers of treats being delivered to the Vatican as cardinals from all over Europe jostle for success during the conclave for the papal election of 1550. International aristocratic marriages mingled retinues as well as the political interests of nations' noble families. When Mary, Queen of Scots, returned from the court of France to assume her throne, she

OPPOSITE Detail from *Banchetti composizioni di vivande* by Cristoforo di Messisbugo, 1549. Full image on page 80.

brought with her a French maître d'hôtel to mastermind the menus for her court. On the great trade routes of the Danube and the Rhine, the scene was even more cosmopolitan, with one German author writing in Augsburg, another of Hungarian origin cooking in Mainz and writing multinational recipes in German, and yet a third to the west working in French-speaking Liège.

Italy emerged as the culinary leader of the century, though France was not far behind and eventually leapfrogged to the lead. Though France published the first cookbook of the period, and its citizens had an avid interest in food, cooking, and health, the Italians showed greater virtuosity in writing and publishing books about cooking and were more open to culinary innovation. Lavish, complex feasts were the order of the day at the court of France under Catherine de' Medici, the houses of the nobility, and the palaces of the church in Italy. Other countries hardly competed. The elegance of the Burgundian court in Dijon had already been engulfed by the political downfall of the Burgundian empire, when wealth and attention shifted to the Low Countries. For a while under King Henry VIII, England maintained a somewhat dated medieval splendor, but under Queen Elizabeth I, attention broadened to include country gentry and the rising merchant class in towns. More and more, England took on the mind-set of an island nation. Prosperity blossomed and with it a conservatism and appreciation of home. On the one hand, recognizing they could not be self-sufficient, the English were getting a head start in exploration and international trade with the Indies and North America; on the other hand, they relished the comforts of their own firesides.

The Italian Trendsetters

The new century dawned with the publication of two enormously influential cookbooks, one in Italian, the other in French. Neither was an original work, instead echoing the very first printed cookbook, Platina's *De honesta voluptate et valetudine* (Of Honest Indulgence and Good Health, 1474). *Platine en françois,* published in 1505, was not a direct translation but a sophisticated adaptation of the original Latin work that added a good deal of new culinary and medical material. *Epulario,* published in 1516, was reputedly by a certain Giovanne Rosselli, but the recipes repeat almost word for word those in *De honesta voluptate.* Venetian publishers seem to have been the moving force behind this book, which proved to be a best seller, and Rosselli's name was dropped in later editions. *Epulario* continued in print for nearly two centuries. Both books illustrate the "family tree" principle that had begun in the 1400s, in which each new cookbook drew on its predecessors. In other examples, Taillevent's *Le viandier* (The Victualler, 1490) and the anonymous *Le ménagier de Paris* (The Householder of Paris, a manuscript from 1393) were echoed in several modest pre-1550 French cookbooks that were also copied from one to another. According to historians Mary and Philip Hyman, "The public could choose between at least five *créations* with some or many recipes in common."[1]

Not until midcentury did an original Italian book on cooking appear. Cristoforo di Messisbugo's *Banchetti composizioni de vivande e apparecchio generale* (Banquets, Composition of Dishes and General Presentation, 1549) is an impressive practical guide for managers in leading households. Messisbugo was the son of a prominent Ferrara family and *scalco* (steward, or *maître d'hôtel* in French or *majordomo* in Spanish) at the spectacular court of Ferrara, where he worked for both Duke Alfonso d'Este and his son Cardinal Ippolito. Renaissance state-of-the-art feasting had been refined to a high art at the court of the dukes of Burgundy, and Messisbugo understood the demands of Duke Alfonso's lavish entertainments to perfection. Along with recording complete menus and recipes for the dishes, he noted details such as the musical instruments to be played at precise points during a feast. This glimpse of the finest ingredients, equipment, and entertainment that money could buy had an influence far beyond *Banchetti*'s debut publication in Ferrara, leading to nine more editions in the sixteenth century and three in the seventeenth.[2]

Banchetti begins with the 1529 wedding banquet for Alfonso's oldest son and future duke, Ercole, an occasion designed to demonstrate to his bride, the French princess Renée, that she would be entertained as well in Italy as at the court of King François I that she had left behind. Messisbugo's eighteen-course, seven-hour banquet menu for the princess featured many typical local ingredients: eggs, cheeses, a rich variety of small fish from the nearby Po River, lampreys, sardines, large crayfish, calamari, rice, mushrooms, oranges, macaroni, asparagus, raw baby artichokes, salads, and fresh fava beans (because the banquet took place on a fast day on the Catholic calendar, no meat could be served). Fried-fish dishes were sprinkled with cinnamon, sugar, and juice from oranges that would have been tarter than today's varieties as they were closer to their wild botanical ancestors.

The Este family was known for the lavish spending that stocked its pantries and transformed its exquisite damask-clothed tables with the glitter of Cellini gold and Murano glass—a Venetian specialty then as now. In a conspicuous use of cane sugar, an expensive imported commodity, twenty-five gilt and colored sugar sculptures of Venus, Bacchus, and Cupid adorned the banquet room alongside a series portraying heroic feats by Hercules.[3] The feast ended in Renaissance fashion with the service of light sweets, including candied Seville oranges, lemons, cucumbers, and almonds to "close" the stomach and aid digestion.[4]

Messisbugo's menus incorporated recipes of varied origins. Some of the dishes for the wedding banquet, such as prawns and carp, were to be served *alla francese*, in the French style—not simply because the host wanted to give Renée a taste of home but also because international influences had moved into the kitchens of affluent households. Indeed, cookbooks would increasingly take on an international flavor throughout the rest of the century.

A number of the French-inspired recipes in *Banchetti* are similar to ones that appeared in cookbooks published in Paris between 1530 and 1545, and their inclusion in

ABOVE In this idealized Renaissance kitchen from *Banchetti composizioni di vivande* by Cristoforo di Messisbugo (1549), a surprising number of details emerge: the carcasses of poultry and animals lie waiting to be cleaned, while others hang from a pole beside sausages ready for cooking. To one side, the pastry cook rolls dough. Two cooks turn spits in front of the fire, and another stirs a cauldron decorated with elegant lions' heads, while an apprentice fans the flames with bellows (his small body reflects not only his physical size but also his lowly place in the hierarchy).

THE CENTURY OF SUGAR

The sixteenth century saw an explosion in the use of sugar. No longer simply a condiment to be used in combination with salt and a wide range of spices, as it had been in medieval cooking, sugar now acquired star status. The impetus came from increased cultivation of sugarcane, first by the Portuguese in Madeira and the Canary Islands in the late fifteenth century, then in Brazil and the Caribbean with the Spanish and English colonial expansion into the New World.[1] By the end of the century, cooks were fashioning sculptures from solidified sugar syrup or sometimes using molds and then chiseling the sugar into shape. These creations were an innovative alternative to the *pièces montées,* obligatory at medieval feasts.

The Este wedding of the future Duke Ercole in Ferrara in 1529 confirmed the sugary trend. In *Banchetti,* Cristoforo di Messisbugo glossed over the technical problems that the elaborate sugar sculptures must have posed. The structures are fragile, all the more when they start to decompose. Tall constructions would collapse under their own weight, even when supported with wires. Moreover, in these days before refined white sugar, sugar syrup would have been a monotone, though not unpleasant, beige. Sugar artists must have added colors such as saffron, the green of herb extracts, and the purple of crushed bilberries, which would have rendered the solidified sculptures even more fragile. The pressure of time and the demand for teams of skilled pastry cooks must have been enormous. No wonder that, later in the century, household staffs set aside special rooms for sugar creations in preparation for their triumphant entrance as the finale to a costly feast.

As the century advanced, sugar became more accessible to prosperous households. A small amount mixed with fruits in preserves and drinks not only boosted the foods' flavor but acted as a preservative to allow longer storage of summer fruits. In his *Opuscule,* Nostradamus described sweetened dishes with even wider appeal, making sugar remedies the foundation of miraculous medicines as well as fashionable luxury foods.[2] With the sugar fad sweeping Europe, he picked up recipes for sugar candy from Genoa and Venice and offered recipes for preserves from Spain, where, he said, sugar was less expensive so cooks had more experience with it.

Sugar had an added boost from New World ingredients such as chocolate. Almost immediately after *Opuscule* appeared in French, translations of Italian books on sugar work and distilling began to appear in London. The art of pastry, and with it the métier of pastry cook, had begun. ♦

1 Sidney W. Mintz, *Sweetness and Power: The Place of Sugar in Modern History* (London: Penguin, 1985), 30–32.

2 Barbara Ketcham Wheaton, *Savoring the Past* (Philadelphia: University of Pennsylvania Press, 1983), 39–40.

By the time *L'art de raffiner le sucre* by Henri-Louis Duhamel du Monceau appeared in 1764, sugar refining had improved to the point that the crystals were sparkling white instead of drab beige. At least a half dozen steps were needed before the syrup could be left to crystallize in cone-shaped molds. Later, the sugar seller cut chunks from the tall blocks for the cook to take home and grate for use.

Food and sex have long been a favorite combination, recognized in this illustration from *De conservanda bona valetudine* by Jean Curion (1545).

Messisbugo's book suggests that an identifiable style of French cooking was already emerging.[5] Indeed, Jean Bruyérin-Champier, the well-traveled court physician to François I, noted in his *L'alimentation*, "The Milanese and those who live beyond the Po have not the smallest aversion to French cooking, which they consume copiously and with enjoyment."[6]

Messisbugo was keenly aware of cooking traditions elsewhere in Europe. In addition to the French recipes served to Renée, *Banchetti* includes a smattering of English, Catalan, and Spanish dishes. A likely influence would have been Ruberto de Nola, fifteenth-century master cook to Ferdinand I of Aragon and king of Naples, whose court from 1479 to 1516 was "one of the most brilliant, sophisticated, and urbane cities in the entire Mediterranean."[7] The Catalan region produced two popes in the fifteenth century, bringing their local culture and cuisine to Rome.[8] The manuscript of Ruberto de Nola's *Libre del coch* (The Cook's Book) was published in the Catalan language in 1520, and in Spanish in 1525 as *Libro de cozina* (Kitchen Book).[9] Catalan cooking of the time showed many Arabic influences, including a love of confectionery and sugar. Nola foreshadows later sixteenth-century treatises in Italian that transformed the way sugar was used throughout Europe.[10]

ANOTHER ITALIAN *SCALCO* TOOK the precepts of Messisbugo several steps further, seeking to define the responsibilities of a princely household in "a Work useful for all." When *La singolare dottrina di M. Domenico Romoli sopranominato Panunto* (The Exceptional Doctrine of M. Domenico Romoli, Known as Panunto, 1560) was published, Romoli had been chief steward both for a cardinal and for Pope Julius III. From a distinguished Florentine family, he showed a partiality for the dishes of Tuscany in his menus. Michele Tramezzino, the Venetian printer of *La singolare dottrina*, was even more renowned as the creator of landmark books on ancient Rome and would soon be celebrated as the publisher of Scappi's *Opera*.

La singolare dottrina includes nearly 150 recipes, but it is much more than a collection of recipes. The book is unique in offering "everyday" menus for 365 days of the year. Here, in real time, is a record of what people in an affluent household actually ate, day by day, fast days and feast days, for the year 1546. March menus accommodate Lent with week after week of dazzling fish dishes supported by a bevy of vegetables and fruits. Other menus herald the occasional festivity, such as a June party *alla francese*, indicating that Romoli sought to create a faithful day-by-day record of the household's activities. November's grand wedding feast for fifty guests, with attendant carvers to provide both service and entertainment, shows the high status of Romoli's master. First came a buffet set out on the *credenza* (sideboard), then guests were seated for a seven-course extravaganza of as many as two hundred dishes large and small. Such

LA SINGOLARE
DOTTRINA DI M. DOMENICO
Romoli ſopranominato Panunto ,

Dell'ufficio dello Scalco, de i condimenti di tutte le viuande, le ſtagioni che ſi conuengono a tutti gli animali, vcelli, & peſci, Banchetti di ogni tempo, &
mangiare da apparecchiarſi di di, in di, per tutto
l'anno a Prencipi.

Con la dichiaratione della qualità delle carni di
tutti gli animali, & peſci, & di tutte le
viuande circa la ſanità .

Nel fine vn breue trattato del reggimento della ſanità .
Opera ſommamente vtile a tutti .

E IL MIO FOGLIO

QVAL PIV FERMO   E IL MIO PRESAGIO.

SIBILLA

Cel Priuilegio del Sommo Pontefice, & dell'Illuſtr.
Senato Veneto per anni XX.

The title page of *La singolare dottrina* by Domenico Romoli (1560) displays a good deal of information but does not mention the book's printer, Michele Tramezzino, who was at least as well known as the author. Tramezzino was renowned as the creator of landmark works on ancient Rome and soon to be celebrated as publisher of Bartolomeo Scappi's cookbook *Opera.* The illegible stamp on the page records an early owner.

THE ANATOMY OF CARVING

Books on carving are enthralling: the words alone intoxicate. Take this ditty from *The Boke of Kervynge*, published in 1508 by Wynkyn de Worde, partner of William Caxton, who brought the first printing press to England in 1476:

The termes of a Kerver be as here followeth:

Breke that dere—
lesche that brawne—
rere that goose—
lyfte that swanne—
sauce that capon—
spoyle that hen—
frusche that chekyn—
unbrace that mallarde—
unlace that conye—
dysmembre that heron—
display that crane—
disfygure that peacocke—
unjoynt that bytture—
untache that curlewe—
alaye that selande—
wynge that partryche—
wynge that quayle—
myne that plover—
thye that pygyon—
border that pasty—
thye that woodcocke—
thye all maner smalle byrdes—
tymbre that fyre—
tyere that egge—
chynne that samon—
strynge that lampreye—
splat that pyke—
sauce that plaice—
sauce that tench—
splaye that breme—
syde that haddock—
tuske that barbell—
culpon that troute—
fyne that cheven—
trassene that ele—
trance that sturgeon—
undertraunche that purpos—
tayme that crabbe—
barbe that lopster.—
Here endeth the goodly terms of Kervynge.

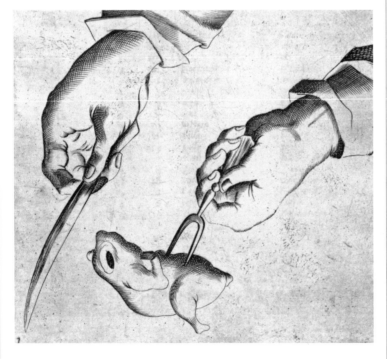

The tools of a carver at work appear in *Il trinciante* by Vincenzo Cervio, 1593.

Each species has its own verb: "Lift that swan, wing that quail, tear that egg, tame that crab." No wonder that writers have copied down these dizzying words through the centuries, starting in medieval times before the printed word. Versions differ slightly, and this one comes from *Antiquitates culinariae* (Curious Tracts Relating to the Culinary Affairs of the Old English, 1791) by the Reverend Richard Warner, who gathered medieval menus, recipes, and commentary into a nostalgic memoir of medieval feasting.

The carver was a high-ranking official in the household hierarchy—a showman whose sleight of hand with knife and fork would entertain the lord and his companions. Only the rich could afford whole animals, birds, and fish on the table, and the display of these specimens was an important part of the pleasure, and ritual, of feasting throughout Europe. An illustration in the fifteenth-century *Très riches heures du duc de Bérri* (Very Rich Hour Book of the Duke of Berry) depicts a carver taking his knife to a charger of little birds. Scappi in his *Opera* (1570) shows a carver at work, knife and fork held high, dismembering a duck to crush in the press beside him.

Vincenzo Cervio's *Il trinciante* (The Carver), first printed in Venice c. 1593, is a masterpiece of the High Renaissance that presents nearly seventy separate instructions for meats, birds, fish, fruits, and vegetables in its flowing italic type. Interspersed with the text are woodcuts of the classic carver's two-pronged fork and slender, tapered blade, several of which are life-size. The longest is a full eight-inch blade molded into a square-cut handle, a wicked weapon designed perhaps for dismembering a pig's head, a turtle, a whole ham, or a baby goat. Cervio's text is exhaustive, with

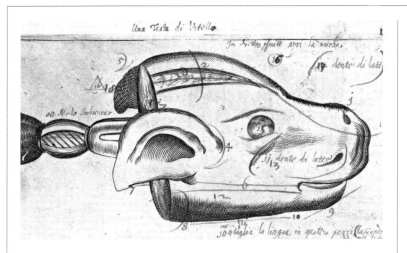

The technique for carving a calf's head is detailed in red and black inks in *Il trinciante* by Mattia Giegher, 1621. The handwritten notations from this first edition were incorporated into the text of later versions.

whole pages devoted to a single item, expressed in the intimate *tu* of one professional to another. Such rare and beautiful books have a provenance, and five different owners have left their names in our copy of *Il trinciante*.

Close by in Padua nearly thirty years later, Mattia Giegher published another *Il trinciante* (The Carver, 1621), a two-color picture book that is perhaps the most renowned of all books on carving. He dedicated it to "Federigo di Polenz, Noble of Prussia, councilor of the illustrious nation of Germany at the University of Jurisprudence in Padua," an international connection that gives a clue to his approach. Adopting a revolutionary design, Giegher demonstrates the knife cuts required to dismember more than forty common birds, fish, and meats, from a capon to a crayfish. Lines and numbers indicate the order of the steps, eliminating the need for words, and thus for translation. The author's decision to build in this versatility hints at a well-traveled career, or at least foreign staff in the kitchen.

Our copy of Giegher's *Il trinciante* has a distinguished provenance,

listed in 1954 as part of the library of Chicago collector Arnold Shircliffe, then passing to Raymond Oliver, a distinguished French chef. It is a first edition with an original drawing sewn in between the printed pages, an apparent afterthought. Even more intriguing are the proofreader's corrections and additions in a contemporary hand, which we have determined were incorporated in later editions. Could this have been the publisher's copy or, even closer to home, have belonged to Mattia Giegher himself?

In later centuries, carving continued to inspire cooks and writers. *L'ecuyer tranchant* (The Carving Steward) is one of a handful of little books on specific subjects that were bound together as a manual in *L'ecole des ragousts* (The School of Ragoûts, 1668). Germany had its *Neu-vermehrt nützliches Trencher-Buch* (New Improved Useful Carving Book, 1657), written by Andreas Klett, a teacher who talks of his students and possibly worked near Nuremberg. In London in 1676, Joseph and James Moxon published a pack of playing cards illustrated by pieces of meat with instructions on dismembering them. Sirloin of beef was king of the pack. A century later, King Charles III of Spain asked his cousin Henrique de Aragon, the Marquis of Villena, to publish an official *Arte cisoria* (Art of Carving, 1766) based on an earlier manuscript of 1423. The book is unremarkable but for the verbal portrait of the marquis: "small of stature, though stout of body … white-complexioned and lively of spirit. Inclined to the arts and sciences rather than guns or horses, he was not a military man."[1] The ideal dinner companion! ♦

1 Don Henrique de Aragon, *Arte cisoria, o tratado del arte del cortar del cuchillo* (Madrid: Antonio Marin, 1766).

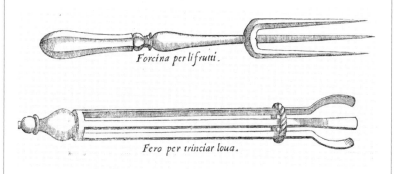

The early image of a three-pronged fruit fork from Vincenzo Cervio's *Il trinciante* (1593 edition) is shown beside a handle for grasping the shank when carving a leg of lamb.

lavish display at this date, particularly the number of serving platters required, marked the wealth of the host.

Like any good private chef, Romoli scarcely repeated himself in his daily menus. Dinner was the main meal of the day, with supper a single course, probably created from leftovers. His appetizing midday menu for the fast day of Tuesday, March 23, 1546, is typical and would not be out of place today:

> *Openers*
> Sweet melons with sugar, walnuts, figs, lettuce and chopped fresh shallots
> Tench [a river fish], turned inside out
> Salted croaker [a variety of drum] and capers
>
> *A Boiled Course*
> Large tench
> A piece of skate wing
> A pebble field of chickpeas with back-meat tuna, flavored with nuts
>
> *A Fried Course*
> Spinach florentine [a kind of pie]
> Mullet, squid, and smelts with sliced lemons and olives
>
> *A Fruit Course*
> Artichokes
> Green mandarins
> Pine nuts, pistachios, and fennel

The year's menus pursue their seasonal course through squash and pears in June to fresh figs and quince in August to the woodcock, wild boar, and other game of fall. Clearly, Romoli had access to excellent markets, for his dishes incorporate pears from France and Sardinia and olives from Spain. A sprinkling of dishes are *alla francese* too, crayfish comes *alla tedesca* (German style), chicken is *alla catalana,* ravioli is *alla lombarda,* and many dishes are *alla fiorentina;* treats come from all over Italy, such as biscotti from Pisa and "little morsels" from Naples.

As an adjunct to his menus, Romoli delves into the background of fine dining, offering notes on how to choose and store meats, fish, produce, and poultry. He mentions "Indian peacock," or turkey, recently arrived from the New World. He devotes one of his twelve chapters to spices and condiments, including vinegar and wine, but he selects a much smaller spice box than had been common a century earlier, including only pepper, ginger, clove, cassia and cinnamon, saffron, nutmeg, and coriander. He discusses household finance and health issues such as the value of exercise and the importance of clean air and water. His menus often list fennel, known to counterbalance the phlegmatic humor, so perhaps one of his patrons felt lethargic.

These foods eaten in Italy were a far cry from those appearing in the menus of Queen Mary of Scots, which emphasized meat, fish, and poultry, the medieval protein overload. Romoli makes clear that Italy has moved away from the complex, heavy dishes of a century before that were still the norm in northern Europe. That he mentions only half a dozen spices is surprising in itself, and his cautious use of them is even more remarkable. His use of sugar is sparing but specific, implying that his sweet dishes such as melon tart and *ciambelle* cookies with sweet icing resembled our desserts today.

TEN YEARS AFTER *LA SINGOLARE DOTTRINA*, *Opera di M. Bartolomeo Scappi* appeared, marking the high point of Renaissance achievement and setting a standard by which all later cookbooks can be judged. The book, printed after Scappi had retired, opens with a magisterial portrait of the great man, bearded and gazing in contemplation out of the frame. Educated and articulate as would befit one of the highest members of an elite Renaissance household, Scappi was a master cook. He headed the influential kitchens of two cardinals and two popes, including Pius IV, a Lombard renowned for his love of puddings and pies as well as, says Scappi, for his appreciation of frogs' legs fried in garlic and parsley. At this time in the mid-sixteenth century, the papal court was a hub of humanist natural philosophy, and the Jesuit community (there and elsewhere) was at the forefront of the new experimental science. Scappi's culinary talents flourished in this extraordinary environment.

Opera is an expansive work that focuses on life in the kitchen, describing the hierarchy of cooks, the layout and operation of the kitchen, the necessary tools, and the contents of the pantry. Scappi provides menus of stupendous meals and presents more than one thousand impressively detailed recipes with sophistication and originality.[11] His recipes draw ingredients from all over Italy, incorporating the specialties of Milan, Genoa, Lucca, Lombardy, the Piedmont, Rome, Naples, Venice, and Sicily and adding regional tags to products such as rice, oil, Parmesan cheese, and fruits. They also embrace foreign influences, making frequent use of Spanish ingredients like olives and ham, for example, and including Hungarian and French dishes.

At this time, the general population still observed fast days, and the collection of fish recipes in *Opera* is detailed and wide-ranging, offering seven pages on the elegant sturgeon and including the humble sea slug.[12] Among the meats, even bear gets its due as a rustic northern specialty, along with water buffalo, boar, and oxen testicles. Italy was always a home for vegetables, and Scappi outdoes Romoli with complex recipes such as cabbage leaves stuffed with nuts, raisins, herbs, and garlic; spiced with saffron; and simmered in meat broth. His leek and onion *minestra* is equivalent to the French *potage* and is bolstered on meat days with eggs

In the style of Leonardo da Vinci, this elaborate spit can be wound like a clock with the handle at left, so that three spits can turn untended for a half hour or more. The image comes from the 1596 edition of Scappi's *Opera*.

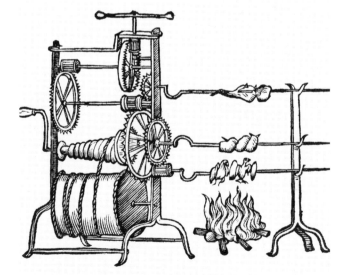

and grated cheese, or a choice of capon or wild boar, simmered in meat broth, saveloy sausage, sugar, and spices, including saffron, all to be served on a generous deep platter.

In *Opera*, Scappi is insistent on training: "The basic foundation on which [the cook] must rely requires knowledge and practical experience of a variety of sorts, so that if a few ingredients may be missing, because of location or season, he can make good substitutions." His opening advice to the master cook could have been written by one of today's top chefs, with their metaphysical approach to food: "Following his sure

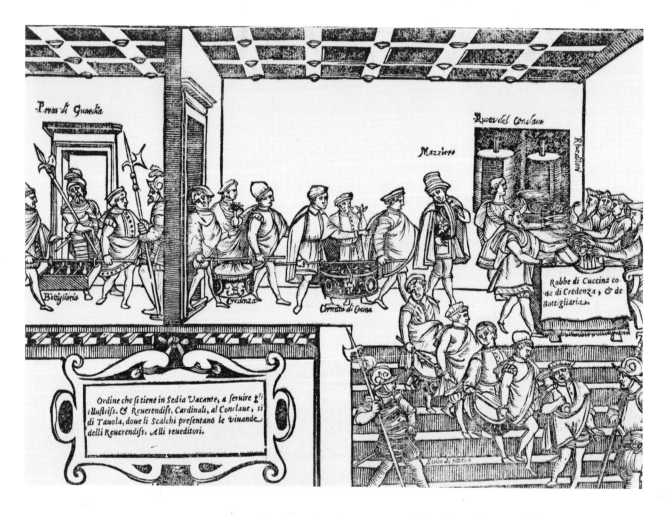

ABOVE As a veteran of papal conclaves, master cook Bartolomeo Scappi could not resist telling the visual story of the election of Pope Julius III in 1550. The focal point of this double-page spread from his cookbook *Opera* (1596 edition) is the procession of servants carrying scarlet and gold hampers of hot food (*cucina*), cold food (*credenza*) for the buffet, and drinks (*bottigliaria*), each emblazoned with a cardinal's coat of arms. To ensure that no messages are smuggled into the conclave, a panel of bishops inspects the food before passing everything through the revolving hatches to the cardinals enclosed in the Sistine Chapel. In the power play of the conclave, fine dining must have been of key importance to participants.

SCAPPI'S RENAISSANCE KITCHEN

Scappi's *Opera* is the archetypal Renaissance book, in this case for the working cook. The twenty-five magnificent plates at the back of the book constitute the first cookware catalog. Thanks to Scappi, we enter a vivid world of steaming stoves, flashing knives, and ingenious spits turning in the convection heat from an open fire in the style of Leonardo da Vinci. Far from being just a picture book, *Opera* is a practical manual. All the images are instantly recognizable today. In the main kitchen, the fluted ravioli cutter lies ready to slice a sheet of pasta dough, a mortar and hefty pestle stand at the ready on a stone column, and bread is stored on a high shelf, safe from prowling animals. Outside in the courtyard, gutted rabbits hang from a beam near a tub of fish, while a knife sharpener spins his wheel, whetted with water from a barrel.

A whole page on knives, their handles riveted for strength, follows *Opera*'s presentation of "diverse tools" that include cauldrons, pots, ladles, mandolins, mortars and pestles, scales, macaroni cutters, cheese graters, pastry cutters, assorted strainers and spoons, casseroles, and frying pans. Scappi's sketch of a knife, fork, and spoon is possibly the first view of these utensils as a set. As a cook himself, Scappi clearly had a penchant for gadgets such as mandolins, nutmeg graters, and picnic hampers; one illustration shows a duck press in action to delight his gourmet audience. His three-tiered roasting spit is turned by a single crank, and he even includes a diagram of how to lift an implausibly giant cauldron with the help of four strong men.

Far more practical is the raised stove of bricks that Scappi shows along one wall, pictured with a pot simmering on top. Heat is provided by logs, or in some cases by glowing charcoal, and smoke drifts out via the nearby door. Such stoves, called *potagers* in France, were to become universal in the following centuries, present in large and small kitchens. No longer did the cook have to struggle, back bent over an open fire. Heat was easier to regulate, making possible more complex soups and sauces. Cooking could now take place at waist level, pans were easy to manipulate, and the cook could monitor progress at a glance. The raised stove, however, did not replace the open fire but was an adjunct to it.

Over the centuries, Scappi's illustrations have formed an invaluable professional inventory. The raised stove, for example, lasted well into the nineteenth century, and reproductions of his tools still dot the pages of modern cookbooks. ♦

With its running water, bank of raised stoves, and amenities such as a firescreen and bale of straw for securing knives, the main kitchen shown in the 1596 edition of Scappi's *Opera* is an idealized fantasy that would inspire cooks for at least two centuries.

THE ART
OF THE BOOK

Mainz was the birthplace of print and the home of a generation of German printers who trekked across Europe to set up presses and teach the craft. The first stop for these traveling craftsmen was often northern Italy, the cradle of humanism and a fount of ancient texts begging to be converted into print. Italian merchants already held a near monopoly on the paper trade, and Venice was a hotbed of humanist bibliophiles ready to invest. By the late 1470s, bankers had stepped in, financing, among others, the famous Aldine Press. Because they owned the presses, investors had considerable say in what got published.[1] They created books not just to be useful but to be beautiful. In a visual rupture with the past, printers invented the roman and italic type fonts that re-created the handwriting of the ancient Greek and Roman books. Humanist aesthetic influence led to easy-to-read pages with white space around the various elements and the use of alphabetizing and indexing. Even pagination

was a humanist advance.[2] *Platine en françois* had echoed the appearance of a manuscript text, but as the sixteenth century advanced, printers, who were in effect publishers, took charge of book design and production. The very look of Italian Renaissance cookbooks such as Messisbugo's *Banchetti* and Scappi's *Opera* signals their modernity. Their text is orderly, and the words are surrounded by clean white space rather than being crammed on the page. The typeface is the new, flowing, reader-friendly italic.

Sixteenth-century authors, including cooks and stewards, did not think of the sales potential of books, instead depending on wealthy patrons for support. *Banchetti*, for example, was made possible by the patronage of Duke Alfonso d'Este. Resident geniuses were symbols of prestige during the Renaissance, and a nobleman or church dignitary, even if not particularly intellectual, would invite talented artisans and cooks as well as artists into his household, elevating their status to "a gentleman in service."[3] A book such as *Banchetti* that celebrates the grandeur of the court of Ferrara

would have been even more prestigious for Duke Alfonso as patron than for Messisbugo himself.

Of all the books in our collection, the 1596 edition of *Opera* by Scappi stands out as a masterpiece of design. The book transcends the centuries not only as a teaching tool but also as a work of art. The 334 pages of this classic of the High Renaissance, first published in 1570, are dense with brilliant black italic script, culminating in woodcuts of a model kitchen of the late sixteenth century that offer stiff competition for today's four-color images. Pots simmer on the raised stovetop, water gushes from the tap, and the turnspit waves his hand behind the protective screen that shields him from the blazing fire.

Opera contains more than a thousand recipes, but *Ein new Kochbuch* (A New Cookbook), by Marx Rumpolt, printed in Frankfurt in 1581, is larger in every way. Germans were among the last to abandon the so-called blackletter Gothic appearance, so *Kochbuch* is a hybrid of new and old. Each section of recipes for living creatures—calf, salmon, turkey, lobster—is illustrated by woodcuts from previously published works of natural history that realistically portray the animals in their natural habitats. Drawings of fruits, vegetables, and even breads seek to imitate nature, eschewing the allegorical and mythical references of the past.

Just a glance at these books, with their view into the future, takes your breath away. They have permanently shaped our perception of beauty and utility—of what a book should be. ◆

1 Lisa Jardine, *Worldly Goods: A New History of the Renaissance* (New York: W. W. Norton, 1996), 128.

2 Lucien Febvre and Henri-Jean Martin, *The Coming of the Book,* trans. David Gerard (London: Verso, 1976), 92–94.

3 Jardine, *Worldly Goods,* 245.

A grotesque fills a gap in the 1633 edition of John Gerarde's *The Herball or Generall Historie of Plantes.*

M BARTOLOMEO
SCAPPI

conception, he establishes solid foundations, upon which he gives to the world unique and marvelous constructions; thus the design of the Master Cook must possess beautiful and precise order, based on experience."[13]

Given the massive scope and rich reservoir of knowledge in *Opera*, Scappi and his publisher likely expected it to be a popular book, but it was possibly less so than might be supposed. Printed earlier, Messisbugo's *Banchetti* went through twenty editions, whereas *Opera* achieved seventeen, though the print runs may have been larger.[14] Possible reasons for the book's relative lack of success could equally well apply today. First, the economic environment was poor. *Opera* was published in the republic of Venice, an oasis of liberty on the disputed Italian peninsula, but by the end of the century, Venetian publishers and their Protestant humanist backers had fallen on hard times and had to shut down their printing presses for lack of funding. Second, perhaps the sheer grandeur of this eight-hundred-page tome on "mastering the art" of the greatest Renaissance kitchens was simply too much for the limited cookbook market to bear. Outside events intervened, too, particularly in France, where civil wars of religion were under way and fierce anti-Italian sentiment prevailed in the late sixteenth century. Nonetheless, a precious copy of *Opera* embossed with the arms of Queen Catherine de' Medici survives to this day in the Bibliothèque Nationale in Paris. Also, many of *Opera*'s recipes were later plagiarized, carrying Scappi's influence to Spain, the Netherlands, England, Denmark, and Germany.[15]

Dignified portraits of the author, called cartouches, were often featured in books of the High Renaissance. At left is Bartolomeo Scappi from the 1596 edition of *Opera;* at right, Cristoforo di Messisbugo from the 1549 first edition of *Banchetti composizioni di vivande.*

Scappi's *Opera* is the last of the landmark cookbooks in Renaissance Italy; cookbook innovation then moved elsewhere. During the following centuries, smaller cookbooks aimed at wider audiences were to appear, but the sweeping focus of encyclopedias such as *Opera* was almost entirely absent until Italian unification in the 1860s. Regional quarrels, invasions by foreign conquerors, religious power struggles, and the inward focus of Italian thought and culture following the brilliance of the Renaissance likely all played a role in dampening cookbook authors' ambitions to publish major works.

Harbingers of a New French Style

The lighter, new cooking that had developed in Italy by midcentury took longer to reach France. Medieval cooking held sway, epitomized by Taillevent's *Le viandier,* which continued until 1604 with nearly thirty editions. The first new cookbook of the sixteenth century, *Platine en françois* (1505), was actually a fresh adaptation and translation into French of Platina's masterwork of three decades before. It too continued in print into the following century, with over twenty editions, the first published in Lyon, which was already a gastronomic center and home for a dozen years to Rabelais, the famed man of letters.

The team that translated Platina's book, headed by Desdier Christol of Montpellier, made significant additions to the text, including new commentary on the foodstuffs and recipes in the original. The 1505 work, which is twice as long as Platina's original, blends the new and old material so seamlessly that it is impossible to know what was added without directly comparing the Latin and French versions. In *Platine en françois,* touches of Spanish, Arab, and Catalan cooking punctuate Platina's Florentine, Venetian, and Roman delights: luxurious pastas, carefully seasoned vegetables, sugared

A giant illuminated *P* opens the first page of *Platine en françois* translated by Desdier Christol, 1505. At this early stage in the history of printing, books did not always have a separate title page.

fritters, and other sweets. The book also touts food as the key to good health, prefiguring a trend that would mark the century. An extensive passage pairs sauces with foods according to the Greek physician Galen's medical theory of the humors. Cooks should not use the same sauce for a boiled meat that they use for a roast, say the French translators: in winter, mustard, ginger, pepper, cinnamon, and garlic are good, but summer sauces must be fresh with verjuice, lemons, orange juice, rose water, and perhaps a little sugar.

Despite its title, *Platine en françois* does not exclusively hark back to the previous century. Hints of a new French style already show through in a greater reliance on seasonal and local ingredients and pursuit of a definably French cuisine, a quest that would intensify in the seventeenth century. Another French cookbook of the time, *Livre fort excellêt de cuysine tres utile* (The Most Excellent Book of Very Useful Cooking, 1508), relies heavily on butter, wine, herbs, and aromatics, combinations we now think of as typical of France. The *Livre de cuysine tres utile* (A Very Useful Cookbook, 1540) includes many vegetable dishes and a recipe for garlic soup. In a final, important glimpse of the future, sweets (cream tarts, pears in the warm spiced red wine called ypocras, quince paste, spiced dragées) were confined to the final course, heralding the changing role of sugar.

As the sixteenth century progressed, interest in cooking spread beyond royal and ecclesiastical circles to the increasingly prosperous bourgeoisie. One harbinger was the court physician Jean Bruyérin-Champier, who published a thick treatise in Latin, *De re cibaria* (On Food), in 1560, the same year that Romoli's day-by-day cookbook appeared in Italy. Bruyérin's book has no recipes, but he details the expanding range of food during the reigns of two French kings, François I and his son Henry II. The author declares that frogs and snails, those two French culinary icons, were formerly consumed by "*bêtes sauvages* (savage beasts). . . . only an *âne* (ass) ate vegetables. . . . But now, in almost the whole of France they are served as delicate dishes on the best tables."[16]

A comparison of the first printed version of Taillevent's *Le viandier* of 1486 with Bruyérin's revelations seventy years later shows how dramatically French dining changed in this time. Gone are the multiple cooking processes and layers of spicing described by Taillevent. For example, to prepare partridges, Taillevent recommended first roasting the birds and then braising them in a pot with lard, beef bouillon, and onions chopped small and fried, adding grains of paradise, other spices, and sugar as needed. He called for thickening the sauce with bread and then adding yet more spices, verjuice, and salt. Bruyérin, in contrast, says that partridges younger than a year are best served simply roasted. They need no elaborate sauce because they produce enough fat and flavorful juices that the cook need only season them with a little verjuice, vinegar, or bitter orange juice. In a similar vein, vegetables such as asparagus, chard, and cabbage are now *just* cooked so that they are still crisp (*croquant*), and salads are expected to maintain "a singular delicacy."[17]

As this new simplicity developed, so did the French conviction of the superiority

EATING LIKE
A QUEEN

By chance, our collection includes household records that belonged to two queens, one the daughter-in-law of the other. The first is a slim, elegant book, its lavish printing surrounded by wide margins, of menus for the court of Mary, Queen of Scots. The second is a single sheet, the inventory of Catherine de' Medici's food supplies for March 30, 1570, for her château at Plesis Macé near Angers on the Loire.

Queen Mary was already installed on her throne in Scotland by the summer of 1562, when the menus for her court and staff of possibly two hundred were compiled. (Her young husband, François II of France, had died in December 1560.) The book is in French, drafted by her maître d'hôtel, Monsieur de Pinguillon, and signed Marie R. by the queen herself in approval of the contents. The book specifies the food plan and financial allowance for each group at court, from the maître d'hôtel and controller to the lowliest *valletz* and *femmes de chambre*. Mary was clearly at home with French habits, having lived fourteen of her twenty years in France at the court of Catherine de' Medici. However, her personal menus show little sign of sophistication, amounting to scarcely more than lists of ingredients. Her first meal of the day, the *ordinaire*, includes three courses, with a fruit course to finish. *Bouil*—related to *bouillir*, to boil—is a kind of hash, while *Rost* refers to whole roast meats.

DISNER

Quatre platz poutaige
[moist broth stews]

Quatre platz entres de table
[small cooked dishes such as sausages, or fricassées]

BOUIL

Ung piece beuf roialle
[a "royal" simmered piece of beef]

Ung hault couste mouton
[a simmered side of mutton ribs]

Ung chappon
[a simmered whole capon]

ROST

Ung membre mouton
[a roast leg of mutton]

Ung chappon
[a roast capon]

Trois poulletz ou pigz
[three roast chickens or possibly pigeons]

Trois gibiers
[three roast game birds]

Deux gros
[two roast pieces of large game such as deer or wild boar]

The list for *soupper* is similar, including a pie, so it may have consisted partly of leftovers, though traditionally these were passed on to the staff. The book does not specify what seasonings and sauces cooks might have used to vary the principal ingredients—beef, mutton, capon, game, fowl, veal, fresh pork, goat, eggs—nor does it mention vegetable garnishes, though they were almost certainly served during the summer months (July to October) covered by these menus. The menus provide for a daily bread allowance of two loaves per person and include wine, normally cut with water, in every meal.

At first glance, the sheet for Queen Catherine de' Medici looks like a menu, but it turns out to be a list of available food supplies, much like a checklist that a sous-chef might use today to take inventory of the cold store. The secretary (his name, Alessandro de Schivonoia, hints at Italian ancestry) lists bakery (*panneterie*), wine (*eschanconnerie*), kitchen (*cuisine*), fruit (*fruiterie*), and

18	MENU DE LA MAISON	1562.

Rost

Vng membre mouton
Vng chappon
Trois poulletz ou pigz
Trois gibiers
Deux gros

SOUPPER

Quatre platz poutaige
Quatre platz entres de table

Bouil

Vng hault couste mouton
Vng chappon

Rost

Vng membre mouton
Vng chappon
Trois gibiers
Trois poulletz ou pigz
Vng paste de iii poulletz ou pigz
Deux gros et demy

TABLE des officiers delad cuisine

DISNER

Quatre platz poutaige

Boil

Deux pieces beuf

The dinner menu for Mary, Queen of Scots, is noted by her head of household, Monsieur de Pinguillon, in *Menu de la maison de la Royne,* 1562.

general supplies (*fourriere*). The kitchen larder contained beef worth seventy-five sols, about eighty-five U.S. dollars today. Bouillon was a paltry seven sols, as was fat. The list in turn values kids, capon, hares, chickens, plover, thrushes, veal, stuffed veal, legs of lamb, tripe, sweetbreads (a favorite of the queen's), beef marrow, lamb's and cow's feet, and veal liver and innards in sols and deniers. The list establishes a budget for fruits and vegetables, with an aide-mémoire of available staples that includes lard, butter, eggs, candle wax, oranges, cheeses, and tarts and pastries (presumably from previous meals and thus to be eaten as soon as possible). Catherine de' Medici herself was renowned for her greed and is said to have almost died from overeating *béatilles* ("tidbits"), a glorious concoction of sweetbreads, kidneys, cocks' combs, and artichoke hearts. ♦

of their cuisine—often demonstrated in a proliferation of dishes. In *L'histoire de la nature des oiseaux* (History of the Nature of Birds, 1555), naturalist Pierre Belon provided a dazzling list of dishes that a French cook could produce for a banquet. As evidence that such a production was possible, he referred his readers to the feast set forth by humanist writer François Rabelais in the fourth book of *La vie de Gargantua et de Pantagruel* (1552). This iconic (and imaginary) Rabelaisian banquet includes four types of bread, nine *fricassées*, sixteen tortes, twenty tarts, seventy-eight dry and liquid *confitures*, and dragées in one hundred colors. In addition, the fictional guests dined on beignets, crêpes, pâtés, soups, hot pots, andouilles, hedgehogs, flamingos, boars' heads, and macaroons, not to mention artichokes, cardoons (a stocky green), ripe peaches, and white wine and claret served chilled in large silver cups, as well as both red and gold warm spiced wine *(ypocras).*

By the early 1570s, in keeping with the visions of Belon and Rabelais, an observer at the royal court in Paris noted that the traditional service of three courses—the *bouilli*, or boiled meat course, the roast, then fruit—was hopelessly old-fashioned. Modish French courtiers expected meats prepared six ways, an array of *pâtisseries*, *salmigondis* (elaborate composed salads of meats, vegetables, and pickles, usually arranged in circles), and a wide selection of other little side dishes.[18] By the time Michel de Montaigne visited the court of Cardinal Caraffa in Rome in 1580–81, the French feeling of superiority was sufficiently entrenched that the essayist could only sniff when the cardinal's Italian cook sought to educate him in the culinary arts: "With magisterial gravity . . . he spelled out for me the different kinds of appetite . . . the organization of sauces, first in general and then the qualities of the ingredients and the effects of each in particular; the different kinds of salad according to the season, what should be heated and what should be served cold, and how they should be garnished and presented in order to make them more appealing to the eye."[19]

The term *terroir,* meaning "taste of the earth," dates from this time, though identifying regional specialty food by place names—an early form of identifying *terroirs*—goes back to the writers of antiquity, notably Horace and Athenaeus. The Renaissance fascination with observation and detail spurred writers to classify the material world in a geographical context. Some even invented an imaginary world, the land of Cockaigne, a mythical land of plenty and a glutton's paradise.[20]

For Charles Estienne, coauthor with Jean Liébault

In this illustration from the 1784 English edition of the *Works of Francis Rabelais,* Rabelais's outsize character Gargantua welcomes his greedy son Pantagruel to the family table.

THE BEST INGREDIENTS: ADVICE FOR THE FARMER

Good cooks are lost without the best possible ingredients, a principle fully recognized in classical Rome but somehow lost in the subsequent shuffle. Several books printed in the sixteenth century tackle the omission by reproducing the classical writings of Pliny, Cato, and Columella on natural history, animal husbandry, and the growing of foodstuffs. The prosperity of the early decades of the sixteenth century, coinciding with a long period of peace in France, gave horticulture and husbandry the stature of serious sciences.[1] The European population at this time was low, giving landowners and peasants access to plenty of land for cultivation. How best to develop these riches was a prime concern, and a clutch of major books came out during the sixteenth century to address the subject.

As early as 1499, *Le grand propriétaire de toutes choses* (The Complete Owner of All Things) set the scene with three chapters on how to hunt and raise both wild and domestic birds; how to use herbs and plants, including their medical properties; and how to hunt game and raise domestic animals. The book describes all manner of plants and instructs readers in their cultivation, though it does not describe how to cook them. The title is metaphysical rather than literal, as this was originally a thirteenth-century

This illustration of a farmer, from *Ein new Kochbuch* by Marx Rumpolt, 1581, shows the close link between cooking and the land.

encyclopedia of general knowledge by an English scholar and bishop, Bartholomaeus Anglicus. First printed in Latin, *Le grand proprietaire* reached a wider audience when translated into French in 1556 by Jean Corbichon.

In the fourteenth century, an Italian lawyer called Petrus de Crescentius had set metaphysics aside to offer practical advice on running an agricultural property. His Latin manuscript, *Ruralia commoda* (Benefits of the Countryside), proved so useful that in 1373, Charles V of France commissioned a translation. Following this international success, the book was early to go into print, seeing publication in Germany in 1471 and France in 1486. A lavish, updated edition appeared in 1540 as *Le bon mesnaiger* (The Good Householder). Pierre de Crescens' (as he is now dubbed) analysis of the "rewards of working the fields, vines, gardens, trees of all kinds" was one of several similar agricultural texts. He explored the "qualities of all herbs that nourish the human body," including more than 130 familiar plants such as coriander, endive, fennel, lentils, and lettuce.[2]

The first contemporary manual reflecting this agricultural prosperity was *L'agriculture et maison rustique*—appearing as *L'agricoltura, e casa di villa* in Italian, *XV Bücher von dem Feldbaw* in German, and *The Countrey Farme* in English. Published in Latin and in French ten years later (1554), the two sumptuous volumes describe a paradise in print, offering a vast storehouse of information on every aspect of country life, with "secrets" scattered liberally among instructions for planting vines and stocking fishponds. Here at last was a book that left behind moral and medical commentary in the fresh, Renaissance air. Authors Charles Estienne and Jean Liébault show an interest in

This illustration to the chapter titled "Various Cabbage Salads, white and green" in *Ein new Kochbuch* shows fruits and nuts, including chili pepper, a pomegranate, apples, cherries, a radishlike root, walnuts, a lemon, pears, and the hop flowers that became crucial to brewing beer.

cooking, not just in cultivating ingredients. In the kitchen, they make *restaurants* to restore health and vitality using the latest medical equipment called a *bain-marie;* they instruct readers in making sugar-based preserves of all kinds, distilling waters and *eaux-de-vie,* and making wine and vinegar from fruits.

A few decades later, fellow countryman Olivier de Serres declared, "The earth and the buildings upon it must adapt to each other."[3] His advice in *Le theatre de l'agriculture et mesnage des champs* (Overview of Agriculture and Land Management, 1600) is exhaustive, and the book's large quarto format made it a prestigious volume for the library of the wealthy landowner. Serres instructs on what to grow, how to cultivate and harvest crops, and how to raise animals and eventually dispatch them from this world. He details the ideal layout of a gentleman's residence to capture light and shade, locating the *basse cour* (farmyard) adjacent to the kitchen door but well away from the master's study to avoid the noise and smells. Many French châteaux of the day were constructed according to his rules.

The progression of these four books (all of them luxurious in size and presentation) illustrates the leap in popular knowledge made possible by printing. They are valuable books for cooks, full of information vital to good cooking. All of them generated multiple editions, as did the *Five Hundredth Pointes of Good Husbandrie* (1573), in which Englishman Thomas Tusser expressed most of his advice in verse. Tusser's creation is invigorating reading, with dictums such as "And he that can reare up a pig in his house, hath cheaper his bacon and sweeter his souse [brine]" and "In winter at five a clocke, servants arise, In summer at foure is verie good guise."[4] This original approach proved so popular that the book remained in print for nearly two hundred years. ♦

1 Le Grand d'Aussy, *Histoire de la vie privée des français,* 3rd ed. (Paris: Laurent-Beaupré, 1815).

2 Petrus de Crescentius, *Le bon mesnaiger* (Paris: Charles Langellier, 1540), title page.

3 Olivier de Serres, *Le theatre d'agriculture et mesnage des champs* (Paris: Huzard, 1804), ch. 1, 17.

4 Thomas Tusser, *His Good Points of Husbandry,* ed. Dorothy Hartley (London: Country Life Limited, 1931), 123, 177.

ABOVE Working the land is the theme of *L'agriculture et maison rustique* by Charles Estienne and Jean Liébault. This illustration from the 1654 edition shows farmers plowing and harrowing the field in preparation for sowing grain.

of *L'agriculture et maison rustique, terroir* was the principal framework for agriculture. *Terroir* was somewhat interchangeable with *terre* ("earth/soil"), but Estienne used the term to describe the taste that travels up from the soil through whatever is planted there—a grapevine or a shaft of wheat—and imparts a particular flavor to the final product, be it wine or bread. Believing that any patch of dirt was equal to the sum of its physical properties, Estienne urged farmers to take a handful of their soil and taste it so that they could select appropriate crops.

Maison rustique connects the geography of terroir with cooking—describing, for example, why the wheat of the Beauce region leads to breads that are very different in taste, color, texture, and aroma from those of Picardie and Champagne. In the same way, Estienne explains that the great variety of French wines is due to the range of soils and climates from Alsace to Bordeaux to Burgundy. Of course, human skill affects taste too: if the baker is careless or the wine is kept in poor condition, the end product will be disappointing. But without good earth, no one can expect to achieve the finest flavor.

Estienne's book inspired other authors. Brescia native Agostino Gallo, in his *Le vinti giornate dell'agricoltura* (The Twenty Days of Agriculture, 1569), compared the plums, figs, melons, and wines grown in various *terroirs* in Lombardy.[21] In nearby Venice, the tradition of ambassadorial reports, or *relazione,* was in place as early as the thirteenth century and supplied a ready formula for listing the geographical attributes of foreign places. Travelers as diverse as Antonio de Beatis, secretary to the Italian cardinal of Aragon; Pierre Belon, the French physician and naturalist; and Scotsman Fynes Moryson habitually described the landscapes of the regions through which they passed, in effect ticking off the contents of the local larder.

Animal heads and root vegetables enliven the pages of *De conservanda bona valetudine* by Jean Curion, 1545.

Cooking along the Trade Routes

With the sixteenth century came an increase in travel, and with it enthusiasm for new foods and recipes. Several cookbooks with an international flavor appeared along the well-frequented trade circuits through the cities of northern Italy, the valleys around Lake Como, Switzerland, the Danube, the Rhine valley, Savoy, and towns across Flanders and the Low Countries. These routes had been active since the Middle Ages, and merchant networks and brotherhoods of itinerant artisans had grown up around them in the fifteenth century, continuing to proliferate into the eighteenth. The famous book fair in Frankfurt and trade fairs in Champagne increased traffic, while overland mountainous routes allowed traders to dodge customs on expensive goods. Peddlers selling luxuries such as wines, truffles, spices, citrus fruits, cheeses, capers, candy—and books—sparked the imaginations of the curious.

The cookbooks that emerged along these busy routes project a very different image from the Renaissance grace of contemporary Italian cookbooks. They are authoritative, delivered in stark black gothic type and commanding headlines. Their mission was to impress as well as to inform. First on the scene was *Ein sehr künstlichs und nützlichs Kochbuch* (A Very Artistic and Useful Cookbook), published in 1544 in Augsburg, a center of trade on a tributary of the Danube. The author, Balthasar Staindl, was a native of nearby Dillingen in Bavaria, a town that thrived economically and culturally under the leadership of the Fugger banking family.[22]

To judge from his writing style, Staindl was a cook himself, possibly an innkeeper or part of the staff in the Fugger household. As a member of the guild system that was strong in the Germanic states, he would have been expected to pass on his skills, and he indeed declares himself eager to make cooking approachable for the layman in "a very artistic and useful cookbook . . . easy for men and women to learn for themselves." He describes mundane procedures such as roasting fish and frying eggs that other cookbooks would have considered self-evident. An impish imagination leads him to color almond cheese bright blue and fashion bright red crabs from marzipan. For a distraction on fast days, he suggests shaping sausages from fish or shellfish and

A voluptuous selection of fruits, vegetables, and game stimulates a traveler's appetite in this evocation of an early sixteenth-century Dutch kitchen by Jacob Maetham (c. 1603). The guests at the table behind them will have to wait for dinner.

Von Krebßen seind drey vnd zwantzigerley Speiß vnd Trachten zu machen.

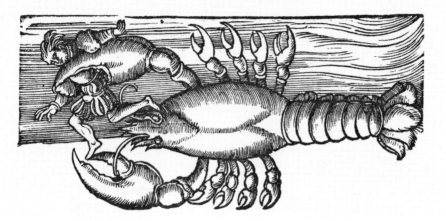

A man is caught in a lobster's claw in this engraving from *Ein new Kochbuch* by Marx Rumpolt, 1581. The lobster was the enemy of serpents, the symbol of sin—hence the predicament of this presumably wicked human.

serving a roast "deer" fashioned from a paste of spiced chopped figs covered in almonds with a sprinkling of ginger and sugar and then doused in melted butter. Most food was still eaten with the fingers, so Staindl's recipes often create pastry packages. In *Fladen,* the filling is layered between two sheets of dough; *Pastete* are shaped like bowls or tart shells; and in *Krapffen,* the dough is wrapped around the filling and baked or deep fried.

The great publishing capital of Frankfurt, near the confluence of the Main and Rhine rivers, lay on the busiest trade route. From here came *Ein new Kochbuch* (A New Cookbook, 1576) by Marx Rumpolt, master cook for the archbishop-elector of Mainz. In contrast to the modest approach of Balthasar Staindl, *Kochbuch* is a masterwork of menus and over two thousand recipes. Prosperous German publishers were among the savviest in using the large format, and the book contains many striking woodcuts. The design and illustrations once again draw on Platina's *De honesta voluptate,* this time in a German translation published in Augsburg in 1542, but the resemblance to Platina's best seller did not make *Kochbuch* outdated; on the contrary, it added prestige.

In Mainz, on the great highway of the Rhine, Marx Rumpolt was cooking for an international clientele, so his recipes are Hungarian, Spanish, French, Italian, and Catalan. However, he kept his eye on his main market, Germany. His book emphasizes meats and game and includes unabashed advice on local table manners (in Germany, unlike in France, well-behaved diners never served themselves). The first forty pages include instructions for household officers, with menus for a range of social levels, from kings and archdukes to farmers and citizens. He describes with precision how to set elite banquet tables, specifying clean, white napkins and a silver fork for every guest.[23] All this good advice suggests an audience appeal beyond fellow court cooks, out to a broad cross section of German society.

Ein new Kochbuch/

Das ist Ein
gründtliche beschreibung

wie man recht vnd wol / nicht allein von vierfüssigen / heymischen
vnd wilden Thieren / sondern auch von mancherley Vögel vnd Federwildpret / dar-
zu von allem grünen vnd dürren Fischwerck / allerley Speiß / als gesotten / gebraten / gebacken / Pre-
solen / Carbonaden / mancherley Pasteten vnd Fällwerck / Gallrat / etc. auff Teutsche / Vngerische / Hispanische / Ita-
lianische vnnd Frantzösische weiß / kochen vnd zubereiten solle: Auch wie allerley Gemüß /
Obß / Salsen / Senff / Confect vnd Latwergen / zuzurichten seye.

Auch ist darinnen zu vernemmen / wie man herrliche grosse Pancketen / sampt
gemeinen Gastereyen / ordentlich anrichten vnd bestellen soll.

Allen Menschen / hohes vnd nidriges Standts / Weibs vnd Manns Personen / zu nus
jetzundt zum ersten in Druck gegeben / dergleichen vor nie ist außgegangen /

Durch

M. Marxen Rumpolt / Churf. Meintzischen Mundtkoch.

Mit Röm. Keyserlicher Maiestat special Priuilegio.

1 5   8 1.

Sampt einem gründtlichen Bericht / wie man alle Wein vor allen zufällen
bewaren / die bresthafften widerbringen / Kräuter vnd andere Wein / Bier /
Essig / vnd alle andere Getränck / machen vnd bereiten soll / daß sie natür-
lich / vnd allen Menschen vnschädtlich / zu trin-
cken seindt.

Gedruckt zu Franckfort am Mayn / In verlegung M.
Marx Rumpolts / Churf. Meintz. Mundtkochs /
vnd Sigmundt Feyerabendts.

In the high Gothic manner,
German printers were worthy
rivals of their Italian counterparts, demonstrated in this
frontispiece from *Ein new
Kochbuch*.

At the same time, not far from Mainz another ecclesiastical cook, Lancelot de Casteau, was cooking in the Liège kitchens of three successive bishop-princes. When his cookbook *Ouverture de cuisine* (Window on Cooking) appeared in 1604, it reflected the half century that had passed since the last new cookbook in the French language. It was printed in clean, roman type, displaying the modern, humanist book design found in Messisbugo and Scappi. Like Rumpolt, Casteau sought to appeal to a broader market, declaring that his recipes were an "initiation in cooking." He even reached out to women cooks "because some women come eagerly into the kitchen, and can be better cooks than men in certain ways; so to please these women, here is a kind of initiation to show them what to do."[24] This is a very early recognition of the value of women in the kitchen by a male professional cook.

Casteau's base of Liège lay on the trade route between Italy and the Low Country coast, leading again to international dishes. His coverage rivals Rumpolt's, with flaky Spanish pastry dough that borrows from Arab cooking and identifiably Italian pastas. He includes *huspot,* the Flemish national one-pot meal, and the Spanish signature stew *olla podrida.* For such a small book, *Ouverture* has a wonderfully fresh and varied collection of recipes. Sugar gets its due in his sugar-paste decorations and garnishes of sugared fruits and flowers. His menus show that perennial favorites such as the medieval *blanc manger* and colored jellies (from a base of wine, sugar, spices, and fish gelatin) and "snow" (made of beaten cream and sugar) were being served in the final course, as was already the custom in France. Such recipes offer further evidence that, as the price of sugar dropped with the increase in cultivation of sugarcane in the New World, sweet dishes were becoming available to a wider audience.

English Tastes: Plain, Not Fancy

At the start of the sixteenth century, English cooking, like that elsewhere in Europe, followed medieval traditions. King Henry VIII not only jousted with François I of France at the Field of Cloth of Gold in 1520 but competed with him at the banquet table. Francesco Chiericati, Italian papal emissary in England, wrote his friend Isabella d'Este in Mantua in 1517 to describe court celebrations that could equally well have taken place a century earlier:

> The banquet . . . was on a magnificent scale; the gold and silver plate piled on the sideboards was worth a king's ransom, and every variety of meat, poultry, game, and fish was served at table. All the dishes were borne before the King by figures of elephants, panthers, tigers, and other animals, admirably designed; but the finest things . . . were the jellies made in the shape of castles, towers, churches, and animals of every variety. . . . To sum up, here in England we find all the wealth and delights in the world. Those who call the English barbarians are themselves barbarians![25]

A WOMAN'S PLACE IN THE KITCHEN

Women's role in the kitchen in medieval times and earlier is shadowy. Their presence was rarely recorded, though pictures show them carrying out traditional tasks in the dairy, herding animals, picking up sticks for the fire, or selling goods in the market. Women are also largely invisible in early cookbooks, with the remarkable exception of *Le ménagier de Paris*, a late fourteenth-century manuscript written for a young housewife. Later, clues to what women were up to in the kitchen appear in John Partridge's *The Treasurie of Commodious Conceits & Hidden Secrets*, which was published by Richard Jones in London in 1573 and directed specifically to women. The following century a wave of English cookbooks for women told them how to entertain well and how to make preserves and distill potions for the sick. All imply that women were involved in a practical sense in home kitchens.

By the seventeenth century in France, trade-guild records from Paris give an idea of women's food-related activities outside the house, showing that the wives of professional cooks often worked beside their husbands. A cook's widow was

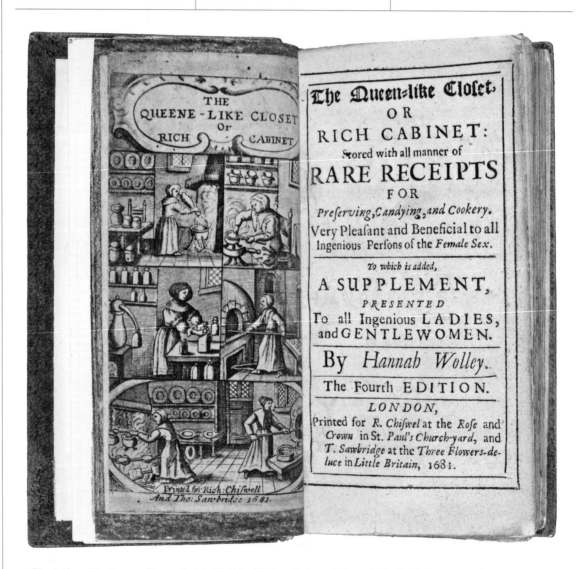

The duties of the housewife are depicted in this 1681 frontispiece of Hannah Woolley's *The Queen-like Closet, or Rich Cabinet: Stored with All Manner of Rare Receipts.*

permitted to stay in business after her husband died, and she could keep her membership in the culinary guild unless she remarried. She was not allowed to train apprentices, but she could hire journeymen cooks—trained craftsmen who were not yet masters—to work alongside her.[1] The daughters, as well as the sons, of guild masters could follow their fathers as apprentices. English guild rules for women were much the same as in France. In England, the law did not forbid women from setting up a business, though local regulations might be restrictive.

Outside the guild system in both England and France, young women could work as cooks in private households, inns, or institutions such as convents and hospitals.[2] Cookshops (establishments that sold cooked food) hired women as domestics, though often relegating them to the ill-paid, menial jobs. Similarly, a young woman might do the same work as a journeyman but for less money. Women wage earners were most often shopkeepers, innkeepers, or sellers of drinks, including fresh water.[3] The seventeenth-century engravings by Nicolas de Larmessin II show women in the roles of *chaudronnière* (pots and pans vendor), *poissonnière* (fishmonger), and many others. Similarly, in England, contemporary engravings of "criers," outdoor peddlers who shouted out their wares in London, show women selling food and drink. Domestic service was one domain in which women cooks had an advantage over men, though motherhood could introduce complications.

Local regulations often restricted a woman from being independent of her family, but in one success story in the early seventeenth century, four brothers who inherited an Oxford tavern left the running of the establishment to their three sisters, preferring to continue their pursuit of careers that offered greater social status. The oldest sister married her father's apprentice, and when he died, she took over the tavern and became one of the most prominent merchants in the city.[4]

In some large German cities, as in Elizabethan England, women worked in market stalls selling the chickens, eggs, milk, cheese, and vegetables they had raised at home. More surprisingly, women in Nuremberg "also served as the retail distributors of items of long-distance trade," such as citrus from Italy, spices from the Orient, and salted fish from Denmark.[5] Northern Europe and England were more tolerant of women in the public eye than were the Mediterranean countries. In most Italian cities, it was unusual to even *see* women in public, such were the conservative restrictions placed on them. In fifteenth-century Florence, for example, women rarely worked in food trades or shops, or even in general employment. The freedom allowed to a respectable woman varied from city to city: in some, daily errands might be a woman's job; in others, the male head of household was in charge of the food buying, either doing it himself or appointing an intermediary such as a male servant, a professional "buyer," or a friend. Often upper-class women could not leave their neighborhoods, as defined by the distance between home and church. Even when employment became more widespread in the seventeenth century, women's work was almost entirely in textiles.[6]

When women cookbook writers began to surface, many came from the traditional domestic and service jobs such as tavern keeping and market vending. Englishwoman Hannah Woolley, whose *The Queen-like Closet, or Rich Cabinet* appeared in 1670, is often credited as the first woman cookbook author, though Anna Weckerin, the wife of a prominent German doctor, had written *Ein köstlich new Kochbuch* (A Delicious New Cookbook) in 1597. Woolley was not just a housewife writing down her favorite recipes; she taught classes in needlework and making preserves. The obstacles for women in writing and getting a cookbook published were daunting, to judge from the few that appeared. For one thing, a man was more likely to have the education to write a book. For another, most women hoped that working in the family shop or cooking in a master's kitchen would be a transitional occupation between marriage and later lives as wives and mothers.[7] ♦

1 Jennifer J. Davis, "Men of Taste: Gender and Authority in the French Culinary Trades 1730–1830" (PhD diss., Pennsylvania State University, 2004), 42.

2 Ibid., 55, 17.

3 Lorna Weatherill, "A Possession of One's Own: Women and Consumer Behavior in England, 1660–1740," *Journal of British Studies* 25, no. 2: 131–56.

4 Mary Prior, "Women and the Urban Economy: Oxford 1500–1800," in *Women in English Society 1500–1800,* ed. Mary Prior (London: Routledge, 1985), 97–99.

5 Merry Wiesner Wood, "Paltry Peddlers or Essential Merchants? Women in the Distributive Trades in Early Modern Nuremburg," *Sixteenth Century Journal* 12, no. 2 (summer 1981): 10.

6 Judith C. Brown and Jordan Goodman, "Women and Industry in Florence," *Journal of Economic History* 40, no. 1 (1980): 78.

7 Sara Maza, *Servants and Masters in Eighteenth-Century France* (Princeton, NJ: Princeton University Press, 1983), 48.

A Booke

A dish of Larkes.
A pasty of red Deere.
Tarte, Ginger bread, Fritters.

Seruice for Fish daies.

Butter.
A Sallet with hard Egges.
Potage of sand Eeles and Lampzons.
Red Hering gréen bzoiled sugar strewed
White Hering. }   (vpon.
Ling.   } Sauce Mustard.
Haburdine.   }
Salt salmon minced sauce mustard and
     Uinagre and a little Sugar.
Powdzed Cunger. }
Shad.   } Sauce Uinagre.
Mackrel.   }
Whiting, sauce with liuer and mustard.
Plaice, sauce sazrel, oz Wine and Salt,
     oz Uinagre.
Thozne back, sauce Liuer and Mustard,
     Pepper and Salt strewed vpon it af-
     ter it is bzused.
Fresh Cod, sauce Gréensauce.
Bace, Mullet.
Eeles vpon Sops.
Roches vpon Sops.

                                   Perch

of Cookry.   3

Perch.
Pike in Pike sauce.
Trout vpon Sops.
Tench in Gelly oz in Grissel.
Custard.

        The Second course.
   ¶ Flounders in Pike sauce.
Fresh Salmon.
Fresh Cunber.   }
Bzit.   } Sauce Uinagre.
Turbut.   }
Holibut.   }
Bzeam vpon sops.
Carp vpon sops.
Soles oz any other fish fried, sauce the
     dzipping.
Rosted Lampzuns. } Sauce galentine.
Rosted Pozpos.   }
Fresh Sturgion. }
Creuice.   }
Crab.   } Sauce Uinagre.
Shzimps.   }
Baked Lampzye.
Tart.   } Chése.
Figges. } Raisins.
Apples. } Pearcs.
                             Almonds

The menus in *A Booke of Cookrye*, by A.W., 1584, sum up the unchanging English taste for substantial, plain food. The "Service at Dinner" (the first course) lists large birds, including bustard, and all the domesticated meats, such as a "pigge," a "loyne of veale or brest," "half a lamb or a kid," and "two pasties of falow deer in a dish."

As the century progressed, English cooks became increasingly independent of the rest of Europe. *Boke of Cokery* (1500) had been a landmark, forming the foundation of recipes in nearly every cookbook published in England during the following hundred years. Though foreign influences were clear in the original text, they were noticeably absent in later versions so that, for example, *A Proper Newe Booke of Cokerye* of 1558 lists only To Make a Stewe After the Guyse of Beyonde the Sea and one dish in the "French fashion." In *The Good Huswifes Jewell* (1585), Thomas Dawson mentions only three international recipes, from France (boiled meat), Spain (preserved peaches), and Holland (boiled chicken and mutton). At the end of the century, *A Booke of Cookrye* (1591), compiled by A.W., included just two foreign references, one each for France (puffin, or puffs) and Spain (quince preserves). Clearly, nationalism had entered the kitchen, and cooks were increasingly convinced that English cooking was best.

In all these books, plain English taste was evident in a fondness for roasted meats and pottages, pies, tarts, and eggs. *A Proper Newe Booke of Cokerye* opens with advice on the seasons for meats: "Lamb and yonge kydde is beste between Christmas and

LITTLE BOOKS WITH A LARGE INFLUENCE

Boke of Cokery, published in London in 1500, is far more important than its unassuming title suggests. This small collection of health tips and medieval-style recipes heralded the arrival of the little book, the antithesis of the high-profile masterworks amassed by great cooks or high-level household stewards such as Rumpolt or Messisbugo. Almost surreptitiously, by mid-sixteenth century little anonymous compila-

A copy of one of the earliest printed English cookbooks, *A Proper Newe Booke of Cookerye*, dates from 1558 and has remained in the library of Corpus Christi College since that time. The text is short, with only fifty recipes, but this reprint from 1913 includes a comprehensive preface and a useful glossary of medieval culinary terms.

tions of recipes on all sorts of subjects began coming off the presses, driven by the entrepreneurial spirit of publishers across Europe. A model for these modest, often cheaply produced collections was the medieval craft book, or book of "secrets," an instructional guide for almost every activity imaginable.[1]

Publishers wasted no time cashing in on the vogue for secrets, initially issuing stand-alone tracts and later printing larger collections of medical and culinary recipes. They hired in-house writers to write, compile, or translate these little books, which often had overlapping content and confusingly similar titles. This redundancy was not just a display of unimaginative marketing; French, English, Italian, and German publishers wanted to exploit the demand for new recipes by supplying titles resembling those of other successful cookbooks. Typically, though the books duplicated many recipes, writers would refresh the text by deleting dated items and adding trendier novelties. The midcentury run of little French cookbooks, each new book drawing from the preceding ones, is an excellent example: *Livre de cuysine tres utile* (A Very Useful Cookbook, 1540), *Le grand cuisinier de toute cuisine* (Master Cook of All Cooking, 1543), and *La fleur de toute cuisine* (The Flower of All Cooking, 1543).[2]

In England, the story was the same. The little book entitled *A Proper Newe Booke of Cokerye* was published in 1545 and continued to be reprinted in various editions over the next hundred years. *A Proper Newe Booke of Cokerye* was based on the earlier *Boke of Cokery* and in its turn formed the basis of two later sixteenth-century cookbooks. Thomas Dawson's *The Good Huswifes Jewell* (1585) supplements the borrowed culinary recipes with

home remedies, and A. W.'s *A Booke of Cookrye* (1591) streamlines the previous book's menus and adds more recipes and detailed cooking instructions. (Several of these little books were republished in facsimile in 1977 by Theatrum Orbis Terrarum in Amsterdam.)

All the little books tended to look alike, printed on cheap paper in the easily read blackletter type font. However, those that came out toward the end of the century adopted significantly modernized language. The earliest *Boke of Cokery* uses the French word *cygnet* for "swan" and calls a boar's head "chef de synglere" (*sanglier*). By midcentury, a "sygnette" had transformed into the more English "swanne." The recommended ingredients also changed dramatically as the century developed. At the opening, most vegetables and fruits—cabbages, onions, pears, and apples—were homegrown, as were flavorings such as rose water, verjuice, and saffron and herbs like parsley, thyme, and sweet marjoram. The midcentury *Proper Newe Booke of Cokerye* cites damsons, strawberries, medlars, gooseberries, wardens (pears), and green apples, whereas Dawson's book adds cherries, quinces, oranges, lemons, peaches, and mulberries and introduces other new ingredients such as olives, capers, and endive. ♦

1 William Eamon, *Science and the Secrets of Nature: Books of Secrets in Medieval and Early Modern Culture* (Princeton, NJ: Princeton University Press, 1993), 7.

2 Philip Hyman and Mary Hyman, "Printing in the Kitchen: French Cookbooks, 1480–1800," in *Food: A Culinary History,* ed. Jean-Louis Flandrin and Massimo Montanari (New York: Columbia University Press, 1999), 394–402.

The Larder, a mezzotint by Richard Earlom, is taken from an earlier Flemish painting by Martin de Vos in 1580. Earlom was renowned for the perspective and details of his engravings, many of which portray foodstuffs in almost clinical detail. He likes to include figures such as this cook hefting a prime rabbit, while out of sight under the table the cat claws a row of dead birds and the hound sniffs a deer.

lente," states the anonymous author. However, "Beife and Bacon is good all tymes in the yere."[26] Common sauces rarely stray from mustard, pepper and vinegar, green sauce, orange sauce, and gravies of drippings. Indeed, such simple, pungent seasonings remain staples in England today. As the century progressed and cooks in the rest of Europe began calling for less sweetness in savory dishes, travelers often noted the black, rotten teeth of the English, blaming it on too much sugar.[27]

To a degree, the English compensated for their conservatism with a variety of meats and fish that could not be matched on the continent. Venison, partridge, grouse, pheasant, duck, and rabbit were commonplace, as elsewhere, but British cookbooks added teal, woodcock, heron, gull, bittern, larks, thrush, and more, some caught by the popular sport of falconry. The saying went that hawks could stock the gentleman's larder better than any of the new matchlock muskets.[28] From the sea came porpoise, halibut, sole, turbot, bream, crabs, and lobsters, and cookbooks specified that some fish, such as sturgeon, salmon, eel, and cod, be fresh, not salted. After all, no point in England is more than sixty miles from the sea.

By the second half of the century, fine fruits and vegetables were beginning to rival English fish and meats. During the fourteenth century, a vast supply of herbs and roots had been growing in England, but they were neglected in the kitchen until botany became a serious intellectual pursuit.[29] In 1587, William Harrison wrote in his *Description of England* that orchards were bearing more good fruit in greater variety than before. He reported seeing not only "delicate apples, plums, pears, walnuts, filberts, etc." but also "strange fruit, as apricots, almonds, peaches, figs . . . cherry trees in noblemen's orchards." Add to these "capers, oranges, and lemons," and, he noted, he had even "heard of wild olives growing here."[30]

At the same time, the famous English aptitude for trade was beginning to develop, with London as a new European center. The city profited from its prime location on the Atlantic trade route and from the misfortunes that befell European cities during raging civil wars of the late sixteenth century. Antwerp, which had outstripped Venice in international commerce, was itself sacked by the Spanish in 1576. The East India Company was founded in 1600 to exploit commerce in the Far East. Elizabethan London became a center for Italianate, French, Dutch, even "Babylonian" styles.[31] Exotica were imported into the kingdom, and Harrison noted with a hint of disapproval the "many strange herbs, plants, and annual fruits . . . daily brought unto us from the Indies, Americas, [Ceylon], Canary Isles, and all parts of the world." Nonetheless, some time would pass before their influence seeped into books about cooking or affected the average English diet.

In a comprehensive herbal such as *The Herball or Generall Historie of Plantes* (1597) by John Gerarde, the hundreds of drawings would be taken from many sources. In the 1633 edition, this image of pomegranates, a favorite sixteenth-century ingredient, is particularly fine.

Toward a New Century: Living Well in Nature and at Home

The English might not have been willing to adopt the new, lighter cooking of the continent, but they were ideally poised to lead the trend toward country living and household comfort. The age of empiricism was in full swing throughout Europe, and the rise in literacy and texts in the vernacular created enthusiasm for do-it-yourself exploration that entered the kitchen as well as the garden and medicine cabinet.[32] Cooking was considered central to early scientific culture, and with the help of a book, anyone who could read could experiment. Books would jumble together subjects such as the stewing of meats and game, confectionery and preserving, medical remedies, domestic economy, and gardening. Some were devoted to a single activity, such as concocting cosmetics and herbal medicines or brewing homemade wines. Unlike the grand books of Scappi or Rumpolt, they made little attempt to organize recipes in coherent categories.[33] The scene is set in Thomas Hill's *The Proffitable Arte of Gardening. . . . To Which is Added Muche Necessary Matter, and a Number of Secretes with Phisick Helpes Belonging to Each Herbe, and That Is Easy Prepared* (1568). Hill pioneered the very English habit of combining homemade drinks, medicines, balms, and other household concoctions with culinary recipes, foreshadowing a flourishing genre that continues to this day.

The frontispiece of *De conservanda bona valetudine* by Jean Curion (1554) shows prosperous gentlemen in furred robes taking pleasure in a generous spread of varied dishes. A female server brings even more food to their table, and the wineskins at the ready in the foreground indicate that these diners plan to enjoy themselves. At a back table for two, a young woman entertains her companion. The perils of overindulgence are portrayed by the bedridden individuals in the back. The cook at the fireplace is an early illustration of a woman at work in the kitchen.

MEDICINE IN THE HOME KITCHEN

In the minds of sixteenth-century Europeans, all knowledge was connected, so that medical, culinary, and household hints could live happily together in what we would think of as illogical confusion. Medicine had been linked to cooking since classical times. "Nourishment should be taken according to the needs of health, not according to individual desires," cautions *De institutis coenobiorum* (On the Management of Monastic Communities), a treatise drafted for a Provençal order of monks in the fifth century. In other words, overeating is a sin.

A millennium later, the first printed cookbook continued the connection by proudly claiming to explore Platina's *De honesta voluptate et valetudine* of 1474. In the 1505 French translation, *Platine en françois,* the translators (several of whom were doctors) declared that to inhale the aromas of particular plants is not just pleasant but vital to absorbing their health-giving properties—early aromatherapy. Washing the hands with scent-infused water not only cleans but aids digestion. Recommended aromatics include orange flowers, myrtle, lavender, iris, and, most popularly, roses.

Thirty years later, Thomas Paynell produced a new translation of *Regimen sanitatis,* the medieval treatise informed by Galen's theories of the humors. Its titular claim to being a "boke techyng al people to governe them in helthe" guaranteed its success.[1] Galen's beliefs in inherited tendencies toward choleric, melancholic, phlegmatic, or sanguinous temperaments dominated medical thought at the time, together with the belief that certain hot, cold, wet, and dry foods could counterbalance them. Picking up on this sixteenth-century obsession with health, another book provided a sales pitch for the natural curative properties of food—"very useful and successful for keeping the human body healthy," announced *Le grand proprietaire de toutes choses* (The Complete Owner of All Things, 1556).

As the century progressed, medicine and cooking became increasingly entwined. "A good cook is half a physician, the chief physick …does come from the kitchen," declared Andrewe Boorde, a former monk and contemporary of Rabelais at the prestigious University of Montpellier. In his *Dyetary of Helth* (1552), Boorde credited two inspirations: the humanist medicine of Galen and the spiritual counsel of Jesus Christ. Individual temperaments vary and so do national ones, he reported. Rough and hearty foods such as bacon and bean bread are fit for the plowman but not the English gentleman, who should eat beef (but only if it is young). The Dutch are suited to drinking beer. Pork gave Boorde pause: Galen praised it; the Scriptures did not. Onions provoke sexual acts (and not in a beneficial sense); artichokes too inspire lascivious inclinations.

The most famous of the century's medical authors was Nostradamus, better known today for his astrological predictions than for his culinary recipes, which he would have regarded as medical prescriptions. In his day, astrology, medicine, and alchemy were considered sister sciences, and as astrologer to Queen Catherine de' Medici, Nostradamus was celebrated for his great success concocting plague cures.[2] His preserves and syrups are packed in a little book with a big title, *Excellent et moult utile opuscule à touts nécessaire qui désirent avoir cognoissance de plusieurs exquises recettes* (An Excellent and Most Useful Little Work Essential to All Who Wish to Become Acquainted with Some Exquisite Recipes, 1552). From the cooking viewpoint, *Opuscule* is a landmark. Nostradamus brought medical precision and highly detailed instructions to his recipes, far ahead of contemporary books written by cooks. Not for another century was such accuracy equaled with the appearance of the anonymous *Le pastissier françois* (The French Pastry Cook, 1653).

At the same time in England, authors such as Thomas Dawson and Sir Hugh Plat were establishing the tradition of household books that cover medicine, drinks, and preserves as well as cooking so that To Make Apple Moyse [Mousse] might run side by side with A Medicine for the Megrime [Migraine]. . . . or Other Diseases in the Head.[3] Typical is *The Widdowes Treasure* (1582) by John Partridge, a collection of culinary and medical recipes that he claimed came from a gentlewoman. Popular authors like Partridge sparked protests from doctors and apothecaries who feared the loss of their monopoly as medical experts.[4] Partridge was not fazed, arguing that these "hidden secrets …[are] not impertinent for every good Huswife to use in her house, amongst her own famelie."[5] As proof, by century's end upper-class gentlewomen were supervising the production of sugar syrup–based health drinks (cordials and juleps) and distilled liqueurs in purpose-built still houses (distilleries) on their country estates.[6]

The links of medicine to cooking lingered into the nineteenth century, sometimes as prescriptions and advice on sensible living but more often in shadowy assumptions about the effects of certain ingredients and preparations on general health. François Marin, author of *Suite des dons de Comus* (1742) was typical in declaring, "Three considerations apply to ingredients, their number, their quality, and their usage, qualities that constantly blend the cook and the doctor."[7] ◆

1 *Regimen sanitatis salerni,* trans. Thomas Paynell (London: T. Berthelet, 1528).

2 Wulfing von Rohr, introduction to *The Elixirs of Nostradamus* (London: Bloomsbury, 1995), xv.

3 Thomas Dawson, *The Good Huswifes Jewell* (1585) (Amsterdam: Theatrum Orbis Terrarum, 1977).

4 Natalie Zemon Davis, "Printing and the People," in *Society and Culture in Early Modern France* (Stanford, CA: Stanford University Press, 1975), 215.

5 John Partridge, *The Treasurie of Commodious Conceits, & Hidden Secrets* (London: Richard Jones, 1573), title page.

6 Anne C. Wilson, "Stillhouses and Stillrooms," in *The Country House Kitchen 1650–1900,* ed. Pamela A. Sambrook and Peter Brears (London: Alan Sutton Publishing, 1996), 129–43.

7 François Marin, *Suite de dons de Comus* (Paris: la Veuve Pissot; Didot; Brunet fils, 1742), 1:x.

EVERYONE LOVES A SECRET

As the ability to acquire information from print broadened during the Renaissance, secret knowledge, formerly closely held by privileged experts, became more widespread. Readers had an insatiable appetite for the little books of "secrets" that publishers produced, including cookbooks touting new ingredients, dishes, and cooking tips. Food and drink were topics of great interest, and recipes were viewed as secrets and personal objects of curiosity to circulate among friends. Publishers were happy to pick up on this interest, freely sprinkling words like *secret, curiosity, conceit,* and *jewel,* as well as *cabinet, closet, rare,* and *experiment* throughout their cookbooks.

Inspiration for these books of secrets arose from the great courts of Renaissance Italy, notably Ferrara, Rome, and Naples, leading to the label *virtuoso* for someone with a particular interest in natural science. The virtuoso gentleman-scholar is an idealized figure in one of the most widely read books of the century, Baldassare Castiglione's *Il libro cortegiano* (Book of the Courtier, 1528).[1] His model of behavior and manners for a virtuoso was widely admired and emulated throughout Europe. Giambattista Della Porta, one of Italy's most famous natural philosophers, pioneered experiments in artificially chilling the new distilled health drinks, while Girolamo Ruscelli, better known as Alexis of Piedmont, described his sugar-work experiments in *Secreti del reverendo donno Alessio piemontese* (Secrets of the Reverend Father Alessio of Piedmont, 1555).[2] *Secreti* became a runaway best seller and was quickly translated into French, English, Latin, and German, then plagiarized for the next two centuries.

Sir Hugh Plat was the embodiment of the virtuoso gentleman-scholar interested in natural science. In Elizabethan London, Plat constructed a "jewel house of best practices, experimental wisdom, and useful information."[3] He wrote down everything in small notebooks, of which twenty survive. Plat "haunted" herbalist John Gerarde's botanical garden and was an avid collector of published books of secrets, where he clearly learned some of the recipes for *Jewel House of Art and Nature* (1594).[4] He wrote about "nature's cabinet . . . her most secret jewels" in terms that average readers could easily understand.[5]

A sidelight on the passion for knowledge was an obsession with "curiosities." Curiosities could be anything rare or unusual—animal, mineral, or vegetable—ranging from tulip gardens and seashells to miniature paintings, recipes for chemical experiments, books, new plants, and foodstuffs. People displayed these curiosities as symbols of wealth, social distinction, and personal connections. Travelers like Thomas Coryat, who first reported on the fork as an eating implement, and lawyer Fynes Moryson alerted readers to magnificent collections such as Rudolf II's *Wunderkammer* in Prague and the cabinets of the Medicis in Florence.[6] On a smaller scale, even modest households boasted curiosity cabinets by the end of the century. ♦

1 Walter E. Houghton Jr., "The English Virtuoso in the Seventeenth Century: Part I," *Journal of the History of Ideas* 3, no. 1: 58–59.

2 On Porta, see William Eamon, *Science and the Secrets of Nature: Books of Secrets in Medieval and Early Modern Culture* (Princeton, NJ: Princeton University Press, 1993), 197.

3 Deborah E. Harkness, *The Jewel House: Elizabethan London and the Scientific Revolution* (New Haven, CT: Yale University Press, 2007), 214.

4 Ibid., 233.

5 Sir Hugh Plat, *Jewel House of Art and Nature* (N.p.: Bernard Alsop, 1653).

6 Paula Findlen, *Possessing Nature: Museums, Collecting and Scientific Culture in Early Modern Italy* (Berkeley: University of California Press, 1994), 99–108.

Jean Corbichon, the translator of *Le grand proprietaire de toutes choses* by Bartholomé de Glanville (Bartholomaeus Anglicus), 1556 edition, is shown in his study.

The diagram of a bull from *L'agriculture et maison rustique* (1654 edition) was to help in the diagnosis of a sick animal, one of the many skills a country landowner needed.

Sixteenth-century writers' obsession with the "secrets" of emerging knowledge in a wide range of fields is personified by Sir Hugh Plat. Plat was an insatiably curious student of Bartolomeo Scappi and Francis Bacon, among others, and the forerunner of a handful of gentlemen—and women—cookbook writers in the following century who believed that knowledge comes from practical experimentation alongside experts in the field. The scientist's laboratory (frequently spelled *elaboratory* in books of the time) was no farther than his kitchen. Plat's early book *Jewel House of Art and Nature* (1594) linked cooking with natural science, which was becoming a respectable activity for learned gentlemen.

AS THE SIXTEENTH CENTURY came to a close, interest in the mysteries of nature went hand in hand with an interest in country living, and home, hearth, and domestic concerns occupied center stage in several European countries. The many books that addressed domestic economy (including home remedies) helped create the idea of the home as a private universe where all of the elements were ordered according to the precepts of nature. Estienne's *L'agriculture et maison rustique* summed up a humanist theory of country living that served as an architectural and social model mirroring a larger society, including the ideal orientation of rooms, courtyards, and gardens:

> I want our country house to be like a Pandora's box, overflowing with all kinds of products and goods to which the neighboring villages may have recourse for all their needs, and perhaps only making a small profit on the sale of foodstuffs that you furnish them daily. I intend that our farmer is the baker, the pastry-maker, the brewer whenever necessary. In short, that he neglects nothing that may engage, sustain, and enrich the household.[34]

Sixteenth-century gardens were still designed in the traditional medieval square, with plants (typically the slow-growing shrub known as box) forming intricate knots such as these patterns proposed in *L'agriculture et maison rustique*. Not surprisingly, these elaborate plots needed a great deal of maintenance.

Heading into the seventeenth century, writers continued to expound on the comforts of home—linens, pewter dishes, tables, chairs, and dishes—holding out privacy and material comfort as the householder's aspiration.[35] Many landowners were members of the "gentle classes [having] full possession of literacy."[36] In France, these readers were the market for *Maison rustique,* and in England, the same audience looked for books of recipes (in the broadest sense) to make a country property a successful, independent enterprise.

With women bearing much of the responsibility for making a house a home, English writers began recognizing housewives as a potential audience for their books. Barber-surgeon John Partridge's *The Treasurie of Commodious Conceits, & Hidden Secrets* (1573) was the first book of recipes and more general household advice directed to English women. He was a good promoter, claiming "hidden secrets . . . gathered out of syndrye experiments lately practiced by men of great knowledge." His theme was simple: knowledge should be open and "good for all to know." Later, Sir Hugh Plat contributed to the genre, publishing *Delightes for Ladies* in 1600. Like his earlier *Jewel House of Art and Nature,* the book recognized the link between cooking and natural science—and in the process women's growing literacy—pointing out the need to test every recipe. Scattered among Plat's handwritten observations and recipes in the manuscript are recipes in another hand, by a person identified only as T. T. Many of these recipes—whether original or copied from other sources—bear the imprimatur "proved by T. T.," offering perhaps the first recorded example of notes from a recipe tester.[37]

Cookbooks for housewives were to be one of the great success stories of the seventeenth century. And as interest in country living and the comforts of home continued into the early years of the century, new authors followed the examples of Charles Estienne, Thomas Hill, and Hugh Plat. Prosperous society was poised to welcome more household and cookery books, which became as popular as they were practical.

THE FOUR PRINTED COOKBOOKS that appeared before 1501 give little hint of the flood that followed. Recipes rapidly take on a wider function than brief instructions for the working cook. The authors are still professionals, but they now occupy far wider fields. For example, Nostradamus, who was a medical doctor as well as an astrologer, created potions and preserves that are a model of accuracy for the kitchen and the sickbed. Messisbugo, steward to the trendsetting Duke Alfonso d'Este of Ferrara, details recipes with both the front of the house and the cook in mind. "Mix this thoroughly before serving," he cautions, and for a pasta dish, he instructs, "this can be served without sugar."

The example of simpler seasonings shown by Maestro Martino in the previous century is slow to take hold, particularly in northern Europe, but by the end of this century, spices are used in less profusion and presumably in smaller quantity (exact amounts are rarely stated). A few national preferences can be discerned: Italians already like to sprinkle finished dishes with cinnamon and sugar, the British love ginger, and all enjoy the heat of black peppercorns. Herbs and green vegetables have become worthy of consideration, and recipes for salads, dressed with oil and a sharpening of citrus or vinegar, appear all over.

With the Europe-wide increase in trade comes the growing use of new ingredients such as oranges and lemons, which gradually replace the medieval verjuice for tartness. A few New World ingredients—turkey, corn, chili peppers, chocolate—are introduced and spread rapidly, and will later revolutionize European eating habits. Above all, this is the century of sugar, which jumps from being a condiment used like salt to being a main ingredient, opening the way to confectionery work. Entertainments are centered on sugar sculptures, sometimes as a part of the main feast and on other occasions segregated on a separate table or even in a different room.

On the main table, the huge pies of medieval times called "coffins," stuffed with all manner of meats and birds, have been refined to more manageable offerings with lighter fillings of fruits and vegetables (Italian cooks often thickened them with fresh cheese). Some are open tarts, and others employ a double crust to maintain the element of surprise. Most recipes call simply for "paste," but a few add doughs that range from little more than a mixture of flour and water to early versions of puff pastry that are rolled and folded for a layered effect. A "Florentine" was a particular shape of double-crust pie. The names of other dishes, such as *potaccio* (a stew) and *pan'unto* (a type of crostino), have survived to this day.

Potaccio alla Italiana

———

Italian-Style Stew

From Cristoforo di Messisbugo, *Banchetti composizioni di vivande e apparecchio generale* (Ferrara, 1549): *Take fat meat cut into pieces that are neither too big nor too small and fry in melted goat fat until brown. Then take a little broth and a few well-washed dried chestnuts and cook them with this meat. And when they are cooked in this broth, mix a little spice of different sorts, but somewhat more of cinnamon, and ground fresh coriander seeds, and half a pound of honey; and let it cook also. When it has taken color, put in the pan with the other things and cook well; and when it is ready to serve, put sugar and cinnamon on top.*

THE "FAT MEAT" CALLED FOR HERE is an excellent background for this sweet and spicy mix of cinnamon, coriander, and caramelized honey. The combination brings Renaissance Italy, with its liveliness and originality, vividly to the plate. To me, fat meat is pork, but in Messisbugo's time it could well have been mature, fat mutton which would have needed long simmering, as in the recipe. For the "different sorts" of spices, just use what you have on hand, such as the pepper and cumin I suggest. Salt is not mentioned by Messisbugo, so I've made it optional. Dried chestnuts can be found at Italian grocery stores, or you can substitute cooked chestnuts, adding them to the pork about 10 minutes before the end of cooking. As was customary in Italy at the time, Messisbugo suggests a final sprinkling of ground cinnamon and sugar. Today, *potaccio* is a regional recipe from the Marche, and refers to a savory stew flavored with rosemary.

Spiced Stew with Chestnuts   *Serves 4 to 6*

2½ pounds (1.2 kg) boneless pork shoulder
2 tablespoons (30 g) goat's milk butter or lard
1 cup (175 g) dried chestnuts
2 cups (500 ml) veal or beef broth
½ cup (200 g) honey
2 teaspoons ground cinnamon, more for sprinkling
2 teaspoons ground coriander
½ teaspoon pepper
½ teaspoon ground cumin
Salt (optional)
Sugar, for sprinkling

Cut the pork into 1¼-inch (3-cm) cubes, discarding the tendons and most of the fat. The cubes should be about twice the size of the chestnuts. Melt the butter in a sauté pan or large frying pan over medium-high heat and fry the cubes in batches, taking about 10 minutes to brown each batch well on all sides. Return all the browned pork to the pan, stir in the chestnuts, and spread the mixture in an even layer. Pour over enough broth to almost cover. Cover the pan and simmer very gently for 30 minutes.

Meanwhile, warm the honey in a heavy-based pan. Stir in the cinnamon, coriander, pepper, and cumin. Bring the mixture to a boil, and boil, stirring only occasionally, until you can smell caramel, 3 to 5 minutes (color is no indication here as the honey is already dark with the spices). Have a bowl of cold water ready and plunge the base of the pan into the water briefly to stop the cooking. Note that caramel scorches easily when overcooked.

While the spiced caramel is still warm and liquid, stir it into the pork and chestnuts, cover, and continue simmering gently until the pork and chestnuts are very tender, another 15 to 30 minutes. Taste and adjust the seasoning, adding salt if you like.

In a small bowl, mix cinnamon and sugar to your taste. Serve with the stew for sprinkling.

From Michel de Nostredame, *Excellent et moult utile opuscule à touts néces-saire qui désirent avoir cognoissance de plusieurs exquises recettes* (Lyon, 1552; recipe from 1555): *Take whatever quince you wish, above all they should be very ripe & yellow, & quarter them, without peeling them (those who trim them, or peel them do not understand what they are doing: for the peel increases their perfume) & cut each quince into five or six pieces: and remove the seeds, because they will jell well without them: & while you cut them, put them in a bowl full of water, because if they are chopped or cut hurriedly, without being soaked in water, they will turn black: & when they are chopped, boil them in a large quantity of water, until they are thoroughly cooked, almost crumbling: & then when they are well done, strain this water through a fresh cloth, which should be thick, & extract as much of this decoction as possible by squeezing hard: & then measure it: & if there are six pounds, you take a pound and a half of Madeira sugar, and stir it into the decoction, & boil it over what you judge to be a medium heat, so that toward the end it will reduce a great deal: & then lower the heat so it does not scorch at the sides, which would give bad color to the jelly: & then when it is nearly cooked, to recognize when it is perfectly cooked, you take a little with a spatula, or a silver spoon, & put it on a dish: & if you see when it is cold, that the drop holds quite round without spreading, the jelly is done, & take it from the fire: & wait until the foam on top subsides: & when still hot you put it in boxes of wood, or glass: & if you want to write something, or shape the bottom of the box, you can do it, because it can easily be seen: for the color will be transparent, resembling an oriental ruby, of similar excellent color, & flavor even greater, this jelly can be given to invalids, and to the healthy.*

NOSTRADAMUS ACCURATELY DESCRIBES this spectacular jelly as "resembling an oriental ruby, of similar excellent color, & flavor even greater." He would have regarded it as a remedy to soothe the stomach at the end of a meal, for he was trained as a physician, and his book belongs to the contemporary genre of medical treatises. No modern recipe could be more meticulous, and the wording has changed little over more than four centuries. We simmer the fruit and measure the correct quantity of sugar as he

Pour Faire Gellée de Coings d'une Souueraine Beaute, Bonte, Saueur, & Excellence, Propre pour Presenter Deuant un Roy, & Qui Se Garde Bonne Longuement

———

To Make Quince Jelly of Exceptional Beauty, Goodness, Flavor, & Excellence, Proper to Present before a King, & Which Keeps a Long Time

does, we stir to avoid scorching, and we test for the setting point in just the same way. Nostradamus has clearly stood over the stove himself, watching the quince syrup boil. He wastes no words, but omits no instructions either, remarkable in any era.

Quinces are so tart they are inedible raw and look like misshapen yellow pears, with fuzzy skin and white flesh—not very promising. However, they cook to a glowing ruby red, with an intense, tangy flavor that highlights rich meats like duck and game, as well as desserts. The fruit is full of pectin, ensuring excellent preserves. Crab apples can be substituted in this recipe, though they will not rival quince.

Quince Jelly   *Makes 4 half-pints (1 liter)*

10 pounds (4.5 kg) quince
4 quarts (4 liters) water, more if needed
About 3½ cups (650 g) brown sugar

Preserving pan, jelly bag, 12 half-pint (250-ml) jelly jars, candy thermometer

Quarter the quinces, leaving the peel and flower ends. Core each quarter and cut into 5 or 6 chunks, dropping them into a bowl of water as you work. Using your hands, transfer the quince chunks to the preserving pan and add the water, with more if needed to cover the fruit generously. Bring to a boil and simmer the fruit, uncovered, until very tender, almost collapsing into a purée, about 1½ hours. Stir occasionally during cooking, and add more water if necessary so the fruit is always covered. Sterilize the jelly jars.

Suspend the jelly bag over a large bowl. Let the fruit and juice mixture cool slightly, then ladle it into the bag and leave it to drain until tepid, at least 1 hour. Squeeze the pulp in the bag by pressing against it with the ladle to extract any remaining juice. Measure the juice. You should have about 7 quarts (7 liters), although the amount will depend on the individual fruits. For each quart (liter), measure ½ cup (100 g) brown sugar.

Put the juice and sugar in the preserving pan and heat gently, stirring occasionally, until the sugar is dissolved. When the syrup is clear, bring it to a boil and cook over medium heat, stirring often, until it is reduced by about half; this may take up to 1½ hours. Meanwhile, put 2 or 3 small saucers in the freezer.

Lower the heat to prevent scorching and continue boiling without stirring until the jelly reaches the jell point, 220°F (105°C) on the candy thermometer. Alternatively, spoon a few drops of jelly onto a cold saucer and leave for a few moments to set. If the pool sets enough to wrinkle when you push the edge with a fingertip, it is ready.

Take the pan from the heat and let the bubbles subside. Ladle the jelly into the sterilized jars and seal them while still warm.

From Domenico Romoli, *La singolare dottrina di M. Domenico Romoli so-pranominato Panunto* (Venice, 1560): *When you have cut the slices of bread in the shape / of kidneys, & toasted them, put them / to fry in butter, turning them once, / spread them out in the pan, & place a slice of fresh provatura cheese on each / cover with the hot lid, and when the provatura / is browned, sprinkle with a little rose water & / sprinkle sugar and cinnamon on top: now / send them to table, taking care above all that they are eaten hot.*

WHY DOMENICO ROMOLI CALLED HIMSELF *pan'unto* in the title to his masterly cookbook is a mystery. In his introduction, he comes across as an assured self-promoter, so the literal meaning of "greasy bread" for *pan'unto* would hardly seem an attractive nickname. Perhaps he had invented this charming crisp crostino himself and wanted to highlight it. Nicknames for chefs were not uncommon at the time. Romoli includes a couple of *pan'unto* recipes, and this one maintains a nice balance of savory fresh cheese with a sweet flavoring of rose water, sugar, and cinnamon, all served on a butter-fried slice of bread. Fresh provatura is a mild, soft cheese resembling fresh buffalo mozzarella, which is the best substitute. *Pan'unto* is an excellent breakfast or brunch dish, delicious with fresh figs.

Fresh Cheese Crostini with Rose Water
Serves 2 as a treat, or 4 as an accompaniment

- 8 ounces (225 g) fresh provatura or buffalo mozzarella cheese
- 1 tablespoon (15 g) sugar
- 1 tablespoon ground cinnamon
- 4 large slices ciabatta, cut ½ inch (1.25 cm) thick
- 3 tablespoons (45 g) butter, more if needed
- 2 tablespoons rose water

Kitchen blowtorch (optional)

Heat the broiler, or have ready a kitchen blowtorch. Cut the cheese in slices ¼ inch (6 mm) thick, and arrange them in a single layer on a rimmed baking sheet. Stir together the sugar and cinnamon. Toast the bread.

Melt the butter in a large, broilerproof frying pan over medium-high heat. Fry the toasted bread, turning once, until crisp and the butter is absorbed, about 1 minute on each side. Using a spatula, transfer the cheese slices to the bread slices, arranging them so each bread slice is covered completely. Transfer the frying pan to the broiler and broil until the cheese melts slightly, 2 to 3 minutes. Alternatively, melt the cheese with the blowtorch. Sprinkle the toasts with the rose water and cinnamon sugar, and serve very hot.

Pan'unto con Prouatura Fresca

Fresh Cheese Crostini

Per Fare Torta di Carote, & d'Altre Radiche, & Altre Materie

———

To Make a Pie of Carrots and of Other Roots and Other Ingredients

From Bartolomeo Scappi, *Opera di M. Bartolomeo Scappi* (Venice, 1570; recipe from 1596 edition). *Wash and scrape the carrots and blanch them in water; remove from the water and cook in a good meat stock, and when done take the carrots and chop finely with a knife adding mint and marjoram and for every two pounds of chopped carrots add a pound of grated Parmigiano di Riviera, and a pound and a half of fatty cheese [possibly full milk cheese] and six ounces of Provatura cheese [fresh buffalo milk cheese], an ounce of ground pepper, two ounces of ground Neapolitan nutmegs, an ounce of cinnamon, two ounces of candied finely chopped bitter orange peel, a pound of sugar, eight eggs, three ounces of butter and make a pie with pastry below and above and a pastry border around, and cook in the oven or under the griddle, and the pastry should be made with sugar and cinnamon and rose water. In this way you can make pies of all sorts of parsnips and parsley roots, having removed the core.*

THIS RECIPE, TOGETHER WITH Pour Faire Tourtes Verdes by Lancelot de Casteau, marks a high point in the creation of savory pies. Earlier, in medieval times, the pastry enclosing the filling was regarded more as a container to hold ingredients during cooking than as an integral part of the finished dish to be eaten. Fillings could be haphazard and large pies were often made with a plain dough of flour and water. By the late sixteenth century, pies closely resembled our modern ones and shapes had become clearly defined. Scappi assumes that the reader has a favorite pastry dough and knows how to make it, calling for "pastry below and above and a pastry border around" the spicy filling of carrot and three cheeses. In Scappi's pages illustrating kitchen equipment, he shows several pans for *tortere* and *torta alte* (tall pies).

The pastry for this impressively spicy pie, says Scappi, "should be made with sugar and cinnamon, and rose water." Many of his recipes have no precise quantities, but here he lists pounds and ounces, which tells us exactly how much sugar and spice he liked in the filling (mainly black pepper, which was then fashionable). Salt is not mentioned, but Parmesan cheese adds balance so that, despite the generous amounts of sugar, to our tastes the pie is a first course rather than a dessert. Turnips, parsnips, or parsley roots can replace carrots, provided the cores are removed. Fresh buffalo mozzarella is a close match for provatura, and I use farmer cheese or whole-milk ricotta for the fresh cheese.

A Pie of Carrots and Other Roots   *Serves 10 to 12*

1½ pounds (675 g) carrots, peeled

2 cups (500 ml) veal or beef broth, more if needed

3 or 4 sprigs mint

3 or 4 sprigs marjoram

1½ cups (330 g) farmer cheese or whole-milk ricotta cheese

3 ounces (90 g) fresh buffalo mozzarella cheese, chopped

2 cups (225 g) grated Parmesan cheese

1 cup plus 2 tablespoons (225 g) sugar

3 tablespoons (30 g) freshly grated nutmeg

1½ tablespoons (15 g) ground cinnamon

1½ tablespoons (15 g) pepper

2 tablespoons (30 g) finely chopped candied orange peel

2 tablespoons (30 g) butter, melted

2 eggs, lightly beaten

1 egg lightly beaten with ½ teaspoon salt, for glaze

PASTRY DOUGH

4 cups (500 g) flour, more for rolling

2 egg yolks

1½ teaspoons salt

¼ cup (60 g) sugar

1 teaspoon ground cinnamon

1 teaspoon rose water

5 to 6 tablespoons (75 to 90 ml) water

1 cup (225 g) butter

11- to 12-inch (28- to 30-cm) tart pan with removable base

To make the pastry dough: Sift the flour onto a work surface and make a well in the center. Put the egg yolks, salt, sugar, cinnamon, rose water, and 5 tablespoons of the water in the well. Pound the butter with a rolling pin to soften it, add it to the well, and work the ingredients in the well with the fingers of one hand until thoroughly mixed. Using a pastry scraper, gradually draw in the flour from the sides of the well and continue working with both hands until coarse crumbs form. If the crumbs seem dry, sprinkle with the remaining 1 tablespoon water. The crumbs should be soft but not sticky. Gently press the crumbs into a ball; the dough will be uneven and unblended at this point.

Sprinkle the work surface with flour and put the dough on it. With the heel of your hand, push the dough away from you, flattening it against the work surface. Gather it up, press it into a rough ball, and flatten it again. This flattening motion evenly blends the butter with the other ingredients without overworking the dough. Work quickly so the butter doesn't get too warm. Continue until the dough is as pliable as putty and pulls away from the surface in one piece, 1 to 2 minutes. Shape it into a ball, wrap, and chill until firm, 15 to 30 minutes.

To make the filling: Quarter the carrots lengthwise, then cut out and discard the cores. Put the carrots in a pan of cold water, bring to a boil, and blanch for 5 minutes. Drain the carrots and return them to the pan with enough broth to cover. Cover the pan and simmer until the carrots are tender, 12 to 15 minutes.

Meanwhile, remove the mint and marjoram leaves from the stems, discard the stems, and chop the leaves. Crush the farmer cheese with a fork in a large bowl, and stir in the mozzarella.

When the carrots are ready, drain them, chop them coarsely, and stir them into the cheese mixture along with the chopped herbs, Parmesan, sugar, nutmeg, cinnamon, pepper, orange peel, butter, and eggs.

To shape the pie: Cut off and set aside one-third of the pastry dough. On a lightly floured work surface, roll out the remaining two-thirds of the dough to a 14-inch (35-cm) round. Fold the rolled dough loosely around the rolling pin and transfer it to the tart pan, using your fingers to press it gently into place. Spread the filling in the pan, and fold the overhanging edges of dough over the filling. Brush the dough edges with the egg glaze. Roll out the remaining dough to a 12-inch (30-cm) round and lift it onto the filling. Roll the rolling pin over the top of the pie; this flattens and seals together the rounds of dough, and trims any excess dough all in one movement. Brush the lid with the egg glaze, then lightly score it with the tines of a fork in a lattice design, or add whatever decoration you like. Chill the pie until the dough is firm, at least 30 minutes. Meanwhile, heat the oven to 375°F (190°C) and put a baking sheet on a low shelf to heat.

To bake: Set the pie on the heated baking sheet and bake until the crust is brown and starts to shrink from the edges of the pan, 50 to 60 minutes. A metal skewer inserted in the center should come out hot to the touch when withdrawn after 30 seconds. Let the pie cool for 10 minutes in the pan, and then unmold it. Serve it warm or at room temperature. The pie keeps well, loosely covered, at room temperature for a day or two.

How to Bake Orenges

From A. W., *A Booke of Cookrye, Very Necessary for All Such as Delight Therin* (London, 1584; recipe from 1591 edition): *Faire peele your Orenges, and pick away all the white that is under the peele, and so lay them in fine paste, and put into them Sugar, very little Sinamon or none at all, but a little Ginger and bake them very leisurely.*

ORANGES, BROUGHT FROM CHINA to southern Europe during the Muslim conquest, were reported to be growing in Sicily at the end of the twelfth century. "Arangus," described by the chronicler Albertus Magnus, were bitter oranges. Sweet ones came later, and by the sixteenth century, oranges of both types were a widespread sign of opulence throughout Europe. The Medici adopted five oranges on their coat of arms, and Henry IV built the first *orangerie* for growing them in France, at his Tuileries Palace. Sauces flavored with orange juice became popular, with Jean Bruyérin-Champier suggesting them as an accompaniment to roast partridge and Marx Rumpolt pairing them with fish. At this date, the line between savory and sweet courses on English menus was not firm, and baked oranges might have been served as part of the second course alongside game, poultry, or fish, or included in the fruit course that closed out the meal.

Until I read this recipe, I had never thought of wrapping an orange in pastry to bake like an apple dumpling, but why not? The spherical surprise package on the plate, topped with an orange leaf as clue to the contents, has enormous charm. A medium loose-skinned orange such as a satsuma mandarin is the best choice; cling-skinned oranges of the navel type are tiresome to peel. (The inner skin of the orange must be left intact or juice will leak into the pastry.) Here I give measures for a simple, sweet *pâte brisée* dough, or you can use your own favorite pastry.

Orange Dumplings *Serves 8*

    8 medium loose-skinned oranges

    6 tablespoons (90 g) sugar

    2 teaspoons ground ginger

    1 teaspoon ground cinnamon (optional)

    6 orange-tree leaves or bay leaves, for decoration

    PÂTE BRISÉE

    3 cups (390 g) flour, more for rolling

    1 egg yolk

    ¾ teaspoon salt

    2 tablespoons (30 g) sugar

    4 to 5 tablespoons (60 to 75 ml) cold water

    ⅔ cup (140 g) butter

    1 egg lightly beaten with ½ teaspoon salt, for glaze

To make the *pâte brisée* pastry dough: Using the quantities listed here, follow the directions in A Pie of Carrots and Other Roots, omitting the cinnamon and rose water. Wrap and chill the dough until firm, at least 30 minutes.

Meanwhile, carefully peel the oranges, pulling away all of the white pith. Be careful not to pierce the thin skin covering the flesh. In a small bowl, mix together the sugar, ginger, and the cinnamon, if using.

To assemble the dumplings: On a lightly floured work surface, roll out the pastry dough to a 10-by-20-inch (25-by-50-cm) rectangle. Cut it into 8 equal squares, trimming any ragged edges. Brush the dough squares with the egg glaze. Set an orange on each square, and sprinkle the top with some of the sugar mixture. Cut the dough on the diagonal from each corner toward the center of the orange, making 4 cuts. Leave the dough joined at the center, under the orange. To shape each dumpling, lift one point to the top of the orange, curving the dough to cover the fruit. Move to the next corner and again lift the point to the top of the orange, like a pinwheel, overlapping the first and second portions of dough and pressing so they adhere. Repeat with the remaining two corners so the orange is completely wrapped. Brush the dumpling with the egg glaze and transfer it to a baking sheet. Shape the remaining dumplings in the same way. Chill until the dough is firm, about 30 minutes. Meanwhile, heat the oven to 375°F (190°C).

Bake the dumplings until the pastry is browned, 30 to 35 minutes (baking time will vary with the size of the fruit). A skewer inserted in the center of a dumpling should be hot to the touch when withdrawn after 30 seconds. Wait for 5 minutes before transferring the dumplings to serving plates. Poke a hole in the top of each dumpling with a toothpick, and insert the stem of an orange leaf. Serve the dumplings warm or at room temperature. They keep surprisingly well for a day.

To Make a Sallet of All Kinde of Hearbes

From Thomas Dawson, *The Good Huswifes Jewell* (London, 1585; recipe from 1596 edition): *Take your hearbes and picke them very fine into faire water, and picke your flowers by themselues, and washe them al cleane, and swing them in a strainer, and when you put them into a dish, mingle them with Cowcumbers or Lemmons payred and sliced, and scrape Suger, and put in vineger and Oyle, and throwe the flowers on the toppe of the sallet, and of every sorte of the aforesaide things and garnish the dish about with the foresaide thinges, and harde Egges boyled and laide about the dish and upon the sallet.*

"WASHE THEM AL CLEANE, and swing them in a strainer," directs Thomas Dawson, painting an engaging picture of the cook swinging his greens in a salad basket, the faster the better, to dry them effectively. In the sixteenth century, the word *herbs* had a wider meaning than it does today. It embraced not just culinary herbs but also what we call salad greens, plus green vegetables such as cabbage, pea shoots, spinach, sorrel, fennel, and artichokes. Most of the herbs we now use for flavoring were available, including parsley, sage, mint, savory, and tarragon. Here, I suggest a representative mix of "herbs" and a few edible flowers. Thomas Dawson undoubtedly would have included anything available from the garden or market. He dresses the salad with the familiar vinaigrette of oil and vinegar, sweetened with sugar, in a taste that still survives in England. The first choice of salad oil, reserved for the well-to-do, would have been imported olive oil, with cider or wine vinegar.

Green Salad with Herbs   *Serves 4*

½ head lettuce or curly chicory (about 6 ounces or 170 g)
2 handfuls cress, sorrel, or spinach (about 5½ ounces or 150 g)
1 handful mixed herb sprigs such as parsley, savory, and mint or tarragon (about 1 ounce or 30 g)
1 handful edible flowers such as nasturtium or rose petals
1 small cucumber or 1 lemon
3 hard-boiled eggs, peeled and quartered lengthwise

VINAIGRETTE
1 teaspoon sugar
2 tablespoons cider vinegar
6 tablespoons (90 ml) olive oil
Salt (optional)

THE SIXTEENTH CENTURY \ RECIPES

Separate the lettuce leaves from the head. Discard the stems of the lettuce leaves and of the cress. Pull off the leaves from the herb sprigs and discard the stems. Wash the lettuce, cress, and herbs thoroughly in 1 or 2 changes of water, then spin them dry in a salad basket or spinner. Dry any remaining moisture with paper towels. Pile the greens and herbs in a large salad bowl. Pick over the flowers, but do not wash them. Peel the cucumber, then halve lengthwise and slice thinly. If using the lemon, pare off the zest and pith, leaving only the flesh. Quarter the lemon and thinly cut the flesh into dice, discarding any seeds. Reserve the hard-boiled eggs.

To make the vinaigrette: In a small bowl, whisk together the sugar and vinegar until dissolved. Gradually whisk in the oil so the dressing emulsifies and thickens slightly. Season it with salt to taste if you like (Dawson does not mention salt).

Just before serving, whisk the dressing if necessary to reemulsify it. Stir the cucumber or lemon into the greens, pour over the dressing, and toss all together. Taste a salad leaf and adjust the seasoning. Scatter the flowers on top, decorate with the eggs, and serve at once.

Pour Faire Tourtes Geneues Verdes

To Make Genoese Green Tarts

From Lancelot de Casteau, *Ouverture de cuisine* (Liège, 1604): *Take two good handfuls of spinach & a handful of mint, & thoroughly chop the two together, & squeeze out the water, then take three ounces of grated Parmesan cheese, mix it with the chopped herbs, put it on pastry the thickness of a finger, then take a half pound of fresh cream cheese, & soften it well with three raw eggs, half a small pitcher of olive oil, a little pepper, & ginger, & mix all well together, & take a spoon, & scoop some white cheese, drop spoonfuls on the herbs three fingers apart one from another, & make the cover thin; the cover should be pierced with little holes with a finger, sprinkle a little more olive oil on top, & cook like other tarts.*

LANCELOT DE CASTEAU'S *OUVERTURE DE CUISINE* was published in Liège in a part of Flanders that is now Belgium. At the time, Flanders was a crossroads of international commerce from all four corners of Europe, and he picks the already-popular Italian combination of greens with fresh cheese, a style he calls Genoese. In contemporary Italian prints, tarts are shown flat on a baking sheet, so I've followed that style here. Casteau explains that the pastry lid must be thin, with holes poked with a finger so steam can escape from the moist contents of spinach, herbs, and fresh cheese. Because today's fresh cheese and cream cheese vary with the type and brand, I recommend you use a farmer cheese or whole-milk ricotta, making sure it is firm. The eggs of today are much larger than eggs were in Casteau's time, so two are quite enough to soften and bind the filling. Depending on the cheese you use, the recipe may lack salt, so it is listed as optional, though not originally mentioned by Casteau. The tart is equally delicious served hot or at room temperature.

Spinach and Cheese Tart with Mint *Makes one 10-inch (25-cm) tart to serve 8*

> 8 ounces (225 g) farmer cheese or whole-milk ricotta cheese
>
> 1 pound (450 g) spinach
>
> 1 large bunch mint
>
> ¾ cup (90 g) grated Parmesan cheese
>
> 2 eggs
>
> 2 to 3 tablespoons olive oil, more for brushing
>
> ½ teaspoon pepper
>
> ½ teaspoon ground ginger
>
> Salt (optional)
>
> PASTRY DOUGH
>
> 3 cups (390 g) flour, more for rolling
>
> 1 egg yolk
>
> ¾ teaspoon salt
>
> 4 to 5 tablespoons (60 to 75 ml) cold water
>
> ⅔ cup (140 g) butter, more for the pan
>
> Cheesecloth

To make the filling: Line a strainer with the cheesecloth, place over a bowl, add the farmer cheese, and leave to drain for 30 minutes. Bring a large pan of salted water to a boil. Remove and discard the tough stems from the spinach leaves. Strip the mint leaves from their stems and discard the stems. Add the spinach and mint leaves to the boiling water and boil until they are wilted, 3 to 5 minutes. Drain them in a colander until cool enough to handle, then squeeze out the water with your fists.

To make the pastry dough: Using the quantities listed here, follow the directions in A Pie of Carrots and Other Roots, omitting the sugar, cinnamon, and rose water. Wrap the dough and chill until firm, at least 30 minutes.

Chop the spinach mixture, place in a bowl, stir in the Parmesan cheese, and set aside. Beat the eggs in another bowl until mixed. Add the drained cheese, in pieces, to the eggs and beat until well mixed after each addition. Beat in 2 tablespoons of the olive oil, the pepper, and ginger, adding more olive oil if needed. The mixture should just fall easily from the spoon. Taste and adjust seasoning.

To shape the tart: Cut the dough in half. On a lightly floured work surface, roll out one half to a 12-inch (30-cm) round. Fold the dough loosely around the rolling pin and transfer it to a buttered baking sheet. Spread the spinach mixture on top, leaving a 1-inch (2.5-cm) border uncovered around the edge. Using a spoon, drop spoonfuls of the cheese mixture on the spinach, keeping them at least 3 fingers' width apart. Brush the border with water. Roll out the remaining dough to a 12-inch (30-cm) round, and transfer it to cover the tart. Press the edges together and flute them with your fingers. Using your little finger or a chopstick, poke holes in the lid in a flower or geometric pattern. Brush the top of the tart with olive oil and chill the tart until firm, about 15 minutes. Heat the oven to 375°F (190°C).

To bake the tart: Bake the tart until the pastry is crisp and very brown, 35 to 45 minutes. A metal skewer inserted in the center should be hot to the touch when withdrawn after 30 seconds. Let the tart cool for at least a few minutes, then transfer it to a board or platter and serve hot or at room temperature.

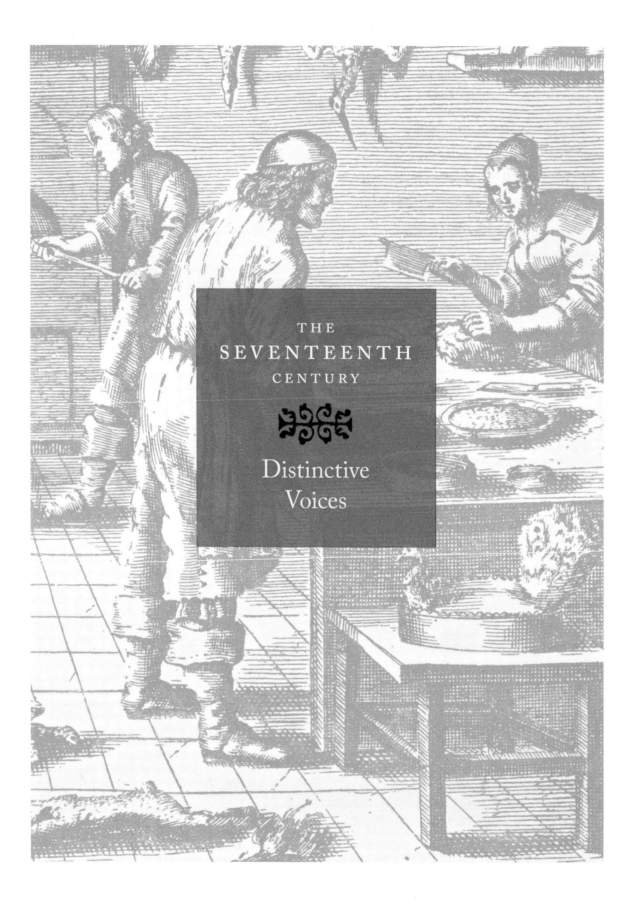

THE SEVENTEENTH CENTURY

Distinctive
Voices

COOKS FOUND THEIR INDIVIDUAL VOICES during the seventeenth century, taking the example from earlier writers and sending echoes down to the present day. The most important genre, already well established, was cookbooks for professionals, often written by maîtres d'hôtel, stewards, or heads of great kitchens. A small but growing group of authors were independent pastry cooks and caterers running small businesses. Domestic cookbooks containing household advice were the exciting new arrival, hinted at in the late 1500s and now in full expansion. English authors, sometimes women, were the pioneers in this field with few rivals in Europe (or indeed America). In France, a sudden burst of creativity in midcentury established classical cooking on the pedestal it occupied for the next two centuries. At the same time, outside in the vegetable garden, the French were applying an intellectual framework to the huge array of fruit and vegetable species now available. Some of these varieties were ancient, some were recently developed hybrids, and most exciting of all were the band of newcomers from the New World.

As the seventeenth century opened, books were no longer primarily luxury items and were becoming commodities, increasingly available to a larger number of people, at least in urban centers. In England and to a lesser extent in the rest of Europe, literacy, and with it readership, had already expanded well beyond noble households and grandees of the church to include a growing group of country gentlemen, men of letters, doctors, and prosperous housewives. Add to them culinary professionals, both men and women, and cookbooks were bound to do well. They proliferated in various genres, written recipes ranged from flights of fancy designed to entertain fashionable readers to the detailed instructions necessary for such specialties as baking and confectionery, conveyed in the aide-mémoire shorthand of seasoned professionals.

Publishers, for their part, were eager to cash in on this widening audience and had already devised a variety of ways to attract readers. To save expense, they often encouraged authors to borrow from earlier published material or piggybacked a book of home remedies onto a book of culinary recipes. One new approach was to issue a second, "economy" edition of a cookbook, set in smaller type and printed on lower-quality

OPPOSITE Detail from *Le pastissier françois*, 1657. Full image on page 161.

Habit de Cuisinier.

Nicolas de Larmessin II came from a family of engravers, and his *Les costumes grotesques et les métiers* of 1695 illustrates artisan trades while mocking the fantastical costumes at the court of Louis XIV. The figure in his *Habit de cuisinier* (Clothing of a Cook) carries a spit as sword with a frying pan as lance, sausages for ribbons, and a crown holding a suckling pig.

paper than the original edition. The small duodecimo format of such books made them more profitable for publishers and more affordable for consumers. Amid this new interest in marketing, authors, too, had a role to play, developing names for themselves that made readers eager to acquire their advice. Recognizing the value of celebrity, publishers were not above tacking a big name onto a book together with a frontispiece portrait, even if actual authorship was dubious. As a further bonus, by midcentury, the cost of copper engravings had diminished enough for even a small practical book such as Nicolas de Bonnefons's *Le jardinier françois* (The French Gardener) to include three attractive full-page illustrations.

Throughout Europe in the sixteenth and seventeenth centuries, much contemporary food writing was still linked to doctors and their remedies. Medical theory continued to reflect Galen's principles of balancing the four bodily humors with appropriate food combinations, concepts that remained deeply ingrained in Western thought but were increasingly considered old-fashioned. Cooks and diners had long been defying the strict principles of dietetics when it suited them, and doctors "prescribed" what their fashionable patients wanted to consume.[1] Despite classical warnings against overeating fruit, wealthy Italians had been indulging in raw fruits as a luxury since the fifteenth century. Melons, cheese, and pastries were particular phobias, and temptations.

Milestones signaling change were everywhere. The sheer increase in the number of books published about cooking was one marker. In their abundance of titles, England and France took a substantial lead over Italy, while Germany and Spain stayed in the background. Another sign was the expansion of science (called natural philosophy) and medicine into everyday life and their close links with cooking. Finally, the century saw the seeds of a new species of food book that flourishes today—the gastronomic commentary. Strictly speaking, books in this genre are not cookbooks at all, though they may include recipes. They cover a wide range of culinary topics, from menus to diet guidelines, use of seasonal ingredients, and current events, always with a secretive hint of insider gossip.

The English Cookbook Boom

The seventeenth century saw a permanent split in English cookbook styles that was to become characteristic. On the one hand were domestic books, often written by women and designed for the housewife running a busy household, who might or might not also be the cook. The recipes in these books were simple, sometimes just a few lines, and they used ingredients that were readily available. Authors covered all the skills needed to run a small household, from concocting remedies for the sick to making cheese and butter. They emphasized preserving, candying, and growing produce at home, and they grounded their instructions in concerns about economy, health, and diet. On the other hand were cookbooks written by professional cooks, almost always male, who controlled staffs into the dozens. They offered creative, fashionable menus designed to please the master or client, making the most of expensive ingredients and gearing their dishes to make an impressive show at table. Readers included not just the master but also fellow professionals, a growing band of caterers, pastry cooks, and vendors of ready-prepared food. Both genres of cookbook flourish today, with offshoots in many directions but still clearly separate audiences.

Domestic economy was first explored early in the century in two stylish cookbooks, Sir Hugh Plat's *Delightes for Ladies* (1600) and Gervase Markham's *The English Hous-wife* (1615). These two slim, practical volumes provided household and medicinal recipes alongside instructions for sugar confections, making their creators the most popular authors of household books. In the countryside, readers ranged from members of the aristocracy and gentry without titles to former merchants on down to tenant farmers. Hampered by bad roads, grand mansions and modest farms alike were often cut off from towns, and even from neighbors; all aspired to self-sufficiency as a result. In response, authors of household books supplemented their cooking instructions with advice on the kitchen garden, the medicinal herb garden, the fruit orchard, and the still room.

Herbals were of enormous influence in the seventeenth-century household kitchen, and we own one of the most famous. John Gerarde's *The Herball or Generall Historie of Plantes* (1597) is resplendent with bold woodcuts of plants on almost every one of its 1,631 pages, epitomizing the sumptuous possibilities of this genre. At the time, herbs might not have ranked high on the European table, but they were well established as remedies, and with the help of herbal recipes the cook was expected to keep a household healthy. As a London surgeon, Gerarde wrote not just to provide medicinal remedies but also to widen people's eating habits.

Gervase Markham covered animal husbandry and gardening as well as cooking,

---

THE

ENGLISH
HOUS-WIFE,
CONTAINING

The inward and outward Vertues
which ought to be in a compleat Woman :

As her skill in Phyfick, Surgery, Cookery, Extraction of Oyls , Banquetting ftuff , Ordering of great Feafts , Preferving of all forts of Wines , conceited Secrets, Diftillations , Perfumes , ordering of Wool , Hemp, Flax: making Cloth and Dying ; the knowledge of Dayries: Office of Malting ; Of Oats, their excellent ufes in a Family : Of Brewing, Bak ng, and all other things belonging to an Houfhold.

A Work generally approved , and now the Eighth time much augmented, purged, and made moft profitable and neceffary for all men , and the generall good of this
NATION.

By G. M.

LONDON
Printed by *W. Wilfon* , for *George Sawbridge*, at the Bible on Ludgate-hill
near Fleet-Bridge. 1 6 6 4.

On the title page of the eighth edition of *The English Hous-wife* (1664), Sir Gervase Markham, writing as G.M., makes clear the priorities of the accomplished housewife: medicine (including surgery) comes first, followed by entertaining, distilling, weaving, dairy work, brewing, baking, and finally "all other things."

This majestic title page sets the scene for the 1633 edition of *The Herball or Generall Historie of Plantes* by John Gerarde. This was just one of countless herbals large and small that were published throughout Europe during the sixteenth to eighteenth centuries.

and his salad recipes reveal a taste for fresh, raw greens and lightly dressed vegetables. Already in Elizabethan times, an English housewife's skill in managing her house and garden was highly regarded, the key to her family's well-being. "Perfect skill in cookery," admonished Markham, is the principal knowledge a wife must possess. "Our Hous-wife is intended to be generall, one that can as well feed the poor as the rich."[2]

Sir Hugh Plat took a different but equally English line, emphasizing elaborate confectionery treats that were right in fashion with genteel women who liked to display their skills. During this era, when a pound of sugar cost the equivalent of two days' pay for a laborer, liberal use of imported sugar reflected economic as well as social privilege.[3] Prices gradually declined throughout the century thanks to more abundant sugar supplies and refineries in the colonies. Sugar was the only important foodstuff to get cheaper, allowing confectionery, and with it a little bit of luxury, to women farther down the social scale.

Gervase Markham was not to be outdone by Plat. "Banquetting stuff," Markham commented, was an array of sugar-rich "conceited dishes, with other pretty and curious secrets, necessary for the understanding of our English Hous-wife." Although these treats—homemade sweetmeats, fresh fruits and cakes, comfits, and marzipan—were "not of general use," he pointed out, "yet in their due times, they are so needful for adornation, that whosoever is ignorant therein, is lame, and but the half part of an Hous-wife." On country properties, this "sugary feast" might take place in specially designed rooms, even in separate buildings.[4]

Many seventeenth-century books that discussed home cooking were part of the explosive interest in books of secrets—a carryover from the previous century's obsession with new knowledge—whose mentions of hidden closets and cabinets tantalized readers. One follower hailed Plat as "the most curious man of his time."[5] With the added attraction of elite authors, these books could set Paris and London abuzz with excitement. The cabinet might be real, inlaid with precious woods and mined with secret pockets, or it might be a metaphorical structure in the title of a book, considered a cabinet for the curiosities and inventions disclosed within.

One of the first such books, *A True Gentlewomans Delight* (1653), was said to be the personal recipe collection of Elizabeth Grey, Countess of Kent, a distinguished name that was ideally suited for aggressive marketing to newly affluent consumers aspiring to upper-class habits. More likely, the cookbook was written by the countess's famous chef, Robert May, or perhaps by her mysterious publisher himself.[6] Published four times within the first year alone, it had gone through twenty-one editions by 1708, a true best seller.[7] The publisher, W. J. Gent, apparently seeking to capitalize on the late countess's reputation as a skilled medical practitioner, offered an expanded edition the first year that combined *A True Gentlewomans Delight* with *A Choice Manuall, or Rare and Select Secrets in Physick and Chirurgery*, providing over a hundred additional pages of medicinal recipes. In another marketing ploy, Gent followed the eighty-one-page luxury edition of culinary recipes with an economy edition that was squashed down

MATTERS OF COURSE

No wonder so many cookbooks include menus. Just looking at an early recipe gives no indication of where to serve it during a meal. At one extreme, a menu might call for spreading all the dishes out on the table at once, with no specification of the order in which they should be eaten, but this approach is rare and usually applies only to simple, family meals. At the other end of the scale, it might spell out a carefully balanced progression, serving one dish at a time in a continuous parade, like the tasting menus of today. This custom, called *à la russe* because it reputedly began with Russian diplomats in Paris, became fashionable only in the mid-nineteenth century. Over the ages, most menus have combined the two approaches, laying out as many as eight courses, with one or more (and sometimes dozens) of dishes in each.

The menus that have come down to us from medieval times, such as those for the feast for the enthronement in England of Archbishop Warham in 1504, typically present a long list of fifteen or more primary ingredients, such as "Carpe in sharpe sauce, Eeales rost, Quynce baked, Fryttor ammel, Tenches floryshed, Lyng in foyle, Fryttor dolphin," and they include only a cryptic indication of how these elements are to be cooked.[1] They specify two or three courses, which were interspersed with sideshows, or *entremets* (meaning "between the courses"). The high point of the meal, which was usually the second course, was a panoply of roasts. This display would follow a less imposing course of sweet or savory dressed dishes, such as beef pies and often soups or broths (*brouets*). The last course was almost as random as the first, though it often contained fruit. *Le ménagier de Paris,* a late fourteenth-century manuscript, mentions the word *desserte,* possibly the first usage. Throughout Europe, at grand feasts, the host might offer a "finish" of fruits as well as savory dishes, and a "sendoff" of spiced wine and a washing of hands was customary.

By the sixteenth century, as we see in the menus that Domenico Romoli provides in *La singolare dottrina* (1560), the sequence of eating was much more reliable, with entrées (or antipasti), including soups, followed by roasts (sometimes two or even three courses of them) and an ending that often involved fresh and stewed fruits, fruit pies, and sometimes more savory dishes. An entremet was now likely to be an edible treat, no longer an entertainment. Everyday menus were much simpler. Even in Mary, Queen of Scots' household, the queen herself sat down to only two courses of Bouil (a kind of hash) and Rost, with a few entrées and potages to begin. The word *dessert* is not mentioned; it did not appear in England until 1633, and then as a pejorative: "Such eating, which the French call desert, is unnaturall."[2]

A certain confusion marks the evolution of courses during the seventeenth and eighteenth centuries. Between *La singolare dottrina* and *L'Escole parfaite des officiers de bouche* (The Ideal School for Household Officers, 1662), 120 years later, the soup and entrée courses have become transposed. François Massialot, author of *Le cuisinier roial et bourgeois* (The Royal and Bourgeois Cook, 1691), introduced hors d'oeuvre, meaning literally "outside the work" and defined more widely as "certain dishes served in addition to those one might expect in the normal composition of a feast."[3] They were hot dishes, smaller than entrées, served as part of the first or second course or hidden among the entremets. *Cuisinier* indicates how complicated menus were now becoming, reflecting the growing number of dishes that might be included. At the turn of the seventeenth century, a typical Massialot menu for twenty guests lists fifteen entrées and fifteen entremets, along with a number of roasts and hors d'oeuvre, to be completed with five bowls and baskets of "Fruit, colloquially known as Dessert."[4] In England around the same date, Charles Carter's seasonal menus contained a similar number of dishes.

Around this time, the *relevé* emerged, initially a large spit-roasted entrée that replaced soup (*potage*) during the first or second course. But the term could also refer to any extra dish that "raised" the impact of a menu. In parallel, the plain roasts were served in one grand climax.

The seventeenth-century search to combine order with elegance led to rules of menu planning. The number of dishes per course needed to reflect the number of diners. For example, a four-course meal for twenty-five should contain one hundred dishes; more diners meant more dishes. The placement of dishes on the table also had to be just right. The arrangement of the first-course dishes established a design, and the dishes in later courses had to be set down in similar positions. By the eighteenth century, this requirement had led to mindless numbers of serving dishes, tureens, condiment sets, bread baskets, spice boxes, and cutlery. Household staffs must have been relieved when dessert coalesced into one, sometimes two, sweet courses that ended the meal.

At the beginning of the nineteenth century, Grimod de la Reynière attempted to sort things out: "We have moved away from such profusion, and with good reason. A glance at this multitude of dishes satiates

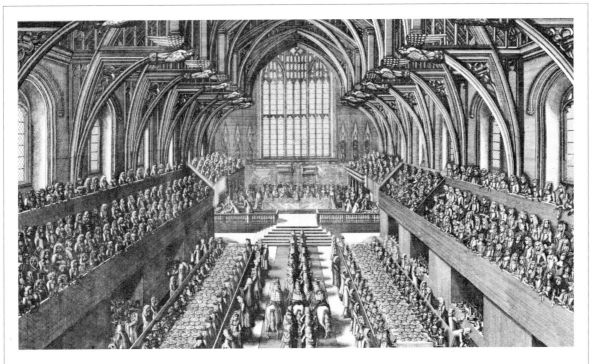

A pictorial record is one way to authenticate a claim, and in 1687, King James II of England commissioned *The History of the Coronation* from Francis Sandford, who was Lancaster Herald of Arms at that time. A contemporary artist detailed the feast for honored guests at the event, overlooked by a crowd from the gallery, while between the tables a grand procession sweeps toward the throne of the newly crowned king. Westminster Hall, with its hammer beams of angels flying over the congregation below, still stands among the Houses of Parliament in London.

rather than tempts; although most of these dishes are duplicates, the overabundance of choice is so confusing that the appetite wanes and the dinner gets cold before one can make up one's mind....Anyone giving such a dinner nowadays would be a laughingstock."[5] Apparently he did not speak for everybody in the culinary world, however. Antonin Carême, the legendary chef who cooked for the prince regent of England, and the prince de Talleyrand, the most famous politician of the Restoration in France, thought nothing of serving a dinner of eighty-four dishes.

In England at the same time, conservative rules continued to prevail. French chef Louis Eustache Ude held to strict categories: an entrée was any dish of meat, fowl, game, or fish that was dressed for the first course. Next to appear were items

he designated as entremets, including vegetable dishes, jellies, pastries, salad, prawns, and lobsters. These dishes were strictly a sideshow for the all-important roast that by this date formed the second course. Despite this seemingly simple guideline, any of these dishes, even a whole course, could be "removed" during the service by a new, fresh alternative. And an underlying guest/dish ratio also still applied. "Supposing you have eight persons at dinner," wrote Ude, "you cannot send up less than four *entrées*, a *soup*, and a *fish*; you must have two removes, viz. for the second course two dishes of roast, next four *entremets*; and if you think proper, two removes of roast."[6] Such dictates were quite a challenge for a modest little dinner party. No wonder this regime was to be swept away by the innovation of *service à la russe* and

one dish per course, presented on a platter to the assembled guests. But this radical change, reflecting social attitudes as well as gourmet perceptions, did not become widespread until after the 1860s. ♦

1 Richard Warner, *Antiquitates Culinariae or Curious Tracts Relating to the Culinary Affairs of the Old English* (London: R. Blamire Sirano, 1791), 107.

2 W. Vaughan's *Direct Health,* quoted in *Oxford English Dictionary* (Oxford: Oxford University Press, 1971), 1:702.

3 *Dictionnaire universel françois et latin: Dictionnaire de Trévoux* (Trévoux: 1704).

4 François Massialot, *Le cuisinier roial et bourgeois* (Paris: Charles de Sercy, 1693), 498.

5 Jean-Louis Flandrin, *Arranging the Meal: A History of Table Service in France,* trans. Julie E. Johnson (Berkeley: University of California Press, 2007), 98.

6 Louis Eustache Ude, *The French Cook* (London: John Ebers, 1818), viii–ix.

to forty-three pages through the use of smaller type. The countess was also perhaps the first woman to merit the expense of an engraved plate: the first edition contained her somewhat unattractive portrait, yet another attempt by the publisher to build on her good name.

An even more prestigious woman, the queen mother in exile Henrietta Maria, was referenced in the title of *The Queen's Closet Opened. Incomperable Secrets in Physick, Chirurgery, Preserving, Candying, and Cookery; As They Were Presented to the QUEEN by the Most Experienced Persons of Our Times* (1655). This personal collection of recipes and notes was compiled by W. M. (probably Walter Montagu, the queen's private secretary), who also wrote the introduction. Later expanded and running to several editions, *The Queen's Closet Opened* contributed to the notion that a woman's name was an asset in publishing. Some editions bore the likeness of the royal personage honored in the book, lending regal authority to its contents.

Among the most famous English cookbooks in the book-of-secrets genre was Sir Kenelm Digby's *The Closet Opened* (1669). Written in the style of a commonplace book,

A cartouche of Elizabeth Grey, Countess of Kent, opens *A Choice Manual*, bound with the 1665 edition of *A True Gentlewomans Delight*. Every aspect of this book is designed to appeal to the upwardly mobile housewife, from its tiny, notebook size to the nobility of the woman author and the subject matter combining medicine with cooking.

this very personal collection of recipes focused on winemaking, soups, and savory meat and fish dishes. Digby's closet was very full indeed, crammed with dishes from a sizable segment of European nobility as well as from the queen mother herself. As Henrietta Maria's attendant, Digby had followed the exiled Stuarts to the continent during the Puritan regime of Oliver Cromwell (but not before being twice sent to jail). Later a founding member of the Royal Society with diarist John Evelyn, Digby was mocked as a man-about-town by the satirist Shadwell, who portrayed him as Sir Samuel Hearty who cross-dresses in order to sell beauty recipes, "also all manner of Confections of Mercury and Hogs-Bones."[8]

Sir Kenelm Digby's travels around the continent seeking financing for the English royalist cause were opportunities for this inquiring spirit to collect recipes: a *pan cotto* "as the Cardinals use in Rome," meathe (a honey drink) from Antwerp, roast wild boar in the Frankfurt style, and a generous collection of French potages, including multiple recipes for the era's most trendy soup, *potage de santé* (healthy soup, usually containing herbs with other ingredients at the whim of the cook). Digby's recipes also use butter and flour as a *liaison* (a roux) in the manner of La Varenne's *Le cuisinier françois* (The French Cook, 1651), where this thickening method first appeared, showing his familiarity with the latest cooking techniques (or at least with current books about cooking). The book also contains one of the earliest recipes for "tea," a kind of eggnog, from a Jesuit who had been in China. The instructions call for beating two egg yolks with sugar and then pouring hot tea over the mixture; the concoction is very good, he says, when one is hungry but has not the constitution or time for a meal.

While this group of titled English cookbook authors was writing for cooks at home, other professionals were writing for their peers. Even in the seventeenth century, the working cook who wanted to get ahead wrote a book. Despite the interruption of the English Civil War, luxury foods and elegant dining were on the rise, though the complex and ostentatious menus and meals in Messisbugo's and Scappi's sixteenth-century works—six to seven courses and three hundred dishes—were excessive for the contemporary audience. Books by cooks published in England had to appeal to a wide range of households far beyond court society. Four professionals dominated the scene, all male and trained or with experience in France and all heading the kitchens—not the dining rooms—of distinguished households. Their cookbooks display their pride in their international experience and wide repertoire of dishes. This international interest was to grow in England as the century progressed.

In *A New Booke of Cookerie* (1615), John Murrell reflected the fascination of elite London society with continental cooking and flaunted cosmopolitan credentials from his extensive travels, proclaiming "the now, new, English and French fashion" of cooking for "an extraordinary, or ordinary Feast." His little book of 125 recipes includes 16 French dishes learned when he worked alongside caterers in Paris. His first recipe is To Boyle a Capon, Larded with Lemmons, on the French Fashion. This and other dishes in which Murrell describes boiling game and fish after "the French fashion"

TEA, COFFEE, & CHOCOLATE: THE ARRIVAL OF CAFFEINE

Within a single century, European drinking habits were revolutionized by the arrival of three ingredients from faraway continents: tea from Asia, coffee from Africa, and chocolate from the Americas. Two ornate little books are evidence of Europe's widespread fascination with this trio of beverages: Philippe Sylvestre Dufour's *Traitez nouveaux & curieux du café, du thé et du chocolat* (New and Inquiring Treatises on Coffee, Tea, and Chocolate, 1685), published simultaneously in Lyon, The Hague, Geneva, and London; and Nicolas de Blegny's *Le bon usage du thé du caffé et du chocolat pour la preservation & pour la guerison des maladies* (The Healthful and Curative Properties of Tea, Coffee, and Chocolate, 1687). The exotic origins of tea, coffee, and chocolate clearly struck a chord, for both books contain charming engravings of a bearded sheik, a Chinese potentate, and an American Indian warrior, each holding a cup of his favorite beverage.

Like sugar in the two previous centuries, the new drinks were first classified as medicines, and their reputed curative properties only added to their exotic appeal. Marco Polo had written of tea in China as early as 1285, but the first commercial load of tea, carried in the ships of the Dutch East India Company, did not arrive in Europe until the early seventeenth century. Once launched, tea drinking spread rapidly, becoming common in France and Russia by the 1630s and in England during the 1650s.[1] In prosperous homes, tea began to replace beer at breakfast (no doubt better for productivity!). The brew was so popular that in 1660 the government decided to cash in and levy a profitable tax upon it.

Tea services were created using the translucent hard-paste porcelain imported from China, some with matching pitchers, teapots, and sugar bowls. The precious tea was stored in locked, foil-lined boxes, the key kept by the mistress of the house. The drink itself was an infusion with water. From the first, it was often sweetened with sugar, but the English penchant for adding milk did not appear until the late eighteenth century. Tea houses opened to savor the new beverage, in parallel with the coffee and chocolate houses that became hotbeds for political and social activity. Early coffeehouse encounters by prosperous men of affairs also promoted business, including the growth of London's city as a financial center. Coffee had originated in Ethiopia among the dervishes and other sects in search of stimulants to sustain them during long religious ceremonies. Europe first heard of it in 1599, when Anthony Sherley described Middle Eastern encounters with "damned infidels drinking a certaine liquor, which they do call Coffe."[2] Once introduced, probably to Venice, the vogue for coffee spread rapidly westward into France, the first report turning up in Marseilles in 1644. The first coffeehouse in Paris, Procope (a café of this name still exists), opened in 1674.

Chocolate had arrived in Spain in 1544, before either tea or coffee, but for about a century, it remained a Spanish taste, ignored by northern Europeans. One reason was the complicated processing of the cocoa beans, which had to be fermented and dried before being ground with other flavorings, usually with sugar, to be turned into a drink. The first book solely dedicated to chocolate, *Libro en cual se trata del chocolate* (Book Which Discusses Chocolate) appeared in Mexico in 1609, written by Juan de Barrios. The Spanish

Typical drinkers of tea, coffee, and chocolate are personified [above and opposite] in *Novi tractatus de potu caphé, de Chinensium thé et de chocolata* by Philippe Sylvestre Dufour, 1699 edition.

continued the Mexican custom of flavoring chocolate drinks with vanilla and chili, introducing spices such as nutmeg and cinnamon to the brew. However, starting in the early seventeenth century, chocolate gradually became available in "cakes" or "leaves" that were easier to use. Dutch merchants were early into trading chocolate cakes and later began processing the beans themselves. Quite suddenly, the taste for chocolate took off, and from midcentury onward, chocolate houses proliferated beside the coffeehouses. Around 1680, Madame de Villars wrote to a friend in France of a wonderful discovery she had made during a trip to Spain: "I am staying with my chocolate diet; to it alone I believe I owe my health. But I don't use it like a madwoman and without precaution....It is, however, delicious."[3]

All three of the new drinks were surprisingly slow to make the transition from drink to flavoring. Early use of chocolate was savory, moving from the Mexican style favored by Spain and Catalonia to meat pies in Italy and a French recipe by Massialot for *macreuse en ragout au chocolat* (wigeon [wild duck] in a ragoût with chocolate) of 1691.[4] Consumption of sweetened chocolate started when the dried, ground beans were mixed with sugar (presumably as syrup) and called "almonds," often flavored with honey and spices. At last, in the mid-eighteenth century, desserts flavored with chocolate became popular—creams, mousses, cookies, and candies—and everyone's favorite dessert flavoring was launched. Coffee was not far behind chocolate; both feature in ice cream

in Emy's *L'art de bien faire les glaces d'office* (The Art of Succeeding with Ices, 1768). Coffee, however, has never moved far beyond ices and dairy-based mousses; even so-called coffee cakes are designed to be served with the drink rather than flavored with the bean. As for tea, from the beginning, it found use as a poaching liquid and as the basis of medicinal possets. However, neither coffee nor tea has ever approached the triumph of chocolate in the kitchen. ♦

1 Kakuzo Okakura, *The Book of Tea* (New York: Fox Duffield, 1906), 15.

2 Alan Davidson, *Oxford Companion to Food* (Oxford: Oxford University Press, 1999), 202.

3 Marie Villars, *Lettres de Madame de Villars & Madame de Coulanges (1679–1680)* (Paris: Henri Plon, 1868), 115.

4 On the use of chocolate in meat pies, see Davidson, *Oxford Companion to Food*, 181.

are essentially broths served over bread (called *soupes* in France), and his use of aromatic herbs with fewer spices parallels the French trends of the time. His sauces favor a combination of verjuice, butter, wine, pepper, and capers, or perhaps a light dressing of butter or bitter orange juice, instead of such medieval standbys as liver and mustard sauce, wine and salt sauce, or verjuice and sugar, all of which were still to be found in Thomas Dawson's recipes in the previous century. However, Murrell's frequent use of sugar still harks back to medieval times; the section on London cookery even lists fine sugar as the first garnish.

In a revised edition of *A New Booke of Cookerie* in 1638, Murrell identified a new readership: the growing number of freelance cooks in cities who were not tied to one household and therefore had to adjust rapidly to current fashion. Lamenting "the general ignorance of most men in the practice of Catering," he aimed this edition directly at fellow professionals who were called upon to perform in other capacities, such as carving and serving. He also added bills of fare "to adorn eyther Nobleman or Gentlemans Table" and (without attribution) the entire text of *Boke of Kervynge,* which had been published in 1508 by Wynkyn de Worde.[9] (Thereafter, Wynkyn's little treatise became a common component of English cookbooks for two centuries.)

Writing forty years later, Joseph Cooper, former head of the Stuart royal kitchens, must have been an enterprising man. "I know this piece will prove your favourite," he boasted of *The Art of Cookery Refined and Augmented. Containing an Abstract of Some Rare and Rich Unpublished Receipts of COOKERY* (1654), which he audaciously published during the English Civil War and the antiroyalist Protectorate of Oliver Cromwell (1653–58). Cooper's recipes use sugar less often than Murrell's, and on occasion the author instructs the cook to add sugar only if the sauce is too "sharp," a technique sometimes associated with French-style cooking. This well-organized collection, refreshing and apparently original, has some of the earliest recipes for posset and syllabub, the milk-based drinks that became so popular in England in the next century. Cooper's recipe for puff pastry uses an English technique in which the cook dots the base layer of dough with pieces of butter—today's English rough puff pastry—instead of the French method of covering the dough with a full layer of butter before folding and rolling.

The leading light of Restoration cooks was Robert May, cook first to prosperous country gentry and later to cookbook author Elizabeth Grey, Countess of Kent. In keeping with the rampant copying typical of the era, May owes more than inspiration to his predecessors: many of his recipes echo those in Joseph Cooper's *The Art of Cookery Refined and Augmented* and W. M.'s *The Queen's Closet Opened.* Like Cooper, May apprenticed in Paris, and *The Accomplisht Cook* (1660) reveals the luxurious inspiration of a nobleman's household. As the mature cook in the frontispiece portrait of *The Accomplisht Cook,* May thought of himself "as an artist," which meant that he "never weighed the Expence."[10] Despite May's training, his recipes are more traditionally English than mid-seventeenth-century French. Calf's head with oysters, red deer,

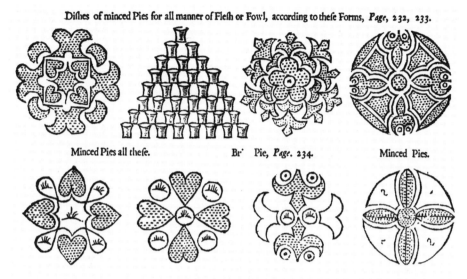

Difhes of minced Pies for all manner of Flefh or Fowl, according to thefe Forms, *Page*, 232, 233.

Minced Pies all thefe.   Br' Pie, *Page*. 234.   Minced Pies.

Pies for all manner of Land or Sea Fowl, to eat hot or cold : one, two, or three in a pie, *page* 214, 215, 216, 217.

Red Deer pies garnifhed, *page* 228.   Lumber pies, *page* 224, 225.

Designs for cutout pastry toppings for tarts, custards, and pies adorn the 1685 edition of *The Accomplisht Cook* by Robert May. May was keen on decorations and what he called "kickshaws," little side dishes named for the French *quelque chose.*

marrow pies, and hare baked with a pudding in his belly are a few examples. His preparations are old-fashioned: some of his sauces hark back to traditional medieval flavor combinations; others seem fixed in the sixteenth-century cooking of Bartolomeo Scappi, especially his "tortelleti, or little pasties" containing meats, Parmesan, sugar, egg yolks, and cinnamon in a dough that includes rose water, sugar, and butter. French, Spanish, and Italian influences are evident, though May does take pains to adapt foreign methods and techniques to suit English tastes.

Cookbooks published in England after the return of the Stuart monarchy in 1660 revealed changes—revolutionary in their minor way. The Civil War had shaken up all classes so that England was becoming more socially mixed. Politicians seeking popular support spent time with constituents, often in taverns, inns, and coffeehouses.[11] In Restoration-era cookbooks, English tastes were melded with international influences, creating dishes that became favorites across social classes, a successful pairing that lasted well into the eighteenth century.

An early harbinger of this blend of influences was a 1661 book by one of Robert May's contemporaries, Will Rabisha. *The whole Body of COOKERY DISSECTED* heralded the monumental menus that were to dominate professional cooking until the French Revolution and beyond. Rabisha directed readers in one edition of his book to burn all other cookbooks because his was the best—a boastful stance typical of many of the professional cooks of the era. He announced that he had written *The whole Body* because it was "desired by many young Practitioners in this Art, and others, for Receipts and assistance therein . . . for the satisfaction of all those that are ingenuous, and desirous to be instructed."[12] The book celebrates the return of the monarchy with seasonal menus of up to seventy dishes each, meant to be displayed, dozens at a time, along the center of the dining table so that guests could take their choice. One menu suggests serving flesh and fish dishes at the same meal, a rare departure from the feasting/fasting divide that was still customary despite gradual relaxation of religious observance since the Reformation. Such elaborate menus must have entailed much advance preparation. Rabisha's book opens with four chapters on pickling, brining, and baking meats and fish to be eaten cold. His hot dishes are often easily reheatable, though they must have cooled quickly on the table display. Like Robert May, Rabisha had done a stint overseas during the Civil War, though he keeps quiet in his book about the foreign influences that have crept into his recipes. His Florendine (a double-crust savory pie), or Made-dish of a Kidney of Veal, is a plausible ancestor of today's steak and kidney pie. In turn, his habit of thickening sauce at the end of cooking with a "lear" or *liaison* is very French, and he calls for sautéing a delicious lemon "amelett" (omelet) and sprinkling it with sugar for serving.

Domestic Cookbooks by Women

Another contemporary of Robert May's, Hannah Woolley, marked a major milestone in cookbook publishing as the first bona fide female author of a book on cooking in England. The two earlier household books attributed to women authors, the Countess of Kent and the queen mother Henrietta Maria, were probably ghost-written by men. A third, disconcerting example was a satire penned anonymously by a writer clearly happy to see the end of Cromwell's Protectorate and to have the royal family back on the throne: *The Court and Kitchin of Elizabeth, Commonly Called Joan Cromwel, the Wife of the Late Usurper* (1664) devotes almost half its pages to a vicious political attack on the Cromwell family. The rest of the little book is a collection of recipes such as pie, buttered eggs, and red quince cake, "most of them . . . common and vulgar," according to the author. Yet another successful cookbook should perhaps be attributed to a woman, Gervase Markham's *The English Hous-wife*. Markham has always had the credit, though a note on the back of the title page does say that he only "approved" the recipes, which were taken from "a Manuscript, which many years agone belonged to an Honourable Countesse, one of the greatest Glories of our Kingdome."[13]

After these works of questionable authorship, Hannah Woolley's works stand out, firmly establishing a professional woman's competence as an author of household books that sold. Writing prolifically in a field dominated by men, she published at least four books in just over a decade, becoming the first Englishwoman to publish a successful book of cookery under her own name in her lifetime. Like Plat and Markham, Woolley was eager to appeal to a broad social base, announcing that the "Bills of Fare" in her books were for "Great Houses" and for "Houses of Lesser Quality." Her books present the now familiar "secret" pattern of eclectic recipes for food, physick, cosmetics, and distilled waters and drinks. They read like commonplace books of household hints gathered over time. Her first book, *The Queen-like Closet, or Rich Cabinet* (1670), was a haphazard repository mingling biblical quotes, riddles, gardening hints, and household remedies with the culinary recipes. Woolley was wildly disorganized, often recycling information from one book to the next and drawing on other sources such as Hugh Plat. Despite these shortcomings, her books sold well, and *The Queen-like Closet* was even translated into German.

Woolley seems to have needed to support herself financially at a time when the possibilities for women were few.[14] Her primary income came not from her publications but from teaching classes in sewing and making preserves. She and Mary Tillinghast, a London cooking teacher and author of *Rare and Excellent Receipts* (1678), showed that respectable English ladies could earn money from their work without losing respect. Mrs. Woolley's culinary repertoire was limited to the English fare of her time, but her worldview was anything but traditional.[15] In *The Gentlewomans Companion* (1673), Woolley lamented the neglected state of women's education and wrote that getting published was "a thing as rare for a Woman to endeavour, as obtain."[16]

In writing for at-home housewives, Hannah Woolley was speaking to a very different audience from the professional cooks addressed by Robert May and other contemporaries. For one thing, domestic cooks had less access to exotica than May's fellow professionals did, so Woolley tended to use ingredients that were more generally available. In the countryside, peddlers traveled from village to village selling small amounts of pepper, saffron, and ginger, so these are Woolley's favorite spices.[17] She favors the herbs found in most kitchen gardens, such as rosemary, savory, chervil, Italian parsley, and tarragon. Root vegetables, such as carrots and turnips, had long

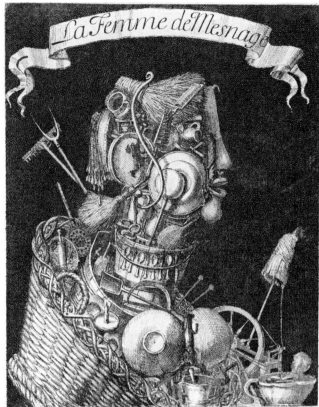

Jadis pendant mes jeunes ans
Grand nombre de Blondins galans
portant canons a triple estage
mettoient la fleurette en usage
sur mes beaux yeux, mes belles dents
sur ma taille sur mon corsage
et le beau teint de mon visage

folle J'escoutay leur langage
et donnay dans le mariage
le plus fascheux des accidens
quel changement: quel tripotage
mille soins et chagrins cuisans
m'ont depuis en cet equipage
rendu la femme de Mesnage

La femme de mesnage (The Cleaning Lady) is a rare print by an unknown French artist, published by Nicolas Langlois, c. 1660–90. The practice of fashioning portraits from the tools of a trade was launched by the Italian mannerist painter Giuseppe Archimboldo in the second half of the sixteenth century. A sad verse below the image recounts the decline of this woman, admired by all in the bloom of youth but now able only to do the cleaning for the household.

WOMEN COOKBOOK AUTHORS ON THE CONTINENT

While Hannah Woolley and other women cookbook authors thrived in England, the situation was less rosy for women in the rest of Europe. They were not idle, keeping unknown hundreds of commonplace books from medieval times onward, but only a tiny handful of books by women devoted to cooking made it into print on the continent before the 1700s. The first known printed cookbook by a woman was a household book of secrets that had appeared in Germany in 1597. Anna Weckerin was in the habit of accompanying her husband, physician Johann Jacob Wecker, on his house calls. In the process, she compiled a book of culinary recipes and home remedies called *Ein köstlich new Kochbuch* (A Delicious New Cookbook, 1597), which appeared after her husband's death. She set forth everyday meals, "innovative" foods, food for the poor, quick meals, even diet meals, a coverage so apposite that it was much copied in later German cookbooks.

Ein köstlich new Kochbuch was a pioneer. Not until almost a century later did two widely read household cookbooks appear in Germany, written by women for women. First came Anna Juliana Endter's *Vollständiges Nürnbergisches Koch-Buch* (The Complete Nuremberg Cookbook, 1691). Frau Endter was married to a successful publisher and invested money to assemble this massive volume of some 1,700 recipes, from soups to the favorite layer cakes of her native region. Under the picturesque title *Freywillig aufgesprungener Granat-apfel des christlichen Samariters* (The Spontaneously Combusted Pomegranate of the Christian Samaritans, 1697), Eleonora Maria Rosalie Lichtenstein combined medicinal and culinary recipes, detailed in admirably precise measurements and instructions.

Frenchwoman Marie Meurdrac also took the English household approach. *La chymie charitable et facile, en faveur des dames* (The Generous and Easy Alchemy for Women, 1666; translated into German in 1676) is a book of home remedies, instructions for distilling, and cosmetic recipes. It is a solid work of domestic economy, containing the kinds of recipes typical of England but rare in France, Italy, and Spain. Madame Meurdrac deserves attention for the careful organization of her book and the precision of her recipes. Distilled waters from fruits such as the *pommes de Reinette* (a tart apple) are refreshing and good for the lungs, she remarks, while adding sugar makes this drink into a delicious lemonade that can be taken in unlimited "dosage."

All four of these books by women echo the new genre of domestic economy that by now was flourishing in England. However, despite the success enjoyed by Endter and Lichtenstein, most women writers in continental Europe would have to wait longer to win the type of recognition that their peers were enjoying in England. ♦

Cooking is a serious business in *The Flemish Kitchen*, an engraving by Guillaume Duvivier dating from the 1740s and based on a painting by Antonio van den Heuvel (1600–77).

been staples of English cookery, as they were easy to grow just about everywhere. She uses apricots liberally, as well as several varieties of sweet berries. In addition, the expanding national market had brought more lemons, oranges, raisins, and almonds into modest kitchens, and even far from London, more and more people could afford sugar.

Writers for professional cooks faced different limitations of ingredients. As the seventeenth century advanced, the recipes of Robert May and others show that supplies of wild game and fish were becoming depleted. Fashions were changing too, and diners were losing their taste for the strong-flavored—some would call them rank— meats and fish. The taste for big birds was easily satisfied by adding New World turkeys to the inventory, with occasional mentions of bustard, a large, stupid bird that still exists, though it is very rare. However, porpoise was harder to replace and is nowhere to be found in the cookbooks for professionals (except for one recipe in Rabisha); nor is there much waterfowl other than duck. Recipes feature safe, less exotic possibilities such as pigeons, eels, and carp. Spices are used less liberally, sprinkled in dishes as accents rather than supplying the principal taste. Colored jellies are decorative elements, with orange and lemon slices and fresh or preserved flowers and petals garnishing dishes. Cheap, garden-grown marigolds replace saffron for yellow color and spicy taste.

This virtuoso depiction of sea creatures called *A Fish Market* is one of a series of engravings by Richard Earlom that includes a fruit market, a game market, and an herb market (c. 1618–20). The scenes are taken from early seventeenth-century paintings by Franz Snyders that belonged to the English leader of fashion Sir Horace Walpole.

INSPIRATION FROM THE NEW WORLD

When the first explorers arrived in the New World, they found a wealth of flora and fauna that intrigued and sometimes repelled them. Spaniards, as the earliest arrivals, were the first to experiment with culinary possibilities after observing what the indigenous peoples put in their pots. As early as 1552, a magnificent herbal called the Badianus Manuscript was compiled in Mexico by an Aztec student, Martinus de la Cruz, and translated into Latin by Johannes Badianus. Renaissance-style color illustrations depict 173 herbs well known to native Americans, and detailed text spells out the plants' medicinal properties and, by implication, their use in foods. To treat diarrhea, for example, the author specified a potion of six different leaves and bark, ground with wood ash, honey, salt, pepper, and "a little fragrant tobacco."

4 *Frumentum Indicum luteum.*
Yellow Turky wheat.

"Turky wheat" (above) and "Virginian potatoes" (opposite) are two of the New World ingredients depicted in the 1633 edition of *The Herball or Generall Historie of Plantes* by John Gerarde.

New World foods that had a close connection with the diet back home caught on quickly. For example, the *Phaseolus vulgaris* bean species (which includes kidney beans) and black beans that resembled favas were welcomed early. One of the first plants adopted in Spain was the chili pepper, an easily grown alternative to the expensive black peppercorns that were in universal use as seasoning. Historical records place chili peppers in Italy in 1526 and in Hungary in 1569 in the form of paprika.[1] However, Giacomo Castelvetro, writing in England in 1614 about the food plants of his native Italy, did not include hot or sweet peppers.

Turkey was one of the first strange ingredients to win acceptance as a satisfactory, indeed perhaps superior, substitute for chicken. Carried to England in the 1520s by the "turkey merchants" who traded with the Middle East as well as with Spain, it mistakenly became called the "turkie-bird." In other countries, the turkey was attributed to the "Spanish Indies," dubbed in France the *coq d'inde* and in Germany the *indianische Henn.* By 1534, turkey was being raised in Alençon, France, by Queen Marguerite of Navarre; in 1541, England's sumptuary laws mentioned turkeys along with other large birds; and in 1560, Domenico Romoli included the birds in *La singolare dottrina* (The Singular Doctrine).[2] Nearly two centuries later, turkey was a routine ingredient in recipes such as Charles Carter's Turkey Sausages with Oysters à la Braise (1736) and Menon's Ailerons de Dindon Diversifiés (Turkey Wings Many Ways, 1748).

Europeans had a complicated relationship with maize (Indian corn) when it reached their shores. The plant is easy to cultivate even on tiny, cottage-sized bits of land, though it needs hot, humid nights, so it did not thrive farther north than central France. By the early sixteenth century, it was widespread in southern Spain and southwestern France, where a tradition of corn dumplings and puddings remains. In Portugal, corn became an integral part of the country bread called *broa,* and in northern Italy, it was established as polenta. Corn was cheap, quickly accepted as fodder, but Europeans noticed that if cornbread or polenta were substituted for millet or barley cakes, epidemics of pellagra, a disease of the skin and nerves, would break out (due to niacin deficiency). Corn was eaten as an adjunct to but not a replacement for existing grains.

In the new territory of America, corn of necessity quickly became a staple. Since it was usually eaten with niacin-rich foods like tomatoes, beans, capsicum peppers, and fish, pellagra was less of a danger.[3] William Byrd, a Virginia-born, English-educated tobacco baron, admired the many varieties of sweet-tasting corn that Indians could grow in *Natural History of Virginia* (1737).[4] No less an American authority than Benjamin Franklin boasted in 1765, "Indian corn . . . is one of the most agreeable and wholesome grains in the world . . . a delicacy. . . . Johny or hoecake, hot from the fire, is better than a Yorkshire muffin."[5] In a reverse flow of ingredients, the early colonists brought a number of new ingredients to the New World, including wheat, barley, rice, and sugarcane, as well as black-eyed peas originally from Africa and citrus fruits from Asia. Beef cattle too came over with the colonists. Imagine an early America without cow's milk and steaks!

When new ingredients did not fit into existing food patterns in Europe, they had a much harder time winning acceptance. Chocolate drinks were already fashionable at the Spanish court by the late sixteenth century, but wider uses for chocolate as a flavoring and then as a main ingredient did not come until a century later. Europeans considered pineapple more of a decorative item than an edible fruit and adopted it as a symbol of hospitality; hosts would compete to display this exotic fruit, and architects used pineapples in stone to crown the gateposts of vegetable gardens. Cassava, a root that has to be grated and boiled to extract poisonous juices before it is edible as tapioca, grew only in hot, humid areas so had limited European circulation. Peanuts, one of the most important crops from the New World, also liked warm and wet climes. They came to Europe first from South America, not North America, moved from there to Africa, and then traveled back to North America, where they were regarded with as much wonder as in Europe.

Incredibly to modern diners, the foods that were met with the greatest suspicion in Europe were the tomato and the common potato. The reason is simple: both are close relatives of the nightshade family, commonly described as "deadly." The tomato must have been the first of these two newcomers to gain favor, as indicated by its early names of love apple and golden apple (*pomodoro* in Italian, still used today). The earliest-known printed recipe for tomatoes in Europe is by Antonio Latini, published in 1692. The French *Dictionnaire de Trévoux* of 1704 reported that Italians ate tomatoes "with salt, pepper, and oil, much as cucumbers," but despite such early appearances, tomatoes did not become common in Italy until a century later, hard to believe in light of today's ubiquity.[6]

Tomatoes appear in mid-seventeenth-century Spanish paintings and were recorded in 1544 by the Italian herbalist Matthioli. However, early Spanish cookbooks have no recipes for tomatoes until 1745, when Juan Altamiras included no fewer than

thirteen in his *Nuevo arte de cocina* (New Art of Cooking), so tomatoes must have been familiar in the kitchen by then. The French were a little slower on the uptake, but in 1803, the French gastronome Grimod de la Reynière offered a few words on the tomato in the *Almanach des gourmands*. "This vegetable or fruit, as we should call it, was almost completely unknown in Paris 15 years ago." He remarks, "It was the influx of people from the Midi brought by the Revolution to the capital, where almost all made their fortune, who introduced it here. At the start very expensive, it became common and last year could be seen in great baskets at La Halle [the central market of Paris]."[7]

The history of potatoes is even more fraught with controversy because they are far more of a nutritional staple than tomatoes. By the late sixteenth century, the Spaniards, who brought potatoes back from Peru, had planted them in Seville, a port city where ships were provisioned for long voyages.[8] They became a staple in Ireland during the seventeenth century. The British, too, were open to eating potatoes, and John Murrell mentioned them in *New Booke of Cookerie* (1615). All of these may have been either the white, so-called Virginia potatoes or the Spanish, or sweet, potatoes; both were used interchangeably in early years. By 1747, Hannah Glasse was including potato cakes, potato pie, and a potato pudding in *The Art of Cookery Made Plain and Easy*. Both types of potato either quickly received a warm welcome or launched confrontations of sometimes epic proportions. Typical of the latter response was the adamant rejection by the citizens of Kolberg in Prussia when, in 1774, King Frederick the Great attempted to relieve a famine with potatoes. France was the ultimate laggard. For twenty years during the 1760s and 1770s, though har-

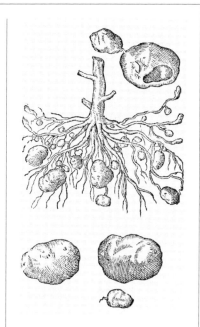

vests were bad and starvation was rampant, Louis XVI's urgings that his people plant potatoes went nowhere. Not until a brilliant promotional campaign by scientist Auguste Parmentier did the royal courtiers reluctantly nibble potatoes. Even after this breakthrough, several decades and the upheavals of the French Revolution had to pass before the potato finally could find a place in the French diet. ♦

1 Susan Pinkard, *A Revolution in Taste: The Rise of French Cuisine* (Cambridge: Cambridge University Press, 2009), 31.

2 On turkeys in England, see Alan Davidson, *Oxford Companion to Food* (Oxford: Oxford University Press, 1999), 810.

3 Reay Tannahill, *Food in History* (New York: Stein and Day, 1973), 248.

4 John L. and Karen Hess, *The Taste of America* (Columbia: University of South Carolina Press, 1989), 21–23.

5 Ibid., 29.

6 Paul Freedman, ed., *Food: The History of Taste* (Berkeley: University of California Press, 2007), 357.

7 Alexandre-Balthazar-Laurent Grimod de la Reynière, *Almanach des gourmands* (Paris: Chez Maradan, 1803), 1:151.

8 Tannahill, *Food in History*, 258.

ABOVE In the 1683 edition of *The Accomplish'd Ladies Delight,* a carefully coiffed woman looks out at her readers from the book's frontispiece. The subject of the portrait was often mistakenly identified as Hannah Woolley, but the book has been shown to be a compilation of other household books of the time and the identity of the anonymous woman remains unknown.

RIGHT Her contemporary, master cook Robert May, projects a more sober image in the frontispiece of *The Accomplisht Cook,* 1685 edition.

For the reader, the contrast between Hannah Woolley's books and those of professionals such as Robert May is marked. Woolley offers shorter recipes with fewer ingredients and less equipment, but May's book is easier to navigate. He uses more expensive ingredients, employs more technical terms, and calls for more equipment and stages of preparation. He liked to lengthen his recipes with alternative versions of the same dish, and his instructions can be unrealistic, not to say impossible. A comparison of the texts for fricassée, a popular dish with a rich, egg-thickened white sauce, offers a window into their different styles. Robert May's A Rare Fricase involves six pigeons, six chicken peepers (small chicks), some lamb stones (testicles) and sweetbreads, with a variety of steps and seasonings, while Woolley simply simmers veal, chicken, and rabbit (any white meat). These fricassées are fundamentally the same dish, but May's entails far greater expense (pistachios, wine, sweetbreads, bone marrow, a French loaf for serving) and a substantial investment of time and equipment (at least six cooking and serving dishes). Woolley's adjusts to what the cook has on hand, with herbs from the kitchen garden, inexpensive flavorings such as anchovies, and a sour note supplied by common barberries. She has eliminated the multistep procedure to allow easy preparation by a cook working alone using a couple of pots.

Whatever the specifics, in adjusting their recipes to suit home cooks, Hannah Woolley and the other English authors writing for women and domestic households had found a winning formula, and the half dozen books they produced became best sellers. Moreover, this new genre separated England from the continental tradition dominated by professional cooks, stewards, and sometimes scientists, who wrote for fellow professionals. (Few women in continental Europe made it into print during this time.) Supported by contemporary English prosperity, publishers were able to develop an unrivaled collection of quirky, amusing, sometimes brilliant household books. Thanks to astute publicity and marketing, all these books ran to multiple editions, some into the dozens. They established a model that flowered triumphantly into the next century and continues with scarcely a pause to this day.

An Independent Europe

On the wider scene in Europe, the great picaresque novel *Don Quixote* (1605) set the tone with a meal that is far from the farcical gargantuan feasts in Rabelais's sixteenth-century novels. Cervantes shows us a particular style of eating—the typical diet of the Spanish rural gentry at the turn of the seventeenth century. The relatively impoverished man of La Mancha dines on quite ordinary fare: "An occasional stew, beef more often than lamb, hash most nights, eggs and abstinence on Saturdays, lentils on Fridays, sometimes squab as a treat on Sundays—these consumed three-fourths of [the gentleman's] income."[18] Despite the vast wealth that had poured in from the Americas, Cervantes shows, by the early seventeenth century, even the landowning classes had been hurt in the badly managed economy at home. In contrast to Spanish poverty, which worsened over the century, the court itself was magnificent, if austere by the standards of other European aristocracy. The wife of the French ambassador to the court of Philip IV, Madame de Villars, remarked on the paradox in a letter of 1680: "With all the gold coming from the Indies, Spain does not seem very opulent."[19] Books about cooking were few and did not break new ground. In *Libro del arte de cozina* (Book of the Art of Cooking, 1599), Diego Granado Maldonado looked back to Scappi and the earlier Spanish author Ruberto de Nola. His huge book of over 750 recipes is pan-European, placing recipes from Scappi side by side with such resolutely Spanish dishes as *empanadas, escabeche,* and the noodles called *fideos.* His readers must have appreciated indigenous dishes as well as international specialties.

The most influential Spanish cookbook of the period, reprinted for more than two hundred years, was *Arte de cocina, pastelería, vizcochería y conservería* (Art of Cooking, Pastry, Savory Pastry and Preserves, 1611) by Francisco Martínez Montiño, Granado's colleague in the royal kitchen. In keeping with the royal determination at this time to rid Spain of Arab and Jewish influences, Montiño's recipes use lard, never olive oil. Spain produced an abundance of citrus and other fruits, chickpeas and beans, green vegetables, mutton, fresh fish, partridges, pigs, sausages, and beef. Montiño describes how to cook them all, including the most famous Spanish dish of the century, *olla podrida.* His style is elegant but not ostentatious, featuring local ingredients, herbs, some spices (including a little sugar), and occasionally garlic. However, his dishes are not as highly seasoned as we would expect given the many accounts by travelers of inedibly overspiced Spanish cooking. Montiño includes a tempting variety of the Spanish sweetmeats that were in demand all over Europe, inspiring confectioners outside Spain to re-create them. English and French cookbooks featured recipes for Spanish candies well into the nineteenth century.

On the other side of Europe, in the Low Countries, cookbook publishing had begun in the early sixteenth century and reached a peak in 1667 with the encyclopedic *De verstandige Kock* (The Sensible Cook). The book was written for prosperous families who could afford to grow good things to eat in their gardens—Dutch gardening was undergoing a revolution at the time—and also covered butchery and confectionery, with even a chapter on mushrooms. Later editions included more text by Frans van Sterbeeck, who was of a patrician Antwerp family.

Germany suffered from unrest during this century. The Thirty Years' War ravaged the countryside, developing from a primarily religious conflict into a power struggle between the Hapsburgs and the Bourbon rulers of France. Famine and disease de-

OLLA PODRIDA, HOT POTS, & POTAGES

Olla podrida! The seventeenth century saw a rage sweep Europe for this massive dish cooked in a cauldron with the curious name of "rotten pot." Originally a meat and chickpea stew from Castille, olla podrida evolved into something altogether grander, "combining the products of farmyard, game park, decoy pond and kitchen garden in one enormous pyramid of boiled meat and fowl."[1] In with the meats and poultry (particularly game birds) would go a variety of root vegetables such as carrots and onion that do well with long, slow cooking. Adding bacon or ham provided a hint of salt and smoke; particularly prized were the hams of the wild acorn-fed pigs of Montánchez in central Spain. Writing in 1611, Francisco Martínez Montiño included only one recipe for olla podrida among the many soups, *potages*, and stews (*cazuelas*) in *Arte de cocina*, but by midcentury, versions were simmering in pots all over Europe.

Under the name *pot pourri* (also meaning "rotten pot") and *ouille*, olla podrida shone in glory on the table of the Sun King, Louis XIV. The Portuguese had their *ollas*, while the Flemish version, the national dish called *huspot*, was unlike the variations in other countries, featuring hashed meats instead of whole pieces. Spanish Olio Podrida is the first recipe in Robert May's *The Accomplisht Cook* (1660), while other English authors, such as Sir Kenelm Digby, used the mundane term *hotchpot*, possibly derived from the French *hocher* meaning "to shake," a necessary step in mixing this vast assemblage of ingredients. Olla podrida and all of its variants derived from *potage*, which origi-nally described anything cooked in a pot, including the pottage for which Esau sold his birthright.

Digby defined it very clearly in *The Closet Opened* (1669): "The ground or body of Potages must always be very good broth of Mutton, Veal and Volaille. Now to give good taste, you vary every month of the year, according to the herbs and roots that are in season."[2] To this basic stock might be added almost any imaginable savory ingredient, including a thickening of bread. One or more potages (the word is the same in both French and English cookbooks) were sure to show up in the first course, and Louis XIV liked to consume up to four of them before embarking on the main dishes (his gourmandise was legendary). By the early nineteenth century, potages had become similar to today's broth soup, flavored with game, particularly game birds, fish, and a wide variety of vegetables. Meanwhile, English pottage (with two *t*'s) had become limited to a thick purée, usually of legumes or grains.

However, in the seventeenth century, olla podrida embodied elegance. Lord Edward Herbert of Cher-bury described a meal in Novara in 1648:

"We were entertained by the governor, being a Spaniard, with one of the most sumptuous feasts that ever I saw, being but of nine dishes, in three several services; the first whereof was, three olla podridas, consisting of all choice boiled meats, placed in large silver chargers, which took up the length of the great table: the meat in it being heightened up artificially pyramidwise, to a sparrow which was on the top: The second service was like the former, of roast meat, in which all manner of fowl, from the pheasant and partridge, to other fowl less than them, were heightened up to a lark: the third was in sweetmeats, dry of all sorts, heightened in like manner to a round comfit."[3] ♦

1 Ivan Day, "Illustrations in British Cookery Books, 1621–1820," in *The English Cookery Book,* ed. Eileen White (Totnes, England: Prospect Books, 2004), 112.

2 Sir Kenelm Digby, *The Closet Opened* (London: H. C. for H. Brome, 1677), 114.

3 Edward Herbert, *The Life of Edward Lord Herbert of Cherbury; Written by Himself: and Continued to His Death* (London: Saunders and Otley, 1826), 191–92.

A resplendent silver serving vessel for "Terrine or Olio" comes from *The Modern Cook* by Vincent La Chapelle, 1733 edition.

creased the population from the Low Countries south into Austria and even down to Italy. Nonetheless, Vienna flourished with the Austro-Hungarian Empire at its height, and according to historian Joseph Wechsberg, "The eating habits of the Baroque were as exuberant as everything else during that epoch; the banquets given in the palaces of Vienna's aristocrats were as splendid as those at the court of Louis XIV in Versailles."[20] The Hungarian gastronomic tradition had been launched two centuries before by Queen Beatrice d'Este of Hungary, who had had her cheeses, onions, and garlic imported from her native Italy. The Thirty Years' War ended in 1648 but brought in its wake no notable cookbook in either Austria or Germany for another forty years.

ABOVE This kitchen in a prosperous Dutch household is crammed with action. A gentleman caller distracts the lady of the house while a dog near her feet awaits any morsel dropped by the cook working at the oven. Birds and animals, dead and alive, writhe among the kitchen tools in a conscious study of form and function. The stuffed peacock to the lady's right is a symbol of pride. The etching, by Claes Jansz Visscher, c. 1605, was reprinted in the late seventeenth century by François Langlois.

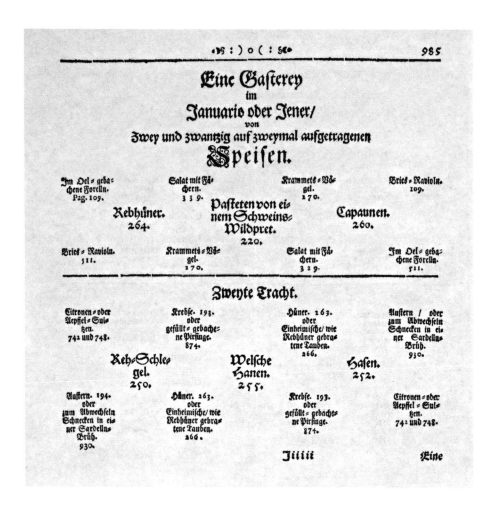

The pullout menu from *Vollständiges Nürnbergisches Koch-Buch* by Anna Juliana Endter, 1691, features a winter tasting in two courses, page-referenced to recipes among the nearly two thousand in the book.

Ultimately, Italy's Antonio Latini, steward to the Spanish court of Naples, deserves credit for producing the final masterpiece of culinary expertise on the continent before the French completed their conquest of European kitchens. His ambitious two-volume household book *Lo scalco alla moderna* (The Modern Steward, 1692–94) not only is impressively comprehensive but also pays homage to a variety of culinary influences.[21] Thanks to his Spanish masters, Latini introduced his readers to novelties such as chilies, and his book contains probably the first printed recipe for tomato sauce—made with finely chopped fresh tomato, onion, and bell pepper and dressed with oil, salt, and pepper, just like today's salsa.[22] As for his expertise in ices, Latini boasted that this was the Neapolitan's birthright.

The French Phenomenon

As the seventeenth century progressed, the national culinary influences that had been perceptible throughout Europe faded in the astonishing culinary revolution that was brewing in France. Early on, the anonymous *Le thresor de la santé, ou mesnage de la vie*

humaine (Treasury of Health, or Management of Human Life, 1607) already signaled a new and different direction, providing a missing link between the theories of Galen and the practical cookbooks that were appearing in ever-greater numbers. Gone was the depressing medical focus on the properties of foods and their effect on health. *Thresor* supplied instead a comprehensive seasonal guide to the joys of eating right. Like many doctors of the time, the author believed that pastries were not healthful, but he could not resist such Parisian treats as *flamiches* (savory breads), *oublies* (wafers), *petites pâtisseries,* beignets, and crêpes. His tempting recipes include pastas from Provence and Italy, one much like Martino's Sicilian macaroni made of fine white flour, egg whites, and rose water. *Thresor* is essentially a guide to healthy eating in the modern style that was to mark the upcoming century.

Although *Thresor* was almost the only new French cookbook for nearly a century, French publishers suddenly sprang into action in the mid-seventeenth century and put out seven in as many years. All of these cookbooks are landmark works of a freshness and originality that were to inspire cooks and diners for generations. First to appear was *Le cuisinier françois* (The French Cook, 1651) by François Pierre de la Varenne; then came two by Nicolas de Bonnefons on gardening and cooking in 1651 and 1654, followed by two books by Pierre de Lune and one by an anonymous French pastry cook. An instruction manual for the maître d'hôtel containing the recipes of an anonymous French court *confiturier* rounded out this formidable cohort of the 1650s. Together, these books were a persuasive invitation to a new way of cooking that took joy in local ingredients and seasonal menus.

Why should so many books on the new French cooking appear at precisely this time? One explanation may lie in the declining power of the traditional trade guilds. Dijon, the Burgundian capital where La Varenne began his career, boasted a growing population of wealthy bourgeois residents and inquiring young gentlemen on the cultural Grand Tour who were interested in luxury foods. Trades such as pastry, butchery, and baking were controlled by guild masters who were often corrupt, limit-

Printers tend to their work in Diderot and Alembert's *Encyclopédie, ou dictionnaire raisonné des sciences, des arts et des métiers*, 1751.

153

THE PARISIAN TRAITEUR

From medieval times, the culinary guilds had dominated the world of professional cooking in France. At the start of the seventeenth century, they were still all powerful, setting their own rules for each branch of public cooking and controlling access to apprenticeships and thus to the professions themselves. Among the earliest guilds were the *rôtisseurs*, the *pâtissiers*, the *charcutiers*, and *cabaretiers* for wine. By the fifteenth century in Paris, the *fournier* would roast your bird, the *oyer* would carve it, and a *saucier* would supply the gravy, together with garlicky *ailée*, mustard sauce, and golden cameline. From the baker came table bread, with waffles and *oublies* (wafers) from the *oubloyer*.

In the seventeenth century, King Henry IV created a guild for *maîtres queux, cuisiniers* and *porte-chappes*, also called *traiteurs* (caterers). Members had the right to cater weddings, feasts, banquets, collations, and "other types of meals that their art depended upon, in royal houses and others, even in the homes of individuals."[1] Henry's act simply recognized a trade that already flourished; sixteenth-century Parisian records show that master pâtissiers were supplying the kinds of dishes later described in *Le pastissier françois* (1653) for official banquets: fish and meat pastries, waffles, biscuits, *pasté à l'italienne, gâteaux feuilleté*, apricot tarts, *jambon de Mayence* in pastry. Because much of the work was seasonal, the caterers would rotate through the kitchens of the nobility and bourgeoisie; senior royal kitchen staff, for example, often served in three-month terms. Lyon and some other cities did not require guild membership for caterers.

Catering could be big business. Travelers and working men could take their meals at auberges, cabarets, and innkeepers' *tables d'hôte*.

Police records show that in 1658, Paris had about five hundred inns/auberges and that by 1730, the number topped two thousand, with dining venues scattered all over the city. (Taverns were drinking houses, allowed to serve only wine; they could not cook food on the premises.) Parisian traiteur and innkeeper Lucien Mignot kept an account book showing that he cooked daily meals for as many as twenty-five people and also catered for neighborhood residents. Blegny's *Livre commode* of 1692 gives the addresses of several auberges that offered customers "three different tables," either fifteen, twenty, or thirty sols for a meal. Many sources list the wide choice of provisions that innkeepers offered for purchase by guests. As historian Daniel Roche has asked, What would the early modern novel, from *Don Quixote* to *Tom Jones*, be without all those encounters at auberges to advance the plot?

Fewer than half of Parisian households had a kitchen or a room of any kind where the family could cook; no wonder cooked foods from outside were so important. A caterer's premises were multipurpose. One room might be set aside for parties and stocked with tables, plates, flatware, glassware, and even linens. Neighborhood families often cooked meals in the caterer's oven for less than the cost of lighting their own fire at home. Cookshops grew up beside most inns, though room service could be expensive, as one Dutch visitor discovered to his chagrin. Writing in his Paris journal in 1657–58, he lamented, "We had food brought to our rooms, but seeing it cost us double we went to take our meals in an auberge which was opposite our lodging."[2] ◆

Outdoor food vendors cater to customers in the street in the frontispiece of *Le nouveau recueil de curiositez* by Sieur d'Emery, 1685.

1 Nicolas Delamare, *Traité de la police* (Paris: Michel Brunet, 1719), 3:496.

2 Philippe de Villers and Prosper Faugère, *Journal d'un voyage à Paris en 1657–1658* (Paris: Benjamin Duprat, 1862), 30.

ing membership by refusing to take new apprentices. Thus, during the years in which La Varenne was coming of age and looking for training, many cooks worked illegally outside the guilds.[23] By midcentury, the guild stranglehold had begun to break down, leaving an opening for artisans such as La Varenne to publish trade secrets without fear of retribution from the masters.

The most conspicuous consumer of the century, Louis XIV (1643–1715), France's Sun King, often gets credit for inspiring classic French cuisine, particularly after establishing his splendid court at Versailles in the 1680s. Court influence may have helped develop French gourmandise, but the culinary innovations that are evident in La Varenne's book of 1651 must have begun decades earlier, long before Louis came to the throne. The cookbooks by John Murrell and Robert May showed that English cooks were traveling to France, Holland, and Italy at the close of the sixteenth century and returning home inspired to write about new influences. French cooks had been working in English kitchens—William Harrison noted the trend in 1577—and were already considered a marker of a sophisticated, wealthy (usually aristocratic) household. The surprise perhaps is that one or more of these French books did not appear earlier.

Habit de la Chaudronniere.

La chaudronniere (The Cauldron Seller) displays her pans and a multitude of metal tools, including strainers, a spit, and a hanging lamp to light the kitchen in an engraving from *Les costumes grotesques et les métiers* by Nicolas de Larmessin II, 1695. Among the hundreds of trades portrayed by Larmessin, he seems particularly partial to those involving food and drink.

The outlines of classical French cooking are clearly visible in La Varenne's remarkable work *Le cuisinier françois,* the first publication indicating that a culinary revolution was taking place. La Varenne gives little clue to his background in the book, noting simply that he learned in the kitchens of his patron, the marquis d'Uxelles, governor of Chalon-sur-Saône in Burgundy and a noted host in his Parisian mansion.[24] He conjures the time-honored image of a young man absorbing accepted techniques as he works beside experienced, older cooks, eventually ending his ten-year career as head of the kitchen. Not until then did he write *Le cuisinier françois:* "Because I love my profession, I am taking care to pass on what I know of it."[25] La Varenne was a distinguished member of the line of cooks, starting with Taillevent and Scappi, whose vocation for teaching made them such a vital source for future generations.

La Varenne makes bouillon, or stock, the basis of his cooking, with recipes for feast and fast days. Other elements he calls *choses généralles* (general things) are equally fundamental: *jus* (reduced natural juices) that heighten the flavors of sauces and a quartet of *liaisons* (thickeners) that depart from the earlier reliance on toasted bread or ground almonds. Many culinary novelties show up here in print for the first time, including *ragoûts,* a new word in the early seventeenth century that described meat-,

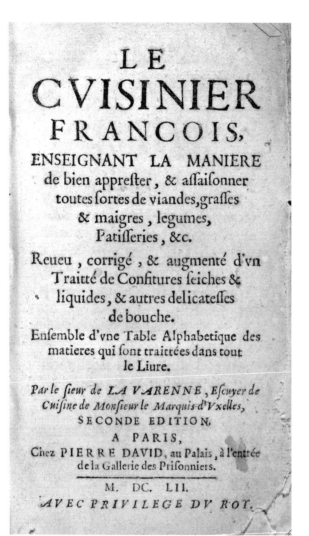

LE CVISINIER FRANCOIS,

ENSEIGNANT LA MANIERE de bien apprefter, & affaifonner toutes fortes de viandes, graffes & maigres, legumes, Patifferies, &c.

Reueu, corrigé, & augmenté d'vn Traitté de Confitures feiches & liquides, & autres delicateffes de bouche.

Enfemble d'vne Table Alphabetique des matieres qui font traittées dans tout le Liure.

Par le fieur de LA VARENNE, Efcuyer de Cuifine de Monfieur le Marquis d'Vxelles,
SECONDE EDITION.
A PARIS,
Chez PIERRE DAVID, au Palais, à l'entrée de la Gallerie des Prifonniers.
————
M. DC. LII.
AVEC PRIVILEGE DV ROY.

fowl-, or vegetable-based preparations with additional flavorings, sometimes garnished and always in a sauce thickened with a liaison.[26] The merits of ragoûts were debated for the next hundred years by rival cooks who claimed not only that the concoctions "disguised" foods but also that they promoted gluttony through their layering of flavors.

La Varenne introduced the butter (or lard) and flour roux then called *farine frite*. He also used flour to thicken liquids during slow simmering so that reductions would concentrate the flavor and texture of his sauces. His *beurre blanc* is a light sauce of butter, salt, vinegar, and nutmeg or pepper, the forerunner of the modern French white butter sauce. Liberal use of mushrooms was new in *Le cuisinier françois*, showing the changed attitude of doctors toward this dangerous food. Most notably, the new cooking no longer depended on expensive imported spices, preferring local and regional ingredients—the herbs, shallots, capers, and other piquant flavorings that are native to France.[27] Sugar scarcely shows up in the book's savory recipes, while ginger and cinnamon— "hot" spices that were ubiquitous in earlier times—are also rare.[28] La Varenne emphasized the need to follow the seasons for good, economical cooking, one of the philosophical underpinnings of modern French cuisine.

With these basics of the new French cooking in place, the book followed tradition in subdividing recipes for meat and fish days by the order of appearance in the meal (starters, entremets, roasts), a structure that was duplicated and expanded in most French cookbooks that followed.[29] La Varenne's recipes use a specialized culinary vocabulary, which had been hinted at more than a century earlier. He can be regarded as the Escoffier of his time, writing a catchy aide-mémoire to hundreds of recipes for cooks who already knew their trade with technical terms such as *miton-*

————

ABOVE The title page of *Le cuisinier françois,* by François Pierre de La Varenne, 1652, declares that this second edition has been "Reread, corrected, and expanded" with a treatise on jams and "other edible delicacies" to increase sales (which were already excellent). By now, recipes for sweets were working their way into the French books written for head stewards (maîtres d'hôtel) and officers of the cold kitchen (*officiers de l'office*), who were in charge of drinks and sweetmeats in elite households. *Le cuisinier françois* ushered in the new French style of cooking that was to become classic.

OPPOSITE The slight tingle left on the tongue after eating an artichoke has long intrigued gourmets. In *Taste,* an etching by Abraham Bosse from *Les cinq sens* (The Five Senses), c. 1638, the artichoke is kept warm on a hot plate. This everyday scene of a husband and wife with their servants and a pet dog is typical of Bosse, in contrast to the allegorical scenes that were popular at the time.

ner (to simmer) and *désosser* (to debone). Thanks to the new closed stoves (*potagers*), cooking techniques could be more varied and sophisticated than was possible when cooks had to work over an open hearth—sautéing is an example. La Varenne's instructions are usually clear and detailed—always specifying how to reduce a sauce or thicken it with a liaison, for example—but without the exact measures that were starting to appear in pastry and sugar work. In a sign of cooks' growing specialization, *Le cuisinier françois* includes no detailed menus or instructions on the presentation of a meal; these tasks would now have been left to the maître d'hôtel. La Varenne was, after all, head of the kitchen and very much a cook—a chef, though the term was not common for another hundred years. By the time he died in Dijon in 1678, the precepts he had set down in *Le cuisinier françois* of an identifiably French cuisine had been established— marked by a structure of core components, methods, and techniques.[30] The great cooks of later generations such as Carême and Escoffier clearly followed his blueprint.

THE STEWING STOVE: PROGRESS AT LAST!

From medieval times until the mid-seventeenth century, kitchens changed remarkably little. The ideal kitchen (almost certainly a fantasy) pictured by Scappi in 1570 shows nearly every cooking installation available at the time, and the accompanying pages illustrate every culinary tool. Almost hidden to the side of one image is a raised stewing stove, but recognition of the convenience of this device was amazingly slow to spread. Two hundred years after Scappi, most cooking still took place over an open hearth, either by spit roasting or by boiling and simmering. (Frying in long-handled frying pans was a cumbersome alternative, horribly hot for the cook and therefore not much used.)

For spit roasting, the whole piece of meat, bird, or fish was impaled on a metal bar supported horizontally in front of a glowing fire by hooked firedogs. The spit was turned by hand, often by children (this was the first task of an apprentice).[1] Mechanical options included a windup weight, a weight jack, or a smoke jack.[2] In 1674, L. S. R., in L'art de bien traiter (The Art of Fine Catering), suggested dog-powered spits for country use and commented that when cranking a spit, the turner would be roasted along with the meat.[3] A pair of firedogs could support three spits, controlled with counterbalanced pulleys, according to Samuel Pepys's diaries of 1660–69.[4] Cooks would place small birds and game animals like rabbits on the top spit for maximum heat and quick cooking and larger, tougher roasts on the bottom one to cook more slowly and thoroughly. Cooking juices and fat were rendered into a drip pan, without browning as in oven roast-

A satisfied diner congratulates the chef, who is still at the stove [above]. Such thanks are "the first duty of an Amphitrion," chides the frontispiece of the 1828 issue of *Almanach des gourmands* by Grimod de la Reynière. The stewing stove can be seen at left, while the traditional cauldron hangs over the fire. In another illustration, an apprentice is shown plucking a bird for the pot [opposite].

ing. Medieval cooks flavored these pure juices with spices, whereas cooks in later centuries preferred milder additions of wine, citrus juices, and herbs.

Despite such improvements, most food was simply boiled in an iron pot over a flaming fire. The pot was suspended on a rope (in early days) or from an iron chain or rod (universal by the late eighteenth century) that dangled from a wooden beam or iron crossbar high up in the chimney. By the 1700s, more advanced hearths sported a swinging crane, or trammel, to allow the cook to load the pot away from direct heat, adding or removing pothooks of varying lengths to adjust the height over the fire. For frying, a spider (a kind of frying pan with legs and a long handle) would be placed over the coals. To achieve gentler, diffused heat, a kitchen helper would bury the pot (often on three legs for stability) in glowing embers. To avoid lifting the lid and losing steam, the cook could judge the progress of cooking by holding a metal skewer in contact with the pot at one end and listening at the other end for the vibration of bubbles.[5] Only wealthy households with several hearths in the kitchen could afford to cook foods separately, as Platina first describes and is found increasingly in cookbooks from Romoli onward.

At last in the sixteenth century, the stewing stove, or *potager,* arrived. Its construction sounds so simple: form a hollow square of fireproof bricks at working level, fill with a layer of charcoal, and cover with an iron grid. Scappi shows two potagers in his 1570 kitchen, and records indicate that one was in use in the papal kitchens in Rome at this time as well.[6] In later centuries, the potager expanded to include up to six "burners," which rested on arched supports of brick faced with decorative tile, with room to store pots or

wood under the arches. By the 1650s, La Varenne and Bonnefons, working for wealthy masters, could assume that their readers would have potagers in their kitchens.

Writing in the late seventeenth century, L. S. R. described the layout of a well-equipped kitchen. It would have two fireplaces, one of which should be large enough for big roasts, high enough for the cook to stand upright, and deep enough for him to turn around. The back wall would be lined with cast-iron plates (firebacks) to reflect heat outward for spit roasting. Each hearth would have a transverse iron framework to support hooks for hanging pots and a shelf on which to set pans to simmer because "as the proverb has it, no one is so preoccupied as he who holds the frying pan handle."[7] The layout would allow for two to four potagers, each with five burners. As for the *batterie de cuisine,* L. S. R. gives an exhaustive list of earthenware pots "of all sizes"; cast-iron *marmites;* copper saucepans "well lined with tin"; fish poachers in round, oval and long shapes; cauldrons; bowls, tart pans, and molds; a slew of spoons; drainers and skimmers; and more.

Potagers improved cooks' ability to control heat: ragoûts could be gently simmered to tenderness, and sauces could be reduced to a glaze without difficulty. However, into the eighteenth century, a potager continued to be an elite installation because it required plenty of space and ventilation for the expensive charcoal necessary to fire it. Domestic kitchens were slow to adopt them, and England lagged behind France. In a small kitchen, the charcoal fumes could be deadly: "it is the charcoal that kills us," lamented Carême, who lived only until he was fifty. Presumably, the potager still saw wide use into the nineteenth century, because he died in 1833. ◆

1 Barbara Ketcham Wheaton, *Savoring the Past* (Philadelphia: University of Pennsylvania Press, 1983), 109.

2 Caroline Davidson, *A Woman's Work Is Never Done: A History of Housework in the British Isles 1650–1950* (Toronto: Clarke, Irwin, 1982), 55.

3 Wheaton, *Savoring the Past,* 109.

4 S. E. Ellacott, *The Story of the Kitchen* (Chatham, England: W. & J. Mackay, 1960), 34.

5 Davidson, *A Woman's Work Is Never Done,* 50.

6 Susan Pinkard, *A Revolution in Taste: The Rise of French Cuisine* (Cambridge: Cambridge University Press, 2009), 110.

7 L. S. R., *L'art de bien traiter* (Lyon: Claude Bachelu, 1693), 66.

The traditional audience for this adventurous new cooking would have been the courtiers of Versailles, the leaders in civilized refinement, but the readership was actually much wider, reaching out to the wealthy bourgeoisie who also cultivated an enviable style of living. Within the cities, food and beverage trades made up the largest section of the working population, and travelers to Paris and London had long commented on the number of freelance cooks who could be hired for special events or to prepare daily meals (much appreciated by single men).[31] Weakened guild control opened up the labor market. This freedom, combined with growing demand for luxury foods, transformed opportunities for cooks—and for gardeners. The products of the vegetable garden and orchard were becoming a priority for well-informed cooks. In parallel with the mid-seventeenth-century outpouring of cookbooks came a similar stream of books on gardening. Professional cooks and gardeners were common, and books published by and for them were big business for the remainder of the century.

The works of Nicolas de Bonnefons, one entitled *Le jardinier françois* (The French Gardener, 1651), the other *Les delices de la campagne* (Pleasures of the Countryside, 1654), detail the wide range of produce that was increasingly available, with exhaustive information on growing each item and some basic notes on cooking the fresh-picked produce. When *Le jardinier françois* appeared, the only serious competitor was a book that had been written fifty years before: Olivier de Serres's *Le théâtre d'agriculture et mesnage des champs* (The Overview of Agriculture and Land Management, 1600). However, *Le jardinier françois* was the first of seventeen new gardening titles published during the next fifty years, signaling a transformation in the French attitude to gardens as well as to vegetables on the table.

ABOVE This elegant gentleman, dressed for gardening and carrying his tools, adorns the frontispiece of the 1661 edition of *Les delices de la campagne* by Nicolas de Bonnefons. He is followed by servants bearing pies and wineskins, the makings of an elegant picnic. For ladies, too, gardening was a fashionable pastime in the city or the countryside. Dinner menus were planned around homegrown vegetables, and new varieties of fruits, particularly pears, were developed by Louis XIV's gardener La Quintinie in the walled garden at Versailles, which still exists.

OPPOSITE A young woman works under the supervision of an older master pastry cook in the 1657 frontispiece of the anonymous *Le pastissier françois*. The hanging display of game and the finished peacock pie are reminders that savory pies were an important aspect of the pastry cook's art.

Two more major cookbooks appeared in Paris in the 1650s: *Le pastissier françois* (The French Pastry Cook, 1653) and Pierre de Lune's *Le cuisinier* (The Cook, 1656), revised three years later as *Le nouveau cuisinier* (The New Cook, 1659). Their audience was the same as La Varenne's—young men who could not find apprenticeships and wanted to learn advanced skills. The anonymous *Le pastissier françois* was likely a product of the consumer demand for prepared luxury foods. Only a very wealthy household could afford a pastry cook. Pâtisserie was (and still is) a specialty left to experts, and even the royal kitchens in the seventeenth century relied upon professionals from shops in town to provision the tables at court with cooked dishes. Likewise in the provinces, pastry shops prospered from increasing demand for savory pâtés and tortes, as well as sweet pastries, cakes, and *petits choux* (cream puffs drenched in melted butter and rose water).[32]

Le pastissier françois is far more than just another book with pastry recipes. The authorship and origins are intriguing. Some editions bear the name of "François Pierre de la Varenne," but this attribution cannot be right. The recipe style of *Le pastissier* is lengthy and explicit, bearing little relation to the sketchy notes of La Varenne in *Le cuisinier*, who wrote as if he were dictating while stirring a pot. It is closer to the style of the scientifically inclined Nostradamus one hundred years earlier. The unknown author asserts that pastry work needs its own *tour* (table, literally "tower"), with tools such as a wooden rolling pin, tart pans (also used for gâteaux), and a waffle iron. Another *tour* is reserved for the mortar and pestle, indispensable for pounding chunks of sugar or salt, crushing the almonds for frangipane, and performing other routine kitchen jobs. To control the heat of a wood-fired oven, explains the author, the cook should prop open the oven door with a stick.

Le pastissier françois, with its meticulous instructions, explanation of terms, and precise measures, was far in advance of any other cookbook at the time. Significantly, it does not discuss sugar boiling, the mark of the confectioner. The anonymous author outlines the basic pastry repertoire, describing the *fontaine*, the well in the center of the mound of flour that is a key basic technique. The *pâte brisée* (pie dough) is the classic formula still used today, and the puff pastry is much like ours, as are the sponge cakes and *génoises*. Indeed, his repertoire is eerily familiar, including *pastillage* (the

COOKING FROM THE GARDEN

During the seventeenth century, an ever-increasing array of fruits and vegetables were reaching markets and thence kitchens in both France and England. In France, the king himself, Louis XIV, took the lead, with his vegetable garden just outside the palace at Versailles. Meanwhile, his subjects nearby in Paris passed leisure hours in their suburban gardens, with some making an active business of growing produce for prosperous bourgeois and the many catering activities of the capital. In England, the new move toward gardening was led by gentlemen, some of whom founded the Chelsea Physic Garden in 1673 in a choice spot on the bank of the river Thames. Now part of central London, the garden still flourishes today.

The surroundings of Paris, with its fertile soil and temperate climate, were ideal nursery gardens for the influx of novelty greens such as chicory and the romaine lettuce whose seeds were said to have been brought back from Italy by Rabelais.

Fresh garden peas became a fad reported by Madame de Sévigné: "There is no end to this interest in peas. . . . Some ladies sup with the king, and sup well at that, only to return home to eat peas before retiring, without any care for their digestion."[1] From the Loire came dozens of new varieties of pear, such as the buttery Vigoureuse, as well as the Reine Claude plums named for the wife of King François I and developed in his garden. New vegetables on the scene included cucumbers, kale, carrots, and cauliflower. Globe artichokes were already familiar in France, imported from Italy and probably descended from age-old cardoons; the Arabs had brought eggplants and spinach to Europe.[2] Other vegetables were arriving from the New World, such as the root artichokes (called *topinambours* in French after a native Indian tribe). La Varenne, whose *Le cuisinier françois* was published the same year as *Le jardinier françois*, suggested braising them and then sautéing them with onions and a grate of nutmeg.

In *Le jardinier françois,* Bonnefons told his readers how to grow all these vegetables and many more. His focus on each fruit or vegetable marked a shift from the medieval ideal of creating a single, unidentifiable flavor from a multitude of ingredients. In his view, "A cabbage soup should taste entirely of cabbage, a leek soup of leeks, a turnip soup of turnips and thus for the others."[3] He was writing, he said, for the Parisian lady whose garden was a source of beauty and color, delicate foods, and fashionable fruits to end her meals. The *petit volume* (as he called it) was just the right size to slip into a lady's dress pocket or the palm of her hand. This refined parcel seemed to elevate the lady gardener above the dirt, sweat, and bugs of the gardening profession. Bonnefons instead sought to

Ladies frolic in the garden in this image from *The Works of the Earls of Rochester*, 1777.

advance the principle of elite urban pleasure. He showed that an accomplished lady gardener could enhance the family economy. She need not splurge on the best fruits in Paris. She could not only grow them herself but preserve them by drying, candying, or macerating them in syrup, or by making salty and sweet jams and jellies.

The dark side of Parisian life that was absent from Bonnefons's first book was a stronger presence in his second, *Les delices de la campagne,* published just three years later. The midcentury civil war, the Fronde, erupted in 1649 and was most destructive in Paris and the new bourgeois neighborhoods surrounding the city. The conflict spread nationally, and two sieges of Paris brought astronomical bread prices along with marauding private armies that exacerbated famine conditions.[4] In *Les delices de la campagne,* Bonnefons struck a note of restrained comfort that made this second volume a useful cookbook for generations. It is the first French cookbook to give economical household recipes for breads, which reportedly were still used by Parisian women in the twentieth-century world wars.[5]

The most famous French gardener of all was Jean-Baptiste de la Quintinie, who created the *potager du roi* (the king's vegetable garden), which he described in *Instruction pour les jardins fruitiers et potagers* (Plan for Fruit and Vegetable Gardens, 1690). The *potager,* with its vast panorama of geometric beds of vegetables punctuated by avenues of espaliered fruit trees, still exists in the outskirts of Versailles, an invitation to a leisurely promenade. La Quintinie designed Louis XIV's garden primarily for the king's pleasure, but il was also a showcase for new hybrids, which then passed into commercial cultivation. The market gardens surrounding Paris and other cities were run as successful businesses. Their specialties—the precocious spring vegetables called *nouveautés* in Bonnefons's day and later known as *primeurs*—were becoming ever more refined and expensive.

Across the channel, in England, the notion of eating vegetables was controversial at the start of the seventeenth century but gradually became more attractive to English diners, especially if they could grow their own produce. Gervase Markham, writing in *The English Hous-wife* (1615), presented salads as a genuine part of an English meal, claiming that his compound salad was fit for "Prince's Tables." He called for serving chives, boiled carrots, lettuce, asparagus, cucumbers, cabbage, purslane, and other herbs on a small plate dressed simply with a little salad oil, vinegar, and sugar; olive oil was preferred. However, at the same date, an Italian exile living in London, Giacomo Castelvetro, was less encouraging: "I am amazed that so few of these delicious and health-giving plants [vegetables] are being grown to be eaten. Through ignorance or indifference, it seems to me that they are cultivated less for the table than for show by those who want to boast of their exotic plants and well-stocked gardens."[6]

At around the same time, William Lawson decided to reveal the "secrets" of English gardens in *The Countrie Housewife's Garden,* announcing that he had labored "forty and eight years" to amass this knowledge. Lawson was an idealist, suggesting a gardener's paradise with six landscaped areas and a stream flowing through, surrounded by a mounded wall. However, his advice on such skills as pruning fruit trees and watering the herb garden was eminently practical, aimed at women, who were often the ones supervising the orchard or vegetable garden (or working there themselves). "How antient, how profitable, how pleasant it is," said Lawson of the orchard. "How many secrets of nature it doth containe, how loved, how much practiced in the best places and of the best."[7]

William Lawson represented the very English tradition of the solitary gardener who spends his life devoted to the soil. John Evelyn—celebrated diarist and amateur naturalist, the multitalented founder of the Royal Society, and a member of the fashionable gardening community in London—was a very different personality. In 1658, Evelyn translated *Le jardinier françois* into English as *The French Gardener,* and forty years later, he praised the swelling ranks of "our Garden-Lovers, and *Brothers of the Sallet,*" in *Acetaria: A Discourse of Sallets* (1699). In this book, he discussed seventy-three pristine leaves, cooked roots, and flowers that are appropriate to use in salads, dressed with fragrant (not rancid) oil, vinegar, and salt, "which doubtless gives it both the Relish and Name of Salad, Ensalada, as with us of Sallet."[8] ♦

1 Marie de Rabutin-Chantal, marquise de Sévigné, *Letters of Madame de Sévigné to Her Daughter and Friends* (London: J. Walker [and others], 1811).

2 Susan Pinkard, *A Revolution in Taste: The Rise of French Cuisine* (Cambridge: Cambridge University Press, 2009), 36.

3 Ibid., 62.

4 Colin Jones, *Paris: The Biography of a City* (New York: Viking, 2005), 156.

5 See William Rubel, "Parisian Bread circa 1654," *Petits Propos Culinaires* 77 (2004): 9–12.

6 Giacomo Castelvetro, *The Fruit, Herbs and Vegetables of Italy* [1614], trans. Gillian Riley (Totnes, England: Prospect Books, 2010).

7 William Lawson, *The Countrie Housewife's Garden* [1617], facsimile edition (Illinois: Trovillion Press, 1948), ix, xvii.

8 John Evelyn, *Acetaria: A Discourse of Sallets* [1699], facsimile edition (Brooklyn, NY: Women's Auxiliary, Brooklyn Botanic Garden, 1937), 22, 4.

ABOVE Women are creating sugary treats from *Le jardinier françois* by Nicolas de Bonnefons, 1666 edition. The sugar in solid cones must be cut with the cleaver, then crushed with the pestle and mortar in the foreground before being dissolved in water for sugar syrup or a coating for dragées. The woman in back is rolling sugar paste, probably with a metal rolling pin.

OPPOSITE In Abraham Bosse's iconic engraving from his series *Les métiers* (c. 1635), the master pastry cook is checking his pies as they bake in the oven, while two young assistants roll out pastry dough. The master's wife sits comfortably to one side and collects money from a customer carrying a baby. The scene gives us a glimpse of the world of the upscale seventeenth-century pastry shop, with its large classical pewter urns filled with flowers, hanging copper pans and molds, outsize oven, and display of ready-to-eat tortes and patés on an elegant white tablecloth marked with folds from the iron.

hard sugar mixture used for decoration), egg glaze, *crème pâtissière*, marzipan, sugar icing, *rissoles* (small croquettes), frangipane, waffles, beignets, a whole range of fruit tarts, and early meringues (although he calls these *pains de citron;* the word *meringue* did not appear in print until later in the century). Like many cookbooks at this time, *Le pastissier françois* is international, including a group of meat pâtés (i.e., wrapped in pastry) from England, Turkey, Italy, and Switzerland, with recipes such as Pafté à la Basque and Petits Paftez à l'Espagnolle. Only the section on cooking eggs, crammed in at the end of the book, seems an anomaly.

The author of *Le pastissier françois* remains a mystery, but the book, so far in advance of any other, must have professional roots. The wording of the recipes confirms this supposition: "the way to make glaze as the pastry cooks do" or "how to make the sweet spice mixture pastry cooks use." Scattered clues suggest that the writer owned or worked in a shop, and he hints that his recipes were the closely guarded secrets of the pastry cooks of the royal court and of Paris. Pâtissiers could be very successful in business; many became wealthy and branched out into hospitality trades such as running an inn. Then, as now, the easiest meal to serve the drop-in guest was an omelet, so perhaps the abundance of egg dishes (seventy-one) in *Le pastissier françois* is no coincidence.[33]

THE FRENCH CONFECTIONER

By the beginning of the seventeenth century in Europe, sugar had been transformed from a favorite flavoring to a lead ingredient. French consumers could not resist it, and cookbooks soon appeared that were devoted to sugar work or confectionery, the latter defined as "a delicacy which is sweet, is usually eaten with the fingers, and keeps for some time."[1] At the turn of the eighteenth century, sugar supplied the largest part of Parisian grocers' income.[2]

One of the earliest French books devoted to confectionery, the anonymous *Le confiturier de la cour* (Maker of Preserves to the Court, 1659), made an unobtrusive debut, for it was bound with Pierre de Lune's *Le maistre d'hostel* and *Le nouveau cuisinier*. *Le confiturier* opens with "The Different Stages of Cooking Sugar," the core of a confectioner's expertise. The repertoire is very different from the pastry work of *Le pastissier françois* of the same decade (and far less eloquently expressed). *Le confiturier* parades fashionable new fruit jellies, fruits in syrup, dragées of fennel, and sugared almonds side by side with liqueurs. The following year, in 1660, *Confiturier françois* (French Preserve Maker) appeared. Though often attributed to La Varenne, the book bears such an eerie similarity to *Le confiturier de la cour* that some experts consider it a second edition.[3]

Confectionery was fast becoming a popular part of professional manuals. Another three-part volume appeared in 1668 under the catchall title of *L'ecole des ragousts* (The School of Ragoûts). In it was a different collection, also called *Le confiturier françois*, this time of fewer than a hundred recipes, that bore no relation to the first book. *Le cuisinier françois* and *Le pastissier françois*

constituted the bulk of the book. The publisher undoubtedly added *Le confiturier françois* to provide one-stop comprehensive coverage of the three disciplines of cuisine, *pâtisserie,* and confectionery for the maître d'hôtel or head of the kitchen; at this time in France, savory and sweet cooking, and its exponents, still overlapped.

François Massialot was at home in all three métiers, which made him a rarity in any generation in any country. Even today, only a few outstanding cooks are equally proficient in the patient exactitude demanded by pastry and sugar work and the hurly burly of savory cooking, and in the days of the open fire, mastering both disciplines was even more difficult. Massialot's *Le cuisinier roial et bourgeois* (1691) was already influencing the future course of French savory cooking. In *Nouvelle instruction pour les confitures, les liqueurs, et les fruits* (New Instructions on Jams, Liqueurs, and Fruits, 1692), he does the same for confectionery, writing with an authority that breathes hands-on experience. In over four hundred pages, he defines the scope of this new métier, covering *confitures* (preserves, particularly jams), chilled drinks based on flowers and fruit, Italian liqueurs (hinting at an Italian origin for this new art of confectionery), meringues, marzipans and caramel candies, and candied flowers and fruits; he ends with some neat little salads that feature preserves, including cornichons. Citing earlier works on confectionery, he declares he need no longer defend "the offering of tasty delicacies," and he lays out a tempting array of these treats in an illustration at the end of his book, arranged on platters or piled in pyramids and all bite-sized for easy eating.[4]

The next big name to come on the confectionery scene in France was François Menon, whose inquiring mind could not resist the intricacies

of sugar boiling. In *La science du maître d'hôtel confiseur* (The Science of the Steward Preserve Maker, 1749), he uses the buzzword of the time, *science*. Menon's content echoes Massialot's but takes each subject several steps further, with detailed instructions and many more recipes, including more than fifty of the ices then at the height of fashion and little treats ranging from cherries in white alcohol to candied green almonds, strawberry marzipan, jasmine biscuits, and caramelized chestnuts. Menon's book also shows elaborate table settings for the display of his creations, with classical vases, statuettes, and even temples for the indoor or outdoor delectation of guests. The transformation of the modern art of the cold kitchen since Massialot, declares Menon, is as great as the difference between Gothic and modern architecture. Today, "an elegant simplicity is what constitutes the beauty and the principal element of our desserts."[5]

Rivaling, and indeed surpassing, Menon in its lavish elegance is *Le cannameliste français* (The Sugar Cook, 1751) by Joseph Gilliers (the name derives from *sucre canne,* cane sugar). Gilliers was head of the cold kitchen for Stanislaus, King of Poland and Duke of Lorraine, who was also father-in-law to King Louis XV of France. He announces that he is writing "for those who wish to learn the métier of the *office.*"[6] Like all books on confectionery, his covers distilled waters, liqueurs, and the chilled drinks that were by this time ubiquitous at fine dinners and balls. His elegant pullout illustrations, drawn with all the assurance of the Enlightenment, overshadow the comprehensive text. Images push invention to such limits as a stalk of asparagus, a whole salmon, even a ham, all molded in frozen ice cream. The dizzying seventeenth-century pyramids of sweets had be-

This print of a pastry kitchen from the *Encyclopédie, ou dictionnaire raisonné des sciences, des arts et des métiers* by Denis Diderot and Jean Le Rond d'Alembert, 1751, was once in the modern collection of author Elizabeth David.

come outdated, and Gilliers favored flowers and fruits made from sugar paste or marzipan, staged in a horizontal presentation on the table with vases of silver or porcelain.

Spanish and Italian cooks were oddly slower than the French to write books on confectionery, though to judge by early references to treatises on sugar, it was they who had launched this vogue. However, toward the end of the century in Italy, monasteries were at the forefront of creative experiments in confectionery. Vincenzo Corrado was a Benedictine monk whose *Il credenziere di buon gusto* (The Steward of Good Taste, 1778) featured hot and cold drinks, candied fruits, preserves, and a whole chapter on *sorbetti*.[7] In Spain, Juan de la Mata's *Arte de reposteria* (The Art of Pastry, 1747) covered sweet and savory pastries, cakes, and chilled drinks as well as confectionery. The English had already taken their own path to comforting pastries and confections that could be cooked at home, and the few books that were written on confectionery spoke to housewives as well as professionals.

By the early nineteenth century in France, the Revolution had changed the book buyers' market. J. J. Machet's *Le confiseur moderne* (The Modern Confectioner, 1803), with its tiny typeface and lack of illustration, is a reminder that styles had moved on, and in time of war a publication had to strike a note of austerity to be successful. Machet wrote for home cooks as well as for budding professionals, and he clearly states the techniques of sugar work for the beginner. His book includes everyone's favorite recipes, from candied apples to violet water, making it the handbook of the working pastry chef for much of the new century. With Machet in hand, the inexperienced pastry cook, or even the housewife, could be proud of the results.

The audience of movers and shakers for Antonin Carême, the most famous confectioner of them all, was very different, and he sensibly waited for the restoration of the monarchy to publish his *Le pâtissier royal parisien* (The Parisian Royal Pastry Chef, 1815). The contents are slightly less exhilarating than the title because his main theme is the essential génoises, almond cakes, and pastries that to this day compose the classic repertoire. Of far greater fame is his landmark *Le pâtissier pittoresque* (The Picturesque Pastry Chef, 1815), a masterpiece of 123 architectural drawings—a Chinese pavilion, a Greek rotunda, a Turkish house of pleasure. All were intended to be cre-

ated in living color—vivid orange, yellow, violet, chocolate, soft green, and crimson—by adding vegetable colorings to the basic dead-white mastic, a pliable paste of sugar and gum arabic that some pastry chefs still use occasionally for *pièces montées*. Despite Carême's instructions, it is hard to imagine even a trained confectioner re-creating these extravagances, which tower a meter or more high. Rather *Le pâtissier pittoresque* is noteworthy for its evocation of the new Empire style, its soaring imagination, and the sheer joy of leafing through page after page of castles in the air. ♦

1 Alan Davidson, *Oxford Companion to Food* (Oxford: Oxford University Press, 1999), 210.

2 On sugar as a share of grocers' income, see Abraham du Pradel (Nicholas de Blegny), *Le livre commode des adresses de Paris pour 1692* (Paris: Paul Daffis de la Bibliothèque Elzeverienne, 1878), 2:6.

3 *Livres en bouche: Cinq siècles d'art culinaire français* (Paris: Bibliothèque nationale de France, Hermann, 2001), 147.

4 François Massialot, *Nouvelle instruction pour les confitures, les liqueurs, et les fruits* (Paris: Charles de Sercy, 1692), i.

5 François Menon, *La science du maître d'hôtel confiseur* (Paris: Chez Paulus du Mesnil, 1750), iii.

6 Joseph Gilliers, *Le cannameliste français* (Nancy: La veuve Leclerc, 1768), title page.

7 Elizabeth David, *Harvest of the Cold Months: The Social History of Ice and Ices* (New York: Viking, 1995), 164–65.

The other major cookbook author of this decade, Pierre de Lune, had headed the kitchens of the duc de Rohan until his master's death forced a change and he turned to writing books. In *Le cuisinier* and *Le nouveau cuisinier,* he talks of the fluid boundaries between private and commercial employment, addressing "young people who travel from town to town to learn . . . the cook's . . . science."[34] Clearly a dedicated teacher, Lune likely wanted his book to educate cooks in domestic service, for he describes it as a teaching tool for cooks who had not learned enough during their time as apprentices and journeymen. Lune's background as a sophisticated Paris cook who had traveled and read widely is different from that of La Varenne, the provincial Burgundian (though La Varenne almost certainly worked much of the year in Paris at his master's mansion). In particular, La Varenne's recipe titles lack foreign names, whereas Lune has dishes of Spanish, German, and Italian origins (such as *choux de Milan en potage* and *oeufs à la milanoise* cooked with sugar syrup and pistachios).

Nonetheless, the similarities between the two writers' recipes are striking. They suggest a standard repertoire that the midcentury professional French cook needed to master, showing that the culinary revolution had already entered kitchen practice and was now taking form in print. The two books share a fundamental dependence on stocks and reduced juices. The names of dishes have become standardized, as has their order in the meal. Bisques, ragoûts, and sausages of all kinds are standard starters (*entrées*), while organ meats, colored jellies, eggs, and vegetables are preferred as entremets. Game, small birds, and very young meat (suckling pig) are considered suitable roasts, but beef, associated with old animals exhausted from work, is not. Some familiar favorites appear in both books, such as beignets, or *pets de putain* (whore's farts), known today more delicately as *pets de nonne* (nun's farts). Lune's recipe for *beurre blanc* echoes that of La Varenne.

The same classic preparations that appeared in the books of Lune and La Varenne turned up forty years later, modernized and refined in *Le cuisinier roial et bourgeois* (The Royal and Bourgeois Cook, 1691) and *Nouvelle instruction pour les confitures, les liqueurs, et les fruits* (New Instruction for Preserves, Liqueurs, and Fruits, 1692), both by François Massialot. Massialot's originality of presentation and voice of authority confirmed him as a worthy successor to La Varenne and Lune, destined to influence cooks well into the next century. By this time, many recipes were standardized, using similar, though not necessarily identical, ingredients and steps. Massialot extended the culinary structure already defined as French, building in recipes that were to become classics, many of them still familiar, such as *bisque d'écrevisses, boeuf à la mode, ragoût de champignons,* and a *crème brûlée* with more than a page of instruction that could not be bettered today.

One of the key preparations underpinning this new cuisine was *coulis* (the name comes from the French *couler,* meaning "to flow"). In the words of Massialot, "Coulis, whether with or without meat [*gras ou maigre*] are used to bind ragoûts and soups [*potages*], and give them a very pleasant flavor."[35] In the fourteenth century, Taillevent was already using the word *coullé* to mean a strained liquid, and during Massialot's time, coulis became an indispensable part of the culinary structure. By the 1729 edition of *Le nouveau cuisinier royal et bourgeois* (the spelling of the title now modernized), coulis had become a kitchen staple; Massialot included nineteen versions, each designed for different background ingredients, often geared to the feast and fast days of the church. Coulis are potent stuff, darker, spicier, and more concentrated than espagnole sauce or our modern brown sauces made from pan juices.

Massialot belonged to the sought-after group of independent Parisian cooks who catered to an impressive clientele, including the royal family.[36] His opening menus in *Le cuisinier roial et bourgeois* served both to advertise and endorse his skills. For example, his staggering menu for a "Grand Repast in the month of May" consists of two gigantesque courses and requires a minimum of 128 serving dishes plus individual plates for the diners. Eighteen cooks and stewards with eighteen aides were needed in the kitchen to prepare the meal, and the *batterie de cuisine* included sixty small casseroles, ten large round casseroles, ten small round casseroles, ten large *marmites* (cauldrons), ten small *marmites*, and thirty spits for roasting meats. Even the wealthiest Parisian residence would hardly have had all these items on hand, confirming that such a feast would require a caterer.[37] A smart businessman, Massialot added the snobbish detail that this meal was hosted at Sceaux, just outside Paris, by the marquis de Seignelai, son of the king's minister Colbert, for "Monsieur and Madame" (the king's brother and his wife) and many distinguished guests.

Massialot was the first cookbook author to present his information as a dictionary, a concise, easy-to-reference style that became popular among Enlightenment writers in the eighteenth century. Early editions of *Le cuisinier roial et bourgeois* give lists of potages, entrées, and entremets, streamed alphabetically without seasonal distinctions.

Roial & Bourgeois. A. 89

INSTRUCTION

EN FORME

DE DICTIONNAIRE,

Où l'on apprendra comment apprêter chaque chose, & comment la servir pour Entrée, pour Entremets, pour le Rôti, ou autrement.

A.

ABBATIS.

Ous avons marqué, page 46. un Potage d'Abbatis d'Oisons. Pour cela, faites-les cuire dans de bon boüillon, assaisonné d'un bouquet de fines herbes, & sel. Etant cuits, coupez-les par morceaux & les passez à la poële, avec lard fondu, persil, cerfeüil, un peu de poivre blanc,

H

ABOVE This dictionary from the 1693 edition of *Le cuisinier roial et bourgeois* by François Massialot is one of the first alphabetical lists of technical terms for professional cooks. The appearance of seventeenth-century French cookbooks underlines their utilitarian purpose. Sturdy, squat, bound in brown calf- or goatskin with a minimum of expensive gilding on the covers, they are destined to be used by working cooks, not to be admired in a gentleman's library. The text is easily legible in italic or roman font, and pages have adequate white space but few, if any, illustrations. Over the centuries, these books have become personalized, often with annotations in the margins or with the name of the owner inscribed proudly on the title page.

STEWARD OF THE HOUSEHOLD, MASTER OF THE FEAST

The French culinary revolution was thoroughly chronicled from the kitchen viewpoint, but the amazing new feats of *service à la française* described in cookbooks clearly needed a stage manager out front, a maître d'hôtel. Maîtres d'hôtel were literate men of good social standing, an appreciative audience for books on the latest manners and styles of entertaining. They were the most prestigious domestic officers of all, outranking the head of the kitchen and symbolizing the grandest houses. The sheer spectacle of the grand meals during the reign of Louis XIV amounted to command performances, demanding that the maître d'hôtel be producer, director, and stage manager of these immensely theatrical occasions. The job included provisioning the entire household, planning menus, and often working hands-on to make some of the great delicacies of the seventeenth-century cold kitchen.

Italy introduced the genre of guides for maîtres d'hôtel with the books of Messisbugo and Romoli. The first French text detailing these duties was *Le maistre d'hostel qui apprend l'ordre de bien server sur table & d'y ranger les services* (A Steward Explains Table Service and Menu Planning, 1659), an unobtrusive forty-page booklet sandwiched between Pierre de Lune's *Le nouveau cuisinier* and *Le confiturier de la cour* to create a single volume. The title page does not specify an author, but the book is dedicated to Lune, suggesting his overall authority. Never before had a cookbook been dedicated to an employee rather than to the author's master, an indication of the prestige of the maître d'hôtel. By packing several texts in what

Delegates from surrounding towns gather in Vienna to feast around a banquet table in *Tafel,* a print from the late seventeenth century by an unknown artist. Note that glasses are limited to a side table.

would now be called a bumper book, the publisher seems to have identified a hole in the market. Within a decade, *Le maistre d'hostel* had twice been packaged with other previously published texts such as *L'escole parfaite des officiers de bouche* (The Ideal School for Household Officers, 1662) and *L'ecole des ragousts* (The School of Ragoûts,

1668), in which it is simply titled *Le confiturier français.*[1]

L'escole parfaite is bound in elegant gold-tooled leather, and its contents are a publisher's grab bag, including, astonishingly, medieval *brouets* not seen since the beginning of the century. By contrast, *L'ecole des ragousts* was small and on low-quality paper, intended for a down-

waves of courses.[2] The next century was to see cookbook diagrams that took a bird's-eye view of dozens, even hundreds, of overlapping dishes on the table. L. S. R. already regales his readers with elegant collations theatrically set on water, in the garden, and in a grotto, "singular and magnificent novelties" worthy of great nobles. He touches on the latest fashion in court dining, a course called *dessert* that until recently had been called simply *les fruits*. The new name derived from the verb *desservir*, signifying the opposite of "to serve," when the last course is cleared and the table is covered with a sumptuous array of basins, plates, and pyramids of fruits and sweetmeats.

The name of one maître d'hôtel has survived from the seventeenth century as a hero of folklore: Vatel, head of household for the Prince of Condé. At a special reception for King Louis XIV, the convoy of carts carrying fish from the coast was late in arriving, and in despair, Vatel committed suicide. He has been characterized variously as a professional who had lost his honor or as a man who lost his sanity. Whatever the reason for his dramatic act, a single observer recorded the event, Madame de Sévigné, who mentioned only the inconvenience Vatel's suicide caused in the prince's household (the guest of honor, the king, had to leave immediately). ♦

1 *L'escole parfaite* (1729) includes *Le maître d'hôtel*, *L'ecuyer tranchant*, *Le sommelier & chef d'office*, *Le chef d'office parfait*, *Le cuisinier parfait*, and *Le patissier parfait*. *L'ecole des ragousts* (1668) includes *Le cuisinier françois et méthodique*, *Le patissier françois*, *Le confiturier françois*, and *La maniere de plier de linge*. *Le confiturier françois* is a simplified version of *Le confiturier de la cour* in *Le maistre d'hostel* of 1659.

2 Barbara Ketcham Wheaton, *Savoring the Past* (Philadelphia: University of Pennsylvania Press, 1983), 138–39.

scale market. It frequently mentions a *chaudron* (cauldron), indicating that the author expected his readers to do more open-hearth cooking than Lune's readers, for example. Lune's book seems to assume that the reader will be working on the waist-level cooking surface of a *potager.* Both *L'escole parfaite* and *L'ecole des ragousts* reused material in ways suited to a wide audience, a formula that proved triumphantly successful. The shelf life of *L'escole parfaite*, for example, took it well into the eighteenth century. The book was revised at least nine times and was also translated into English as *A Perfect School for the Officers of the Mouth* (1682).

L'art de bien traiter (The Art of Fine Catering, 1674) was the first full-scale cookbook to choreograph the multicourse feasts described by La Varenne and Pierre de Lune. The author, known only by the initials L. S. R., provided exacting instructions to enable maîtres d'hôtel to set out painstakingly coordinated

Francesco Novelli's *Pancake Woman* echoes a Rembrandt etching of 1635. People, not food, had captured Rembrandt's interest in this study of half-turned faces.

Massialot also moved beyond the aide-mémoire style of La Varenne and Lune to write recipes in substantial detail. Indeed, by the time his two-volume and then three-volume editions were published in 1712 and 1748, respectively, Massialot's publisher had created a truly encyclopedic work.

The last household book of importance to appear in the seventeenth century in France was Nicolas Audiger's *La maison réglée* (The Well-Ordered House, 1692). Though not as ambitious as Latini's comprehensive *Lo scalco alla moderna*, published at the same time in Italy, the book boasted an author of impressive credentials. Audiger was maître d'hôtel to several prominent households but also spent a good part of his career as a Parisian *limonadier* selling refreshing drinks in a shop in the famous Palais Royal. Audiger knew from the inside how important caterers and specialty food shops could be to large urban households. In *La maison réglée*, he instructs the maître d'hôtel how to contract with the baker for a daily bread supply. In addition to acquiring uncooked meat from the butcher, he explains, the maître d'hôtel needs to buy already-roasted poultry from a professional *rôtisseur* and to arrange with a *charcutier* to provide fats such as lard, various sausages, "and other things used for entremets." To check on correct prices, he will also need to oversee purveyors of raw kitchen ingredients.

TOWARD THE END of the seventeenth century, an innovative genre of food writing appeared, characterized by a newsy style that prefigures the host of shopping, restaurant, and tourist guides of today. Typical was *Le mercure galant* (The Elegant Shopper), a periodical that began in 1672 to report on the tables of the rich and royal. Readers all over France avidly absorbed the stories about the court festivals at the Palace of Versailles. By the end of the century, the urban bourgeoisie craved catering services, cookbooks, the latest dining accoutrements, and more. To meet these needs, a shopping guide to Paris, *Le livre commode des adresses de Paris* (The Book of Useful Paris Addresses), was launched in 1692 to showcase the finest shops for crystal, silver, faience, and tapestries, as well as the best confectioners (in the rue des Lombards).[38] In it was a listing for a boutique on the rue Saint Denis that specialized in ingenious little

insulated carafes of cork, ideal for chilling wine and liqueurs because the ice evaporated slowly. The reader could also buy bread from the baker who supplied the duc d'Orléans, the king's brother. Such insider tips made the *Livre commode* the indispensable guide for smart Parisians and visitors to the city.

These fashionable periodicals of Paris set the scene for the new genre of gastronomic commentary that would emerge in the early nineteenth century. But in their voyeurism, they also encapsulate their own era. In the seventeenth century, ordinary people throughout Europe gained titillating glimpses into the enviable lifestyles of their more privileged compatriots—from the semiroyal grandeur of the duc de Rohan's court to the prosperous middle-income homes of Hannah Woolley's readers. Books on cooking bear witness to the socioeconomic changes at the end of the century that were harbingers of developments in the eighteenth. They indicate who could afford the luxury of a maître d'hôtel and who could not, who could afford exotic ingredients and who, indeed, might be adventurous enough to try them. The trickle-down effect of the growth in overseas trade was generating wealth in western Europe: families were living well and had the money to entertain, cultivate ambitious gardens, and hire domestic help. The success of so many books about cooking indicates that both cooks and their customers were enjoying themselves inside and outside the kitchen.

Diners sit cross-legged in Middle Eastern fashion in Nicolas Guerard's *A Reception for Mehmet Celebi*, the Turkish ambassador to Paris in 1720. With wine being forbidden under Muslim law, says the inscription, a "sorbec" of lemon water and sugar was served after dinner, followed by pipes of tobacco, then coffee. By this time, sorbets were a popular chilled drink served in cafés in many European cities.

THE ICEMAN COMETH

"Italy in the early decades of the seventeenth century was entering a new Ice Age," writes Elizabeth David.[1] Indeed, across Europe at this time, preserving snow and ice for chilled fruit drinks was a hot topic. Two trends had come together, one the vogue for distilling flavored waters and making syrups at home, the other the European fascination for all things Arab. Travelers returned with tales of sherbets, which were drinks, not the firm concoctions of today (the name comes from the Arabic *sharâb*). By midcentury, five shops in Florence were selling a new beverage, *sorbetto,* based on fruit or vegetable juice.[2] Sorbettos were flavored with honey or sugar and possibly a spice; some were concentrated essences or pastes, to be diluted with cold water.[3] Thanks to the vigorous English trade with the Middle East, these refreshments had arrived early in London, advertised by Morat's coffeehouse in 1662 as "sherbets made in Turkie of Lemons, Roses and Violets perfumed."[4]

The fine art of making cold-room ices is summed up in the frontispiece of *L'art de bien faire les glaces d'office* (1768). Cherubs crush ice from the conical ice houses in the background, chill the ice cream or sorbet mixture in buckets of ice and salt, and then scoop spoonfuls into handled cups and fly off to an invisible table of eager guests.

At the beginning, sherbets were not necessarily chilled. Credit for chilling these drinks with snow, long a Turkish practice, probably goes to Naples, where Mount Vesuvius could provide a year-round supply. Neapolitan Giambattista Della Porta explored freezing techniques in the 1589 edition of *Magia naturalis* (Natural Magic), where he declared to household stewards, "If their masters were clamouring for ever colder and icier wine, here was the way to achieve it."[5] Italians were also in the habit of drinking their wine chilled, sometimes mixed with snow, a practice that was noted by Catherine de' Medici's son Henri, future king of France, during a visit to Venice in 1575.

The French were quick on the uptake. By the mid-seventeenth century, the anonymous *Le confiturier de la cour* (Maker of Preserves to the Court, 1659) had given recipes for *les eaux d'Italie* (Italian waters)— flavored with jasmine, orange flowers, roses, coriander, cherries, cinnamon, anise, and more—most of which were to be served chilled. In this book was the first printed recipe for sorbet, Sorbec of Alexandria, a meat-based syrup with sugar. To our tastes, the result is a strange mix of veal broth sweetened with sugar syrup; moreover, the recipe gives no instructions for chilling. Other *sorbecs* featured a mixture of vinegar and mint sweetened with rose sugar from Turkey. *Le confiturier de la cour* was probably aptly titled, as chilled drinks in France were the domain of the wealthiest aristocrats. Exoticism was the rage.[6] In *Voyage de Levant* (1674), Jean de Thevenot describes the practice of making sorbet in bulk from clarified syrup flavored with lemon juice, rose water or violets, and ambergris. Another popular taste sensation was wine that had been flavored with ambergris and musk, two pungent ingredients found today only in perfumes. Old drinks took on new life when chilled; *ypocras,* for instance, remained popular long after its medieval medicinal associations were forgotten.

The very first sorbets as we know them, firm frozen concoctions that hold their shape, appear in Antonio Latini's *Lo scalco alla moderna* (1692–94). By this time, ices were already being sold in the streets of Naples.[7] These treats were semifrozen, very sweet sherbets, in contrast to the hard, glassy water ices of Paris of the same period. The stirring of half-frozen sherbet to break down crystals—ancestor of today's sorbets—is the "new way" referred to in an undated booklet published in Naples about the same time, entitled *Brieve e nuovo modo da farsi ogni sorte di sorbetti con facilità* (Short New and Easy Method of Making Every Kind of Sherbet).

The fashion for iced drinks, and later the more solid iced desserts, spread rapidly. French doctor Pierre Barra, writing in 1675, noted with disapproval the public sale and excessive use of snow throughout the Turkish Empire and Italy; it was equally common in Castille and Constantinople.[8] In parallel, wealthy Spanish, Florentine, and Roman households had been constructing fairly sophisticated ice houses since the end of the sixteenth century.[9] Barra insisted that Rome "was the place . . . where greed caused the creation of many inventions."[10] Nicolas Audiger ran one of the new beverage shops in the Palais-Royal, and in *La maison réglée,* he describes Italians' pleasure in their ice-cold flavored drinks and announces that he had returned from Italy with hopes of becoming the apostle of ice in France. The growing use of ice in France is evident from a new 1701 tax on the sale of ice and snow in the Paris region, though the government admitted that outside Paris, the revenue would not amount to much: "using snow and ice in summer is, without doubt, pure luxury."[11]

Soon a new frozen fashion reached the table—ice cream. Massialot, writing in 1692, includes *fromages glacés* among his ices and sorbets. These ice creams were enriched with cream and eggs and called *fromages* because they were chilled in the same round, shallow molds as cheese.[12] Chocolate and coffee were among the flavorings that would become classic. In England, the taste for dairy desserts like syllabub made ice cream an easy transition, and soon well-off households acquired the necessary churn and molds to make ice creams at home. Hannah Glasse provides one of the first English ice cream recipes in *The Compleat Confectioner* of 1760, though her instructions do not mention a churn. As historian Ivan Day has pointed out, "With such a strongly established taste for these rich dairy foods, it was no wonder that the English took so readily to ice cream, the ultimate luxury sweet."[13]

L'art de bien faire les glaces d'office (The Art of Succeeding with Ices, 1768) by a former steward called Emy was the first French book devoted solely to ices and ice creams. This immensely readable instruction manual for professionals (cold-room stewards and sellers of cold drinks) took the scientific approach typical of the Enlightenment, even for such a luxury as ice cream. Monsieur Emy insists that no one can make perfect ice cream without understanding and controlling the scientific principles of freezing. He writes proudly that "our ices are superior to those that were made twenty years ago," and his frontispiece of cherubs attending to the freezing of ice cream in one of the new mechanical churns must be one of the most charming visual openings to a cookbook in any century.

Making and serving ice cream called for the creativity that eighteenth-century confectioners relished as a chance to demonstrate their skills. In Paris, the *Gazetin du comestible* announced in January 1767 that chez Maillot in the Palais-Royal offered ices and ice creams flavored with pineapple, spinach, or brown bread. Menon's suggestion to send ice cream to the table in decorated sugar paste or almond-paste imitation snuffboxes (with little lids) may well have been the most elegant idea.[14] Snuffboxes were all the rage in shops selling luxury novelties in Paris and London. Silver ice cream spoons, hand-painted porcelain ice cream cups, cut-glass dessert sets, and fine earthenware sets were all new consumer items in the mid- to late-eighteenth century that gave dessert eating an extra dimension of modern luxury. ♦

1 Elizabeth David, *Harvest of the Cold Months: The Social History of Ice and Ices* (New York: Viking, 1995), 57.

2 Judith C. Brown and Jordan Goodman, "Women and Industry in Florence," *Journal of Economic History* 40, no. 1 (March 1980): 75–76.

3 David, *Harvest of the Cold Months,* 74.

4 Ibid., 156.

5 Ibid., 74.

6 Laura Mason, *Sugar-Plums and Sherbet: The Prehistory of Sweets* (Totnes, England: Prospect Books, 2004), 153–56.

7 Elizabeth David, *Italian Food* (New York: Penguin Books, 1999), 263.

8 Pierre Barra, *L'usage de la glace, de la neige et du froid* (Lyon: Chez Antoine Cellier fils, 1676), 16–19.

9 David, *Harvest of the Cold Months,* 25.

10 Barra, *L'usage de la glace,* 65.

11 *Recherches et considérations sur les finances de France* (Basel: Frères Cramer, 1758), 2:127–28.

12 Jeri Quinzio, *Of Sugar and Snow: A History of Ice Cream Making* (Berkeley: University of California Press, 2009), 32.

13 Ivan Day, "The Art of Confectionery," www.historicfood.com (accessed October 2009), 27.

14 Menon, *Les soupers de la cour* (Paris: Guillyn, 1755), 3:280.

RECITPES

ECIPE STYLES BECOME DISTINCTIVE in the seventeenth century. Some remain just a few lines, little throwaway ideas like John Murrell's apple pufs (a type of pancake) and La Varenne's sautéed asparagus finished with herbs and cream. Others are very long indeed, several hundred words of intricate explanation of processes such as making bread or puff pastry. As a result, the length of a recipe text conveys a much better idea of how much more, or less, work is involved than in the past. The two-day procedure described by Nicolas de Bonnefons for kneading, raising, and proofing the rich dough for brioche tells it like it is—a lot of hard work.

By now, ageless favorites are emerging and sounding very familiar. Some are linked to medieval standbys, such as blancmange and macaroons; others develop from the new, lighter style of eating that had been pioneered in sixteenth-century France and Italy. A dish like spicy *gallina morisca* (Moorish chicken), for example, has clear parallels with today's coq au vin. La Varenne stuffs mushrooms, and the anonymous author of *Le pastissier françois* bakes a Savoy sponge cake just as we do. National links are common: England still has its syllabubs and hot pot, France its *ragoûts*, Germany its *Krapffen* pastries. The basic recipes underlying a finished dish are being defined: beef broth (later to be called consommé), *liaisons* for thickening sauces, butter pastry dough, and pastry cream. *Coulis,* an immensely elaborate forerunner of *sauce espagnole*, brown sauce, and gravy, invades both the professional and domestic kitchen.

Recipe titles are becoming more descriptive. Expressions such as ragoût, *en casserole,* and *au court bouillon* tell the reader what to expect, and to some extent what equipment will be needed. A hot pot will call for a cauldron; a cake or torte implies the use of a mold. The key equipment in most kitchens—revolving spit, pot hanger, mortar and pestle—has changed little, however, though the basic pots, frying pans, knives, forks, and spoons proliferate in well-to-do households and trickle down to modest establishments. Whisks, strainers, colanders, and the like are now taken for granted, and a few aids to manual labor appear: Nicolas de Bonnefons mentions a *broyeur,* a type of pounder, for kneading bread dough.

It also becomes customary to highlight the main (and most costly) ingredient by leading with the name of the fish, bird, or cut of meat in a recipe title. Garnishes or flavorings, such as green herbs, chocolate, or strawberries, may be mentioned, too. The arrival of exotic foods, such as turkey and pineapple, can be tracked through their appearance at the head of a recipe. But like food magazines today, many old cookbooks were trendsetters, evoking the curiosity and envy of their readers, rather than documenting their current tastes. They led the way into the future, but, to judge from written menus, acceptance of alien flavors usually took time, even a generation or two.

From Francisco Martínez Montiño, *Arte de cocina, pastelería, vizcochería y conserveria* (Barcelona, 1611; recipe from 1750 edition): *Roast a pair of chickens, and then cut them into fourths: and chop a little bacon into very small dice, and fry very well until they are white, and throw a little onion cut very small, and smother the chickens with this bacon and onion, pour in broth as needed to cover it, with a little wine, and a little vinegar: and if available you can add a little fresh butter. Season with all spices: in this stew do not add eggs. It should be served slightly sour: You can if you wish sprinkle in a few chopped vegetables.*

Gallina Morisca

Moorish Chicken

AS HEAD COOK for the extravagant, dissolute Philip III of Spain, Francisco Martínez Montiño would have been a leader of fashionable dining in what was still one of the most powerful nations in Europe. When he visited Barcelona in 1603–4, Frenchman Barthélemy Joly, a prelate and advisor to Henry IV, enjoyed himself: "The Spanish have great appetites and like highly flavored foods. . . . The largest meats, like turkeys, rabbits, capons, chickens are never whole, but cut into pieces in the kitchen, so much so that when there is to be a large dish or two of turkey, the master of the hall composes each plate by cutting the meat into small pieces and putting two or three pieces, with sauce, on each one. . . . Among all this there is a service where everyone has his own little bowl of yellow broth of almond milk, very spicy and sugared, but without a thickening of bread."

In line with this description, chickens for *gallina morisca* are cut into quarters after roasting, then cooked again in a sauce that is a forerunner of Catalan *sofregit*, a flavoring mixture of onion and bacon to which Montiño suggests adding other vegetables at will. (Our eighteenth-century copy of *Arte de cocina* happens to have been published in Barcelona, capital of Catalonia, but differs little from the first Madrid edition of 1611.) "All spices" called for in the recipe reflect the Moorish influence that remained firmly implanted in Spain after seven centuries of conquest (the Arabs were finally expelled only at the end of the fifteenth century). In common use were sesame, cinnamon, nutmeg, cloves, and saffron (it would have been homegrown). I'm also including garlic, a Spanish favorite, as a spice, and parsley for color. Most important of all is pepper, freshly ground from black peppercorns. In Montiño's day, long pepper (a relative of black pepper) would have been an alternative.

Montiño sprinkles on spices at the end of cooking for aromatic effect, and specifically states that the chicken "should go out a little sourly." He includes wine, for the Spanish court had abandoned the Muslim ban on alcohol. "The wine is smoky and not delicate like ours," remarks Barthélemy Joly. "It is necessary to drink more than usual because of the great quantity of pepper that they put on all their food, in addition to that put on the table, like salt . . . they do not cease to add spice to aid, as they say, good digestion." You'll find that the last-minute dash of pepper, wine, and vinegar he suggests much enlivens this sauce.

Spiced Chicken with Red Wine, Vinegar, and Bacon   *Serves 4 to 6*

    2 chickens (about 3 pounds or 1.35 kg each)

    2 tablespoons (30 g) butter, more if needed

    Salt and pepper

    4-ounce (110-g) piece bacon, cut into small dice

    4 onions, chopped

    5 or 6 garlic cloves, chopped

    1 cup (250 ml) full-bodied red wine, more for sprinkling

    ¼ cup (60 ml) red wine vinegar, more for sprinkling

    2 cups (500 ml) chicken broth

    1 teaspoon aniseeds

    2 teaspoons black pepper, more for serving

    1 teaspoon ground cinnamon

    1 teaspoon freshly grated nutmeg

    Large pinch of saffron threads

    1 to 2 tablespoons chopped fresh parsley

    Kitchen string

To roast the chickens: Heat the oven to 400°F (200°C). Wipe the chickens inside and out with damp paper towels, then truss them with string. Set them, breast side up, in a roasting pan just big enough to hold them. Melt 1 tablespoon of the butter, brush it over the chickens, and sprinkle them with salt and pepper.

Roast the chickens until they start to brown, 15 to 20 minutes. Turn them breast side down and continue roasting, basting often and brushing with more butter if they look dry, about 45 minutes. Turn the birds again onto their backs, baste them, and continue roasting until they are done, 10 to 20 minutes longer. To test if the chickens are done, lift one of them with a two-pronged fork and carefully pour the juices from the cavity; they should run clear, not pink. Transfer the chickens to a cutting board. Leave the oven on, and keep the roasting pan handy, as it will be reused. (The chickens can also be roasted on a spit.) Let the chickens rest for 10 minutes.

Meanwhile, fry the bacon in a frying pan over low heat, stirring often, until the fat runs, 5 to 7 minutes. Stir in the onions and continue frying gently without browning until very tender, 8 to 10 minutes longer. Stir in the garlic and cook for 1 minute more. Remove from the heat.

Cut each chicken into quarters (2 leg and 2 breast pieces), discarding the backbone. Pack the chicken pieces back in the roasting pan, overlapping them. In a small bowl, mix together the wine and vinegar. Spoon the mixture over the warm chicken pieces so it is partially absorbed. Spread the onion mixture on top. Pour enough broth down the side of the pan almost to cover the chickens, and dot with 1 tablespoon

(15 g) butter. Return the pan to the oven and bake until the broth boils and the chicken pieces are very hot, 10 to 15 minutes.

To finish: While the chickens are baking, crush the aniseeds in a mortar with a pestle or the end of a rolling pin, then stir in the pepper, cinnamon, nutmeg, and saffron and pound them all together. Sprinkle the spice mixture over the chicken pieces and return them to the oven until hot and fragrant, about 5 minutes longer.

Transfer the chicken pieces to a warmed platter, cover with aluminum foil, and keep warm. Skim any excess fat from the roasting pan and place the pan on the stove top. Boil the cooking juices over high heat until reduced by half. Remove from the heat and stir in the parsley. Taste and adjust the seasoning with a little more wine and vinegar to pick up the flavor.

Spoon the sauce over the chickens and sprinkle more pepper on top. Serve hot.

To Make Apple Pufs

From John Murrell, *A New Booke of Cookerie* (London, 1615): *Take a Pome-water or any other Apple that is not hard, or harsh in taste : mince it small with a dozen or twenty Razins of the Sonne : wet the Apples in two Egges, beat them all together with the backe of a knife, or a Spoone. Season them with Nutmeg, Rosewater, Sugar, and Ginger : drop them into a Frying-pan with a Spoone, frye them like Egges, wring on the juyce of an Orenge, or Lemmon, and serve them in.*

AS A PROFESSIONAL COOK, John Murrell must have appreciated a little throwaway recipe like this that calls for a couple of eggs, an apple, and flavorings found in most kitchens. He is totally precise on execution: the variety of apple must be sweet and soft so it needs no extra cooking; the eggs are to be broken up with a spoon or the back, not the cutting edge, of a knife. (Note that our four-tined table forks, which whisk eggs quite efficiently on a saucer, had not yet appeared in the kitchen.) "Razins of the Sonne" could have referred to the plump purple muscatel raisins from Málaga, in southern Spain, still a local specialty, or to regular dark raisins. For the one ingredient, an orange, that might have been scarce, Murrell suggests the alternative of a lemon.

The pancakes resemble a delicious sweet omelet, and they should be mixed and fried at the last minute. At the time, dinner normally consisted of three courses, with a varying number of dishes in each. This recipe would have been served as part of a second course. Murrell mentions roasted eel, fried oysters, and buttered parsnips as among the twenty other dishes that might have accompanied this one.

Apple Pancakes   *Serves 2*

    1 medium dessert apple, peeled, quartered, and cored

    2 tablespoons (15 g) dark or golden raisins

    2 eggs

    ¼ teaspoon freshly grated nutmeg

    ½ teaspoon rose water

    2 teaspoons sugar

    ½ teaspoon ground ginger

    2 tablespoons (30 g) butter, melted

    1 orange or lemon, halved

To make the batter: With a large knife, slice the apple quarters, and then coarsely chop the slices. Chop the raisins, add the chopped apple, and then chop them together until quite fine and clinging to each other, about 2 minutes. In a bowl, whisk the eggs until frothy, then stir in the apple mixture, nutmeg, rose water, sugar, and ginger. You must cook the batter at once, as the apple discolors quickly.

To cook the pancakes: Heat a well-cured frying pan or a nonstick frying pan over medium heat until a drop of batter sizzles immediately on contact. Brush the pan with some of the melted butter to prevent sticking. Using a large spoon, drop egg-sized spoonfuls of batter into the hot pan to form 2-inch (5-cm) pancakes, patting lightly to flatten them. Fry them until browned on the first side, flip, and brown the other side, 1 to 2 minutes' total cooking. Transfer to a plate and keep warm. Cook the remaining batter in the same manner, wiping out the pan and brushing with more butter between batches.

Divide the pancakes between 2 warmed plates, sprinkle each serving with a squeeze or two of orange juice, and serve at once.

Asperges à la Crême

———

Asparagus with Cream

From François Pierre de la Varenne, *Le cuisinier françois* (Paris, 1651; recipe from Brussels 1698 edition): *Cut them [the asparagus] very small, leave nothing but the green, sauté them with fresh butter or melted lard, parsley, green onion, or a bouquet of herbs; after that simmer them very gently with crème fraîche, serve if you like with a little nutmeg.*

LA VARENNE, COOK TO the marquis d'Uxelles, and his contemporaries pay an attention to vegetables that was to revolutionize the French table. La Varenne liked to teach; in his own words, "valuing particularly those of my Profession, I thought to pass on to them a little of what I know." In *Le cuisinier françois* he finds religious fast days (*jours maigres*) a convenient heading for a dozen vegetable recipes, such as fried artichokes, spinach tart, a ragoût of truffles, and this simple little asparagus in a sauce of crème fraîche. La Varenne seems to have used green asparagus, but white is good, too.

Asparagus in Cream and Herbs   *Serves 3 or 4*

2 pounds (900 g) asparagus

2 tablespoons (30 g) butter or lard

2 to 3 tablespoons chopped fresh parsley

2 green onions, sliced, or a bouquet garni of 4 or 5 parsley stems, 4 or 5 sprigs
   thyme, and 1 bay leaf

Salt and pepper

1 cup (250 ml) crème fraîche

Freshly grated nutmeg (optional)

Cut the green stalks of asparagus on the diagonal into 1-inch (2.5-cm) slices, discarding the tough ends. Melt the butter in a sauté pan or shallow saucepan. Add the asparagus, parsley, and green onions or bouquet garni and season with salt and pepper. Cover the pan and let the asparagus sweat over very low heat in its own juices, stirring occasionally, until it is almost tender when pierced with a knife, 8 to 10 minutes.

Add the crème fraîche and leave the asparagus to simmer very gently, uncovered, until just tender, about 5 minutes longer. Do not let too much of the crème fraîche evaporate or the asparagus will scorch. Discard the bouquet garni if using. If you like, sprinkle the asparagus with grated nutmeg. Taste and adjust the seasoning, and serve hot.

From Nicolas de Bonnefons, *Le jardinier françois* (Paris, 1651; recipe from 1666 edition): *A boisseau [about 12 quarts/liters] of the very best wheat flour is needed, of which you take a quarter to make the Starter, mixing a sponge with Beer Yeast and hot Water; you leave it to rise in a wooden bowl that has been warmed, & should be carefully covered in Winter; while it rises, you mix the remaining three-quarters of the flour with quite hot Water, though you must be able to hold your hand in it, & put in it a quartron [4 ounces or 110 g] of Salt, a pound of fresh Butter, & a Fresh cheese; two hours later you refresh the Levain with this second Dough as described in the recipe for Bread [below]; then put it again to rest in the bowl, & when risen, you mix it all, & knead it well, that is you work it on the Table, or in the bread Trough with the palm of your Hand, flattening it and then folding the sides to the center; if you have a Broyoire [club for pounding] use it after having worked the dough thoroughly, then you shape it on the Peel, that you will use for transferring it to the oven, & let it rise well; when ready, you glaze it, & put it in the oven, closing it tightly as for Bread.*

When it is done, remove it, and set it gently on a round wooden board, or on a wicker tray, so it cools without fear of splitting. Glaze is made simply with eggs beaten without Water; some cooks like to add a bit of liquid honey, but then it must be baked in a lower Oven.

To make the most delicate [bread] called Cousin [a term used for brioche in the Paris region], from a boisseau of flour, only half a quarter should be taken for the Starter, & the rest of the

Pain Benit & Brioches

Blessed Bread & Brioches

Dough should be mixed with three pounds [1.35 kg] of good Butter, two soft Cheeses, & half a quartron of eggs [the equivalent of 1 large egg], if the Dough is too stiff add good milk; let the dough rise twice, then continue as before.

If you want to work reliably, always try out what you want to do, that is to say, put a small piece in the oven, so if something is missing, you can rectify it before shaping the rest.

To Refresh the Levain [these directions come from Bonnefons's general remarks on bread making, page 6]: The following day, at daybreak, you add the rest of your flour [a dough in the case of pain benit] to the starter, and work the dough, kneading it thoroughly, keeping it quite firm; for the softer it is, the more bread you will have [i.e., it will rise better]; but also when you make it lighter and less hard, the more of it they will eat.

SEVERAL SEVENTEENTH-CENTURY FRENCH COOKBOOKS, including *Le pastissier françois* of 1653, have recipes for *pain benit*. The term originated with the blessed bread that was distributed to all who attended Sunday religious services. By midcentury, *pain benit* retained its religious association and was still served on Sundays, but it had become deliciously enriched with butter, sometimes with eggs, and often with fresh cheese, as suggested here by Nicolas Bonnefons. The term survives in the expression *C'est pain bénit*, meaning "to get what is deserved."

The specialist trade of the baker is clear in this recipe by the number of words that have no everyday equivalent. *Détremper* means literally "to soak," and here refers to mixing flour with water, often also with yeast, to make a soft dough. The wheat flour used for bread varied enormously from place to place and season to season, and the finest was by no means inferior to ours. The *levure de bière* mentioned in early bread recipes comes from partially fermented beer. Low alcohol, or "small," beer was often brewed at home, and the surface foam would be skimmed for yeast to make bread. By the early seventeenth century, brewer's yeast, *Saccharomyces cerevisiae*, literally "brewer's sugar fungus," had been introduced into Parisian bakeries. Great debate ensued about whether it was fit for human consumption, however, so it was slow to be adopted. Because brewer's yeast is more reliable than airborne yeasts, it helps to solve the difficulties of working with doughs that are heavy with eggs and fat. To add similar flavor here, I've dissolved dry yeast in light ale instead of water.

Levain is the starter, the soft, yeast-laden sponge that is mixed into the rest of the dough to leaven it. It can also be a portion of dough retained from a previous batch of bread that has been left to rise, so the yeast multiplies before the *levain* is mixed with the rest of the flour. The use of a sponge leads to the even texture that is noticeable in this recipe, while the cheese contributes moisture and a soft crust. By this date, salt is a routine ingredient in bread, added both for flavor and as a preservative. In earlier times, when salt was expensive, plain bread often went unsalted. Fresh cheese is only a day or two old and can vary in style from region to region. Here, the phrase *un formage mol* most likely means fresh cheese that is just firm enough to hold a shape after draining. French-style *faisselle* or *fromage blanc* that has been drained in cheesecloth or drained plain yogurt is an option here. As no weight is given, I've added the same amount as butter.

For a household, bread would have been made in the largest batch that a single person could conveniently knead. The Bonnefons recipe makes eight 2½-pound (1.15-kg) loaves, a quantity that I have reduced to a single impressive round loaf. As always, the quality of bread depends on the flour used, and I strongly recommend you seek out stone-ground flour; most artisanal mills offer a white version. We are so used to fresh bread that Bonnefons's thrifty advice on developing a dry dough so the baked loaf is more filling sounds like a joke. Not so. As a child I was forbidden delicious fresh pastries on the day of baking because I would eat too much.

Luxury Bread   *Makes one 2½-pound (1.15-kg) round loaf*

⅔ cup (150 ml) light ale

2 teaspoons (5 g) active dry yeast

6 cups (780 g) unbleached stone-ground white flour, more for kneading

¼ cup (60 g) fromage blanc or plain whole-milk yogurt

1½ cups (375 ml) tepid water, more if needed

1 tablespoon (15 g) salt

4 tablespoons (60 g) butter, at room temperature, more for the bowl

1 egg lightly beaten with ½ teaspoon salt, for glaze

Cheesecloth

To make the starter: Warm the ale in a small pan to about body temperature. Sprinkle the yeast on top and leave for 5 minutes. Stir and set aside until the yeast froths, 5 to 10 minutes more. Sift about one-fourth of the flour into a warmed bowl and make a well in the center. Pour in the yeast mixture and stir with your hand, gradually drawing in the flour to make a soft, slightly sticky dough. Cover the bowl and leave it in a warm place until well risen and almost bubbling, 1 to 2 hours. Meanwhile, line a strainer with cheesecloth, add the fromage blanc, and leave to drain over a bowl.

To mix the dough: Sift the remaining flour onto a work surface, and sweep a wide well in the center with the back of your hand. Add the water, salt, butter, and drained fromage blanc to the well, and work with the fingertips of one hand to mix. Using a pastry scraper, gradually draw in the flour, mixing with your hand to form a dough. If the dough is sticky, add a little more flour.

To combine and knead the dough and let it rise: Flatten the dough on the work surface and tip the starter onto it. Pull the edges of dough on top to cover the starter, then knead to combine the two. Continue kneading, pushing away with your hand, then pulling toward you to peel the dough from the work surface. Give the dough a quarter turn and continue working in this way until the dough is very smooth and elastic, 5 to 8 minutes. The dough can also be mixed and kneaded with an electric mixer fitted with the dough hook. Transfer the dough to a buttered bowl, then flip the dough over so the top is buttered. Cover the bowl with plastic wrap and leave to rise in a warm place until doubled in bulk, 1 to 2 hours.

To shape the loaf: When the dough has risen, knead it lightly on a floured work surface to knock out the air. Shape it into a loose ball, then fold the sides over to the center, turning to make a tight round ball. Flip the ball onto a baking sheet so that the smoothly rounded, unseamed side is upward. Let the loaf rise uncovered in a warm place until well risen, 45 minutes to 1 hour. Meanwhile, heat the oven to 400°F (200°C).

To bake the bread: Brush the loaf with the egg glaze, and slash the top in a pound sign so the dough rises evenly. Bake until the loaf is browned and sounds hollow when tapped on the bottom, 45 to 55 minutes. Transfer to a rack to cool.

The bread is best eaten the day of baking, but it keeps surprisingly well for up to 3 days when tightly wrapped in plastic wrap and stored at room temperature.

Brioche   *Makes one 3-pound (1.35-kg) round loaf*

When the butter and fresh cheese in *pain benit* are pushed to the limit, Bonnefons calls his loaf "brioche," a cakelike bread quite similar to the rich butter-and-egg-laden brioche of today.

> ⅔ cup (150 ml) light ale
>
> 2 teaspoons (5 g) active dry yeast
>
> 6 cups (780 g) unbleached stone-ground white flour, more for kneading
>
> ¾ cup (170 g) fromage blanc or plain whole-milk yogurt
>
> ¾ cup (175 ml) milk, heated to tepid, more if needed
>
> 1 tablespoon (15 g) salt
>
> ¾ cup (170 g) butter, at room temperature
>
> 2 eggs
>
> 1 egg lightly beaten with ½ teaspoon salt, for glaze

Make the starter and drain the fromage blanc or yogurt as directed in Luxury Bread, above. Combine the ingredients for the dough using the same method, adding the milk instead of the water, and the eggs with the drained fromage blanc and butter.

Continuing as directed, combine the starter and dough, knead the dough, and leave it to rise in a warm place until doubled in bulk, 1 to 2 hours. Knead the dough lightly in the bowl to knock out the air, then cover and leave to rise a second time until doubled, about 1 hour.

Shape, glaze, and bake the loaf as directed, allowing 50 to 60 minutes for baking, then cool completely before serving. Brioche keeps even better than Luxury Bread, up to 5 days, and is also delicious toasted.

From Robert May, *The Accomplisht Cook* (London, 1660): *Fill your Sillabub pot half full with sider, and good store of sugar, and a little nutmeg, stir it well together, and put in as much cream by two or three spoonfuls at a time, as hard as you can, as though you milkt it in; then stir it together very softly once about, and let it stand two hours before you eat it, for the standing makes it curd.*

An Excellent
Syllabub

WHEN WINE OR HARD CIDER is stirred into cream or unpasteurized milk, the alcohol and acid thicken it to syllabub, a delicious froth similar in consistency to eggnog. Fresh syllabub can be drunk from the glass, or if left to stand, it separates into a feisty liquid topped by creamy mousse. Specially made syllabub glasses designed specifically for this confection have a deep bowl to display the double layers, with a characteristic short stem and one or two loop handles, a shape that dates back to the time of this recipe.

Syllabub was enormously popular in the seventeenth century, no doubt because it could be made by any household with access to a cow. Early recipes are renowned for requiring milk to be streamed straight from the beast into the bowl of wine. I had always dismissed this as a flight of fancy until I saw the recipe being field-tested in colonial Williamsburg thanks to a cow called Hannah. It turns out that the warmth and force of the jet of milk helps the syllabub to froth and thicken. For the same result in the kitchen, the milk or cream must be warmed to body temperature, then poured from a height into the wine. In this archetypal recipe, Robert May uses only three ingredients, cream, sugar, and apple cider. For the syllabub to thicken, the cream must be as rich as possible, and the cider must be alcoholic, known as hard cider (not just apple juice). I prefer one with a tart finish.

Apple Cider Syllabub   *Serves 8*

2 cups (500 ml) demi-sec hard cider

½ cup (100 g) sugar, more to taste

2 cups (500 ml) heavy cream

8 syllabub glasses or stemmed wineglasses

In a bowl, whisk together the cider and sugar until the sugar dissolves. Warm the cream to room temperature, testing it with your finger, then transfer it to a pitcher. Gradually whisk the warm cream into the cider, a few spoonfuls at a time, pouring it from a height of at least 6 inches (15 cm). When all the cream has been added, continue whisking for 1 minute. (You can also use an electric mixer fitted with the whisk attachment.) Taste and adjust the sugar.

Spoon the mixture into the glasses, cover loosely, and leave in a cool place. It will soon start to separate into a layer of cider punch topped with creamy mousse, two treats in one. Syllabub can be kept for a day or two in the refrigerator and the flavor will mellow. Serve it cool, or chilled.

Another Hotchpot

From Sir Kenelm Digby, *The Closet Opened* (London, 1669; recipe from 1677 edition): *Take a pot of two gallons or more, and take a brisket rand of Beef; any piece of Mutton, and a piece of Veal; put this with sufficient water into the pot, and after it hath boiled, and been skimmed, put in a great Colander full of ordinary pot-herbs, a piece of Cabbage, all half cut; a good quantity of Onions whole, six Carrots cut and sliced, and two or three Pippins cut and quartered. Let this boil three hours, until it be almost a gelly, and stir it often, lest it burn.*

HOT POT, THE ENGLISH edition of the grandiose Spanish *olla podrida* and the French *ouille*, should not be mistaken for a random jumble of ingredients. Beef, mutton, and veal are commonly combined in such recipes, but Sir Kenelm Digby takes care to leave out pork, considered an outsider for simmering because of its fat. Note that he specifies mutton, as it is firmer and tastier than young lamb, which may disintegrate during long cooking. Veal, and above all a cut that includes bone, is valued for the rich gelatin it adds to a broth. A "rand" is a strip or long slice of meat or fish, and after boning is the shape of a beef brisket. Robust vegetables that hold up well to long simmering, such as onions and carrots, are a must. Herbs and spices may be added but play a secondary role. Digby makes no mention of salt, but I have added it to suit contemporary taste.

Hot pots, or *ollas podridas*, demand a giant pot, descendant of the medieval cauldron (a stockpot comes in handy). Key to them all is trimming ingredients to the right size to cook evenly, and then adding them in stages so they will all be done at the same time. The definition of "done" can vary. Digby relishes his meats tender enough to cut with a spoon, but his vegetables too are simmered for three hours, far beyond the firm texture we prefer. I have followed his lead, so the hot pot is served as a melting mélange of vegetables surrounding three large cuts of meat. "Half cut" cabbage I assume to mean in chunks, with thick slices of carrot and herbs in sprigs.

Pot herbs referred to roots and vegetables, not to plants like thyme or sage that add fragrance to a dish. They were defined by a contemporary herbalist, William Coles, as "those we boyle or eat raw, whether roots, fruits, or tender stalks, and leaves, as Turneps, Carrets, Radishes, Leeks, Onyons, Cives, Cucumber, Melons, Pompions, Lettice, Parsly, Sorrell, &c." Apples are an unusual addition to a hot pot, and here they fall apart to thicken the broth lightly, balancing and concentrating the flavor.

Hot pot can be served several ways. In the seventeenth century, the meats would almost certainly have been presented whole on top of the vegetables on a single large platter as a magnificent spread, with the broth in a separate bowl. Hot pot can also be served with the broth as an opening course, followed by a main course of sliced meats arranged with the vegetables. As a third alternative, broth, meat, and vegetables can be served together as a stew in individual bowls—simpler but also less eye-catching.

An English Hot Pot   *Serves 8 to 10*

2¼ pounds (1 kg) boneless beef brisket, rolled and tied

2¼ pounds (1 kg) boneless lamb shoulder, rolled and tied

2¼ pounds (1 kg) veal shank, cut into slices 2 inches (5 cm) thick

6 quarts (6 liters) water, more as needed

A colander (about 7 ounces or 200 g) of aromatic herb sprigs such as
   fresh parsley, thyme, oregano, sage, and lovage

½ medium head white cabbage (about 1½ pounds or 675 g)

6 to 8 medium onions (about 2¼ pounds or 1 kg total)

8 large carrots (about 2 pounds or 900 g total), peeled and cut into
   slices ¾ inch (2 cm) thick

2 or 3 dessert apples, peeled, quartered, and cored

2 tablespoons (30 g) salt, more to taste

Kitchen string

Put the beef brisket, lamb shoulder, and veal shank in a very large pot. Add water to cover and bring very slowly to a simmer, taking about 30 minutes. Poach, uncovered, at a very gentle simmer for 1 hour, skimming away any foam and adding water as needed to keep the meats covered.

Meanwhile, prepare the herbs and cabbage: Pull the herbs into small sprigs, discarding the stems. Cut the cabbage into 1-inch (2.5-cm) chunks, discarding the core. Add the herbs, cabbage, onions, carrots, and apples to the pot, stirring them into the meats and adding water if needed just to cover all the ingredients (though the apples will float). Add the salt and continue poaching until the meats are tender enough to cut with a spoon, 2½ to 3½ hours. Toward the end of cooking, stir and turn the meats so they remain moist. The veal and lamb may be done before the beef; if so, lift them out and set aside, adding the beef to the other meats when it is done.

When all the meats are done, ladle a bit of the broth over them to keep them moist and cover them loosely with aluminum foil. Boil the remaining liquid to reduce it by about half. This can take from 15 to 45 minutes, depending on how much water has been added. Return the meats to the pot to warm before serving. The hot pot can be prepared up to 2 days ahead and the flavor will mellow. Store the meats and vegetables in the broth in a covered container in the refrigerator.

To serve, slowly reheat the broth and meats on top of the stove, allowing about 30 minutes. To serve the hot pot in two courses, transfer the meats to a board and cover loosely with foil to keep warm. Spread the vegetables and herbs on a large platter, cover, and keep warm. Taste the broth for seasoning, adjusting if necessary. Snip the strings, then cut up the meats, discarding any excess fat or sinew. Pile them on the vegetables, and keep the platter warm while serving the broth as a first course. Alternatively, pull the meats and vegetables into chunks, stir them back into the broth, and serve in bowls as a stew.

To Make a Pasty of a Breast of Veal

▪▪▪▪ From Hannah Woolley, *The Queen-like Closet, or Rich Cabinet: Stored with All Manner of Rare Receipts* (London, 1670; recipe from 1681 edition): *Take half a Peck of fine Flower, and two pounds of Butter broken into little bits, one Egg, a little Salt, and as much cold Cream, or Milk, as will make it into a Paste; when you have framed your Pasty, lay in your Breast of Veal boned, and seasoned with a little Pepper and Salt, but first you must lay in Butter.*

When your Veal is laid in, then put in some large Mace, and a Limon sliced thin, Rind and all, then cover it well with Butter, close it and bake it, and when you serve it in, cut it up while it is very hot, put in some white Wine, Sugar, the yolks of Eggs, and Butter, being first heated over the fire together; this is very excellent meat.

To make good Paste

Take to a peck of fine flower, 3 pound of Butter, and three Eggs, and a little cold Cream, and work it well together, but do not break your butter too small, and it will be very fine crust, either to bake meat in, or fruit, or what else you please.

HANNAH WOOLLEY LED WHAT was to become a particularly English specialty: domestic cookery books written by women for middle-class households. Her practical recipes contrast strikingly with cookbooks of the same time written by men, which tend to call for multiple ingredients with complex instructions. Compared with Kenelm Digby's Another Hotchpot, for instance, not to mention La Varenne's Pain Benit & Brioches, this breast of veal in pastry is child's play. When I first read the recipe I almost dismissed it, convinced that the butter-and-cream dough encasing an equally fatty boned breast of veal would end in a soggy mess. Mrs. Woolley seasons only with mace and sliced lemon, ignoring aromatics such as onion or herbs. Yet the finished pasty is a triumph, a visual delight that can be served hot or cold, with varied accompaniments or a simple salad.

Long, slow cooking is needed for veal breast to be tender, a process that turns out to be perfectly possible in a pastry crust, provided it is covered to avoid scorching. Mrs. Woolley's dough is mixed with cream instead of water, giving it a pliable texture that is ideal for wrapping the long, flat veal breast. I am assuming she favors the English (and American) method of mixing in a bowl, rather than the continental practice of working on a flat table. She seems to have been generous in her allowance of dough, and here I've reduced the quantities. "Large mace" is blade mace, the papery skin wrapped around a whole nutmeg. It is much used in England and is available online or from specialty-spice stores. In its absence, ground mace can be substituted. You may want to add a couple of teaspoons of salt to the dough, though none is listed in the original recipe.

Interestingly, Mrs. Woolley measures flour by volume, a method we now associate with America. A peck is two gallons, a volume measure that was commonly used for dry ingredients until the early twentieth century. The gallon varied from place to place (the U.K. gallon is still a fifth larger than the U.S. gallon), and in Mrs. Woolley's time the London peck measure of flour probably weighed about 4½ pounds (2 kg).

You might ask your butcher to bone the veal breast, though it is not hard to do at home, using a boning knife with a sharp point to outline and cut away the rib bones. Mrs. Woolley's sauce thickens to resemble lemon curd without the lemon. A spoonful or two per person adds delicious richness to the meat, though to our taste it is oddly sweet for a savory meat dish.

Breast of Veal in Pastry *Serves 8 to 10*

1 whole breast of veal, about 8 pounds (3.6 kg) with the bones

3 to 4 tablespoons (45 to 60 g) butter, melted, more for the pan

Salt and pepper

1 tablespoon (7 g) mace blades, finely chopped, or 2 teaspoons ground mace

1 lemon

PASTRY DOUGH

8 cups (1 kg) flour, more for rolling

2 teaspoons salt (optional)

2 cups (450 g) butter, cut into pieces

1 egg

1½ cups (375 ml) light cream, more if needed

1 egg lightly beaten with ½ teaspoon salt, for glaze

SAUCE

6 tablespoons (90 g) butter

½ cup (125 ml) medium-dry white wine

3 tablespoons (45 g) sugar

6 egg yolks

To make the pastry dough: Sift together the flour and the salt, if using, into a large bowl. Add the pieces of butter and cut them into the flour using a table knife in each hand. When cut as small as possible, rub the butter into the flour with your fingertips to form coarse crumbs, taking care not to overwork it. Make a well in the center. In a small bowl, whisk together the egg and cream until mixed, pour into the well, and stir with a fork to form large, moist crumbs. If they seem dry, add a bit more cream. Press the dough together lightly with your hand. It should be soft but not sticky. Wrap and chill it for at least 30 minutes.

To trim the meat: Strip the skin and all but a very thin layer of fat from the veal breast. With a short, pointed knife, strip out and discard the rib bones. Trim off the cartilage and excess fat to leave a long, tidy strip of meat.

To wrap the veal in pastry dough: Butter a rimmed baking sheet. Divide the dough in half. On a lightly floured work surface, roll out half of the dough into a rectangle 2 inches (5 cm) longer and wider than the veal. Transfer the dough to the prepared baking sheet. Brush the surface of the dough with half of the melted butter, leaving a 1-inch (2.5-cm) border uncovered around the edge (the butter moistens the veal during cooking). Sprinkle the rib side of the veal generously with salt and pepper and lay it, seasoned side down, on the dough. Brush the top with the remaining butter and season it also. Sprinkle with the mace. Cut the unpeeled lemon in the thinnest possible slices, discarding the ends and any seeds. Arrange the lemon slices on the veal.

Brush the edges of the dough with water. Roll out the remaining dough into a rectangle the same size as the first. Wrap the dough around the rolling pin and unwrap it on top of the veal. Press the borders of dough together with your fingers to seal them, trimming and reserving the excess dough. Flute the edge of the pastry with your fingers, and brush the entire surface with the egg glaze. Make 2 or 3 airholes in the dough with the point of a knife, and insert chimneys of aluminum foil so they remain open. Roll out the dough trimmings and cut out leaves, stars, or rounds to decorate the dough and disguise the airholes. Brush the decorations with the glaze. Chill the shaped pastry until the dough is very firm, at least 30 minutes. Meanwhile, heat the oven to 400°F (200°C).

To bake the pastry: Bake the shaped pastry until brown, about 30 minutes. Discard the foil chimneys and wrap the pastry quite tightly in aluminum foil. Reduce the heat to 350°F (180°C), and continue baking until the veal feels tender when poked through an airhole with a two-pronged fork, 1¼ to 1¾ hours. Rotate the baking sheet from back to front once or twice during baking to ensure even cooking. When done, a skewer inserted in the center of the meat should be very hot to the touch when withdrawn after 30 seconds, or an instant-read thermometer inserted in the thickest part should read 200°F (95°C). Note that the meat must be very thoroughly cooked to be tender. When done, transfer the pastry to a board or platter, cover, and keep warm.

To make the sauce: Melt the butter in a small pan. Let it cool, then whisk in the wine, sugar, and egg yolks. Whisk the sauce over very low heat until lightly thickened, 2 to 3 minutes. Do not let it get too hot or overcook it or it will curdle.

Pour the sauce into a warmed bowl. Carve the veal pastry at the dining table, spooning a little sauce over each slice.

Per Fare Altr' Acqua di Fravole

To Make Another Strawberry Water

From Antonio Latini, *Lo scalco alla moderna* (vol. 1, Naples, 1692): *Take really ripe Strawberries picked a day or so ago; put the Strawberries in water, then crush them after washing your hands well; or use a Spoon for this, as you wish, and when the Water has turned a good color, add to it a little pomegranate juice; color it with Cheese, or with Cream, leave it for a little while, to develop the flavor of Strawberries; add enough Sugar to it, chill it, and serve it as you like.*

SORBETS FIRST CAME TO EUROPE from Turkey. In his *Travels to the Middle East*, published in 1555, the French naturalist Pierre Belon remarked, "the ambassadors of France, Spain, Venice, Ragusa, Florence, Transylvania, and Hungary, who are more particular about their drinking than the Turks, do not wish to mix snow in their wine, so they immerse the wine in water chilled by snow, and in this way they enjoy cold drinks all summer without putting snow or ice in their stomachs" (as quoted by Elizabeth David in *Harvest of the Cold Months*).

A hundred years later, the creation of iced drinks and desserts had spread throughout the continent and was a high art at the court of Naples, where Antonio Latini was working. Latini talks of *acque* (waters) and *sorbette* (chilled drinks rather than today's crystalline creations) that are flavored with cinnamon and sour cherries, as well as our favorite lemon and chocolate. *Lo scalco alla moderna* (The Modern Steward, 1692) was the first book to feature recipes for another innovation, Neapolitan ices, called by London publisher Joseph Addison one of the "natural curiosities of Naples."

In those days, sorbets might contain little or no sugar, though I've added some here to satisfy contemporary tastes. Technically speaking, mascarpone or heavy cream transforms a sorbet to an ice cream, so I've mixed in just a few spoonfuls to lighten and enrich the finished ice without obscuring the taste of the strawberries. Following Latini's method of crushing rather than liquidizing the fruit gives the ice a pleasantly rough feel on the tongue. For the appropriate, soft texture, serve the ice within a couple of hours, as it hardens on standing.

Strawberry Ice *Makes 1 quart (1 liter) ice to serve 6 to 8*

1 pound (2 pints or 450 g) strawberries, hulled

1 cup (250 ml) water

½ cup (125 ml) pomegranate juice, more to taste

½ cup (125 ml) mascarpone cheese or heavy cream

¾ cup (150 g) sugar, more to taste

Ice-cream maker

In a large bowl, combine the strawberries and water and crush the berries with a fork or your fingers, pulling them apart to form a coarse purée. Stir in the pomegranate juice. In a small bowl, whisk the mascarpone with 2 to 3 tablespoons of the purée until smooth, then stir this mixture into the remaining purée with the sugar. Cover and chill for at least 1 hour until very cold.

Taste and adjust the flavor with pomegranate juice and sugar. Freeze the purée in the ice-cream maker until firm. For the best texture, serve the ice within an hour. If freezing longer, transfer the ice to the refrigerator for an hour to soften before serving.

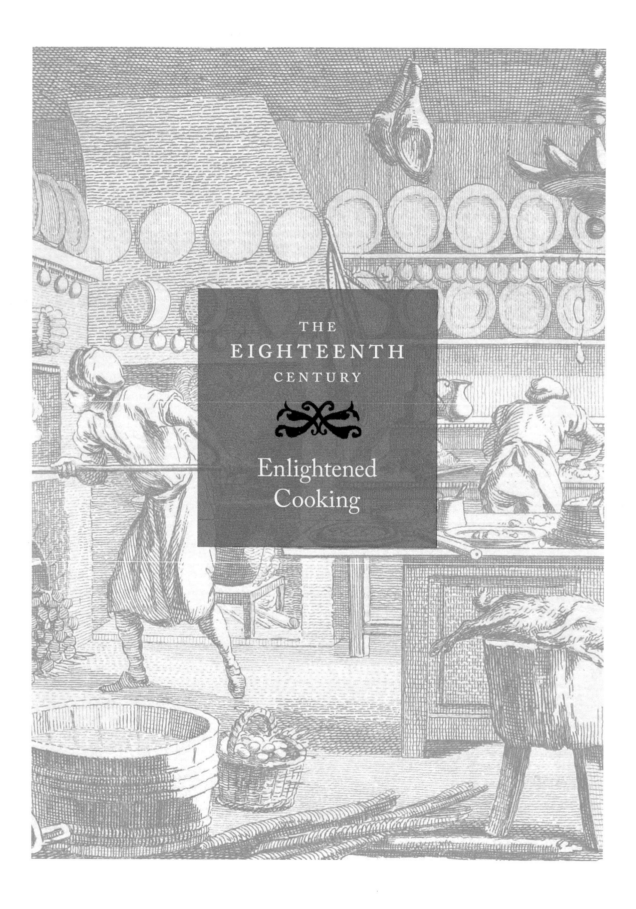

THE
EIGHTEENTH
CENTURY

Enlightened
Cooking

TWO STRONG FORCES were at work in eighteenth-century European society, one intellectual and centered on the philosophical ideas of the Enlightenment, the other material and propelled by the eagerness of consumers. Enlightenment thought, led by the French *philosophes* Voltaire, Montesquieu, and Diderot, sought a new order based on reason and science. This view played out in a variety of ways throughout Europe, ultimately undermining previously entrenched traditions, engendering democratic revolutions in France and America, and filtering into every realm of scientific, social, and political thought, including ideas about food and cooking. At the same time that the Industrial Revolution gained momentum, publishers were able to produce books in greater quantities and at lower prices, making cookbooks more accessible to the growing market of literate customers.

In keeping with Enlightenment notions, most food writers in the early part of the century believed that cooking was a science to be approached systematically, according to a codified set of rules, preferably under the guidance of someone "professed," who had already been trained by a mentor. In practical terms, the professed cook was usually a man, French or French trained and likely associated with the great house of a wealthy aristocrat. Professed cooking reached a high point with François Massialot, whose works bridge the seventeenth and eighteenth centuries. His cookbooks invaded British kitchens almost as soon as they were published in France.

Indeed, France and England (now Great Britain, united with Scotland in 1706) dominated the culinary scene during this period, at first sharing influences but then taking increasingly divergent paths as the century wore on. At the start of the century, English cooks, many with French training or connections, were enamored of French cuisine—a holdover from the restoration of King Charles II in 1661, which had inspired a taste for all things French. As late as 1753, the Duke of Newcastle waxed eloquent on his former French cook's "little hors d'oeuvre or light entrées . . . plain simple dishes that he used to make me, and which are so much in fashion here—for instance, tendons of veal, fillets of young rabbit, pigs' and calves' ears, and other little dishes of that sort."[1] However, with England and France at war off and on for nearly half the century,

OPPOSITE Detail from Denis Diderot and Jean Le Rond d'Alembert, *Encyclopédie, ou dictionnaire raisonné des sciences, des arts et des métiers*, 1751. Full image on page 167.

193

this enthusiasm gradually turned to antipathy. Cooks, along with their readers, became caught in the cross fire, and their nationalistic fervor pervaded food and books about cooking.[2] British cooks and diners began labeling any complicated cooking as "French" and therefore unpatriotic. This war of words over cuisine and identity spilled out of cookbooks and into mainstream publications, satirical prints, and even drinking songs.

In England, the business of "housewifery" became a major focus for both male and female cookbook authors. The target audience for such books was the country's more affluent households. The running of a sizable household, and especially the daily cooking (which included everything from pickling and preserving to gathering fruits and vegetables, preparing poultry, and raising rabbits), was hard physical work. Servants, therefore, were considered not luxuries but integral players in the operation of the well-run household. Many of the recipes in eighteenth-century cookbooks would have been difficult, if not impossible, without help as well as equipment.[3]

Along with this focus came a new market in England for books about cooking: women. Starting with a few notable pioneers, from midcentury onward almost all notable cookbooks in England were written *by* women, *for* women, a genre that did not develop in France until the following century. After a tentative beginning, British publishers were quick to recognize the importance of women as both authors and readers, so that their ideas came to lead culinary writing. Women also took the lead in the new American market, first in reprints of books originally published in England and finally, at the end of the eighteenth century, with the appearance of the first American cookbook.

Meanwhile, in France, the influential *Encyclopédie, ou dictionnaire raisonné des sciences, des arts et des métiers* (Encyclopedia, or Definitive Dictionary of the Sciences, Arts and Trades, 1751–1780) by Denis Diderot and Jean le Rond d'Alembert inspired French cooks to adapt its practical, scientific approach to their métier. They could also turn to *Dictionnaire des alimens* (Dictionary of Ingredients, 1750), signed cryptically M. C. D., for advice on ordering their kitchens with the help of a convenient alphabetical listing of foods and instructions for cooking them. The culinary scene, however, was dominated by the towering figure of François Menon, who was the first cookbook author to use the term *chef de cuisine* to describe his position as head of the kitchen. His magisterial body of work—encompassing as many as ten titles, several in multiple volumes—exemplifies the influence of Enlightenment thinking within the household.

Menon was refining the building blocks of French haute cuisine, shaping today's familiar divisions that were a carryover from Massialot's still-elaborate style. Around this time, a countermovement against refinement itself was taking place both inside and outside of France. It was linked to the *cuisine bourgeoise* of towns (*La cuisinière bourgeoise* was another Menon title) and to the countryside, later to be known as provincial or regional cooking.

England: From Ragoûts to the Art of Housewifery

Throughout the eighteenth century, English cookbook writers kept an eye on their French counterparts, whether seeking to emulate them or rebelling against them. Massialot's *Le cuisinier roial et bourgeois* (The Royal and Bourgeois Cook, 1691) appeared in English as *The Court and Country Cook* in 1702, and his influence is clear in a handful of English cookbooks, three published in the first third of the century and one closing out the era. All were by men who claimed to present cooking in the logical, structured manner of the Enlightenment, and to a large extent, they succeeded in their task. To today's eye, their books are easy to follow, presented in familiar alphabetical or subject-driven formats and sometimes even including lists of their contents and indexes to show the way.

An early convert to the new French style was Henry Howard, former cook to the Duke of Ormond, head of one of Ireland's leading Protestant families, and author of *England's Newest Way in All Sorts of Cookery, Pastry, and All Pickles That Are Fit to Be Used* (1703). At first glance, the title reflects Howard's reassuringly English repertoire of puddings, pickles, potted meats, and fish, with a generous portion of syllabubs, possets, and creams and all kinds of cakes, preserves, and candies. Yet a closer look into its savory dishes reveals that his flavorings are French: mushrooms, chives, shallots, sweet herbs, truffles, bay leaves, lemon juice, and cream, together with the favorites of both cuisines: oysters, capers, and anchovies. He instructs that his fricassées and

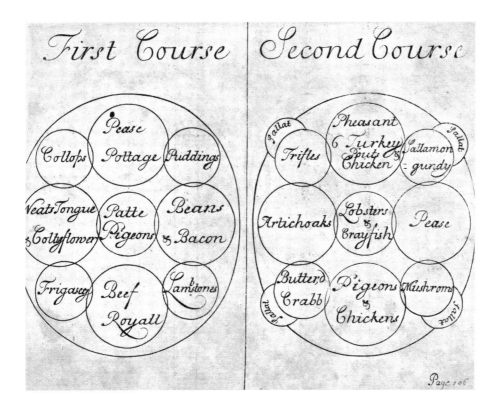

Simple English taste prevails in this dinner menu from *England's Newest Way in All Sorts of Cookery, Pastry, and All Pickles That Are Fit to Be Used* by Henry Howard. Both first and second courses mix fish with game, meats, and poultry, showing that under the Protestant monarchy, the rules of feasting and fasting were no longer observed.

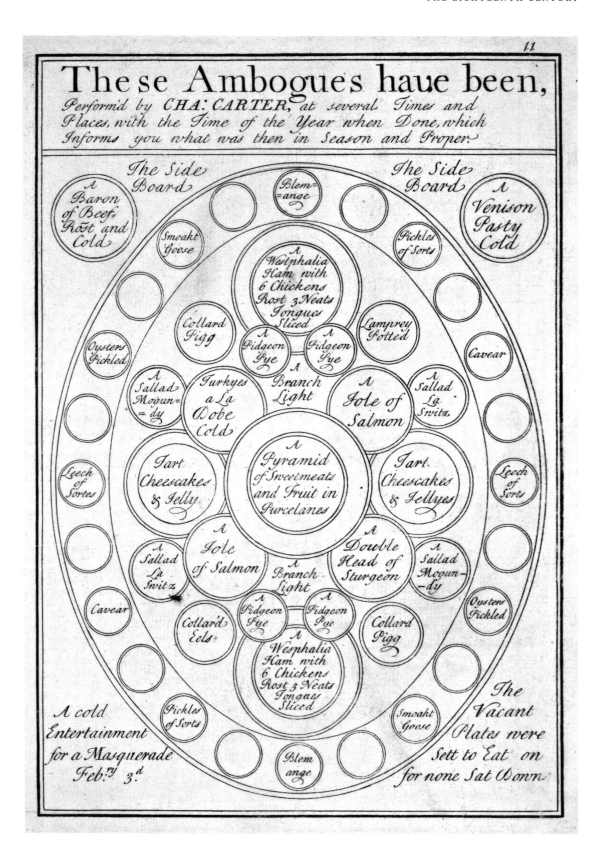

ragoûts be highly flavored, a very French admonition. Howard's book was popular, running to five editions, and it is easy to see why. His deft combination of the familiar with the surprisingly fresh was ideal for the table of a well-to-do household that wanted to be stylish without identifying with foreign ways.

Another fan of French cooking was Patrick Lamb. His fifty-year career in the English royal kitchens spanned the reigns of Charles II (who had spent nine years at foreign courts during his exile from England) in the seventeenth century and Queen Anne in the eighteenth. Echoing Massialot, Lamb reorganized the second edition of his *Royal Cookery or, The Compleat Court-Cook* (1716, first edition 1710) alphabetically and also copied recipes wholesale. Lamb brought a touch of French snobbery to traditional English recipes for an increasingly prosperous group of wealthy merchants, urban professionals, and rural gentry. His recipes show a preference for French-style stewed and braised dishes over the boiled staples of seventeenth-century England. He declares his intent to present the "Grandeur of the English Court and Nation," but he in fact draws heavily on the French models preferred by King Charles. Lamb's roasted meats served with "ragoos" are typically French, and his book devotes an entire section to "cullis" (coulis). His recipes add French seasonings and use a butter and flour *liaison* for sauces, all characteristic of French cuisine at the turn of the previous century. They also feature Massialot's favorite flavoring of mixed herbs with two combinations, one savory, one sweet.

Like the work of Henry Howard and Patrick Lamb, Charles Carter's first book, *The Complete Practical Cook: or, a New System of the Whole Art and Mystery of Cookery* (1730), is resplendent with illustrations of the elaborate menus that were now the style. Rather than listing dishes, Carter provides diagrams showing complex arrangements of the fifty or more dishes he specifies for a course. Placement reflected the lofty or lower rank of diners as established on the seating plan. Two courses, each with a multitude of dishes, were the norm, though sometimes a meal would include as many as five courses of fewer dishes. Carter's recipes were the edible expression of rising Georgian prosperity, with its Adam décor, Chippendale furniture, and *Water Music* by Handel, composed for a royal concert on the river. To guide the cook further, Carter dates each menu "with the Time of Year when Done, which Informs you what was then in Season and Proper." His recipes feature such typically French dishes as bisques,

---

OPPOSITE Charles Carter embellished *The Complete Practical Cook: or, a New System of the Whole Art and Mystery of Cookery*, 1730, with page after page of dishes arranged in the elaborate style called *à la française*, in which the food itself formed the table decoration at each course. "A cold Entertainment for a Masquerade Feb. 3d" illustrates the orchestration of several "removes" during which the table would be completely cleared and reset with different dishes. Carter boasts he has performed this "ambogue" (from the French *ambigu,* on the diagonal) at different times of year, taking advantage of the seasons. His book was an expensive production in large octavo format with sixty "curiously-engraved [i.e. intricate] copper plates," each of which cost £10 to £20, the equivalent today of $1,400 to $2,800.

SETTING THE TABLE

Until the late sixteenth century, all but the most aristocratic European dining tables remained remarkably bare. The medieval trencher of bread gradually was replaced by a simple round plate or shallow bowl of pewter or pottery, with silver for the wealthy. Drinking goblets continued to be shared, commonly made of pottery or wood; only the very rich had their own, made of precious metals. Goblets were stored on a side table, to be passed by servers, as were flasks of drinks, including water. The few platters and serving vessels were displayed on a tiered side table (later called a *credenza* in Italy, a buffet in France). Diners ate with their fingers, aided by a knife and spoon that were usually personal possessions they had brought to the feast.

The first big change was the addition of the fork, a controversial item that even had religious connotations, with its two prongs seen as a symbol of the devil. "God preserve me from forks," Martin Luther purportedly exclaimed in 1518.[1] Eating forks had existed for centuries but only became popular among the Italian upper classes in the late fifteenth century. Forks traveled north from Rome into France, but they still did not spread rapidly. Catherine de' Medici reportedly owned a crystal-handled fork, but nearly a century later, King Louis XIV, a trendsetter and renowned gourmand, was still eating with his hands. Queen Elizabeth I owned a set of forks but preferred to use her fingers, finding the spearing action of a fork uncouth.

Toward the end of the sixteenth century, forks became fashionable with the trendsetting nobility for sweetmeats, luxurious whole preserved fruits that "featured in a special *banquette* course that followed the main meal. A small, two-pronged fork proved highly useful for eating these sticky treats."[2] Two-pronged forks, which echoed the shape of the traditional large kitchen and carving forks, soon developed a third prong to aid in carrying food to the mouth (it was particularly handy for avoiding the huge ruffs of Elizabethan times).

The sparseness of table settings determined what kind of food could be served. Until the spread of forks in the mid-seventeenth century, sauces had to be thick enough not to spill onto clothing. Whole roast meats and fish were presented on a platter and then dismembered by the professional carver so that guests could nibble on elegant bite-sized morsels. (Just in case, each diner tied a generous napkin around the chin or tucked it into the collar.) Given the lack of table cutlery, guests usually brought their own; boxed individual sets were popular. Louis XIV was reportedly the first host to provide guests with a complete table setting, and Charles I of England had silver sets of knife, spoon, and fork made so that his children could practice using them. By the late seventeenth century, most hosts provided flatware for their guests, though the custom of carrying one's own continued.

Glasses were conspicuously absent from the tables of the seventeenth and even the eighteenth centuries. Instead of reaching for an individual wineglass at his seat, a diner would summon a footman when he wished to drink.[3] One sixteenth-century author attributed the virtue of moderation to this practice among the nobility, noting that it discouraged "idle tippling."[4] Indeed, drinking glasses did not become a fixture of formal table settings until the mid-1800s, reinforced a century later by the advent of *service à la russe*, when they took their place among the proliferation of flatware and dishes necessary to supply the diner through a succession of courses.

The spread of the table fork coincided almost exactly with the appearance of a separate room for dining, the *salle à manger* mentioned in a 1647 French architectural house plan.[5] Until then, great feasts had taken place in special banqueting halls (still to be seen in Oxford and Cambridge colleges) that also served as meeting halls and living quarters. In wealthy establishments, people took their everyday meals in personal apartments or in the living room or kitchen of more modest households. With the introduction of a special room for dining, households could store tableware there from one meal to the next.

Now the way was opened for the *service,* a matched set of silver serving dishes placed along the center of the table. The pioneer piece was a *pot à ouille,* an oval tureen for displaying the fashionable *potages.* Soon "there was a steady progression towards an ever greater unity of effect through the use of matching containers for various dishes."[6] The era of *service à la française,* marked by lavish spreads of dishes, had begun. France was particularly famous for its silversmiths, who exported silver services to the courts of Russia, Austria, Spain, and Portugal.

With the new serving dishes, the landscape of the table changed. A distinctive style emerged *en pyramide,* which lasted from the early seventeenth century until well into the eighteenth. France buzzed with stories about the court festivals at the Palace of Versailles, and word traveled abroad as well. In 1671, Cosimo III de' Medici had been so curious about new French dining fashions that he sent one of his Paris agents to observe a royal feast and report back to him in Florence.

This seven-tiered buffet from Carême's *Le maître d'hôtel français* (1823 edition) includes whole fish and birds in aspic, sweet and savory jellies, towering savory molds crowned with decorative skewers, and two of the *pièces montées* in pastillage, at least three feet high, for which Carême was so famous. The buffet surely was never assembled, for it would have collapsed under its own weight. A fish in aspic (detail, next page) illustrates Carême's perfectionism.

Cosimo had heard about the "ingenious" symmetry of the French table and the courses, and his high-society spy did not disappoint, describing in detail the intricate horizontal pattern of different-sized porcelain platters and crystal dishes and—something new—a vertical aesthetic supplied by square, tiered pyramids and "nine candelabras having nine candles each" placed strategically down the length of the table.[7]

This fashion for pyramids sometimes went over the top. The chatty Madame de Sévigné quipped that at Versailles, "doorways need to be made taller to accommodate the pyramids of fruit. Our predecessors could not have foreseen these sorts of displays."[8]

L'art de bien traiter (The Art of Good Catering, 1674) was the first cookbook to describe in detail how the amazing new feats of *service à la française* should be stage-managed by the domestic officers in grand households, using the new table utensils. The book relies on the culinary methods and techniques familiar from La Varenne and Pierre de Lune, but its author, known only by the initials L. S. R., takes the subject a great leap forward with his intricately choreographed (in words) multicourse feasts. In time, cookbooks in both France and England began to include diagrams that maîtres d'hôtel could use to set the table and serve a succession of courses with requisite military precision.[9] The dozens, sometimes more than a hundred, serving dishes in the table plans suggested by Charles Carter (early 1730s) and other authors indicate that wealthy households had to muster huge amounts of tableware, whether owned, rented, or borrowed. Dining was at the heart of this consumer revolution, and with it, the new fashionable accoutrements of the table. ▸

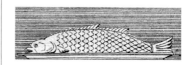

Cookbooks were not just instruction manuals in cooking; they also had a voyeuristic element, showing upwardly mobile householders how to keep up with the neighbors.

The style spread rapidly to less affluent households. By the mid-eighteenth century, the display of household silver had moved from the sideboard to the table, including, for those who could afford them, tureens, sauceboats, castors for sprinkling sugar, pepper pots, and the new *épergnes* (centerpieces). The salt cellar, in medieval times a main item of decoration as well as utility, had by now diminished in size and multiplied in number to be within reach of all guests. Less wealthy households added silver piece by piece as their means permitted: a normal accumulation was sometimes interrupted by the edicts of rulers who were short of funds. Both Louis XIV in the Nine Year's War and War of Spanish Succession and Charles I during the English Civil War ordered their subjects to melt down the family plate. In the interim, the dining table was stocked with blue and white delftware, colorful faience, and later with porcelain.

Here Germany led the way, with Augustus the Strong of Saxony ordering the first fully fledged European porcelain dinner service made by the Meissen factory. The table took on a colorful, festive air, with porcelain-handled knives and decorative figurines among the dishes. Floral designs on tableware reflected the increased interest in botany and gardens.[10] Until the 1740s, all porcelain had been imported from China, a rarity available largely in London, but by midcentury, beau-tiful tableware was manufactured and available all over Britain, including Wedgwood china, cut glass, and Worcester and Chelsea porcelain.[11] In another spur to innovation, new beverages like tea, coffee, and chocolate led to the creation of covered pots to keep the liquid hot, with teaspoons, coffee and chocolate spoons, caddy spoons, cream ladles, and sugar tongs for serving. The size of teaspoons increased as the cost of tea dropped over the decades.[12] The English vogue for punch and hot toddy led to punch bowls of silver or porcelain, with long-handled ladles and mugs to match.

A century later, Antonin Carême was both instructing the pastry cook and tempting his master with fantastic architectural drawings of Egyptian temples and Gothic follies, all to be constructed in edible pastillage and displayed on the table—descendants of the medieval entremets sideshows. "These pièces montées," wrote Carême, "should from now on be the ornament of the most opulent tables in Paris."[13] Almost equally out of this world were his savory charlottes and gâteaux, to be served on massive *socles* (bases) of classical design, which he suggested decorating with fresh flowers to perfume the table as well as add color. This early use of flowers on the dining table was to become a universal fashion.

From the beginning, in the New World the approach was different. Pilgrims saw forks as affectations, to be used only by the English elite. Still, the colonists had a desire to display possessions and manners to rival Europe's. George Washington (who wrote *Rules of Civility and Decent Behaviour* in 1746 at the age of fourteen) ordered a fashionable set of matching silver knives and forks from England in his twenties, but in general, early colonial tables were simpler than those in the Old World. Epergnes and pièces montées were not in the style of the new nation, but the first half of the nineteenth century saw an explosion of practical tableware that reflected American prosperity and ingenuity. A profusion of eating utensils appeared, with special servers for such diverse dishes as macaroni, ice cream, fried oysters, potato chips, lemon slices, and poached eggs. Diners reached for tiny asparagus tongs, scissors for cutting grapes from their stems, sandwich forks, mayonnaise ladles, and—a novelty in any country—butter knives.[14] ◆

1 Carolin C. Young, "The Sexual Politics of Cutlery," in *Feeding Desire: Design and the Tools of the Table 1500–2005*, exhibition catalog, Smithsonian Institution, ed. Sarah D. Coffin, Ellen Lupton, and Darra Goldstein (New York: Assouline Publishing, 2006), 111.

2 Darra Goldstein, "Implements of Eating," in ibid., 118.

3 Jancis Robinson, ed., *The Oxford Companion to Wine*, 2nd ed. (Oxford: Oxford University Press, 1999), 244.

4 Raphael Holinshed, quoted in Joan Thirsk, *Food in Early Modern England* (London: Hambledon Continuum, 2007), 310.

5 Roy C. Strong, *Feast: A History of Grand Eating* (Orlando, FL: Harcourt Publishing, 2002), 242.

6 Ibid., 237.

7 Correspondence from Paris to Florence, 1670–71, Archivo di stato, Florence, Mediceo des principato, 4815 (CAB). See also Barbara Ketcham Wheaton, *Savoring the Past* (Philadelphia: University of Pennsylvania Press, 1983), 138–43.

8 Madame de Sévigné, quoted in Alfred Franklin, *La vie privée d'autrefois: Les repas* (Paris: Librairie Plon, 1889), 77.

9 Wheaton, *Savoring the Past*, 138–39.

10 Sarah D. Coffin, "Historical Overview," in *Feeding Desire*, 65.

11 Lorna Weatherill, *Consumer Behavior and Material Culture in Britain 1660–1760* (London: Routledge, 1988), 86.

12 Goldstein, "Implements of Eating," 129.

13 Antonin Carême, *Le pâtissier pittoresque* (Paris: J. Renouard; Chez Mansut; Chez Tresse; Chez Maison, 1842), 7.

14 Goldstein, "Implements of Eating," 143–45.

terrines, ragoûts, and soups that resemble French potages. But Carter also includes a wide range of English recipes for pickles, potted meats and fish, creams, and puddings. Writing for "noblemen, gentlemen, and their professed cooks," he trumpets the nobility of his courtly cooking and himself as a "thorough-bred Artist," easily the equal of any cook from "a neighbouring Kingdom" (France).[4]

The Complete Practical Cook was grand indeed in presentation, with sixty plates showing dishes arranged for a wide variety of dinners and weddings. However, in *The Compleat City and Country Cook: or, Accomplish'd Housewife* (1732), published just two years later, Charles Carter looked toward the future. While not eschewing self-promotion, he demonstrated an excellent sense of the market. Home, however defined, had become central to the Englishman's yearning for health and prosperity, and *City and Country Cook* was a classic repackaging deal, offering a cut-price version of his earlier work for less affluent home cooks—in particular, the sensible, prosperous women of England. He sought

> to promote good Housewifery [not] Luxury . . . to instruct how to order those Provisions our Island is furnished with, in a wholesome, natural, decent, nay, and elegant Manner. . . . It gives not Directions so much for Foreign Dishes, but those we have at home; and indeed, we have no need of them, nor their Methods of Cookery, whose Scarcity of what we enjoy, obliges them . . . to supply by Art, what is deny'd them by Nature.[5]

To serve this new audience, Carter selected a different publisher, which issued the new book in the smaller octavo format, presented the original engraved plates on single pages rather than foldouts, and incorporated two hundred recipes "in physick and surgery" from the "Collection of a Noble Lady Deceased." The family-style recipes, such as Spanish Olio the Cheap Way and Spanish Tureen the Easy Way, are simpler versions of many of those in his first book.

The fourth male cookbook author to leave his mark on the "new" Britain of the Enlightenment, Richard Briggs, wrote for a readership whose views about cooking had changed dramatically since the first three authors had written their books.[6] By the mid-eighteenth century, a British backlash against French culture was in full swing. It had been brewing almost a hundred years, since the Stuart Restoration in 1660, when no English estate could be considered sufficiently grand until a Frenchman was in charge of the kitchen.[7] Now years of strife over Catholic succession to the British throne had aroused widespread religious animosity against the "popish" French, who were reputedly a threat to freedom-loving British Protestants. With typical British patriotic fervor, William Shipley founded the Anti-Gallican Association in 1745 "to promote British Manufactures, to extend the commerce of England, to discourage the introduction of French modes and oppose the importation of French commodities."[8]

Food, too, had become a matter of politics and religion. "Ragoût" was a catchall category that many thought unhealthy. It included all sauced dishes flavored to excite the appetite with pungent herbs and highly reduced essences such as *jus* and cullis added to provide depth of flavor. However, things French remained fashionable. The household of the Duke of Newcastle was notorious for its extensive—some said scandalous—retinue of French servants. Thomas Turner, a shopkeeper and friend of the duke's gardener, wrote in his diary, "What seems very surprising to me in the Duke of Newcastle is that he countenances so many Frenchmen, there being ten of his servants, cooks, etc., which was down here of that nation."[9]

By the time Richard Briggs wrote *The English Art of Cookery*, in 1788, most people in Britain, regardless of social or economic class, enjoyed eating the same things, which they defined as "traditional" cooking. Things French and "fancy" were out of style, particularly French cooking. In this return to honest British cooking, basic recipes were easy to adjust: porridges, hot pots, pies, creams, or cakes could be dressed up or down just by choosing more or less expensive ingredients, which was not true of the more elaborate, specific recipes of French cuisine. Hasty pudding in William Ellis's *Country Housewife's Family Companion* (1750) is simply milk and flour mixed and boiled; when the mixture is off the fire, the cook can add butter or sugar or both. For a "rich" baked pudding, one would use cream rather than milk and water and add eggs and other expensive extras like marrow, almonds, and dried fruits. Many of the variations in British cooking marked regional preferences as well as economic constraints. A Yorkshire lardy cake would not have been found down south in Devon.

In this environment, Briggs sensibly wrote his sturdy, cloth-bound book of more than five hundred pages for a more modest audience of "all Housekeepers," a group that likely also attracted the thousands of women then working as cooks in inns, coffeehouses, cookshops, and private houses throughout the nation. The book contains a definitive collection of English recipes from Beef Cheek to Mutton Chop, Calf's Feet Jelly, and A Fine Seed or Saffron Cake. He included sections on carving (roasts were always an English specialty), salting meats, pickling, brewing, and, unusually, baking English and French bread. The book opens with seasonal menus of two courses, each consisting of nearly twenty dishes neatly laid out on a rectangular table, the sort of repast Briggs must have presented in London's White Hart Tavern in Holborn and the Temple Coffee-house, where he had been head cook. His brisk, economical style gives the reassurance that nothing can go wrong while he—or his book—is in the kitchen.

OPPOSITE "Their Majesties Dinner" for August 18, 1791, in the time of King George III, seems surprisingly spartan. Fewer than a dozen meats and poultry are removed with a handful of vegetables, and the second course consists of a half dozen "made" dishes, including scholar's eggs and apricot tart. Depending on their rank, other members of the household ate less varied fare, with the "Queens Dressing Servants" at the bottom of the list restricted to roast beef, salads, cucumbers, and French beans.

Thursday August the 18 1791.

Their Majesties Dinner

Harris	Soupe de Navet
Gardiner	Chickens boild Parsly Sauce
Harris 10/4	Cutlets of Veal glacé
Gardiner	Croquets 2 Pullets
Harris 4	Collops of Sweetbreads
Roberts	Giblet Pye 3 Pair
Feed 10½	Fillet of Mutton roasted

Remove

Potatoes Oll
Pease 2 Ducks
Sallad 4
Cucumbers 2
French Beans ½

Harris 6	Crimped Scate boild Shrimp Sauce
	Cold roast Beef
	Grouse cold from Mr Dyson

Second Course

Feed	A Capon roasted
Gardiner	Lettuce stewed 24 1P
Harris	Scholars Eggs
Roberts	Apricot Tart
Harris	Herring Salade 1 Pullet
Gardiner	Mushrooms Stewed 2 Pullets
Feed 4	Pigeons roasted from Richm.d Gardens

Supper

2 Pullets minced
2 Lobsters
Tart
Artichokes 6 & 1P
2 Pheasant Polts cold

Pages Dinner

3 Soles boild Shrimp Sauce
2 Pullets boild
13½ Beef roasted — Potatoes 6 lb / Sallad 1 / Cucumbers 2 / French Beans ½ — 1P
Tarts of Sorts

Supper

2 Pullets roasted
2 Breasts of Lamb fricassee
Artichokes 8 1P

Princep's Serv.ts Dinner

8½ Beef roasted — Sallad 1 / Cucumbers 2 — 1P
Pudding

Supper

2 Ducks roasted
French Beans ½ & 1 Pick 1P

Offices

20 Beef roasted — Cabbages 12 / French Beans 1 / Sallad 1 / Cucumbers 2 — 1P
17 Mutton boild

Footmen

11 Beef roasted — Sallad 1 / Cucumbers 2 / French Beans ½ — 1P

Kings Grooms

10½ Beef roasted — Sallad 1 / Cucumbers 2 / French Beans 1 — 1P

Queens Grooms

7½ Beef roasted — Sallad 1 / Cucumbers 2 / French Beans ½ — 1P

Queens Dress. Serv.ts

6½ Beef roasted — Sallad 1 / Cucumbers 2 / French Beans ½ — 1P

Richard Briggs's clarity and comprehensive coverage also brought him success in recently independent America, where his book was printed in three cities. His was the only cookbook by a male author to achieve such distinction at that time.

WHILE MALE COOKBOOK AUTHORS dominated the scene in Britain early in the eighteenth century, women gradually took over as the century progressed. In many ways, the distinction between men and women authors is artificial. Women authors used the term "professed cookery" in their titles, male cooks often plagiarized from women's books, and vice versa. Readership was similar, embracing cooks (both men and women), housewives, housekeepers, stewards, butlers, and kitchen maids, whether in an aristocratic establishment of forty people or in a modest family with two domestics. However, women writers were not easily accepted, either professionally or socially, prompting Hannah Glasse, for example, to conceal her identity as the author of the best-selling *The Art of Cookery Made Plain and Easy* (1747) as "By a Lady." Men were quick to criticize women's lack of training or "profession." No less a personage than Samuel Johnson, author of the celebrated *Dictionary of the English Language* (1755), groused, "Women can spin very well; but they cannot make a good book of Cookery."[10]

Despite Dr. Johnson's dyspeptic view, nearly half of the sixty or more books about cookery published in Britain during the eighteenth century were written by women or by men with women in mind. Many of the books resemble each other, offering similar recipes spiced with household hints and medical remedies. Indeed, authors often copied from one another, and more than one complained of plagiarism. For example, in the second edition of *Professed Cookery* (1754), Ann Cook accused Hannah Glasse of stealing "from ev'ry Author to her Book, Infamously branding the pillag'd Cook, with Trick, Booby, Juggler, Legerdermain."[11] Most of the cookbooks of this century provided detailed recipes, often with quite lengthy instructions, but gave exact measurements only for baked and dessert recipes, where accuracy really mattered. In savory dishes, writers assumed that cooks knew their trade and would adjust quantities according to their taste and the availability of ingredients. Some books contained supplemental sections on subjects such as confectionery, brewing, curing meats, carving, and even growing fruit trees and tending poultry.

The Compleat Housewife (1727) by Mrs. E. Smith (her first name may have been Eliza, but this is not certain) is a fine example of how the popular English household book was evolving early in the century. From the seventeenth-century books of secrets such

OPPOSITE In the frontispiece of *The British Housewife* by Martha Bradley, c. 1755, the mistress of the house lends a hand in the kitchen: "Behold, ye Fair, united in this Book, The Frugal Housewife, and experienced cook." The book's title is an early use of "British," as the union with Scotland had only taken place in 1706.

as Hannah Woolley's haphazard *The Queen-like Closet* (1670), eighteenth-century cookbooks moved on to adopt a recognizably modern organization with mainly culinary recipes designed for trained home cooks. Mrs. Smith contrasts good, honest, frugal English cooking with dishes that do not suit "English Constitutions," promising her readers only what is best, natural, wholesome, and "most agreeable to English Palates."[12] At least a third of the book focuses on "made wines," cordial waters, and home remedies. Such books fit a dual market: social instruction for the genteel woman who was expected to direct her household staff with confidence, and professional guidance for the hired housekeeper, usually a woman, responsible for running her employer's household, overseeing the kitchen, and often cooking as well. *The Compleat Housewife* was vastly popular and is notable as the first cookbook to be printed in colonial America (Williamsburg, 1742).

Two other women were remarkably successful in reaching the growing British audience for household cookbooks. Economy was an ideal and a common sales pitch for books about cooking. Sarah Harrison, author of *The House-Keeper's Pocket-Book, and Compleat Family Cook. Containing above Three Hundred Curious and Uncommon Recipes* (1733), assured the "House-Wives in Great Britain" that her recipes were "for preparing the nicest Dishes, to avoid all unnecessary Expence, and, as far as the Thing was practicable, to unite Frugality into Elegance in Eating." She noted that careful housewifery could compensate for lack of "a large and plentiful Estate."[13] Authors occasionally used the words *housewife* and *housekeeper* interchangeably, so it is not always clear if the writer is addressing the mistress or a servant. Celia Fiennes, an adventurous traveler in the days when women travelers were few, watched the making of oat clap bread and commented, "As we say of all sorts of bread there is a vast deal of difference in what is housewifely made and what is ill made."[14]

Elizabeth Moxon placed a similar emphasis on economy in *English Housewifery* (1749), "a book necessary for Mistresses of Families, higher and lower Women Servants," supplying many "Measures of Frugality."[15] Mrs. Moxon's cooking was a hybrid of the French flavors popular at the opening of the century and traditional British favorites. The book begins in the French style with soups, features butter-based cooking, and takes advantage of both a stewing stove and an open-hearth fire. Recipes use very little cream, and spices (cinnamon, cloves, nutmeg) appear only in forcemeat mixtures—patties and pies—or in puddings, not generally in savory dishes, which rely on mushrooms, shallots, oysters, capers, and anchovies. Her frequent call for

---

OPPOSITE In this frontispiece from the 1742 edition of *The Compleat Housewife* by Mrs. E. Smith, the lady of the house instructs her female housekeeper, who in turn will instruct the harried-looking cook by the fire, while the server rushes dishes to the table. The housekeeper's look-alike dress had perhaps belonged to her mistress; cast-off finery was a perk of higher-ranked servants.

COMMONPLACE BOOKS

A commonplace book is, much as its name suggests, a handwritten collection of passages that its creator wants to remember—the equivalent of today's personal journal or scrapbook, or possibly a blog. The habit of writing in such books began early, before the establishment of printing. The term comes from the Latin *locus communis,* referring to a place of general interest. Proverbs, rhyming ditties, prayers, and recipes all fall into the mix.

Culinary and medicinal recipes were favorite material. Wedding menus, recipes from neighbors, household hints, optimistic cures for the bites of a mad dog, notes on the best planting season for crops, prescriptions for a long life, riddles and conundrums—all were jotted on the page. Often entries were listed in chronological rather than subject order, as they came to the attention of the writer. A long-lasting commonplace book can illustrate the progress of a busy lifetime, even of a family over a couple of generations.

Hannah Woolley's first book, *The Queen-like Closet, or Rich Cabinet* (1670), is a prime example of the seeming lack of logic in such collections. By the seventeenth century, a commonplace book was considered a mark of accomplishment. Anyone literate was likely to keep a commonplace book, and hundreds, even thousands, of these books survive today. The most famous American commonplace book is a seventeenth-century family manuscript inherited by George Washington's wife, Martha, in 1749, and passed down to later generations. In *Martha Washington's Booke of Cookery,* Karen Hess points out that this collection of recipes had "long since become a family heirloom and . . . had not served as a working kitchen manual since the beginning of the century, perhaps earlier. Many of the recipes must have seemed old-fashioned to Martha.[1]

A half dozen commonplace books in our collection focus on cooking—in essence they are cookbooks. "I Began to Ritte it the 12 day of febery in the yeare of our Lorde 1672," declares Katherina Elisa Harington in her embossed vellum-bound volume of family recipes and medical remedies. (Katherina came from a distinguished family that could afford such a luxurious binding for an important project.) Though the order of her entries is far from logi-

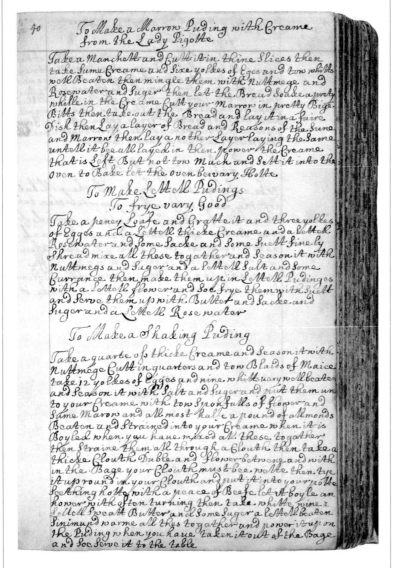

Katherina Elisa Harington recorded To Make A Shaking Pudding among the five hundred recipes in her commonplace book of 1692.

cal, she does leave space for future additions by subject, so about a third of the book remains blank, parts of it filled in with another, less generous script. For more than five hundred pages, her looped, admirably clear hand details recipes such as Almond Cakes Like Biskett Vary Good and How to Make a Fresh Sullibube Excellent Well. Like many authors of cookbooks of the time, she quotes her sources: "Cosen Hamond" is a frequent one, together with "Aunte Pigotte" and "Dr Burges."

Another vellum-bound example is the impeccable manuscript by Thomas Hayton, which he left "To my Cousen Susann Acrod The Eldest Daughter of my sister Catharine Acrod as soon as Possible after my Death it is my most Ernest Desire, Aprill 23:1711." Hayton must have copied much of the material from an existing manuscript because he left not a correction nor a spare line in his impressive collection, apparently written for a large household. The book opens with medical potions and goes on to culinary recipes that are typical of the turn of the century: pies of pigeon, lamb, chicken, turkey, artichoke, and potato, a vegetable by now widespread in English kitchens. Hayton must have been a countryman, for his book includes homey recipes for rabbit hash and roast pike among the customary sweet puddings, custards, and cheesecakes. He too credits his sources, including his sister and housewifely neighbors.

More typical of the average commonplace book is the well-thumbed volume by Katherina Bull, dated 1715. The book is written from both ends, meeting in the middle; pages are dropping from the binding, and words seem to spill from the page. This was a working book: a receipt for five guineas, half a year's rent

in 1802, falls from the pages. Some recipes look to be scribbled on the run, like "Excellent small cakes, the King himself has eat of them." Elizabeth Elenner Hapsell, writing in 1727, was a very different character. Her book is adorned with swirls of penmanship, little sketches to enliven the endpapers, and imaginative recipes. She clearly enjoyed preserving, and among the routine cucumber pickles and quince paste is a Clarett Catchupp laced with horseradish, savory, marjoram, ginger, shallot, and anchovy. For her medicine for "obstructions," she preserves garlic cloves in sugar syrup. She made "mushrooms" of egg white and sugar (i.e., meringue) and shaped "almonds" of chocolate, sugar, and gum arabic, flavored with rose water—an early use of chocolate as a candy.

Odd man out in our little collection of commonplace cookbooks is the anonymous *Méthode pour faire la cuisine* (How to Cook) of 1775. The author was clearly a professional, possibly a man, judging from the small size of the handwriting, but he gives no clue to his identity or workplace. A hint may reside in his recipe for soupe à la graisse, which is typical of Normandy. In a compact volume on lined paper, he conveys in just a few pages all the aspects of planning quite sophisticated meals, from advice on marketing to costing, with a neat little drawing on how to set the table. His recipes such as Petits Pâtés, Salmis, Pigeons en Crapaudine, and Boeuf à la mode underline the existence at that time of an established French cuisine that was to become classic.

For their writers and readers, these commonplace books were a means of personal communication, a way to highlight enthusiasms—"excellent good" and "very goode as can be" were typical comments. A touch of

snobbery comes through in attributions to "My Lady Aline" or "Miss Marton of Abotts Langly." From the handwriting to the binding to the pages battered by the years, each book is unique. Most of all, a commonplace book conveys a personal message down the years from the eager cook who took the time to inscribe specialties and secrets for future generations in the kitchen.

On a larger scale, reflected in printed cookbooks such as *The Queen's Closet Opened* (1655) by W. M., the commonplace book writers reached out to a wide audience, exploring networks of like-minded people who continually exchanged recipes and formed social and intellectual bonds with the most distinguished and interesting people of the day. These ties explain why writers noted the provenance of so many of the recipes they entered in their books. Many recipes in *The Queen's Closet Opened* bear the words "proved" or "approved," sometimes even noting by whom: Lady Arundel's special remedy for the stone, a cordial water of Sir Walter Raleigh, and "Mr Ferene of the New Exchange Perfumer to the Queen, his rare Dentifrice so much approved of at Court."[2] ♦

1 *Martha Washington's Booke of Cookery*, transcribed by Karen Hess (New York: Columbia University Press, 1981), 7.

2 Betty S. Travitsky, Anne Lake Prescott, and Patrick Cullen, eds., *The Early Modern Englishwoman: A Facsimile Library of Essential Works. Essential Works for the Study of Early Modern Women,* Series 3, Part 3 (Burlington, VT: Ashgate Publishing, 2008), 315.

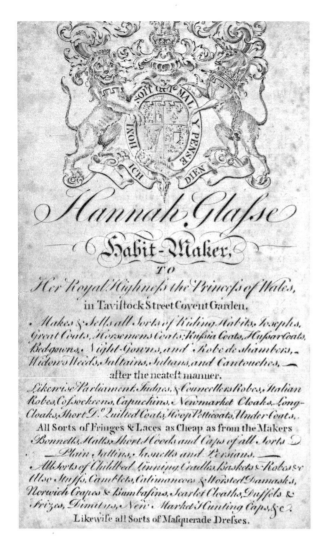

truffles and morels seems extravagant until we learn from her contemporary Richard Bradley that these ingredients were common but underappreciated and "in most places are looked upon as Incumbrances."[16]

Early eighteenth-century authors took for granted the background skills needed to run a kitchen successfully. While Smith and Moxon encouraged their readers to eat according to the seasons, they did not give much advice on shopping in the market. By midcentury, when Hannah Glasse wrote *The Art of Cookery Made Plain and Easy* (1747), the scene was changing and publishers were putting out many more new cooking and household books, which indicates that demand for these books was growing at a healthy pace. Novice cooks relied on book learning to supplement their apprenticeships with experienced cooks. Publishers tended to be small firms with a natural aversion to risk, so they often grouped together in consortiums to pay for the printing and distribution of books. They appealed to an ever-increasing audience of professional female housekeepers who were eager to fend off male competition.

Mrs. Glasse's instructions on "How to market, and the Seasons of the Year for Butcher's Meats, Poultry, Fish, Herbs, Roots, &c, and Fruit" were so apposite that they became standard in later cookbooks. The ignorant servant girl was a prime mark for dishonest food merchants, and with the expansion of towns, many young people grew up not knowing how to pick out sound apples nor what the meat of a healthy, just-slaughtered calf looked and smelled like. Mrs. Glasse also supplied timely "rules" on

ABOVE Until this advertisement appeared in the front of the fourth edition of *The Art of Cookery Made Plain and Easy*, 1751, the author of the most successful English cookbook of the eighteenth century had been referred to simply as "By a Lady." Even with this revelation of Mrs. Glasse's name, the family background of the author remained a mystery until the twentieth century, when her origins in the north of England were tracked down.

OPPOSITE Subscription lists at the front of books, like this one from Hannah Glasse's *The Art of Cookery Made Plain and Easy*, name the individuals who contributed to the cost of printing the book. Subscription was a common eighteenth-century strategy for writers to get into print, and some one hundred thousand individuals contributed to the cost of printed books during the century. Prominent names vouched for the quality of the cook and the book. Other cookbooks printed by subscription included Vincent La Chapelle's *The Modern Cook* (1733). In France, subscription publishing was called *la manière d'Angleterre*. The first edition of Diderot and Alembert's *Encyclopédie* in 1751 had four thousand subscribers, despite its high price (1,000 livres).

SUBSCRIBERS

TO THIS

BOOK.

A

Mrs. ALLGOOD
Mrs. Adams
Mrs. Atwood
Mrs. Armorer
Mrs. Ayliffe
Miſs Ayliffe
Dr. Anderſon
Mr. Anderſon
Capt. Aſh.

B

Mrs. Butler
Mrs. Bedford, *Broad-ſtreet Hill*
Mrs. Bedford, *Chancery-lane*
Mrs. Bury, *Norfolk-ſtreet*
Mrs. Bury, *Peckham*
Miſs Amy Bury
Miſs Bedford
Mrs. Berrysford
Mrs. Bertie
Mrs. Barker
Mrs. Bugby
Mrs. Bathus
Mrs. Beckly
Mrs. Bromfield
Mrs. Brown
Mrs. Bird
Mrs. Bowman
Mrs. Brown, *Chancery-lane*
Mrs. Blunckley
Mrs. Bowdler
Mrs. Barrit
Mrs. Barlet
Mrs. Baker
Mrs. Boys
—— Barnet, Eſq;
Dr. John Bedford
Mr. Back
Mr. Blanco
Mr. Bluck
Mr. Brickhill.

C

Hon. Mrs. Carmecheal
Mrs. Claxton, ſen.
Mrs. Claxton, jun.
Mrs. Crofts
Mrs. Carter, *Hay-Market*
Mrs. Carter, *Biſhopſgate-ſtreet*

Mrs. Churchill
Mrs. Cooke
Mrs. Coteſworth
Miſs Coumbs
Miſs Clokenhints
Miſs Carlton
Mrs. Cheyney
Mrs. Cuttlar
Mr. Collice
Mr. Cove.

D

Lady Dudly
Mrs. Duan
Mrs. Driddon
Mrs. Deucon
Mrs. Dawſon
Mrs. Denton
Mrs. Dent
Mrs. Dalows
Mr. Daverel.

E

Mrs. Edgerton
Mrs. Ebleſo.

F

Mrs. Farmer
Mrs. Fitzwater
Mrs. Finch
Rev. Mr. Finch.

G

Lady Gunſton
Mrs. Griffith
Mrs. Gandy
Mrs. Glaſſe, *Cary-ſtreet*
Mrs. Gordon
Mrs. Gritton
Mr. Glaſſe, Attorney at Law
Mr. Grear.

H

Mr. Hoar, *St. Martin's-lane*
Miſs E. Hoar
Miſs M. Hoar
Mrs. Hill
Miſs Haſtens
Mrs. Herriſs
Mrs. Hatten
Mrs. Hendrick
Mrs. Harriſon
Mr. Hanyſut
Mrs. Ann Hooper

the cleanliness of pots and pans; hygiene had become an important theme after accidental poisonings from worn-out tin linings in copper pots. Most books about cooking from the second half of the century carried boilerplate advice on how to avoid serving something deadly for dinner. Precise cooking times were another advance in *The Art of Cookery*. Older books typically instructed that the food be cooked "for the time it takes to say an Ave Maria," or "until it is enough." Hannah Glasse instructed her readers to fry for "a few minutes," boil "a quarter of an hour," or roast a small mutton breast "Half an Hour at a quick Fire." Not surprisingly, studies on consumer goods record an increase in the number of clocks in urban households after the 1740s.[17]

The Art of Cookery was one of the most successful cookbooks of the century. It ran to at least twenty-one editions, outselling both Mrs. Smith's and Mrs. Moxon's books, and it was still in print as late as 1852. Hannah Glasse was an able marketer, and she reached out to trend-conscious buyers by placing her cookbook in toy shops (which stocked all kinds of little mechanical gadgets) and chinaware shops, two of the places selling luxury consumer goods. Indeed, it was quite the fad for ladies to give books as gifts to their maids and servants.[18] Mrs. Glasse also took advantage of the fashion for distributing to a list of subscribers. She had her finger on the pulse of the nation, and her rhetoric was stridently anti-French, in tune with the debate about the debilitating qualities of French cuisine—with all its physical, financial, and even social costs—that had begun fifty years earlier. Much of British society likely agreed with Glasse's famous diatribe, "Such is the blind Folly of this Age, that they would rather be imposed on by a *French* Booby than give Encouragement to a good *English* Cook."[19]

The ultimate English manual for domestics was written by Elizabeth Raffald, appropriately entitled *The Experienced English Housekeeper* (1769). It was so successful that it remained in print until 1834. The book was published by subscription for the first two printings, and Mrs. Raffald claimed to have eight hundred subscribers, far more than Hannah Glasse. Her book was so popular that she was able to sell her copyright to the well-known London publisher Richard Baldwin for £1,400, a sum in line with those received by some of the better-paid male writers of her day and the equivalent of about $200,000 today. Her charisma was such that Baldwin added a cartouche, an engraved frontispiece of Raffald holding out a book to the reader. She may have made a mistake in selling her rights, for her book ran to well over twenty editions, though the number of copies printed each time may have been small.

With Raffald, cooks at last had clear and consistent measures (a teacupful, a gill, a teaspoonful, three quarts, two ounces) and often precise cooking times. Her instructions are clear, and she offers general observations about a category of food before launching into recipes, building on her basic preparations. Such cohesive structure was a long time in developing. Like Glasse, Raffald wanted to "be an Instructor to the young and ignorant, as it has been my chiefest Care to write in as plain a Style as possible, so as to be understood by the weakest Capacity."[20] Mrs. Glasse, like other authors of the time, had been vague, calling for "a little" of this and "a handful" of that. No author paid attention to portions beyond the occasional remark such as "for a feast day," on the assumption that an experienced cook would know how many people a lamb shoulder or a hare would serve. Generous quantities were the rule, because even a small household needed to feed an extended family and servants. Thus, a recipe might call for three rabbits, a seven-pound sturgeon, or a cake with a dozen eggs.

Mrs. Raffald's record for the greatest number of editions of a household book held for a half century, until the appearance in 1806 of *A New System of Domestic Cookery* by Mrs. Rundell. The author was something of a mystery until a few years ago, when archives from her publisher, John Murray, were released. Even her first name was not known for certain. We now know that Maria Eliza Rundell was the widow of a surgeon from Bath, in southwestern England. She collected her information to help her seven daughters and then donated it free of charge (but unedited) to the Murray family, who were personal friends. Apparently she later regretted her generosity, complaining bitterly that her material had been "miserably prepared." Despite her misgivings, the book became a household bible, with sixty-seven recorded editions before 1846. In America, Mrs. Rundell had similar success, with her book running to fifteen editions between 1807 and 1844.

THE

Experienced Englifh Houfe-Keeper.

CHAP. I.

Obfervations on SOUPS.

WHEN you make any Kind of Soups, particularly Portable, Vermicelli, or brown Gravy Soup, or any other that have Roots or Herbs in, always obferve to lay your Meat in the Bottom of your Pan, with a good lump of Butter; cut the Herbs and Roots fmall, lay them over your Meat, cover it clofe, fet it over a very flow Fire, it will draw all the Virtue out of the Roots or Herbs, and turns it to a good Gravy, and gives the Soup a very different flavour from putting Water in at the firft: When your Gravy is almoft dried up fill your Pan with Water, when it begins to boil take off the Fat, and follow the Directions of your Receipt for what Sort of Soup you are making: When you make old Peafe Soup, take foft Water, for green Peafe, hard is the beft, it keeps the Peafe a better Colour: When you make any white Soup, don't put in Cream 'till you

Mrs. Rundell had a distinctive tone of voice: "There was a time when ladies knew nothing *beyond* their own family concerns, but in the present day there are many who know nothing *about* them." To judge from Jane Austen, few young women thought beyond the wedding day, and Eliza Rundell was intent on remedying this situation. In the twenty pages of somewhat intimidating "Observations," she cautioned, "Perhaps few branches of female education are so useful as a great readiness at figures." She announced that the art of carving was among the many skills that a housewife (not a housekeeper; this book is not written for the wealthy) should acquire, lest "the dish goes away with the appearance of having been gnawed by dogs."[21] Her steady, if somewhat terse, common sense must have reassured many a young wife on both sides of the Atlantic.

Counterfeit editions of popular books were so common in the eighteenth century that authors took to signing their names to verify that a copy was authentic, as did Elizabeth Raffald on the first page of her *The Experienced English House-keeper*, 1769.

ENGLISH BAKING & CONFECTIONERY AT HOME

In England, confectionery, with its focus on sugar, became separated from the more general skills of the pastry cook long before the eighteenth century. Already in the early 1600s, pastry work clearly involved flour, eggs, and often butter or some other fat along with sugar. Pastry was homey stuff involving pies (sweet or savory), large and small cakes, cookies (then as now called biscuits), and the kinds of welcoming treats that endear a mother to her family. There were high-flying pastry cooks too, professionals who catered to the affluent, but in England, far more than in France or Italy, pastry baking was done at home. Domestic cooks might make some simple candies and comfits, but the sophisticated art of *confiserie* described by French authors was not an English trait. As time progressed, confectionery in England became an increasingly narrow, mainly professional field. Moreover, little bread baking (*boulangerie*) took place at home. Throughout Europe from the beginning of the millennium, the large ovens and heavy manual work required to produce yeast breads on any scale had led to a separate professional trade.

The first English cookbook to separate sweet recipes from savory ones was the small but hugely influential *Delightes for Ladies* (1600) by Sir Hugh Plat. "Of musked sugar I intend to write," he declares, "affording to each Ladie, her delight. I teach both fruites and flowers to preserue, and candie them, so Nutmegs, Cloves and Mace." Molded sugar animals or sugar-paste sculptures, fancifully colored and gilded, made attractive presents to friends. Emphasizing the importance of this

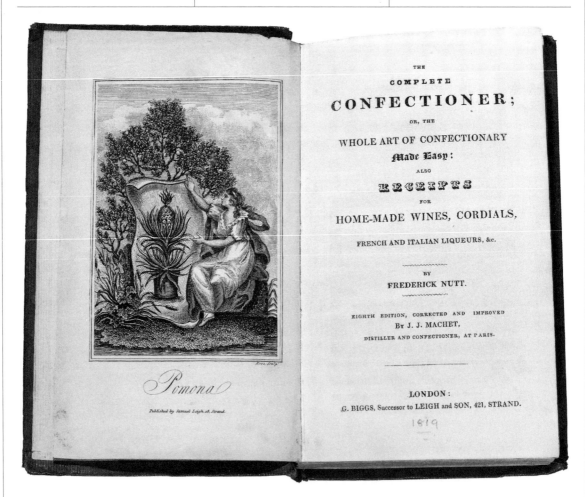

Pomona, the Roman goddess of abundance, displays a pineapple as the symbol of hospitality in the 1819 frontispiece of *The Complete Confectioner* by Frederick Nutt.

new subject, Plat opened his book with the classic candying method that calls for several syrups of increasing concentration, using roots such as elecampane (a digestive) instead of the chestnuts or whole fruits we would expect. Many of his recipes are distinctive, such as lumbolds (later called jumbles), almond paste that is rolled into knots, baked, and iced with sugar and rose water to keep "all the yeere."[1]

Right around the same time, John Murrell, a professional caterer, was writing for the ladies who banqueted and took classes in cooking and confectionery. In the letter of dedication for *A Daily Exercise for Ladies and Gentlewomen* (1617), Murrell wrote, "Wee alter our Fashions and outward Habits daily.... So, our Cookery, Pastry, Distillations, Conserves, and Preserves, are farre otherwise now, than not long since they were; Daily Practise and Observation finding out....to make new much more pleasing and profitable."[2]

Murrell's recipes for candies and sweetmeats, as well as cordials for consumption or a cough, are strikingly detailed about the amounts of ingredients, timing, temperature, and consistency of the cooked sugar. He describes the required chafing dish, earthen pan, alabaster mortar, and other specialty equipment and dries sweets in a "stove," probably the portable charcoal stove used by pastry cooks and apothecaries. Alert to a marketing opportunity, he offers a note at the beginning of his book informing readers that his special molds (snakes, snails, frogs, roses, shoes, keys, letters, and gloves) will be available wherever his little book is sold.

By this time, most home cooks had decided that complex sugar work was best left to the professionals. In *The Queen-like Closet* (1670), Hannah Woolley was typical in devoting more than half her book to savory cookery, the rest to candying and preserving. Sweet recipes follow a cautious path of syrups, jellies, pickles, and a few wines, with cakes and desserts added to the mix. No lesser cook than Mrs. Mary Eales, confectioner to Queen Anne, took a similar track. Her elegant little book *Receipts* (1718) focuses on fruits, with enticements such as To Make Quince Chips and To Candy Little Green Oranges.

With her usual prescience, Hannah Glasse also jumped in to explore confectionery for the housewife in depth. *The Compleat Confectioner* (1760) is a remarkably down-to-earth compilation, justifying its subtitle of "The Whole Art of Confectionary Made Plain and Easy." Like many cookbooks of its time, it draws heavily on other sources. Starting with the stages of sugar boiling, from the thread to caramel, Mrs. Glasse turns to preserves of citrus fruits, stone fruits, berries, pomegranates, and figs. Her cakes range from cheesecakes to "plumb" cake with a trifle along the way. Her single ice cream is chilled over ice and salt, without benefit of one of the new churning devices. The book closes with distilled waters such as rose water and some very British drinks, including cider, raisin wine, mead, and the spiced wine called malmsey. "Those who have hitherto bought of the Confectioners will soon find that a vast expense is to be saved by the use of this book," says Mrs. Glasse with satisfaction.[3]

In parallel, to remedy the shortcomings of home confectionery, professional shops had proliferated in London and other English cities. When Domenico Negri, an Italian confectioner in London, created a "grand dessert" for the fourth Duke of Gordon in 1765, it included an elaborately fashionable structure with glass fountains and other orna-

ments, and naturally the sweetmeats, at a cost of just over £25, the equivalent of about $3,550 today.[4] In 1770, the confectioner to the Spanish ambassador in London, Borella, published *The Court and Country Confectioner: or, The House-Keeper's Guide,* which he described as "the French and English guide to all sorts of confectionary." Borella's recipes give clear clues to the correct color and texture of each procedure, key for his target audience, "the House-keepers of Great-Britain," whose job opportunities increased with superior confectionery skills.

Frederick Nutt, author of *The Complete Confectioner* (1789), was also a professional. He had worked for Negri at his Berkeley Square shop, The Pot and the Pineapple, which may account for the proliferation of sweetmeats that he identifies as Italian and Spanish.[5] His recipes show that the English repertoire had expanded to include ice creams and water ices (the English term for sorbets) and candies such as hard caramels, barley sugar, and the very English "drops" of flavored hard sugar. His cookies (called biscuits) are clearly different from the French petits fours. *The Complete Confectioner* was so popular that it was one of the first cookbooks to be published, in 1807, in the new America. ♦

1 A 1624 edition of *Delightes for Ladies* by Sir Hugh Plat was bound with a separate book called *A Closet for Ladies and Gentlewomen, or The Art of Preserving, Conserving, and Candying* (1608) also by Plat.

2 John Murrell, *A Daily Exercise for Ladies and Gentlewomen* (London: Printed for the widow Helme [1617]).

3 Hannah Glasse, *The Compleat Confectioner* (London: Mrs. Ashburn, 1760), opening page.

4 Ivan Day, "The Art of Confectionery," www.historicfood.com/The%20Art%20of%20Confectionery.pdf.

5 See Ivan Day, "Which Compleat Confectioner?" *Petits Propos Culinaires* 2 (1998): 44–53.

France: The Next Generation

In parallel with the eighteenth-century English boom in domestic cookbooks, in France several giants in the culinary world were to influence the direction of all future cooking within the country and well beyond. These cooks refined haute cuisine and launched a fresh style they called *nouvelle cuisine*. The trend had begun at the start of the century with Massialot, and he was joined by Vincent La Chapelle, a Frenchman who, as head cook to the Earl of Chesterfield, worked in England and the cultural center of The Hague, picking up ideas on both sides of the Channel.

La Chapelle is hard to categorize. He was bilingual, publishing his multivolume cookbook first in slightly fractured English as *The Modern Cook* (1733) and two years later in French as *Le cuisinier moderne* (1735), by which time he had become cook to the Prince of Orange in The Hague. Roughly a third of La Chapelle's recipes were taken from Massialot, and others came from Nicolas Audiger's *La maison réglée* (The Orderly Household, 1692), while several coulis and broths came word for word from Charles Carter.[22] Derivative though it is, La Chapelle's work is a treasury of eighteenth-century French cooking. Almost every one of the fifteen hundred recipes is complete in itself, giving far greater coverage than the recipe count implies. The complexity of La Chapelle's cuisine and menus shows he was used to a large, prosperous household staff, and his instructions make clear that he was cooking on one of the new stewing stoves, or *potagers*.

The term *nouvelle cuisine* postdates La Chapelle's cookbooks, but he is acknowledged as one of its creators. His work bridges the old and the new; for instance, his old-style turkey *à la crème*—roasted and pounded to a complicated farce involving veal, bacon, cow's udder, and mushrooms with half a dozen seasonings, then reshaped around a ragoût of sweetbreads, cocks' combs, and mushrooms—is in radical contrast to his simple version of the same dish, larded with bacon and ham, simmered in milk, then finished on the spit, basted with the milk, and sprinkled with a little flour until "crusty" and "golden brown," a technique called frothing that is still sometimes used. He published his work by subscription—that is, by finding his own financing—a not unusual practice. What was surprising was his failure to find a publisher to buy his copyright once the book proved a best seller. Despite this setback, La Chapelle left a long-term impression in the collective memory of French and British professional cooks. He stands out as an eighteenth-century culinary powerhouse, no matter how much he may have borrowed from Massialot.

Following Massialot and La Chapelle, a new generation of cooks in Paris began pushing a provocative, modern agenda, a *nouvelle cuisine* that would build on the classic foundations of *cuisine ancienne* but be lighter and more delicate. François Marin and François Menon were the leaders of the movement, creating a style that is recognizably modern even today. Both men were part of inner court circles; for example, Marin was maître d'hôtel for the duc de Rohan, an intimate of Louis XV and a frequent guest at the king's famous private suppers. Both published their first books in 1739, in which they aimed to pin down the techniques and dishes of an haute cuisine that continued to develop into the nineteenth century.

Though Menon was the primary architect of nouvelle cuisine, his rival Marin was the first to coin the phrase in print, in 1739. Marin describes the relationship between modern cooking and chemistry in a lengthy preface to his cookbook *Les dons de Comus, ou les délices de la table* (The Gifts of Comus, or the Pleasures of the Table). The preface was probably contributed by a couple of Jesuit priests, though the themes were certainly sparked by Marin himself. He evokes the new quintessences that concentrate most nutrition in the smallest possible essence. The new cuisine, he writes, means "fewer preparations, less fuss. . . . [It is] simpler and cleaner."[23] For him, the good cook is as

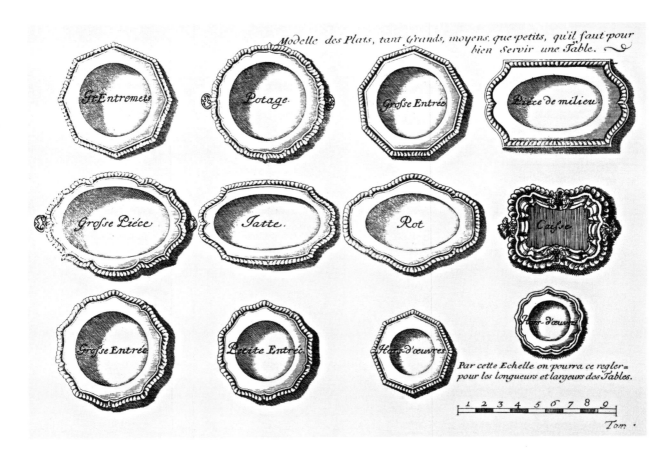

ABOVE The 1742 edition of *Le cuisinier moderne* by Vincent La Chapelle has a foldout frontispiece showing the correct platters for certain dishes. Bills of fare, instructions on seasonality, and diagrams for laying out meals were useful elements of eighteenth-century cookbooks. Advances in engraving technology allowed images to be incorporated into all kinds of print media. French technology was in the lead, but by midcentury, English cookbooks routinely included at least a few illustrations, ranging from fairly crude to elaborate.

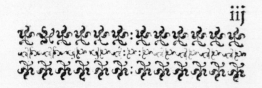

iij

AVERTISSEMENT.

LA cuifine, comme tous les autres Arts inventés pour le befoin ou pour le plaifir , s'eft perfectionnée avec le génie des peuples, & elle eft devenuë plus déli- cate à mefure qu'ils fe font polis. Comme je n'entre- prens pas d'en faire l'Hif- toire , je ne m'arrêterai point à fes commencemens. La vie des premiers hommes a dû reffembler à celle des peuples de l'Amerique, qui, bornés

a ij

much scientist as artist, skilled at updating the old com-plex dishes to make them both healthier and more ethe-real. The concept was sufficiently controversial to provoke an almost immediate response, a parody called *Lettre d'un pâtissier anglois* (Letter of an English Pastry Cook, 1739).[24] The dialogue continued in Marin's revised edition, *Suite de dons de Comus* (Sequel to Gifts of Comus) of 1742, to which he added a few introductory pages affirming that nouvelle cuisine was both healthy and agreeable on the palate. Directly addressing charges that might be leveled against the new cooking, Marin stated that none of his sauces were intended to revive jaded taste buds and en-courage gluttony. More importantly, he added two more volumes with hundreds of recipes, many of which were scarcely mentioned in the first book.

François Menon was the most influential and prolific French cookbook author of the eighteenth century. Dur-ing his time, today's familiar categories of French cooking were emerging, and Menon was a master of them all: nouvelle cuisine (a term that each generation redefines); haute or classical cuisine; and cuisine bourgeoise. He even wrote the first French cookbook devoted specifically to a woman cook (*La cuisinière bourgeoise* [The Bourgeoise Cook], 1746). The only style not defined by his fluent pen was regional cooking, which did not emerge until the nineteenth century. Nothing is known about Menon's professional life (even his first name is uncertain), but his close knowledge of fashionable dining shows he must have cooked for a distinguished audience. In the course of his landmark writings, he covered almost every field of the professional cook, in-cluding the maître d'hôtel, laying out a new view of kitchen positions in the process.

Menon first described the new cuisine in detail in the third and final volume of *Nouveau traité de la cuisine* (New Treatise on Cooking, 1742). In contrast to traditional

---

ABOVE In the preface to the 1739 edition of *Les dons de Comus*, François Marin launches his views on his new style of cooking, soon to be called *nouvelle cuisine*. "Cooking, like all the other arts invented out of need or pleasure, has been perfected by civilized society." He heralds a cuisine with "fewer prep-arations, less fuss," sparking controversy that inflamed the culinary world and even a couple of Jesuit priests.

cooking, he wrote, the key to nouvelle cuisine was delicacy. Sauces were lighter but at the same time more nourishing; seasonings aimed to enhance rather than mask lead ingredients. Many dishes were to be prepared *au naturel*, to be healthy, delicious, and elegantly simple. Nonetheless, he followed his predecessors in several respects, choosing seasonal ingredients, reinforcing French kitchen disciplines by emphasizing knife skills, and continuing to rely on the building blocks of French haute cuisine—béchamel, velouté, and espagnole sauces, meat glazes, reductions, and techniques such as blanching and braising—and to assign pastry an important role in both sweet and savory recipes.

Menon not only wrote about the practicalities of nouvelle cuisine; he was also concerned with philosophy, linking his mission closely to that of the leading thinkers of the Enlightenment: to advance and disseminate knowledge that allows humankind to live in a state of nature perfected. Toward this end, he attended to the health properties of food, relying heavily on the popular book by French physician Louis Lemery, *Traité des aliments* (Treatise on Foods, 1702), which put forth the new theories that combined the principles of the humors with new discoveries about the chemistry of acids, alkalis, and salts.[25] According to Lemery and others, food falls into three categories—spirits (air), solids, and liquids—and four principles—oil, salt, earth, and water. Food can be simple, so that it nourishes and restores the body; or medicinal, so that it not only nourishes but also corrects any imbalance.

In his introduction to *Science du maître d'hôtel cuisinier* (Science of the Steward Cook, 1749), Menon details his theory of medicine and cooking.[26] Today's wise cook, he insists, knows how to consult nature to create "a judicious mélange & heighten natural flavors . . . [to] offer you a preparation that is healthy and delicious." His soups, many of them *maigre* (without meat) for fast days, sometimes consist of just three or four ingredients. As for the ragoûts, which many traditionalists considered unhealthy, he specifically avoids "great outlays" while preserving their delicacy. Echoing Enlightenment treatises, Menon is partial to "discourses" and "observations" on healthy eating and he goes much farther than La Chapelle's and Marin's restorative bouillons in including physic in French cookbooks. He set a trend, and a variety of practical octavo-sized dictionaries of cooking and food were published over the following decades that included "Medicinal Observations" along with recipes.

Menon's most elegant and approachable book is *Les soupers de la cour* (Court Suppers, 1755), published in four elegant leather-bound volumes decorated with gilt lettering and flowers on the spine. In them, Menon describes himself as a chef rather than a cook, the first to assign the term to the head of the kitchen. By this time, the intimate supper had overtaken dinner as the most fashionable style of eating in eighteenth-century Paris, and Menon observes that little now distinguishes dinner (midday) from supper (evening). In some ways, *Soupers de la cour* harks back to the old order, with a casual assumption of unlimited time and ingredients. However, the elegant simplicity

THE RISE OF
REGIONALISM

Regional cooking, as distinct from bourgeois or country cooking, became fashionable only in the twentieth century. However, the concept of a style of cooking with a specific geographical identity existed long before books on the subject appeared. The saltless bread of Tuscany dates back before Dante, and the medieval city-states of Italy each had their own breads, a tradition that continues to this day.[1] In England, many eighteenth-century cookbooks referred to foods available in particular areas, whether produced on the spot or brought in on a regular trade route. Cambridge professor of botany Richard Bradley, in *The Country Housewife and Lady's Director* (1727), carefully detailed the regional cheeses of England, optimistically giving recipes for cheeses that would taste like those of Cheshire and Gloucestershire. Books also reveal variations in dishes from place to place. William Ellis's charming *The Country Housewife's Family Companion* (1750) often connects particular recipes with "the Hertfordshire way."

In France, the remarkable variety and excellence of products throughout the domain of King François I and his son Henri II had been noted by Jean Bruyérin-Champier, whose observations on regional products in *De re cibaria* (On Food, 1560) were centuries ahead of any other. Culinary sophistication accelerated with the death of Louis XIV in 1715, and during the Regency that followed, elite dining was no longer tied to court display. Regional specialties emerged as part of the new, more intimate style of dining. Dishes took on local identities, and thanks to the French love of intellectual organization, recipes were given catchy names that served as shorthand language in a busy kitchen. Both Marin's *Les dons de Comus* (The Gifts of Comus, 1739) and Menon's *Nouveau traité de la cuisine* (New Treatise on Cooking, 1739–1742) are rife with ideas such as *à la provençale, gasconne, périgourdine, lyonnaise,* and *bourguignonne.* Cookbooks were spreading the word, and by mid-eighteenth century, place-names for regional dishes were common.

The identification of provincial dishes brought increased demand from outside a region for the foods within. The Bureau du Comestible, which debuted in 1767, was a remarkable business venture. Through its *Gazetin du comestible,* the bureau launched a mail-order service offering a monthly list of items and prices; anyone in France could order "everything connected with table service," from natural products such as Marennes oysters and hams from Bayonne to fabricated ones, including andouille sausages from six towns throughout France. "Everything" for the table in fact meant luxury items, probably previously unknown, and certainly unavailable, for a wider public. The truffles for Menon's *truffes à la Périgord* were obtainable in Normandy at last. In the eighteenth century, it was not enough to dazzle guests with out-of-season fruits and vegetables, as in the time of Louis XIV. Now members of the provincial elite could display their connoisseurship with

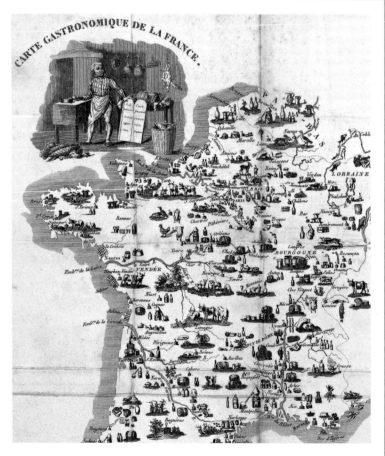

This gastronomic map of France (above and opposite) appeared as the frontispiece to Charles Louis Cadet de Gassicourt's *Cours gastronomique* (1809).

an impressive dish of fresh ingredients that had traveled hundreds of kilometers just for their guests' pleasure.

The *Gazetin du comestible* not only united the producer and the consumer, but it liberated consumers from greedy and unscrupulous intermediaries with its promise of fair prices paid and charged. The bureau was one of many organizations that proliferated to serve the Enlightenment goal of encouraging French agriculture and commerce, proclaiming that it benefited the nation and created happiness for individuals. Farmers and artisans did well. The renowned meringues from Montargis could be ordered and sent anywhere. In January, anyone could order the same ready-prepared *perdrix rouges aux truffes vertes* (red partridges with fresh truffles) from Nérac that were sent regularly by postal coach to the king of Denmark. In March, customers could order raw or cooked crayfish from Beauvais; those from Molsheim in Alsace would arrive alive. Trout from Lake Geneva were cooked before shipping but were guaranteed to be "very good to eat."

The upheaval of the Revolution put an end to this novel enterprise, but it had created a taste for regional fare. In the *Almanach des gourmands* (1803–1812), Grimod de la Reynière offered regular reports on such treats as the dried fruit preserves of Clermont-Ferrand and the "excellent" liqueurs of Madame Marie-Brizard of Bordeaux, a trade name that still exists. Grimod's readers began to take for granted that certain products—butter, for instance, or macaroons—were at their best when raised or made in certain places. In 1809, the first gastronomic map of France appeared as the frontispiece to Charles Louis Cadet de Gassicourt's *Cours gastronomique* (Course in Gastronomy),

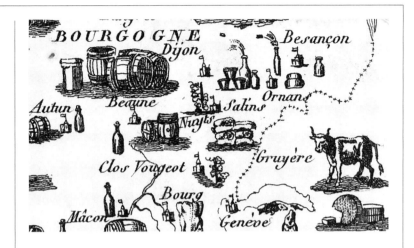

with icons of pâtés, pots of mustard, gamboling rabbits, and wheels of cheese beside the place-names, setting the scene for the first cookbook devoted to the regional cooking of France.

Several books raised false hopes of regionalism, such as the culinary dictionary *Manuel de la cuisine* (Manual of Cooking, 1811), originally published anonymously but now known to have been written by A. Bauvillers, and *Le cuisinier Durand* (Durand the Cook, 1830), a dictionary and anthology from Nîmes. Both touch tangentially on regional cooking via local products or dishes, but neither clearly defines what recipes from a specific region represent the indigenous foods and heritage. Véry's *Le cuisinier des cuisiniers* (The Cook for Cooks, 1825) provides six pages of lists spelling out where to find regional specialties all over France, but the author makes little mention of any of his recipes' regional roots. At last, the anonymous *La cuisinière du Haut-Rhin* (The Cook of the Upper Rhine, 1842) from Mulhouse states with pride, "Travellers agree that in Alsace, in Switzerland, in Swabia, and in neighboring regions, the cooking is good."[2] Even so, the regional focus is by implication rather than overt statement, with two opening recipes for snail

soup and crayfish soup, a dozen dumplings, generous mention of the cabbage family, pâtés including foie gras, and a dazzling collection of recipes for stone fruits. By the end of the nineteenth century, books from the French regions—Gascony, Savoy, Burgundy, and the Landes—were proliferating, but only with the arrival of the twentieth-century motor car did regional cookbooks truly bloom.[3] ♦

1 Carol Field, *The Italian Baker* (New York: Harper Collins, 1985), 110–11.

2 *La cuisinière du Haut-Rhin* (Luzarches, France: Librairie Daniel Morcrette, 1981), 3–4.

3 Julia Csergo, "The Emergence of Regional Cuisines," in *Food: A Culinary History,* ed. Jean-Louis Flandrin and Massimo Montanari, ed. English edition Albert Sonnenfeld (New York: Columbia University Press, 1999), 502.

of Menon's recipes, with their pared-down garnishes and carefully balanced flavors, is very characteristic of the new style of haute cuisine. Even after completing *Soupers de la cour*, Menon did not stop; he published two more books in the late 1750s, one on the background and practice of cooking and the other on cooking and health.[27]

Along with tapping into new ways of thinking about food, Menon's books reflect changing practices in the kitchen. He recognized that the positions of *maître cuisinier* and *chef d'office* were beginning to merge so that these two key positions could function in harmony, each complementing the skills of the other. Thus, he started giving menus specifically for the chef, clearly indicating the increasing reluctance of even the rich to employ a maître d'hôtel, a *chef de cuisine*, and a *chef d'office*.

Like many new ideas, Menon's nouvelle cuisine provoked a counterreaction. Attacks against oversophisticated cooking surface throughout Diderot and Alembert's *Encyclopédie*. In keeping with the encyclopedia's mission of documenting the trades and mechanical arts, it includes many entries on taste, cooking, cheese making, and other artisanal processes, but in doing so, it is more interested in promoting French technology and expertise than the sensual pleasures of the table.[28] One eats to live, one does not live to eat, and the entry entitled *"Nourriture"* (Food) is more medicine than cookery. Nor did Voltaire, who was something of an epicure, think much of the new cooking. "I confess that my stomach cannot adjust itself to the nouvelle cuisine. I cannot endure calves' sweetbreads swimming in a salty sauce. . . . I cannot eat a stew composed of turkey, hare, and rabbit which they try to make me believe is a single meat."[29] And on another occasion, "Ah, my friend, how good fat partridge are, but how hard to digest! My cook and my apothecary are killing me."[30]

Menon faced his critics head-on, insisting in *Nouveau traité de la cuisine* that the new, refined cooking with its lighter ragoûts was a benefit, not a hindrance, and would not destroy one's health. Quite the contrary. Indeed, despite such influential opposition, Menon's message was so powerful that later chefs took it for granted. "The delicacy of our tables was raised, during the last century, to such a level of perfection, that to surpass it would be extremely difficult," exclaimed Beauvilliers, one of the leading restaurateurs of the First Empire, in 1814.[31] And almost thirty years later, the *Biographie universelle* (Universal Biography) of 1843 noted that Menon's "writings are, without question, consulted more often than any others."[32]

AT THE SAME TIME that nouvelle cuisine was finding its footing, another style of cooking was emerging for the growing bourgeoisie. By the early eighteenth century in France, the term *bourgeois* had long since quit its original and simpler legal meaning of town dweller and had come to represent a wide range of classes below the aristocratic but above the artisan. The word had turned up a few times in recipe titles of the seventeenth and early eighteenth centuries, but not until the late 1730s did professional cooks, led by Marin and Menon, recognize *à la bourgeoise* as a specific style, one marked by hearty, rich, and potentially showy dishes. Whereas at the turn of the century, Massialot had one such recipe *(veau à la bourgeoise),* Menon provided six in *Nouveau traité,* and Marin included fifteen in *Les dons de Comus* and later added a section entitled "Cuisine & economie Bourgeoise," designed for "those of average fortune." By mid-century, a contemporary dictionary was giving this style its due, outlining the three major types of French cooking: simple and natural dishes for the bourgeoisie, more costly preparations for the rich, and a lighter, more delicate style for sensualists.[33]

As the lifestyle of the provincial bourgeoisie changed, so did the tasks of their cooks, more and more of whom were women. The lack of women cookbook authors to address this audience in eighteenth-century France is a puzzle. To some extent, the gap was filled by men, who made it clear that well-to-do French women, *bourgeoises,* in towns and the countryside shared with their British counterparts such concerns as good domestic management; homemade pastries, sweetmeats, and wines; and the preparation of attractive and stylish meals for friends and family. Nicolas de Bonnefons had talked of women readers in the previous century, but the noted agronomist Louis Liger was the first Frenchman to write a book specifically for them, thus acknowledging the presence of female cooks *(cuisinières)* in many bourgeois households in France. Liger's *Le ménage des champs et le jardinier françois accommodez au gout du temps* (Agriculture and the French Gardener Adapted to Modern Tastes, 1711) includes advice on gardening, but his focus is on the kitchen and how to cook the produce of the vegetable garden and orchard.

Liger's recipes are less sophisticated than those of Massialot, whose books were circulating at the same time, but the basic techniques, such as butter and flour roux, bouillon, and a beef jus to add depth *(nourrir)* to ragoûts, are recognizably French. Significantly, the extravagant coulis that marked the sophisticated urban cook is missing. *Le ménage des champs* instructed the reader in an art of dining that dated from the seventeenth century, with "a proper meal" for company that was to include potages, entrées such as *tourtes à la viande* or *poisson, pâtez chauds,* ragoûts, *hâchis,* and a variety of things roasted on the grill. Such menus show that the dining style that had developed in upper-class urban kitchens was filtering down into less affluent homes everywhere.

Writing early in the century, Liger reflects a pivotal moment in French society. Whereas in 1654, Bonnefons had explained in detail the method for killing and butchering animals, Liger assumes that all meat will be bought ready for cooking from the butcher, noting that offal can be purchased at the *tripier.* The country wife was clearly buying more of the family's foodstuffs in convenient, and genteel, forms. In a later, much-revised edition, Liger turned his attention to professional cooks, who were also changing focus. The downsizing of household staff meant that more food was bought outside the home, in turn creating opportunities for independent cooking businesses such as pâtisseries, charcuteries, auberges, cabarets, *traiteurs* (caterers), hotels, cafés,

and later restaurants.[34] All offered prepared food to eat in or
to take out, with differing levels of service and social status.

By the time that Menon's *La cuisinière bourgeoise suivie de
l'office* appeared in 1746, almost fifty years after the publication
of *Le ménage des champs,* the French publishing industry had
realized that bourgeois family cooking could no longer be
ignored. The title in French is deliberately ambiguous, and as
Menon himself said, can be read as either bourgeois *cuisine* or
a bourgeois *woman cook.* Either way, as the first French cookbook to hint at a female cook, it appeared to answer a real
need in France, for it became the best seller of the century,
running to thirty-two editions between 1746 and 1789 alone,
with an untold number of pirated versions, and it continued
in print until 1865.[35]

For a variety of reasons, by midcentury the French economy
had gone into the decline that was to end with the explosion
of the Revolution. Every social level was affected, and one way
for households with servants to cut back was to employ
women. Menon had found the proverbial gap in the market.
In the last decades of the Old Regime, many aristocrats in
Paris and all over France lived in fragile circumstances, jug-
gling debts and investments in risky new colonial ventures,
keeping up appearances with perhaps no more than "a woman
cook, a femme de chambre, two footmen and a coachman."[36]
After the Revolution, in the 1790s, 80 to 90 percent of servants
in French households were women.[37] Even the legendary
Antonin Carême acknowledged the importance of the femi-
nine market: "[The housewife's] reading will disclose an infi-
nite number of easy things to do; she can instruct her cook in sensual flavors; she can
prepare delicious dinners with her own hands, which will draw warm praise from her
guests."[38]

OPPOSITE The multitude of tasks necessary to maintain a country property are summed up in the
frontispiece of *Le ménage des champs et le jardinier françois accommodez au gout du temps* by Louis Liger,
1711. Clockwise from top left: treading grapes for wine, milking a cow, herding sheep, hunting rabbits,
setting an outdoor buffet, stocking the larder with hanging game and supplying the still room behind
the door, baking, cooking at the raised *potager* stove, plucking game, and harvesting fruit. The owners
of the house in the center of the image have plenty to show their guests.

ABOVE Our 1748 copy of Menon's *La cuisinière bourgeoise* has his signature on the title page. Menon
signs his book with only his family name, though "François" is often added by bibliographers to
acknowledge his nationality, a common practice in France when authors' first names were unknown.

THE POTATO
& PARMENTIER

Many books have been written about the romantic, sometimes tragic, history of potatoes. The suspicion with which the tubers were regarded when explorers first brought them to Europe from Colombia in the mid-sixteenth century offers no hint of the staple they have become. Spanish and Italian cooks found them watery and slightly bitter. Two other New World tubers were more acceptable, root artichokes and sweet potatoes, which bear no botanical relation to the common potato. The English, however, were more welcoming: in *The Herball* (1597), John Gerarde declared them "a meate for pleasure, equall in goodnesse and wholesomenesse unto the same."[1]

During the seventeenth century, reactions to the potato were mixed, varying from disdain in Germany and France to guarded acceptance in England and Ireland. "A very useful Root," remarked Richard Bradley in *The Country Housewife and Lady's Director* in 1727. "Being either boil'd or roasted in hot Embers. And after it is boiled . . . and beaten in a Mortar, it is used to thicken Sauces, and for making rich Puddings."[2] By this time, potatoes in English cookbooks had become more prolific. For ex-

ample, Hannah Glasse in *The Art of Cookery Made Plain and Easy* (1747) included ten recipes, and most other contemporary authors offered at least one or two potato dishes.

One of the oddest characters in the history of cookbooks is Frenchman Antoine-Augustin Parmentier, the archetypal scientist. His name is indelibly associated with the potato, beginning in the Seven Years' War, when he was imprisoned in Prussia and fed largely on potatoes, then considered the poorest possible diet.[3] On his return to France, his ensuing good health encouraged him first to experiment with the potato and then to propose it as a cheap, nutritious food. Results were mixed. As distant relatives of the deadly nightshade family, potatoes were still popularly regarded in France as poisonous. Even in parts of Great Britain, they were deemed inedible. Protestants wouldn't plant them because they were not mentioned in the Bible, though Irish Catholics dodged the question with a sprinkling of holy water and Good Friday plantings.[4]

A marketing genius, Parmentier began a series of publicity stunts for which he remains famous. First he held a series of dinners, inviting notables including scientist Antoine Lavoisier. Next he presented a bouquet of potato flowers to King Louis

XVI on his birthday, August 23, 1785, a gesture that persuaded the monarch to serve the tubers at court.[5] By 1778, Parmentier had published a massive treatise on baking, *Le parfait boulanger* (The Perfect Baker), in which he praised potatoes and launched a potato bread that contained no grain starch whatsoever. He even sent a loaf to Benjamin Franklin, the American commissioner in Paris at the time. Meanwhile, Parmentier had obtained permission to plant potatoes in some waste ground near Paris at Les Sablons (the name means sandy). In a stroke of brilliance, he arranged for soldiers to guard the field by day, which left it open at night for the curious to steal this seemingly valuable foodstuff.

Aided by his sister, Parmentier tested dozens of recipes using potatoes, including soup, potatoes with fresh cheese, a potato preserve, an "economical cake," and a "very delicate" sweet cookie made with potato starch. Parmentier directed the health service under Napoleon's Empire and was awarded one of the first Légion d'Honneur medals.[6] He epitomizes the new men of his time who were able, by their brilliance and versatility, to bridge the gap between pre- and post-Revolutionary France. ♦

1 John Gerarde, *The Herball or Generall Historie of Plantes* (London: Adam Islip Joice Norton, 1633), 928.

2 Richard Bradley, *The Country Housewife and Lady's Director,* ed. Caroline Davidson (Totnes, England: Prospect Books, 1980), 138.

3 Anne Muratori-Philip, *Parmentier* (Paris: Plon, 1994), 9.

4 Alan Davidson, *Oxford Companion to Food* (Oxford: Oxford University Press, 1999), 627.

5 John Reader, *Potato: A History of the Propitious Esculent* (New Haven, CT: Yale University Press, 2009), 119–22.

6 Larry Zuckerman, *The Potato: How the Humble Spud Rescued the Western World* (Boston: Faber & Faber, 1998), 82.

In this early nineteenth-century portrait by Francois Dumont (1751–1831), the crusading scientist Antoine-Augustin Parmentier holds emblems of three staple foods—ears of wheat, a cob of corn, and potato flowers.

Pier Leone Ghezzi, widely regarded as the first professional caricaturist, drew this satirical print, "Madame Petit et Son Cuisinier," in 1722.

Menon's book launched the concept of a simple bourgeois cuisine that was good for both health and household finances. This notion overlaps with the concept of *cuisine de femme,* though the term was not yet coined—the welcoming, simple food that is cooked by a grandmother at the stove of every French family, at least in the imagination. He lived up to his promise to provide recipes that were simple, good, new, and clearly explained. For example, *La cuisinière bourgeoise* contains bills of fare and "instructions for people who wish to keep a respectable table" *(une bonne table bourgeoise).* The second part of the title is *Suivie de l'office* (Followed by the Cold Kitchen) because, Menon explains, often a woman cook must combine the roles of cook and head of the cold kitchen, and employers will only keep female cooks who can master the skills of both. Thanks to Menon's attentions to the bourgeois cook and his hearty, simple recipes, the term *bourgeois* came to be associated with honest food, and to this day, the French word lacks the English, often pejorative, connotation of conservative affluence.

On the Sidelines

Elsewhere in Europe, fewer writers turned their attention to the kitchen, reflecting a century preoccupied with intermittent wars. In the Germanic states, cookbooks centered on cities and the regions surrounding them—Salzburg, Brandenburg, Leipzig, and Hamburg are examples. Several were substantial tomes, and more than one of them harked back to the fifteenth century and *Küchenmeisterei* for inspiration. Spain had its own problems, with its empire faltering, and only one notable cookbook emerged, written by a Franciscan monk, Juan Altamiras. *Nuevo arte de cocina* (New Art of Cooking, 1745) reflects such popular tastes as seasoning with the medieval favorites cinnamon and sugar. This is a small book, written with modest cooks in mind, and includes hearty fare for the simple household.[39] The distinguishing feature is a dozen groundbreaking recipes for tomatoes, showing an early acceptance in Spain of this New World novelty.

On the Italian peninsula, the Kingdom of Naples was at this time a flourishing center of culture, famed for its confectionery and ices chilled by the snows of Vesuvius.

Vincenzo Corrado must have been quite a character. From the title of his book *Il cuoco galante* (1773) to the plaudits below his romantic portrait, he captures the imagination. Who could resist recipes from a "practical genius" and "arbiter of good taste"?

IL CUOCO GALANTE

OPERA MECCANICA

DELL' ORITANO

VINCENZO CORRADO

Di varie capricciofe vivande nel fine de' loro ifteffi Trattati accrefciuta.

IN NAPOLI MDCCLXXVIII.

NELLA STAMPERIA RAIMONDIANA.

These innovations were the topic of Vincenzo Corrado's *Il credenziere di buon gusto* (The Confectioner of Good Taste, 1778), a book that was widely read throughout Europe. Surprisingly, given these sybaritic subjects, Corrado was a lay monk and scholar from the region surrounding Naples. His works ranged from a treatise on potatoes to an early book on vegetarian cookery, and he championed Neapolitan cooking as a rival to French on the international scene, first doing so in *Il cuoco galante* (The Elegant Cook, 1773).

Corrado's fellow Neapolitan Francesco Leonardi enjoyed an international career, for a few years acting as steward to the splendid court of Catherine the Great. Leonardi collected recipes from all over Europe, including *baccalà alla provenziale* (salt cod provençale) and *ragù di gamberi alla tedesca* (ragoût of shrimp in German style), and he too included tomatoes, this time with pasta, though decades would pass before his countrymen were prepared to adopt the dish. His energy is reflected in his style, with one reader observing that he "wrote with that naive want of reserve peculiar to distinguished cooks."[40] Leonardi's *L'Apicio moderno* (The Modern Apicius, 1790) was the most important Italian cookbook to

228

be published since Bartolomeo Scappi's *Opera,* with more than three thousand recipes, and it undoubtedly influenced the great Italian nineteenth-century classic by Pellegrino Artusi, *La scienza in cucina* (Science in Cooking, 1891).

"Ma che fritto" (What wonderful fritters) declares this English print of Italian street food, from 1820, artist unknown.

The American Adventure

An ocean away, the American colonies gradually forged a separate identity while sharing the heritage of the Old World. Many features of the new land challenged its citizens: flying sand in Florida, a limited amount of specie (hard cash) in circulation, extremes of climate, recurring friction with the indigenous population. The European Romantic movement celebrated nature, but the New World *was* nature: pristine, savage, and idealized. Much colonial wealth was built upon slave labor, while white European-Americans struggled to create a genteel society. For at least the first half of the eighteenth century, Britain's American colonies did their best to emulate the lifestyles of the mother country, and in 1705, tobacco planter Robert Beverley wrote of his fellow Virginians, "The Families being altogether on Country-Seats, they have

Just three years before his death, Quaker Edward Hicks (1780–1849) painted this idealized scene, *The Residence of David Twining 1785*, from memories of his childhood on the Twining family farm in Newtown, Pennsylvania. Collection American Folk Art Museum, New York.

their Graziers, Seedsmen, Gardiners, Brewers, Bakers, Butchers, and Cooks within themselves: they have a great Plenty and Variety of Provisions for their Table; and as for Spicery, and other things that the Country don't produce, they have constant supplies of 'em from England. The Gentry pretend to have their Victuals drest, and serv'd up as Nicely, as at the best Tables in London."[41]

Upwardly mobile colonists of even modest means followed British trends, reproducing at a distance the latest London fads, with manufactured goods re-creating a comfortable material life in the New World. By midcentury, keeping a fine table at all levels of society was a well-established, if simpler, American ideal.

Up to this point, about five British cookbooks had been reprinted in America, and many others had been imported from the Old World. Not until 1796 did an American cook publish a homegrown American cookbook, a small volume that appeared in Hartford, Connecticut, unpretentiously titled *American Cookery* by Amelia Simmons,

EARLY DAYS IN NEW ENGLAND

The French gastronome Jean Anthelme Brillat-Savarin painted a vivid picture of the food of New England during his visit to America in 1794. A farmer and his four daughters set down a classic country spread: "a superb piece of corned beef, a stewed goose, a magnificent leg of mutton, a vast selection of vegetables, and at either end of the table two huge jugs of cider."[1] The "made" dishes such as cucumber *ragoût* or hashed beef with oysters that were the pride of English contemporaries were absent. Colonial cooks had no time for such "kickshaws." "If provisions were precarious and cooking rough-and-ready on the frontier, it can be seen that in the settled areas, Americans of the seventeenth and eighteenth centuries ate extremely well," says Karen Hess, an expert on Amelia Simmons.[2] A comfortable abundance can be inferred from Amelia Simmons's *American Cookery* (1796), but luxury it certainly was not, at least away from major towns.

"Dismal indeed was the life of a cook in early America," reports one authority, though American cooks were working in conditions scarcely more onerous than in England.[3] Typical kitchens featured a large fireplace for cooking, outfitted with the customary hooks, trammels, boiling pots, frying pans, spits, and mechanical jacks. Wherever possible, households must have assigned the nasty chores to servants or slaves. Kitchen gardens were as popular in America as in England, providing easy access to parsley, sweet herbs, and onions. Cattle imported from England yielded plenty of meat and dairy products. Mace, nutmeg, cinnamon, and pepper arrived regularly from the West Indies. Some of the recipes for home remedies that still appeared

The Chowder Party, an engraving in the style of Winslow Homer, appeared in *Ballou's Pictorial,* a weekly newspaper published in the 1850s.

in eighteenth-century British books would have been useful, although Native American herbal remedies were also published by American naturalists.

Far earlier than Amelia Simmons and the first American cookbook, English women cookbook writers of the eighteenth century had shaped the fashionable cooking of the New World. English cookbooks had become spectacularly popular New World imports—notably E. Smith's *The Compleat Housewife,* printed in Williamsburg as early as 1742, and Susannah Carter's *The Frugal Housewife,* published in Boston in 1772 with engravings by Paul Revere.[4] Almost all these books were written by women, though male cooks were represented by Richard Briggs's *The English Art of Cookery,* published as *The New Art of Cookery* in Philadelphia in 1791.[5] Scholarly studies have shown that at least one Virginia family had Robert May's seventeenth-century *The Accomplisht Cook* and John Evelyn's *Acetaria* (1699) in its library. Others owned Elizabeth Raffald's *The Experienced English Housekeeper* (1769),

though there is no record of advertisements for its sale by booksellers.[6] Benjamin Franklin's library contained a well-thumbed copy of Menon's *La cuisinière bourgeoise.* ♦

1 Jean Anthelme Brillat-Savarin, *The Physiology of Taste: or Meditations on Transcendental Gastronomy,* trans. M. F. K. Fisher (New York: Everyman's Library, 2009), 58.

2 John L. Hess and Karen Hess, *The Taste of America* (Columbia: University of South Carolina Press, 1989), 31.

3 Elizabeth Donaghy Garrett, *At Home: The American Family 1750–1870* (New York: Harry N. Abrams, 1990), 99.

4 See Eleanor Lowenstein's chronology of cookbook printing in America, *American Cookery Books 1742–1860* (Worcester, NY: American Antiquarian Society, 1972). American Philosophical Society, *Benjamin Franklin on the Art of Eating* (Princeton, NJ: Princeton University Press, 2004), 35.

5 Other cookbooks by women that were recorded in early America are Hannah Glasse's *The Art of Cookery Made Plain and Easy,* published in Alexandria, Virginia; Sarah Harrison's *House-Keeper's Pocket-Book;* and Martha Bradley's *The British Housewife: or, The Cook, Housekeeper's and Gardiner's Companion.*

6 Jane Carson, *Colonial Virginia Cookery* (Williamsburg, VA: Colonial Williamsburg Foundation, 1985), xii-xvii.

AMERICAN COOKERY,

OR THE ART OF DRESSING

VIANDS, FISH, POULTRY and VEGETABLES,

AND THE BEST MODES OF MAKING

PASTES, PUFFS, PIES, TARTS, PUDDINGS,
CUSTARDS AND PRESERVES,

AND ALL KINDS OF

CAKES,

FROM THE IMPERIAL PLUMB TO PLAIN CAKE.

ADAPTED TO THIS COUNTRY,

AND ALL GRADES OF LIFE.

By Amelia Simmons,

AN AMERICAN ORPHAN.

PUBLISHED ACCORDING TO ACT OF CONGRESS.

HARTFORD:

PRINTED BY HUDSON & GOODWIN.

FOR THE AUTHOR.

1796.

"an American Orphan." Mrs. Simmons wrote in her preface, "The orphan . . . will find it essentially necessary to have an opinion and determination of her own," and this book was hers—in its small way another declaration of American independence.[42] The book lived up to the title, though it borrowed from previously published English recipes: the chapters on syllabubs and preserves are lifted wholesale from Susannah Carter's *Frugal Housewife* (1772). It contains fewer than fifty pages, exact measurements for ingredients are scanty, and many recipes are just a few lines long.

The joy of Amelia Simmons's book is what was new in it, not what was old. Corn looms large in her dishes. In the first printed recipes using cornmeal, Mrs. Simmons mentions Indian slapjacks, "johny" or hoecakes, and three versions of Indian pudding (at the time, cornmeal was often referred to as Indian meal), and she also uses corncobs to smoke bacon. She suggests cranberry sauce as an accompaniment to turkey, and the recipe for "pumpkin" turns out to be a sweet pie, another colonial innovation. Oddly, Mrs. Simmons lists only a few homey soups and stews, but a later edition of *American Cookery,* published the same year, has a superb array of cakes, including Independence Cake and Election Cake, the latter using twenty pounds of flour and four dozen eggs. What a task it must have been to beat the batter!

A number of colonial families, like their European forebears, kept manuscript recipe books called commonplace books, so the dishes that are new in print in Simmons's *American Cookery* had probably been old favorites for some time. However, the contemporary English cook would have found some of Simmons's vocabulary unfamiliar: Crookneck or Winter Squash Pudding was a newcomer. Fat (probably a mixture of lard and butter) for making pastry was "shortening," and biscuits have become "cookies," from the Dutch *koekje.* Simmons was the first to use a chemical raising agent called pearl ash, a substance akin to baking soda and derived from potash, the ashes of a wood fire. This led directly to the quick breads, such as her Molasses Gingerbread, that became so characteristic of American cooking. Before then, cooks had had to rely on brewer's yeast (Simmons calls it "emptins") to raise their breads, a slower-acting and often unreliable ingredient.

Mrs. Simmons was writing, she said, "for the improvement of the rising generation of *Females* in America, the Lady of fashion and fortune," as well as those who "are reduced to the necessity of going into families in the line of domestics."[43] With no provision for training, this was a very different world from the structured hierarchy

---

OPPOSITE The modest title page from *American Cookery* by Amelia Simmons, 1796, epitomizes the contents. The first American cookbook was an artisan production with none of the fancy illustrations and bindings of contemporary European cookbooks. However, its forty-eight pages contain a culinary revolution, making generous use of American ingredients such as corn, squash, pumpkin, and pearl ash (the forerunner of baking powder).

AT HOME ON
THE RANGE

Sometime in the eighteenth century, the iron firedogs that had long been used to prop up logs in an open fire developed into a grate, a horizontal rack that would hold small as well as large logs. Over time, this setup grew more complicated, with additions such as trivets attached to the front bar to hold a kettle or Dutch oven. The size of the fire could be adjusted by contracting or opening the "cheeks" of the grate or by folding down its front bars. These monster cooking assemblies were called open ranges, and coal, which had become more affordable during the eighteenth century, was key to their development. The coal firing of cast iron allowed the production of cheap, sturdy open ranges. And coal, hotter and more compact than wood, was used to stoke the fire itself. The way was clear for the great eighteenth-century revolution of the closed range.[1]

The closed range is associated with Count Rumford, a peripatetic American born in 1753 in Massachusetts, who emigrated to Bavaria and later to England after the Revolution. Rumford was a scientist, an expert in chimney design. In his ranges, placement of a hot plate on top of the open fire created an enclosed cooking chamber, eliminating the need for a suspended pot: a variety of pots and pans could now be heated simultaneously on the flat surface. The engineering of a closed range could be quite complicated, with an arrangement of flues and dampers to control ventilation. An oven and a tank for water might be added at each side of the fire. Some designs enclosed the coals and others left them open to view, but either way, the new ranges mitigated the hot, sweaty aspect of cooking over an open fire. They allowed more accurate control of cooking, and one person could easily oversee a multiplicity of pots. They were also cleaner and easier to stoke than an open fire, though they did call for skill in regulating the ventilation,

which would vary with the direction of the wind. The whole apparatus required frequent, thorough cleaning (a twenty-four-hour job as the range had first to be left to cool).

Though the early nineteenth-century ranges marketed under Rumford's name were said to be "a travesty of what he had actually recommended," it was ultimately thanks to him that the role of the cook in both domestic and professional kitchens was transformed.[2] Throughout the history of kitchens, the cook's creativity and skill have been limited by the equipment at hand. Sometimes it is hard to know which came first, the technology or the dishes that demanded it. Did the even heat of a closed range inspire the delicate sautés, cooked in just a few tablespoons of sauce, made famous by Carême in the early 1800s? Who is to know? ♦

1 Caroline Davidson, *A Woman's Work Is Never Done: A History of Housework in the British Isles 1650–1950* (London: Chatto & Windus, 1982), 60.

2 Ibid., 63.

Long before this kitchen scene from *Modern Domestic Cookery* "By A Lady" (1853), the gadgets and conveniences depicted by the artist had been proliferating in the domestic kitchen.

of Europe. Simmons's recipes are simple but by no means superficial. Reflecting the scattered settlements of the Northeast in the late eighteenth and early nineteenth centuries, over the next decades *American Cookery* was printed in a half dozen New York and New England towns—Albany, Troy, Poughkeepsie, Northampton, Salem, Walpole, Brattleborough—and finally in New York and Baltimore in 1822. Despite this geographic spread, the book seemed to achieve only limited success, perhaps because of competition from the authoritative British housewives who had earlier cornered the market.

Nevertheless, Mrs. Simmons's recipes enjoyed much wider circulation than might appear at first glance. In 1805, *The New American Cookery, or Female Companion* by "An American Lady" was published in New York and circulated widely in the northeastern colonies. The book included an exact reprint of Simmons's second edition of *American Cookery,* followed by some twenty pages on wines and cheese making taken mostly from *The Frugal Housewife.*[44] Copies of this rare edition are hard to find. Another plagiarized version of *American Cookery* (from the Troy, New York, edition of 1808) appeared in the same year with the title *The New-England Cookery.* At least the writer, Lucy Emerson, admitted openly in her preface, "It is with diffidence that I come before the public as an Authoress, even to this little work; I have no pretensions to the originality of the whole of the receipts herein contained, it is due to those LADIES who have gone before me." To her title, Mrs. Emerson added a sweeping summary of the modest contents: "the Art of Dressing All Kinds of Flesh, Fish, and Vegetables, and the Best Modes of Making Pastes, Puffs, Pies, Tarts, Puddings, Custards and Preserves, and all kinds of Cakes, from the Imperial Plumb to Plain Cake."[45] She clearly was a woman of self-confidence.

THE

NEW-ENGLAND COOKERY,

OR THE

ART OF DRESSING

ALL KINDS OF FLESH, FISH, AND VEGETABLES,

AND THE

BEST MODES OF MAKING

PASTES, PUFFS, PIES, TARTS, PUDDINGS, CUS-
TARDS AND PRESERVES,

AND ALL KINDS OF

CAKES,

From the Imperial PLUMB
TO PLAIN CAKE.

Particularly adapted to this part of our Country.

COMPILED BY LUCY EMERSON.

Montpelier:

PRINTED FOR JOSIAH PARKS.
(Proprietor of the work.)

1808.

ABOVE Plagiarism was as common in early America as it was in Europe. The title page as well as the contents of *The New-England Cookery* by Lucy Emerson (1808) are almost identical to those of Amelia Simmons's *American Cookery,* though Mrs. Emerson does acknowledge in her preface, "I have no pretensions to the originality of the whole of the receipts herein contained, it is due to those LADIES who have gone before me."

The stylish comfort of prosperous households in early-nineteenth-century Boston is highlighted in *The Dinner Party* by Henry Sargent, c. 1821. Photograph © 2012 Museum of Fine Arts, Boston.

Why was the wait so long for the first American cookbook? One reason was the convenience of imported British cookbooks. Their recipes were easily replicated in colonial kitchens, and since the majority of settlers were of British descent, they were only too happy to continue the culinary traditions of the old country, whether from a printed cookbook or a treasured commonplace book handed down through generations. Eating familiar puddings and pies boosted morale, while tried-and-true recipes

236

for pickling and potting were just as applicable in British America. As for strange New World foods, there is ample evidence that colonial settlers learned from Native Americans how to handle them in their new home. Further instruction was not needed: a housewife would have recorded these new ideas in her commonplace book for reference.

A practical reason for the late appearance of *American Cookery* was the slow progress of setting up printing presses. The colonial population was small, and presses in seventeenth- and early eighteenth-century America were few. Printers made their living with modest jobs printing laws, almanacs, prayer books, and leaflets, and most received wages from representative assemblies that claimed precedence for their favored publications.[46] Cookbooks were not high on the list of priorities.

Well into the next century, colonists continued to rely on plain, honest British cooking, not least in order to retain their good health in their new surroundings. In both England and America, the eighteenth-century philosophy of health and diet was still influenced by the theory of the humors. Many learned writers expressed concern that the heat in the American South and the West Indian islands might contribute to settlers' physical and moral degeneration. Naturalists and doctors believed that food was vitally important to protect northern Europeans from "creolization," or transformation into a race dissipated by the environment of this strange new world.[47] It was no coincidence that the most popular English early cookbook writers in America, Mrs. E. Smith and Hannah Glasse, were also the most stridently patriotic.

MOVING INTO THE NINETEENTH CENTURY, cooks and authors were experimenting with new ideas and outlets. In America, cooks were gradually to transform their colonial English dishes with the ingredients they found in their new homes, as well as to adopt recipes brought by the waves of immigrants from other countries. The British continued to widen the gap between cooking inside and outside the home. In France, cooks pursued the innovations of nouvelle cuisine, while out in the dining room, gourmands were adapting their dining habits to the new, postrevolutionary regime. Kitchen staffs were reduced while their masters and mistresses dined increasingly in the restaurants that animated the dining scene. This animation was to bring a small, brilliant crop of remarkable books about food and cooking, developing new genres in the ever-enthralling subject of eating.

RECIPES

D URING THE EIGHTEENTH CENTURY, national culinary repertoires become more clearly defined, and indeed familiar to us. France is famous for its sauces and the structured garnishes that are integral accompaniments to its meats, fish, and fowl. François Menon's Filet de Boeuf à la Gendarme is a classic example: slices of beef tenderloin are marinated with onion, garlic, and mushroom; roasted on a spit; and then served with a complex sauce created from the cooking juices, a glass of Champagne, fresh herbs, and a thickening of already-made coulis. Basic preparations such as coulis and roux that had been developed in the previous century now play a wide role in flavors that are characteristically complex. The French shorthand for describing dishes, such as veal *à la bourgeoise* (in a rich sauce, often with carrots and onions) and *à l'indienne* (with powdered spices), is at its most inventive.

England takes a simpler route, preferring plainly cooked meats (often roasted) with vegetables on the side. Sauces and accompaniments are more like condiments, hot with mustard or horseradish and sweet with fruits. A center of maritime trade, England becomes expert in preserves and pickles, many flavored with spices brought from the Indies. Potting, a slow-cooking method of preserving meats and fish that resembles French confit, is characteristic. Savory and dessert pies remain a specialty, almost always covered with a top crust and often a bottom crust as well. Fillings are simplified from the great medieval "coffins" that were carried in procession through the dining hall, but vestiges linger in recipes like Yorkshire Christmas pie, in which five domestic birds are boned, spiced, wrapped one inside another, and baked with assorted wild birds and a boned hare inside a robust butter crust. The pie is served cold so that its slices display a wonderful mosaic of meats.

In the pastry kitchen, French and Italian cooks reign supreme, turning out everything from little sugar, fruit, and almond petits fours to tickle the taste buds up to astonishing sugar constructions several feet high that delight the eye and fire the imagination. Spain is famous for its sweet confections, and responsible for bringing the chocolate that now spreads throughout Europe, first as a drink, then as a dessert flavoring. This is the century in which sorbets and ice creams sweep Europe. At first sorbets were drinks chilled with snow, but by the mid-eighteenth century, the freezing properties of adding salt to ice have been discovered, and cookbooks burgeon with ices, most of them sweet but some savory too. Cooks crave a hand-cranked churn for freezing, with an ice house hidden among the trees on up-to-date country properties.

This is also the century in which the kitchens of the New and the Old Worlds become closer. Foods such as potatoes, tomatoes, and corn are increasingly found in

Europe, though the rate of acceptance on the table varies enormously from country to country. Early America relies on imported English cookbooks for printed recipes, and an English style predominates in the domestic kitchen. However, the first American cookbook, *American Cookery* by Amelia Simmons, published in 1796, contains a handful of staple new recipes that had been quietly developing. One is To Alamode a Round, in effect a pot roast; others use the squash and pumpkin that grow so abundantly in the vegetable garden; and several call for cornmeal, already a basic ingredient in dishes like Indian slapjacks and johnnycakes.

Artichaux Frits

Fried Artichokes

From Louis Liger, *Le ménage des champs et le jardinier françois accommodez au gout du temps* (Paris, 1711): *One fries artichokes, & for that, one cuts them in slices, one removes the choke, & one cleans them well.*

Then one cooks them in water, when done, one dips them in a light batter, made of fine flour, salt, pepper & an egg; then one fries them in lard or melted butter.

One can if one wishes simply flour the artichokes, & put them to fry, to serve with fried parsley as garnish.

One serves Artichokes à la Crème, one takes only the bottoms, that one cooks in boiling water, then one tosses them in butter in the saucepan, or with bacon, and a bunch of fresh herbs; then one adds cream, all well seasoned; when they are cooked one serves them hot.

Artichokes are included in most ragoûts, & are one of the principle garnishes.

THE EUROPEAN FASCINATION for globe artichokes continued for centuries, dating back to the mid-1400s, when they arrived in Naples. A mid-seventeenth-century engraving by Abraham Bosse shows a happy couple feasting on a single giant artichoke to illustrate "Taste," one of the five senses. A half century later, Louis Liger feels he has to include this edible member of the thistle family with such fashionable vegetables as asparagus, cardoons, pumpkin, beans, and green peas, but is clearly bored. "I say nothing here of the common way to prepare artichokes," he remarks. "Nor how to make a sauce, as no one who has the smallest knowledge of housekeeping is not informed. Here are other methods which will be good to learn." All are elegantly expressed in the third person, perhaps to emphasize Liger's background as an agronomist rather than a working cook, and this recipe for fried artichokes *à la crème* is only one of his handful of ideas.

Fried Artichokes with Bacon and Cream   *Serves 4 as a first course*

1 lemon, halved

4 large globe artichokes

Salt and pepper

1 tablespoon (15 g) lard or vegetable oil

4 or 5 thin slices bacon, diced

3 tablespoons mixed chopped fresh herbs such as savory, sage,
or thyme with parsley and chives
1 cup (250 ml) crème fraîche or heavy cream

To trim the artichokes: Prepare a saucepan of cold water made acid with the juice of the lemon. Break the stalk from the head of an artichoke. Pull back and snap off all the large bottom leaves from the head, leaving a cone of soft, small leaves in the center. Using a small knife, trim any remaining green parts where the leaves were attached. Trim the soft cone level with the artichoke bottom, leaving a bit of the central choke attached. At once drop the artichoke bottom into the saucepan of water before it discolors. Repeat with the remaining artichokes.

To cook the artichokes: Add a little salt to the water in the pan, cover, and bring to a boil. Simmer until the artichoke bottoms are just tender when pierced with the point of a knife, 15 to 20 minutes. Drain them and let cool. Scoop out the inedible choke with a teaspoon and cut the bottoms into slices ¼ inch (6 mm) thick.

Heat the lard in a frying pan and fry the bacon, stirring often, until lightly browned, 2 to 3 minutes. Add the sliced artichokes and stir gently to mix. Stir in the herbs and crème fraîche with some pepper, then heat gently until very hot, 3 to 4 minutes. Taste and add salt if needed. Serve at once while very hot, as the artichokes quickly absorb the cream.

A Rich Seed-Cake, Call'd the Nun's Cake

From Mrs. E. Smith, *The Compleat Housewife* (London, 1727; recipe from 1742 edition): *Take four pounds of your finest flour, and three pounds of double-refin'd sugar beaten and sifted, mix them together, and dry them by the fire till you prepare your other materials. Take four pounds of butter, beat it in your hands till it is very soft like cream, then beat thirty-five eggs, leave out sixteen whites, and strain out the treddles of the rest, and beat them and the butter together till all appears like butter; put in four or five spoonfuls of rose or orange-flower-water, and beat it again ; then take your flour and sugar, with six ounces of carraway-seeds, and strew it in by degrees, beating it up all the time for two hours together; you may put in as much tincture of cinnamon or ambergrease as you please ; butter your hoop, and let it stand three hours in a moderate oven.*

HOW CAKE MAKING HAS BEEN REVOLUTIONIZED! As a child in rural Yorkshire, I would join in making the Christmas cakes following almost exactly the ritual described by Mrs. Smith. Our stout, old cook Emily would rise before the sun to stoke the wood-burning fire that heated the oven beside it. After five hours or more of preheating, the oven temperature would have mellowed to the desired even, medium level that Emily would test with a leaf of newspaper; when it took one minute to scorch, the heat was just right.

Meanwhile, the ingredients were prepared. The flour was spread on a baking sheet, set before the fire, and stirred from time to time to dry out the all-pervasive winter damp. The sugar was sifted to eliminate lumps, again caused by damp. The whites of our farm eggs had fertilized threads in them, so they needed to be strained. Dried fruits and nuts (not called for in Mrs. Smith's seed cake) were picked over, rinsed, and drained. The cake pan was lined with more newspaper for insulation, then with a layer of buttered parchment.

At last the mixing began. By then all the ingredients, and we ourselves, were at warm room temperature. Emily would install me in a low chair, where I clutched the largest pottery mixing bowl in the house to my chest. First the butter: I would squish with my fingers, then curving my hand like a spoon would beat it to a cream, the warmth of my little, eager hand helping the mix. Then came the eggs, beaten into the butter one by one. By now muscle power was needed and Emily would take over, beating rhythmically and taking turns with each hand. Finally came the flour, beaten in too with no effete nonsense about "folding as lightly as possible." Once the cake was in the oven, we would creep about the house lest a banging door create a draft on the fire, causing the cake to fall. A fallen Christmas cake betokens a death in the house in the coming year.

The sheer muscle power needed to beat as much cake batter as Mrs. Smith describes is prodigious. Old Emily and I never ventured beyond a couple of pounds of flour and sixteen eggs, half Mrs. Smith's quantities. Here I've quartered them, revealing almost-perfect proportions for a classic pound-cake batter. I urge you to try mixing by hand. The direct contact with the batter as it develops from a soft cream to a smooth, fluffy batter is an experience not to be missed. If you use an electric mixer, the batter is fluffier but the cake emerges from the oven less moist and with a darker crust. Ambergris, a waxy secretion from a sperm whale, was once used to perfume foods. As it is now a rare ingredient, I've opted for Mrs. Smith's second suggestion, of cinnamon, which marries unexpectedly well with caraway.

Rich Seed Cake with Caraway and Cinnamon *Makes one 9-inch (22-cm) cake*

3½ cups (450 g) flour
1⅔ cups (330 g) sugar
6 tablespoons (45 g) caraway seeds
5 eggs
4 egg yolks
2 cups (450 g) butter, more for the pan
1½ tablespoons rose water or orange-flower water
2 teaspoons ground cinnamon

9-inch (22-cm) springform pan

Heat the oven to 325°F (160°C). Butter the springform pan. Sift together the flour and sugar into a medium bowl, and stir in the caraway seeds. Separate the whole eggs, putting all the yolks together and straining the whites into a small bowl to remove the threads.

To make the batter: Cream the butter either by hand or with an electric mixer fitted with the paddle attachment. Add the yolks two at a time, beating well after each addition. Beat in the rose water. Whisk the egg whites just until frothy, then beat them, a little at a time, into the egg yolk mixture. Beat in the cinnamon. Finally, beat in the flour mixture, sprinkling it a little at a time over the batter. This should take at least 15 minutes by hand, 5 minutes with a mixer. The batter will lighten and become fluffier. Transfer the batter to the prepared pan.

To bake the cake: Bake until the cake starts to shrink from the sides of the pan and a skewer inserted in the center comes out clean when withdrawn, 1¼ to 1½ hours. Let the cake cool in the pan on a rack to tepid, then unmold it and leave it to cool completely on the rack. When carefully wrapped, it keeps well at room temperature for several days and the flavor will mellow.

Chocolate Cream (au Bain Marie)

From Vincent La Chapelle, *The Modern Cook* (London, 1733): *[Take a Quart of Cream, put in it a Bit of Sugar, a Stick of Cinnamon and a Bit of green Lemon-Peel, with a quarter of a Pound of Chocolate broken in pieces. Let it boil all together. Your Chocolate being well mixt and boil'd, and your Cream palatable, take it off . . .] Your Cream being boil'd and order'd as aforesaid, place your Sieve upon your Dish, and put in it six Yolks of Eggs, with your Chocolate Cream prepar'd as before. Then strain it through a Sieve, put a Stew-pan full of water on the Fire, let the Bottom of your Dish touch the Water, put your Cream in it, and cover it with another Dish with Fire over it. Your Cream being taken, put it in a cool Place, and serve it up for a dainty Dish, either cold or hot.*

BY THE TIME VINCENT LA CHAPELLE wrote this recipe in 1733, chocolate as a flavoring for sweet desserts was high fashion, and even today the preparation seems quite modern in its focus on simplicity and purity of flavor. Just as we might do, he melts his chocolate in cream with a bit of sugar, then infuses it subtly with cinnamon and with lime zest (he calls it green lemon), a trendy ingredient at the time. Lime and lemon juice had recently been discovered to prevent scurvy on long sea voyages.

To set the cream, La Chapelle bakes it in a shallow dish, partially immersing it in a water bath (a bain marie), and places a tray of hot coals on top so the custard is surrounded by low, even heat. In today's ovens the process is much simpler. To highlight the shimmering surface of the custard, you should use a plain shallow baking dish, of porcelain if you have one. The precaution I suggest of covering the custard with corrugated cardboard ensures that the surface does not crack or spot with drops of moisture. The silken texture of the cream is best at room temperature as an accompaniment to fresh fruit such as pears or strawberries.

Chocolate Cream with Lime   *Serves 6 to 8*

1 quart (1 liter) heavy cream

4 ounces (110 g) dark chocolate, coarsely chopped

3 tablespoons (45 g) sugar

2-inch (5-cm) piece cinnamon stick

Pared zest of 1 lime

6 egg yolks

1-quart (1-liter) shallow baking dish

Put the cream in a saucepan with the chocolate, sugar, and cinnamon stick. Give a bartender's twist to the lime zest to release the oil and drop it into the cream. Place over medium-low heat and stir with a wooden spoon until the chocolate melts and the sugar dissolves. Simmer gently until well flavored, about 10 minutes. Let the cream cool for 5 to 10 minutes.

Heat the oven to 350°F (180°C). Put the egg yolks in a bowl, whisk them until mixed, and stir in the chocolate mixture. Strain the custard into the baking dish, place the dish in a roasting pan, and pour hot water into the pan to reach halfway up the sides of the dish. Bring the water bath to a boil on top of the stove. Cover the dish with a sheet of cardboard so steam cannot reach the surface of the custard. The cardboard protects the custard, absorbing steam so it bakes without condensation marring the mirror-smooth surface.

Carefully put the water bath in the oven and bake until the cream is set and shivers only slightly when the dish is shaken, 45 to 55 minutes. Take the dish out of the water bath and let it cool for at least 3 hours, still covered with cardboard to keep the surface moist. The chocolate will set and the cream will stiffen. The cream is best at room temperature. It can be stored, tightly covered, for a day or two in the refrigerator, but you should let it come to room temperature before serving.

A Yorkshire Christmas-Pye

From Hannah Glasse, *The Art of Cookery Made Plain and Easy* (London, 1747): *First make a good Standing Crust, let the Wall and Bottom be very thick, bone a Turkey, a Goose, a Fowl, a Partridge, and a Pigeon, season them all very well, take half an Ounce of Mace, half an Ounce of Nutmegs, a quarter of an Ounce of Cloves, half an Ounce of black Pepper, all beat fine together, two large Spoonfuls of Salt, mix them together. Open the Fowls all down the Back, and bone them; first the Pigeon, then the Partridge, cover them; then the Fowl, then the Goose, and then the Turkey, which must be large; season them all well first, and lay them in the Crust, so as it will look only like a whole Turkey; then have a Hare ready cased, and wiped with a clean Cloth. Cut it to Pieces, that is jointed; season it, and lay it as close as you can on one Side ; on the other Side Woodcock, more Game, and what Sort of wild Fowl you can get. Season them well, and lay them close; put at least four Pounds of Butter into the Pye, then lay on your Lid, which must be a very thick one, and let it be well baked. It must have a very hot Oven, and will take at least four Hours.*

This Pye will take a Bushel of Flour; in this Chapter, you will see how to make it. These Pies are often sent to London in a Box as Presents ; therefore the Walls must be well built.

A Standing Crust for Great Pies.

Take a Peck of Flour, and six Pounds of Butter, boiled in a Gallon of Water, skim it off into the Flour, and as little of the Liquor as you can ; work it well up into a Paste, then pull it into Pieces till it is cold, then make it up in what Form you will have it. This is fit for the Walls of a Goose-pye.

CHRISTMAS PIE HARKS BACK to the legendary medieval *rôti sans pareil,* in which a dozen or more birds were boned and stuffed one inside the other, starting with a thrush enclosing an olive and ending with a peacock in full plumage. To open a feast, such edible collages were carried in formal state by a young woman with flowing, unbound hair to signal her virginity. Hannah Glasse's much later version involves five different birds, all boned and stuffed inside one another, then baked in a raised pie crust made with melted butter. The finished pie is a masterpiece, a specialty of northern England, where Mrs. Glasse was raised. "These Pies are often sent to *London* in a Box as Presents," she remarks, "therefore the Walls must be well built." (London was then a four-day journey by coach.) I like to imagine her as a young woman, before she left home to try her luck in London, decorating these edible sculptures at whim with leaves, roses, manikins, or signs of the zodiac.

Enough is enough, so here I have cut down on both the pastry and the filling for what is still a gargantuan pie, leaving out the hare and game birds that Mrs. Glasse uses to fill gaps at the sides of her giant poultry package. Even as it is, you'll need an outsize 10-quart (10-liter) oval vessel to mold the dough. All the birds are boned by the same method, and I would start with the turkey, as a large bird is easier to handle than a small one. When boning is finished, you will have a great pile of bones, the foundation for a big pot of stock.

For the pastry "walls," Hannah Glasse would have used raised pie pastry dough, a butter or lard and hot water dough that is still used for English pork pies. When warm, the dough is malleable, then it stiffens as it cools to a firm, freestanding pastry case (for a pie as big as this, for safety's sake I support the dough with foil). Mrs. Glasse's recipe uses a whole peck of flour, measuring two gallons, so the base and sides of her pie must have been very thick; I have cut quantities by more than half but nonetheless your pie will have walls ½ inch (1.25 cm) thick. Because today's birds are so fat, I have drastically reduced the quantity of butter added to the pie to moisten them.

The full recipe for Christmas pie is an all-day affair, calling for friends in the kitchen and at least one experienced cook. After baking, the pie must cool for six hours or more before slicing it to display the contrasting layers of white and dark meat. I've only made the grand original a couple of times, but a scaled-down version is quite easy to do. Simply reduce the number of birds to two or three, bone and season them as described, pack them into a big pot, and instead of creating walls of dough, bake them under your favorite pie crust.

The pie can be served warm or cold. A fruit chutney and a big pot of braised cabbage are good accompaniments to a warm pie. When served cold, the pie keeps well for up to a day at room temperature (during which it will develop its full fragrance), or two to three days in the refrigerator. Your favorite mustard, a cranberry or other sweet chutney, and a salad of root vegetables or peppery greens are good accompaniments. Either way, you're in for a feast. The golden, crusted pie resembles a giant modern terrine mold of earthenware, but Yorkshire Christmas Pie is totally, eminently, edible. To take it apart, first cut around the lid and remove it. Then make two vertical cuts through the pie and filling on either side of the "equator." Cut each hemispherical end in wedges. The remaining central piece can be cut lengthwise or across in slices ¾ inch (2 cm) thick. By our standards, the pastry is substantial, moist, and rich with butter and meat juices. In the 1700s, I have no doubt, every morsel was eaten, but for us a small wedge of pastry may be enough.

Yorkshire Christmas Pie of Five Birds *Serves 10 to 15*

One 12- to 14-pound (about 6-kg) turkey

One 8- to 10-pound (about 4-kg) goose

One 4- to 5-pound (about 2-kg) chicken

1 partridge or Cornish game hen

1 squab

2 whole nutmegs or 2 tablespoons (15 g) ground nutmeg

2 tablespoons (15 g) mace blades or 1 tablespoon (7 g) ground mace

2 teaspoons whole cloves or 1 teaspoon ground cloves

2 tablespoons (20 g) peppercorns or 2 tablespoons (15 g) ground pepper

¼ cup (75 g) salt

1 cup (225 g) butter, softened

RAISED PASTRY DOUGH

16 cups (2 kg) flour, more for rolling

4 cups (900 g) butter

2 tablespoons (30 g) salt

1½ quarts (1.5 liters) water, more if needed

1 egg lightly beaten with ½ teaspoon salt, for glaze

10-quart (10-liter) oval casserole

To bone the birds, starting with the carcass: Place the turkey on a cutting board. Trim off the wing tip and middle section, leaving the largest wing bone. With the breast of the bird down, slit the skin along the backbone from neck to tail. Cut out the wishbone. Carefully cut and pull the flesh and skin away from the carcass, working evenly with short, sharp strokes of the knife. After each cut, ease the flesh and skin away from the carcass with your fingers. Cut the flesh from the saber-shaped bone near the wing, and remove the bone. When you reach the ball-and-socket joints connecting the wing and thigh bones to the carcass, sever them so that they are separated from the carcass but still attached to the skin. Continue cutting the breast meat away from the bone, working around the tail, until you reach the ridge of the breastbone, where the skin and bone meet. Turn the bird around and repeat on the other side. When you have finished, the meat will be completely detached from the carcass and the skin will cling only along the ridge of the breastbone. Pull gently to separate the breastbone and carcass from the flesh (the skin tears easily).

To remove the leg and wing bones: Lay the skin and flesh of the bird flat, skin side down. Holding the outside of the wing bone in one hand, cut through the tendons, and scrape the meat from the bone. Pull out the bone, using the knife to free it. Holding the inside end of the leg bone, cut through the tendons attaching the flesh to the bone. Use the knife to scrape the meat from the bone, pushing it away from the end of the bone as if sharpening a pencil. Continue cutting to free both bones from the skin. If any sinews still remain in the leg, cut them out. Repeat on the other side, then push the legs and wings skin side out. Lay the boned bird on the board. Most of the skin will have meat attached to it; trim any excess skin and fat.

To assemble the poultry package: Put the whole nutmegs in a plastic bag and smash them with a rolling pin. Put the smashed nutmeg, mace, cloves, and peppercorns in a small food processor or coffee grinder and work them to powder, or crush them in a mortar with a pestle. Stir in the salt. (If using ground spices, stir them all together with the salt.) Sprinkle about one-fourth of this seasoning mix on the turkey. Using another cutting board, bone the goose and lay it on top of the turkey. Sprinkle it with more seasoning mix. Continue boning and seasoning the other birds until all are used, laying them one on top of another and sprinkling each one with some of the seasoning mix. Fold over the short sides of the turkey skin, then pull the long sides to the center to make an oval package. Secure the edges of skin with toothpicks (neatness is not important at this point). Chill the package in the refrigerator while you prepare the dough.

To make the raised pastry dough: Put the flour in a bowl and warm it in a very low oven for 15 to 20 minutes. Combine the butter, salt, and water in a pan, bring just to a boil, take from the heat, and skim off the froth. Make a well in the flour, pour in the very hot liquid, and stir rapidly with a wooden spoon, drawing in the flour to make a smooth dough. If the dough seems dry, add a few more spoonfuls of hot water. Press the dough into a large ball. Knead it, pushing away with the heel of your hand, then pulling it toward you to peel the dough from the work surface. Give it a quarter turn and continue working in this way until the dough is smooth and holds together, working in more flour if the dough seems buttery. This will take 3 to 5 minutes. It is important to keep the dough warm, moist, and pliable as you work. If it cools and stiffens, warm it in the microwave.

To shape the pastry case: Pleat to double thickness a wide band of heavy-duty aluminum foil that is about 1 inch (2.5 cm) higher and 5 inches (13 cm) longer than the circumference of the casserole. This will enclose and support the pie during cooking. Line the sides of the casserole with the foil and secure it with toothpicks, folding any excess foil over the edge of the vessel. Set aside about one-fourth of the dough for the lid. On a lightly floured work surface, roll out the remaining dough to an oval about 10 inches (25 cm) larger all the way around than the base of the casserole; it should be thicker in the center than at the sides. Sprinkle the dough generously with flour and fold it in half, forming a semicircle. Roll the thicker part so the dough flattens to form a pouch. Lift the dough package into the casserole, and shape it in the base and around the sides with your fingers, draping the edges of the dough over the rim.

To fill the pastry case: Remove the poultry package from the refrigerator and carefully lower it, seam side up, into the dough-lined casserole. This is easier with two people. Fold the draped dough edges over the poultry. Line a baking sheet with foil or plastic wrap and set it, lined side down, on the poultry. Turn the casserole upside down onto the baking sheet to invert the poultry and pastry. Lift off the casserole. Butter another baking sheet and set it, buttered side down, on the pie. Invert the pie again so the open side is upward, and remove the first baking sheet. (Again, two people are helpful for this maneuver.) Discard the toothpicks from the poultry. Press the overlapping dough up to form a rim.

To add the lid and decorate the pie: Spread the 1 cup softened butter on top of the poultry. Roll out the remaining dough to a lid 2 inches (5 cm) larger than the top of the pie, fold it loosely around the rolling pin, and transfer it to the top of the pie. Press the dough down onto the poultry package and right up to the dough walls, pressing the edges together. Trim with scissors to neaten the edge and flute it using your fingers. Brush the whole lid with egg glaze. Poke 2 or 3 good-sized airholes into the dough with the point of a knife, and insert chimneys of foil so they remain open. This allows steam to escape. Roll out the dough trimmings and cut out leaves, flowers, or other decorations to decorate the dough and disguise the airholes. Brush them also with the glaze. Chill the pie until the dough is firm, at least 1 hour.

To bake the pie: Heat the oven to 400°F (200°C). Set the pie on a low shelf in the oven and bake until golden brown, 40 to 50 minutes. Reduce the heat to 350°F (180°C) and cover the pie with foil. Continue baking until a metal skewer inserted in the center of the pie is hot to the touch when withdrawn after 30 seconds, 6 to 6½ hours. An instant-read thermometer inserted in the center through an airhole should read 170°F (77°C).

Take the pie from the oven and let it cool for at least 3 hours before discarding the foil. (The internal temperature will continue to rise for about 30 minutes.) The pie can be served warm or at room temperature.

Filet de Boeuf
à la Gendarme

*Beef Tenderloin
à la Gendarme*

From François Menon, *Les soupers de la cour* (Paris, 1755): *Cut a filet of beef in the thinnest slices you can: put them to marinate with oil, parsley, green onion, a garlic clove, some mushrooms, all finely chopped, salt, and coarse pepper, then you spear them on a brochette with all the marinade, and wrap in paper; cook on the spit, and serve with a sauce made with a little coulis, a glass of Champagne wine, salt, and coarse pepper; boil it a few moments, and when serving add a pinch of blanched ravigote herbs, very finely chopped.*

FRANÇOIS MENON WAS the most influential and prolific of all eighteenth-century cookbook authors. He not only focused on the nouvelle cuisine of the day with its emphasis on health, but also wrote books for maîtres d'hôtel, explored the science of cooking, and, with *La cuisinière bourgeoise*, was the first French author to suggest a woman in the title. His *Les soupers de la cour* (Court Suppers) deliberately evokes the narcissistic brilliance of the court of Louis XV. By midcentury, intimate dining with a few friends had become the latest novelty, and with it arose a vogue for simple recipes like this one. Sometimes dishes were named for celebrities, such as the marquis de Béchamel (white sauce); the duc de Soubise was renowned for the savory pheasant and partridge egg omelets he whipped up in his private apartments. The concept of a simple supper remained relative, however, and a menu created for the king and Madame de Pompadour for Friday, November 4, 1757, shows four courses, each featuring a dozen or more dishes focusing on fish, it being a fast day.

Ravigote is an aromatic, piquant sauce that traditionally includes vinegar with a variety of herbs. I particularly enjoy this milder version with tarragon, chervil, chives, and burnet, the acidity imparted by green onion. The sauce acts as both a marinade, deliciously permeating the meat with the flavor of fresh herbs, and an accompanying gravy. Menon's recipe implies a whole beef fillet should be used, but I have cut quantities down to fit a household spit. After slicing and marinating, the fillet is reshaped and wrapped in paper to hold it together and retain the juices. It should be cooked quite rapidly, preferably in front of an open fire or over a barbecue, close to the heat so the surface of the meat is done while the center remains rare. The beef can also be roasted in a 450°F (230°C) oven, allowing 25 to 30 minutes and turning it once. In the sauce, I've substituted a few spoonfuls of meat glaze for the coulis, the rich brown sauce much used in the eighteenth century; meat glaze is available in upscale markets and on the Internet. If the herbs are scarce, you could settle just for tarragon.

Spit-Roasted Fillet of Beef with Herbs and Mushrooms   *Serves 6*

5 or 6 button mushrooms (about 4 ounces or 110 g)
3 to 4 tablespoons chopped fresh parsley
2 green onions, green tops only, finely chopped
1 garlic clove, chopped
3 tablespoons (45 ml) vegetable oil, more for brushing

248

Salt and pepper

2¼-pound (1-kg) piece beef fillet

SAUCE

4 or 5 sprigs each tarragon, chervil, and burnet

1 small bunch chives

2 tablespoons meat glaze

¼ cup (60 ml) Champagne or other dry sparkling white wine

Grill with spit, brown paper bag or sheet of heavy brown paper,
   long metal skewer, kitchen string

To prepare the marinade: Trim the mushrooms and coarsely chop them. Add the chopped parsley, green onion tops, and garlic and chop all together until quite fine. This is best done by hand. Mix these aromatics in a bowl with the oil, salt, and pepper.

To prepare and roast the beef: Trim any membrane or fat from the beef and slice it across the grain as thinly as possible with a very sharp knife. Add the beef slices to the marinade and toss and turn with your hands until the beef is thoroughly coated. Leave the beef at room temperature for 15 minutes. Light the spit.

Spread the sheet of brown paper on a work surface and brush it with oil. Spear the beef slices on the skewer so the beef fillet is reshaped, making sure each slice is coated with marinade. Push the slices snugly together on the skewer, wrap the fillet in brown paper to form a cylinder, and securely tie the ends with string. Spear or attach the package to the spit.

Roast the beef quite close to the heat, catching the drippings in a drip pan. The ideal distance from the embers will vary depending on the heat of the fire (do not let the fire ignite or scorch the package). The timing will depend on the fire, as well. In general, allow 25 to 30 minutes for rare meat, or 30 to 35 for medium. To test, poke a hole in the paper and look between the meat slices. When the beef is done, take it from the grill and leave it in the paper for 10 minutes.

To make the sauce: While the beef is resting, bring a pan of water to a boil. Strip the herb leaves from the stems and blanch the leaves in the boiling water until wilted, about 1 minute. Drain, rinse them with cold water, and drain them on paper towels. Finely chop them. In a small saucepan, combine the meat glaze, Champagne, and drippings from the beef and bring just to a boil.

Detach the package from the spit and set it on a platter; remove the paper and pull out the skewer. Pour the juices from the platter and any juices left in the paper into the saucepan holding the sauce and simmer for 2 minutes. Stir in the blanched herbs, taste, and adjust the seasoning with salt and pepper. Serve the beef with the sauce in a separate bowl.

Des Glaces

On Ices

From François Menon, *Les soupers de la cour* (Paris, 1755): *All ices are put on ice to freeze in the same way; in your churn [salbotière] you put the liqueur or fruit that you want to freeze, & put the churn in a bucket of appropriate size, & all around & above put finely crushed ice, mixed with saltpeter or salt; you must take care from time to time to scrape the mixture that has set from the sides with the ice pick [houlette] so that it freezes evenly; you present them in goblets at the moment of serving, & so they are not frozen solid, you work them with the ice pick, stirring briskly until you see no ice crystals are left; if your ices are made some time before serving, you leave them on ice & only work them when you are ready to serve.*

Lemon Ice: For an hour infuse the zest and juice of 5 lemons, three quarters of a pint of water, three-quarters of a pound of sugar, & strain through a napkin.

Juniper Ice: Bring to a boil half a dozen times a pint of water with half a pound of sugar, a little cinnamon & a small handful of juniper; strain it at once through the fine sieve & put it to freeze on ice.

Coffee Ice Cream: You make three good cups of coffee with water, so they are very strong; two ounces of coffee are needed for each one, left to rest & strained clear, boil it with a pint of thick cream, & a half or three-quarters pound of sugar, after having boiled seven or eight times, & and having cooled you put it in the churn so it freezes to ice, work & finish it as above.

THE EIGHTEENTH CENTURY SEES a flowering of sorbets and frozen desserts, thanks partly to a better understanding of freezing techniques and to the spread of sunken icehouses for preserving blocks of ice during the summer. For the first time, a whole book is written on ices and ice creams, the charming *L'art de bien faire les glaces d'office* (The Fine Art of Making Cold Room Ices, 1768) by Monsieur Emy, who describes himself as an *officier*, or steward, in charge of the cold kitchen. François Menon devotes a whole chapter to ices in *Les soupers de la cour* (Court Suppers), and here are three. Two of them—the lemon and juniper flavors—we would call sorbets, as they contain only sugar, water, fruit juice, and spice. The third is a luscious coffee ice cream that would have been set in the same mold that was used for cheese, hence the name *fromage*.

By today's standards, all three ices contain a great deal of sugar, so they freeze at a relatively low temperature. For processing in modern machines, the mixtures must be thoroughly chilled in the refrigerator before they can be churned, and even then all of them remain slushy when chilled, holding a shape but not firmly set like today's ices. They hark back to the original Arab sorbets, which were described as frozen drinks rather than desserts needing a spoon.

I suggest using an ice-cream maker for the Lemon Sorbet, Juniper Sorbet, and Coffee Ice Cream, though you can chill the Lemon Sorbet in the freezer without stirring. All three recipes do fine in the freezer for up to a week, where they will harden but will not develop the ice crystals that are common with less sugary mixtures.

Lemon Sorbet *Makes 1 quart (1 liter) sorbet to serve 6 to 8*

This lemon mixture is so heavy in sugar that it can also be frozen directly in the freezer as granita: Stir once or twice as it freezes and it will set to the perfect soft, slightly granular texture. When serving, simply scrape curls of the lemon mixture into chilled glasses, using a spoon.

> Pared zest and juice of 5 lemons
> 3 cups (750 ml) water
> 1⅔ cups (330 g) sugar
>
> Ice-cream maker

Put the lemon zest, juice, water, and sugar in a saucepan and heat gently, stirring, until the sugar dissolves. Bring just to a boil, then cover and leave over low heat to infuse just below the boil for 30 minutes. (I find this is long enough, though Menon suggests an hour.)

Let the syrup cool, strain it, and freeze in the ice-cream maker. Transfer to a chilled bowl, cover tightly, and store in the freezer. The sorbet will remain smooth in the freezer for up to 1 week.

Juniper Sorbet *Makes 1 quart (1 liter) sorbet to serve 6 to 8*

The warming, winter flavors of juniper and cinnamon make this unusual sorbet, sweet but with a pungent aftertaste, a good accompaniment to apple pie. To pick up the juniper, add a splash of gin at serving time.

> ½ cup (45 g) juniper berries
> 1 quart (1 liter) water
> 2 cups (400 g) sugar
> 2 cinnamon sticks
>
> Ice-cream maker

Put the juniper berries in a plastic bag and crush them with a rolling pin or the base of a heavy saucepan. Put the water and sugar in a saucepan and heat gently until the sugar dissolves, stirring occasionally. Add the crushed juniper berries and cinnamon sticks and bring just to a boil. Remove from the heat, let cool for 2 minutes, then bring back to a boil. Repeat the boiling and cooling 6 times.

Let the syrup cool completely and strain it through a fine strainer. Freeze in the ice-cream maker. Transfer the sorbet to a chilled bowl, cover tightly, and store in the freezer. The sorbet will remain smooth in the freezer for up to 1 week.

Coffee Ice Cream *Makes 1 quart (1 liter) ice cream to serve 6 to 8*

Menon's coffee ice cream is deliriously rich, a perfect balance of cream and fragrant coffee, simpler to make than the usual custard. We are accustomed to less sugar nowadays, but if you reduce the amount, the ice cream consistency is less unctuous.

2 cups (500 ml) very strong brewed espresso

1¼ cups (225 g) sugar

2 cups (500 ml) heavy cream

Ice-cream maker

Put the coffee and sugar in a saucepan and heat gently, stirring until the sugar dissolves. Stir in the cream and bring the mixture just to a boil. Let it cool for 2 minutes, skim, then repeat the boiling and cooling 7 to 8 times, skimming as needed.

Let the coffee cream cool completely, then freeze in the ice-cream maker. Transfer the ice cream to a chilled bowl, cover tightly, and store in the freezer. The ice cream keeps well for up to 1 week.

A Rich Potatoe Pudding

From Mrs. Martha Bradley, *The British Housewife: or, the Cook, House-keeper's and Gardiner's Companion* (London, c. 1755): *Boil two Pounds of fine Potatoes till they are thoroughly done, taking Care they do not break ; take them up, and lay them on a Sieve to cool ; peel them, put the pure Pulp into a Mortar, and beat it to a Mash; add a Gill of Sack to soften it, and then drive it through a Sieve.*

Melt Half a Pound of fresh Butter, and mix it with this Pulp of the Potatoes.

Break ten Eggs, beat up all the Yolks with three of the Whites, mix these with the Potatoes and Butter, and then add six Ounces of the finest Sugar in Powder; add last of all another Gill of Sack, and Half a Pint of the richest Cream, grate in a third Part of a Nutmeg, and then stir all very well together that it may be perfectly mixed.

Make some fine Puff Paste, cover the Bottom of a Dish, and raise a Rim round the Sides, pour in this Mixture, and send it to the Oven; let it be baked with a moderate Heat to a fine Brown. It is a very elegant baked Pudding. Some add Sweetmeats, and some Currants, but they utterly destroy the true Taste of the other Ingredients.

MARTHA BRADLEY WAS ONE of the many housewives who published cookbooks during the second half of the century. She is distinguished as the consummate cooking teacher, designing *The British Housewife, or, the Cook, Housekeeper's and Gardiner's Companion* as a cooking course that starts with the basics and builds in complexity. Whether Mrs. Bradley had potatoes or sweet potatoes in mind for her pudding is unknown, as even at this late date they were rarely separated. But her recipe works for both. We would call it a pie because she lines a pan with puff pastry and fills it with the potatoes, puréeing them liberally with butter (she calls this a "rich" pudding), then mixing them with eggs, sugar, sweet sherry, and cream. Her potatoes would have been small and hard, which is perhaps why she instructs to "drive [them] through a Sieve" to purée them. For similar effect, I've suggested using firm new potatoes. A puff pastry case tends to be soggy if it is not prebaked, as I do here, though Mrs. Bradley does not mention this precaution.

To our tastes, Sherry Potato Pie is neither sweet nor savory, so when to serve it is a conundrum. In Martha Bradley's time it would have been presented on the table with many other savory and sweet dishes in one of two or three courses *à la française*. I've much enjoyed the pie in a savory role with roasted or sautéed vegetables, and with roast pork; a place beside the roast Thanksgiving turkey would be perfect. In the role of dessert, the pie would agreeably partner with poached plums or pears.

Sherry Potato Pie *Makes one 10-inch (25-cm) pie to serve 8*

12 ounces (330 g) prepared puff pastry dough

Flour for rolling

1 pound (450 g) small new potatoes or sweet potatoes, unpeeled

¾ cup (175 ml) medium-sweet sherry

½ cup (110 g) butter, melted, more for the pan

4 egg yolks

2 eggs

6 tablespoons (90 g) sugar

½ cup (125 ml) heavy cream

1 teaspoon freshly grated nutmeg

10-inch (25-cm) deep quiche pan or round baking dish

To make and blind bake the pastry shell: Chill the puff pastry dough for 30 minutes and butter the quiche pan. On a lightly floured work surface, roll out the dough into a thin round and use it to line the prepared pan, pushing up the edge and fluting it. Prick the dough with a fork so it does not rise. Chill the lined pan in the freezer for 15 minutes. Meanwhile, heat the oven to 375°F (190°C) and put a baking sheet on a low shelf to heat.

Line the chilled pastry shell with parchment paper, then fill with dried beans to hold the dough in place. Set the pan on the heated baking sheet and bake until the dough is set and the edges of the shell are browned, 15 to 20 minutes. Remove the paper and beans and continue baking the shell until dry and firm, 5 to 10 minutes longer. Set the pastry shell aside to cool completely. Lower the oven temperature to 350°F (180°C).

To make the filling: While the pastry shell is baking, put the potatoes in a pan of salted water, cover, bring to a boil, and simmer until very tender when pierced with a knife, 20 to 25 minutes. Sweet potatoes will take 10 to 15 minutes longer to cook. Drain, then arrange the potatoes on a rack and let cool for 5 minutes.

Peel the potatoes, return them to the pan, crush them with a potato masher, and work in half the sherry. Push the potatoes through a flat strainer or food mill into a bowl. (A food processor will make the purée gluey.) Stir in the melted butter. In a small bowl, whisk together the egg yolks and eggs until mixed, and stir them into the potatoes, along with the sugar. Stir in the remaining sherry, the cream, and the nutmeg.

Pour the filling into the cooled pie shell and bake until the filling is set, 30 to 35 minutes. An extra 5 to 10 minutes of baking is needed if you are using sweet potatoes. Serve the pie hot or at room temperature directly from the pan. It keeps well for a day or two in the refrigerator and should be warmed just before serving.

To Alamode a Round

From Amelia Simmons, *American Cookery* (Hartford, CT, 1796): *Take fat pork cut into slices or mince, season it with pepper, salt, sweet marjoram and thyme, cloves, mace and nutmeg, make holes in the beef, and stuff it the night before cooked ; put some bones across the bottom of the pot to keep from burning, put in one quart Claret wine, one quart water and one onion ; lay the round on the bones, cover close and stop it round the top with dough ; hang on [the pothook] in the morning and stew gently two hours ; turn it, and stop tight and stew two hours more ; when done tender, grate a crust of bread on the top and brown it before the fire ; scum the gravy and serve in a butter boat, serve it with the residue of the gravy in the dish.*

POT ROAST, CALLED "ALAMODE," must already have been an American favorite by the time *American Cookery*, the first American cookbook, appeared. Amelia Simmons includes two recipes with detailed instructions, and she piles on the aromatics—sweet herbs, cloves, and mace—and lards the meat with fat pork or bacon. She adds the handy trick of propping the meat on some bones so it does not scorch on the bottom of the pot. This version calls for a whole quart of claret wine, which means it must have been intended as a festive dish. The pot roast would have been simmered over the enveloping heat of an open fire, and I'm suggesting an oven as the nearest equivalent. A dough of flour and water, known as luting paste, is used to seal the pot so no juices evaporate, a wise precaution when cooking over an open flame.

If you can cook pot roast ahead, so much the better, as flavor improves and fat is easy to skim from the gravy if chilled overnight. Root vegetables would have been the natural accompaniment. When ordering the bones, ask the butcher to cut them in smaller pieces that will fit nicely in a pot. I've used a piece of salted fatback for Mrs. Simmons's pork fat, assuming hers would have been salted, and I've been sparing with added salt.

Pot Roast of Beef with Red Wine   *Serves 8 to 10*

5 ounces (140 g) salted pork fatback
1 tablespoon chopped fresh thyme
1 tablespoon chopped fresh marjoram
2 teaspoons salt
1 teaspoon pepper
½ teaspoon ground cloves
½ teaspoon ground mace

½ teaspoon freshly grated nutmeg

5- to 6-pound (about 2.5-kg) piece boned top round of beef, rolled and tied

2 pounds (900 g) beef bones

1 onion, cut into chunks

1 quart (1 liter) red Zinfandel wine

1 quart (1 liter) water, more if needed

LUTING PASTE

2½ cups (300 g) flour, more for rolling

1 cup (250 ml) water, more if needed

Kitchen string, large Dutch oven or casserole

To lard the beef: Cut the pork fat into large dice. Work it in a processor with the thyme, marjoram, salt, pepper, cloves, mace, and nutmeg to a coarse paste, 1 to 2 minutes. With the point of a small knife, slash ¾-inch (2-cm) incisions in the beef and insert the seasoned fat. Cover the beef and refrigerate it overnight.

To make the luting paste: Put the flour in a small bowl and make a well in the center. Add the water and stir gently, adding more water if needed to make a soft, rough paste. Do not overmix or the paste will shrink in the heat of the oven.

To cook the beef: Heat the oven to 325°F (160°C). Lay the beef bones in the Dutch oven, set the meat on top, and arrange the onion chunks around the meat. Pour in the wine and water. The meat should be two-thirds covered by liquid; if it is not, add more water. Cover the pot with its lid. Halve the luting paste; set one-half aside and cover it tightly. On a lightly floured work surface, using your palms, roll the remaining paste into a long rope. Use the rope to seal the gap between the rim and the lid of the Dutch oven.

Place the pot in the oven and cook the beef for about 2 hours. Break off and discard the luting paste, remove the lid, and turn over the meat. If necessary, add more water so that the meat is covered again with liquid by about two-thirds. Cover and reseal the pot with the remaining luting paste. Continue cooking for about 2 hours, then break the seal again. The beef should be very tender, almost falling apart, when pierced with a two-pronged fork. If not, continue cooking until it is done.

Transfer the meat to a cutting board, cover it with aluminum foil, and keep warm. Strain the gravy from the pot into a saucepan, and skim any scum from the surface (Mrs. Simmons would have left the fat). Taste and if the gravy is thin, boil it for 10 to 15 minutes to concentrate the flavor. Taste again and adjust the seasoning.

Carve a part, or all, of the roast in generous slices, and arrange the slices, overlapping them, on a platter. Spoon over some gravy and serve the rest separately. The flavor of pot roast mellows after refrigerating it for a day or two. It reheats well on top of the stove over low heat.

THE EARLY
NINETEENTH
CENTURY

Celebrity
Epicures

POLITICS DROVE THE DIRECTION of cooks and cookbooks in the first part of the nineteenth century, with the French and American revolutions creating more egalitarian views of cooking. Taste vacillated between the simpler fare considered seemly in this new era and the more luxurious dining preferences of the rich and famous—represented by the fashionable cooking of the first celebrity chef, Marie Antonin Carême. In turn, the overthrow of Napoleon and restoration of the French monarchy in 1815 not only encouraged the rise of nationalism throughout Europe but helped create an environment in which art, literature, and gastronomy could thrive. Books devoted to regional and national cuisines made their appearance, offering hints of the varied fare that would proliferate in the modern cookbooks to come. In addition, cookbooks by the first restaurateurs emerged early in the century, and gourmet guides became popular. Only the British remained true to tradition, relishing their roast beef and the comforts of a familiar, well-run household. By the nineteenth century, these comforts had become embodied in a very English institution, the gentlemen's club, where congenial companions met to enjoy conversation over the very best of food and wines.

During this era, the terminology in cookbooks changed, causing a dip in the popularity of some of the older genres. Books on cooking that advised readers on how to live a healthy life became a rarity, and treatises on Galen's theory of the humors at last gave way to a more "scientific" approach to cooking, most notably with the publication of Nicolas Appert's *L'art de conserver, pendant plusieurs années, toutes les substances animales et végétales* (The Art of Preserving, for Several Years, All Animal and Vegetable Matter, 1810). This pioneer work on the art of canning helped transform the winter diet of Europe and North America, appearing the following year in English and German and a year later in America. Very quickly, the expression *culinary science* replaced the word *remedy* as the fashionable mantra for authors to mention in their prefaces (more rarely in the body of the text). In the twentieth century, the word *diet* would become the most frequently used term, applied to ingredients or dishes supposed to have specific effects on the body.

OPPOSITE Traditional and modern dress for a cook from Antonin Carême, *Le maitre d'hôtel français*, 1823 edition. Full image on page 282.

France: After the Deluge

The Revolution of 1789 fundamentally changed the culinary scene, as it did so many other fields. The great royal and noble kitchens disappeared, while conspicuous consumption was imprudent for anyone else, particularly after the bloodshed of the Terror that started in 1793. A few chefs fled to England, but most, particularly the younger men, adjusted to the new conditions (women cooks were less at risk, concealed among the other domestics in a household). The narcissistic self-praise of prefaces to earlier cookbooks was left behind. This was a time of comradery within the culinary community, when cooks stood by each other to survive. Antonin Carême describes how colleagues would arrive the night before a great dinner to help with preparations for the stocks and sauces that were the foundations of so many of the dishes. (By now, espagnole had replaced coulis as the basic brown sauce, but it still took up to eighteen hours to simmer to perfection.)

Cooks and authors experimented with new outlets, and gourmands changed their dining habits. Alexandre Viard was the first to chronicle the new constraints, in *Le cuisinier impérial* (The Imperial Cook, 1806): "as a choice is not always available, I have

By the early nineteenth century, a little dalliance in the kitchen was quite the fashion. "Holding the pan handle creates a tricky situation" runs the caption to this late-eighteenth-century color print by an unknown French artist.

thought it best to describe only how to use what one has."[1] To judge from his practical knowledge, Viard must have been a professional cook at one time, but he described himself simply as an *homme de bouche* (food expert), probably someone in charge of catering for a large household. Despite his book's impressive title, Viard declared he was writing for "all levels of fortune" in this egalitarian society of *citoyens*, and indeed the polished text includes such basics as pea soup, quick-cooked rabbit, and salt cod provençale. At a higher level, he was the first cook to describe the classic, puffy soufflé, flavored with chestnuts, frangipane, white coffee, vanilla, or potato (still a novelty), that became such a symbol of France. The book did well, even when the restoration of the French monarchy required a hasty title change to *Le cuisinier royale* (The Royal Cook), and the "year of revolutions" in 1848 precipitated another change, this time to *Le cuisinier national de la ville et de la campagne* (The National Cook of Town and Countryside)—only to revert to *impérial* once more under Emperor Napoleon III. The text, too, underwent hundreds of additions, first by Viard and later by colleagues, allowing it to remain in print until 1875.

The freedom of thought and action following the Revolution also gave impetus to the evolving concept of the restaurant, which had begun as a largely "restorative" establishment in the 1760s but now was becoming associated with fine dining. Proprietors helped promote business by writing cookbooks, and diners consulted the first-ever restaurant reviews that appeared in *Almanach des gourmands* in 1803 (published each year until 1812). Antoine Beauvilliers, who had opened a restaurant in his own name as early as 1780, decided in 1814 that he needed "to pin down the ideas that are so fugitive and changeable," publishing his two-volume *L'art du cuisinier* (The Art of the Cook).[2] His were the first restaurant recipes to appear in print, ahead of a distinguished band of nineteenth-century chefs who eventually paved the way for Auguste Escoffier and those of our own times. His menus were gargantuan, reflecting the old style of the table d'hôte, designed to be displayed on a single Rabelaisian table, always laden with more dishes than the number of guests. (Additional dishes were swapped in and out during service.) Despite Beauvilliers's renown, his book ran only to three editions.

The greatest chef of the era was Antonin Carême, "the chef of chefs" and international superstar who dominated the French culinary scene from the Restoration to almost the end of the nineteenth century. Carême had an enviable career working for the rich and famous. He started at the Congress of Vienna in 1815, where he cooked for the French diplomat Talleyrand, one of the most sophisticated and articulate gourmets of the day. From there, Carême moved on to England and the kitchen of the prince regent, the future George IV; he visited Russia at the invitation of Tsar Alexander I; then he moved on to the British embassy in Vienna, where he found the cooking "second only to that of Paris"; and finally back to Paris. In 1823, he entered the service of the Rothschilds "at a salary beyond what any sovereign in Europe might be able to pay."[3] Not a fan of either British or Russian cooking, he nonetheless seemed

"Heavy birds fly slowly" reads the caption for this 1791 cartoon of Louis XVI by Isaac Cruikshank and John Nixon, entitled *Le gourmand*. "I couldn't care less about all that, leave me in peace to eat," protests the king to the obsequious official who has come to arrest him in his flight from Paris on June 21, 1791. "My dear Louis, haven't you finished your two turkeys and drunk your six bottles of wine," rebukes Marie-Antoinette as she preens in the mirror, while the little dauphin stamps his foot.

to please all his employers. England's prince regent remarked graciously, "Dinner last night was superb, but you will make me die of indigestion." Carême is rumored to have quipped, "Prince, my duty is to tempt your appetite, not to control it," an attitude very different from that of fifteenth-century cooks, who took responsibility for preserving the health of their masters.

Like many great chefs, Carême trained in the discipline of pâtisserie before moving into the freer forms of savory cuisine, and pastry remained a lifelong obsession. Consequently, his first two books, published back to back, are on pastry. *Le pâtissier pittoresque* (The Picturesque Pastry Cook, 1815) contains dozens of designs for *pièces montées:* rustic pavilions, ruins, temples, forts, and other ornate confections in pastillage (a paste of sugar and gum arabic) and marzipan, survivals of medieval subtleties. A self-taught draftsman, he produced the elaborate full-page drawings as well as the recipes himself. *Le pâtissier royal parisien* (The Parisian Royal Pastry Cook), published the same year, is more conventional though still highly illustrated—a practical recipe collection of cakes, pastries, petits fours, and desserts. The book that crowned his reputation, however, was *Le maître d'hôtel français* (The French Maître d'Hôtel, 1822), which told the behind-the-scenes story of his years working for his illustrious employers, complete with gigantesque menus and recipes.

Each of Carême's books is definitive, a peak of creativity in its own field. *Le pâtissier pittoresque* displays the gothic revival style in a dazzling array of castles, follies, Roman ruins, and Egyptian cascades, all a meter or more high and designed to be shaped in sugar paste in shocking colors of orange, purple, green, and many more. *Le pâtissier royal parisien* documents the art of savory and sweet pastries, great pies, and elaborate gâteaux that delighted diners of the time. *Le maître d'hôtel français* offers an irresistible inside glimpse of the lifestyles of the elite.

Carême earned his fame on his own merits. His energy was prodigious and his creative imagination boundless. He rarely repeated dishes from meal to meal, and no two dishes are the same in any of his menus, which routinely set forth more than one hundred choices. We know exactly how he cooked and what he thought about it—his menus, his recipes, even sometimes the names of guests at his dinners—because he wrote everything down each night in a diary. He even discusses *service à la russe,* the

A wistful, idealistic side of Antonin Carême shows in the portrait from his *L'art de la cuisine française au dix-neuvième siècle* (1854 edition).

new style of table service he had come across in Russia, in which each guest is served the same succession of dishes, one at a time. However, he found the style lacked the magnificence and freedom of choice of the existing *service à la française*, with its lavish spread of dishes on the table, and probably did not practice it himself.

Carême's last work, the five-volume *L'art de la cuisine française au dix-neuvième siècle* (The Art of French Cooking in the Nineteenth Century, 1833–35), is the definitive guide to the sauces, ragoûts, garnishes, and full panoply of classic French cooking that by now was dominant throughout Europe. He insists that his cuisine is simpler than that of the previous century, and though this statement seems a stretch given the complexity of some of his dishes, he did codify much of the cooking vocabulary we use today and defined the structure and many of the archetypal French recipes that still survive. In this sense, *L'art de la cuisine française* provided a bridge to the great culinary encyclopedias of the later nineteenth century.

For the French, their cuisine had become a national pride and pastime, and their cooks, now known as chefs, were the acknowledged leaders of style and influence. People read Carême's cookbooks and Grimod de la Reynière's *Almanach des gourmands* as eagerly as fashion magazines for gossip about the rich and famous, savoring Carême's lavish menus, whether in their imagination or on the plate. This emphasis on luxury was to ebb and flow throughout the century, from the popular movement of the 1848

Gastronomic commentator Grimod de la Reynière sent a mildly erotic letter to his wife, Mademoiselle Feuchère, on June 5, 1791, during the revolutionary violence just before the arrest of King Louis XVI. "Turning to happier matters, tell me. . . . how are those two charming columns of alabaster, and the little stomach that is so smooth, and the two pretty globes of love crowned each with a strawberry? All that is in good order? And ready to receive your humble servant?"

TALKING OF TASTE: GASTRONOMIC COMMENTATORS

The confusion of the Revolution brought a new genre of culinary writing to France—the gastronomic commentary. Hints had already surfaced a century before with the chatty French periodical *Le mercure galant* (The Elegant Shopper, first issued in 1672) and a shopping guide, *Le livre commode des adresses de Paris* (The Book of Useful Paris Addresses, 1692). From the sixteenth century onward, travelers such as Michel de Montaigne had complained about the strange menus and manners in the country inns where they had been forced to sleep, and diarists like Madame de Sévigné chattered about what they ate. In 1782, Le Grand d'Aussy had published a massive *Histoire de la vie privée des français* (History of the Private Lives of the French People), an exhaustive study of food, feasting, and table manners from the Middle Ages to his own time. Now, after the Revolution, times were different; the new restaurant scene was growing so fast that it needed a chronicler. Parisians had to know what and how to eat, and where to eat it.

The *Almanach des gourmands* (Gourmand's Almanac) by Alexandre-Balthazar-Laurent Grimod de la Reynière, man about town, incurable eccentric, and inveterate gossip, provided the answer. The first issue of the *Almanach* in 1803 presented a catalog of the gourmand's ideal "library [of] every type of food provisions, including a suckling pig, pâtés of several kinds, enormous *cervelat* sausages and other treats, accompanied by a generous number of wines and liqueurs, with jars of fruits, both candied and in *eaux de vie*. From the ceiling [of this model pantry] hangs a lantern, in the shape

A panel of food critics is at work in the *Séances d'un jury de gourmands dégustateurs,* the frontispiece in the 1805 issue of *Almanach des gourmands* by Grimod de la Reynière.

of a giant Bayonne ham."[1] The table is set with similar delicacies, but the gourmand himself is not shown, on the hunt perhaps for more treats to be listed in the next issue. After this first issue, Grimod continued to publish the *Almanach* almost yearly until 1812.

Grimod's observations make amusing, very modern reading. He reports that in January, hares born the previous year make fine eating in hot and cold pâtés, daubes, and in sauces *à la bourgeoise* or *à la suisse*. Hare is the lightest, tenderest, and most digestible of the dark meats. Rabbit, in contrast, though succulent, can be tasteless when raised domestically, only worth buying if one's finances are in bad shape. In his entry for December, Grimod goes on a tour of fashionable restaurants, remarking how these have flourished, increasing fivefold since the Revolution. Women used to be full of the vapors, drinking only tea and tisanes, whereas now they hold their own and eat chicken wings and ham with their male escorts. Gourmet food shops have expanded too, he says, but for every ten, three are for show and four are simply out to make money.

Grimod did not just pursue the gastronomic news created by others, he created it himself. After training as a lawyer, he had begun to achieve notoriety when he issued invitations announcing his own death, creating a *souper scandaleux*. On inheriting money from his father, he opened food stores in several French cities under the name Société Grimod et cie. In 1808, his *Manuel des Amphitryons* (Amphitryon's Manual) appeared, which he declared was "an indispensable work for all who are eager to eat well and offer the same to others." By 1811, he had trod on too many political toes in the capital and had to take refuge in the countryside. He managed to bring out one last edition of the *Almanach* in Paris, organizing a wake, complete with coffin, for yet another joke about his own funeral, and then retired to the provinces, where he died on December 25, 1837.[2]

Even more famous than Grimod is his contemporary Jean Anthelme Brillat-Savarin, a lawyer whose reputation rests on twenty aphorisms written on two pages at the start of a somewhat tedious book entitled *Physiologie du goût* (The Physiology of Taste, 1826). Brillat-Savarin was at his best when he wrote about food—in his discussion of the many roles of sugar, in his praise of truffles, "the diamond of the kitchen," and in his enjoyment of a wild turkey hunt and subsequent feast during a visit to the new postcolonial America. Brillat-Savarin had escaped the Revolution, then spent two years in New York teaching languages and playing in a theater orchestra before returning to Paris to become a judge under Napoleon and during the restoration of the monarchy.[3] The astuteness of such dictums as "Tell me what you eat, and I will tell you what you are," "The destiny of nations depends on how they eat," and "The discovery of a new dish gives more pleasure to the human race than the discovery of a star" has delighted readers for nearly two centuries. Not only are his truths timeless, they are easy to translate into other languages.

Germany had its own gastronomic writer, Baron Carl Friedrich von Rumohr, whose *Geist der Kochkunst* (The Essence of Cookery) was published in 1822. Von Rumohr's scholarly knowledge of cooking Europewide was backed up by practical expertise, for he traveled a great deal and took a keen interest in the kitchen, particularly the scientific aspects of the behavior of foods. "It is the height of achievement to cook with grace, and combine appeal and ornamentation with nutrition," he declared.[4] Though he included no specific recipes in his book, he offered a mass of invaluable culinary information, written in engaging style. "If [Von Rumohr] had been writing in English, French, or Italian," says Alan Davidson, "the advice which he offers would have been more than sufficient to assure him a very wide audience and enduring international fame."[5] Thanks to the inquiring minds and keen palates of Grimod, Brillat-Savarin, Von Rumohr, and their ilk, the new style of culinary writing prospered, to become a flourishing independent genre. ♦

1 Alexandre-Balthazar-Laurent Grimod de la Reynière, "Sujet du frontispiece," *Almanach des gourmands*, vol. 1 (Paris: Charles-Béchet, 1803).

2 Alan Davidson, *Oxford Companion to Food* (Oxford: Oxford University Press, 1999), 355.

3 Harold McGee, *The Curious Cook* (San Francisco: North Point Press, 1990), 273.

4 Carl Friedrich von Rumohr, *The Essence of Cookery*, trans. Barbara Yeomans (Totnes, England: Prospect Books, 1993), 62.

5 Davidson, *Oxford Companion to Food*, 675.

revolution through the opulence of the Second Empire, down to the Franco-Prussian War, when Parisians were forced to eat elephant and other denizens of the zoo, only to rebound with Prosper Montagné, Auguste Escoffier, and the Belle Époque.

Home Cooks in Europe and America

While France was establishing the classics of cuisine and pastry, England triumphantly led the way with books on household economy, most of them written by women, for women. The tone of these books continued to be encouraging but tinged with the self-righteousness that was to characterize Victorian culture. Mrs. Rundell's *A New System of Domestic Cookery* (1806), with its almost intimidating detail of what the well-informed housewife should and should not do, was a forerunner of the classic household encyclopedia. She opens her "Miscellaneous Observations" with the bracing "In every rank, those deserve the greatest praise, who best acquit themselves of the duties which their station requires." Her recipes catalog the classic English repertoire that continues today—dressed crab, scalloped oysters, boiled fowl with rice, bread-and-butter pudding, beef olives, queen of puddings, and orange marmalade are just a few—written in a direct style that assumes only basic culinary knowledge.

A New System of Domestic Cookery was published in several cities in America, setting the standard for New World as well as Old World household cookbooks, which proliferated on both sides of the Atlantic as the century progressed. The British kitchen goddess of the 1860s, Isabella Beeton, followed Mrs. Rundell's example with particularly exacting instructions on how to treat servants in her *Book of Household Management* (1861), a version of which remains in print today.

A contemporary of Mrs. Rundell, Frenchman Louis Eustache Ude had been cook to Louis XVI but had had the good sense to emigrate during the Revolution. Ude became a lone male voice among England's many women cookbook authors. He headed the kitchens of the Earl of Sefton and then the Duke of York before branching into a new career as the director of the prestigious Crockford's, a gambling club near St. James's Palace in London. By now, English gentlemen's clubs were in their heyday, and Crockford's was as famous for its dining as its card tables. Like the casinos of today, the club kept the finest dishes at the ready at any hour for gamblers who, notoriously, gained or lost fortunes in a single night. Ude dedicated *The French Cook* (1813) to "the genuine amateurs of good cheer." Though he wrote that he was chided by his women customers for using too many French cooking terms, he led the way for one of the most colorful and influential cooks of the nineteenth century, Augustus Soyer, whose many adventures included anchoring the kitchens of the Reform Club and cooking beside Florence Nightingale for wounded soldiers during the Crimean War.

In France, women's cookbooks fared less well than in England. The ray of light beamed by *La cuisinière bourgeoise* (1746) did not inspire other contemporary authors to write a major book on home cooking. Women cooks had to wait until the early years of the twentieth century and the success of Madame de Saint'Ange, a cooking teacher and editor of the food magazine *Le Pot au Feu*. Her *Le livre de cuisine* (The Book of Cooking, 1927) far eclipsed Mrs. Beeton's in its exhaustive descriptions of each tiny step in making such treats as *blanquette de veau* and *côtelettes de porc charcutière*. Though the two women's visions were different, both sought to help the cook create a well-ordered kitchen, the foundation of a happy family. Can it be an accident that the first editions of both their books, one dark green, one a deep maroon, are shaped like thick, squat bricks?

Until the latter half of the nineteenth century, the Italian and German states were hampered (or helped, depending on how you view the importance of regional cooking) in developing a single culinary style by their lack of national unity. National cuisines

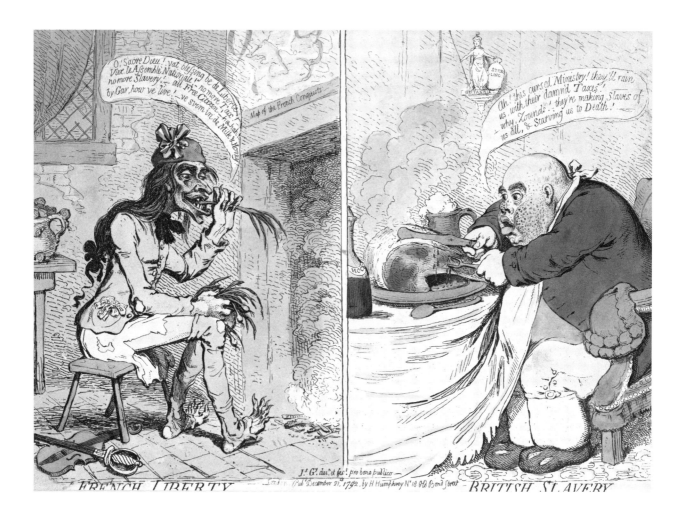

ABOVE Franco-British relations were summed up in this hand-colored etching by James Gillray, 1792, titled *French Liberty, British Slavery*. "Dear God!" exclaims an emaciated Frenchman, chewing on a bulb of garlic before a miserable fire. "Ah! this cursed Ministry! they'll ruin us with their damn'd Taxes!" ripostes his British counterpart as he attacks a vast roast rib of beef.

Perhaps Nephew. as you are Hungrey. you would like some Soup before Fish.

"Perhaps Nephew," inquires this formidable aunt in *Frugality without Meanness* by William Heath, 1804, "as you are Hungrey, you would like some Soup before yr. Fish?"

did not emerge in either area, but regional cooking based on local ingredients and cultural backgrounds flourished and continue to do so, particularly in Italy. Catalan cooking, in its heyday an international culinary leader, had lost impetus as early as the seventeenth century, leaving only vestiges today in the pungent anchovy and garlic-laden sauces of the Balearic Islands and along the Mediterranean coast near Barcelona. The Kingdom of Naples, the European birthplace of sorbets and ices and the home of luscious Arab-inspired pastries, lost its autonomy for good in the early years of the nineteenth century—and therefore its cachet as a center of culture—lapsing into provincial obscurity. As for Spain, the characteristic Castilian style of cooking that had developed in the seventeenth century scarcely moved forward, a lack of progress reflected in the paucity of important books on cooking printed in Spain during the next two centuries.

In America, ironically, it was not Amelia Simmons, the author in 1796 of the first native cookbook, but her plagiarist, Lucy Emerson, who pointed the way to a future of regional cooking with *The New-England Cookery* (1808). Emerson's was the first of many American cookbooks with regional titles, followed by the likes of Mrs. Mary Randolph's *The Virginia Housewife: or, Methodical Cook* (1824). These books were more approachable for American housewives than the English imports, as underlined by Sarah Rutledge, author of *The Carolina Housewife* (1847), who declared that French and English cookbooks "almost always require an apparatus either beyond our reach or too complicated for our native cooks."[4] American cookbooks developed a sense of independence and a form of culinary national pride. Under the nascent republic, the woman's role as head of household and educator of the family took on new importance, with each woman responsible for developing her children into the next generation of proud citizens. As a result, women's literacy skyrocketed.

For their part, the imported English household books continued in circulation, encouraging the self-reliance that was so important in the early American household. Mrs. Rundell in particular had struck a tone that was echoed by writers such as Lydia Maria Child in *The Frugal Housewife* (1829) and Catherine Beecher in *Miss Beecher's Domestic Receipt Book* (1846), who expressed "all directions so minutely as that the book can be kept . . . and be used by any domestic who can read, as a guide in *every one* of her employments in the kitchen."[5] Yet the most widely read American household book during the first half of the nineteenth century was not a book that focused on cooking but rather Catherine Beecher's best-selling *Treatise on Domestic Economy* (1841), a book that emphasized both efficiency and Christian values and offered advice on everything from constructing one's house to maintaining good health.

By the mid-nineteenth century, and often much earlier, the many genres of cookbook that we know had already taken hold. Throughout Europe and America today, we expect to find a cookbook of some kind in almost every kitchen. Take any one off the shelf, open it, and the chances are that its origins are already nearly two centuries old.

RESTAURANTS REVIEWED

The term *restaurant* originated in Paris as a name for the restorative broths (*bouillons*) that had long been offered by simple eating houses also called bouillons. The story goes that in 1765, a M. Boulanger started offering more substantial dishes, including sheep's feet in a creamy *sauce poulette,* to bolster his broths; the restaurant was born.[1] Before that, inns would offer routine bills of fare at a communal table called *table d'hôte,* served at fixed times of day. In a restaurant, a customer could sit at a personal table and at any time of day order from a list of individually prepared dishes. This new concept of eating what you wanted, when you wanted, with only your friends, quickly caught hold.

By the Revolution in 1789, top positions in large, wealthy households were declining, and enterprising cooks had begun to move into the public sphere. Typical was Antoine Beauvilliers, a chef who opened the Grande Taverne de Londres in 1780 and later published his recipes in *L'art du cuisinier* (The Art of the Cook, 1814). Brillat-Savarin remarked of Beauvilliers, "He was the first to have an elegant dining room, impeccably dressed waiters, a select wine cellar, and superior food . . . and he seemed to pay special attention to his guests."[2] The scale of offerings by restaurants grew rapidly, so that in 1825, when Monsieur Véry printed the *carte* for his restaurant Véry Frères, the main courses numbered almost 150, along with a list of nearly 50 vegetables and an equal choice of desserts and cheeses.[3] Diners could order beefsteak prepared seven different ways, six wild birds in addition to domestic chicken and duck, and more than a dozen roasts. "Not available today, sir," must surely have been a frequent waiter's comment.

A Table d'Hôte, or French Ordinary in Paris, a hand-colored aquatint by Thomas Rowlandson, 1810, shows the daily host's table offered to travelers throughout Europe at the time, a popular theme of satirical prints. In his *Travels through France and Italy,* Tobias Smollett, who would have dined at many a table d'hôte, points out that one man's meat is another man's poison: "A true-bred Frenchman dips his fingers, imbrowned with snuff, into his plate filled with ragoût. It must be owned, however, that a Frenchman will not drink out of a tankard, in which, perhaps, a dozen of filthy mouths have slabbered, as is the custom in England." Here Parisian diners are not shy about helping themselves to potluck, with a motley collection of male and female guests vying for morsels with an equally hungry dog.

local seasonal foods, later helped drive the creation of regional specialties.

Elsewhere in Europe, a more traditional scene prevailed. A meal outside the home often implied street food—pies, kebabs, fruits, drinks—picked up on the move. The sellers depicted in the series of contemporary engravings called the Cries of London evoke a vivid, and noisy, outdoor community. People could sit down for a meal at an inn frequented by travelers or at a tavern (selling alcoholic drinks), or they could opt for a more modest refreshment at one of the new coffee or chocolate houses. Caterers specializing in roasts or charcuterie played a big role, particularly in cities such as London, where only the well-to-do had good kitchens, so many people relied on cooked dishes delivered to the house. In general throughout Europe, the essentially urban concept of the restaurant took longer to spread than in France. New York City, however, was early into the business in 1830 with an elegant French restaurant, Delmonico's, one of the first outside Paris.[5] ◆

1 Le Grand d'Aussy, *Histoire de la vie privée des français* (Paris: Laurent-Beaupré, 1815), 1:387. See also Rebecca L. Spang, *The Invention of the Restaurant* (Cambridge, MA: Harvard University Press, 2000), 9.

2 Jean-Louis Flandrin and Massimo Montanari, eds., *Food: A Culinary History,* ed. English edition Albert Sonnenfeld (New York: Columbia University Press, 1999), 475.

3 V...Y, A.M. (Véry), *Le cuisinier des cuisiniers* (Paris: Audin, 1825), 437–44.

4 Philippe Meyzie, *La table du sud-ouest et l'émergence des cuisines régionales (1700–1850)* (Rennes: Presses Universitaires de Rennes, 2007), 72.

5 Michael Batterberry and Ariane Batterberry, *On the Town in New York: A History of Eating, Drinking and Entertainments from 1776 to the Present* (New York: Charles Scribner's Sons, 1973), 71–75.

The restaurant was a Parisian invention that quickly spread to the provinces. Bordeaux, for example, was a growing regional capital already well served by cafés, caterers, and auberges when restaurants began to open there in the mid-1780s. A 1784 newspaper for the city carried the announcement that a Monsieur Fromentin, who ran a café in Place Saint Rémi, had installed restaurant tables at his vast Café de la Marine. Monsieur "has hired an excellent cook, and you will find all the foods that are seasonally available, along with an assortment of wines and liqueurs."[4] For customers attached to their regular habits, Fromentin still held his *table d'hôte* as usual. Such experiments in the French provinces, featuring

RECIPES

FROM THE EARLY NINETEENTH CENTURY

LIKE SO MUCH IN the early nineteenth century, recipes turn a corner. A conversational, practical style becomes the norm, featuring ingredients where needed, with clear instructions for cooking them and a scattering of helpful, often personal tips. By now most authors realize the value of exact quantities when drafting their recipes. They are more consistent in giving detailed instructions, in the appropriate order of work. Of course, there are naïve (or careless) exceptions, but by and large as the nineteenth century unfolds, recipes in the vast majority of cookbooks reflect the same priorities of precision and logic that we look for today. Even in laggard America, by the 1830s cookbooks had developed from the three-line recipes of Amelia Simmons in 1796 to the orderly prose of later writers who had spread along the Eastern seaboard, up to the Great Lakes, and south to Louisiana.

Writing for professionals, Antonin Carême offers exhaustive details, such as how to thoroughly dry the apple purée for his feather-light Soufflés Parisiens aux Pommes de Reinette. In *Le pâtissier royal parisien* (1815), he explains how to glaze the top by rubbing with a dampened forefinger, with a caution against forgetting a soufflé in the oven lest it "turn ugly from this lack of care." In a similar, firm voice, Mrs. Rundell sets the stage for a succession of authors who are writing for less sophisticated domestic households (she is the mother of several daughters). "When whites of eggs are used for jelly, or other purposes, contrive to have pudding, custard, &c. to employ the yolks also," she advises in *A New System of Domestic Cookery* (1811). And carving the famous British roast sirloin of beef "may be begun either at the end, or by cutting into the middle. It is usual to inquire whether the outside or the inside is preferred."

Some of the dishes in early nineteenth-century cookbooks may seem old-fashioned to us, but Mrs. Rundell's Pickled Lemons are right back in style. Like Antoine Beauvilliers, we might wrap our quail in barding fat and roast them with bay leaf. However, when it comes to pudding, we lack the imagination of our forebears. Of the 230 recipes in Lucy Emerson's *New-England Cookery,* 30 are for puddings. Most kitchens in both Europe and America were constrained by the need to bake over an open fire, so preparing a shallow, moist pudding was less risky than attempting a molded cake. More versatile, too: a pudding could use almost any binding ingredient, with different flavorings for variety. Forget the narrow English definition we think of now: in the old days, "pudding" covered a multitude of main or side dishes that could be made savory or sweet at will. They might feature a vegetable, like the squash pudding here, or carrots, rice, barley, millet, almonds, apples, or pears, and that is only a start.

Early nineteenth-century recipes show us the beginning of the modern kitchen. An open fire and a shortage of pots and pans might have limited possibilities, but cooks learned to improvise. Most people still ate what had been raised close by, but that might include a surprising variety of game, fish from rivers and ponds, and a wide range of fruits and vegetables. Town dwellers might have had access to exotica such as truffles or imported cheeses, at a price, but most cooks had a handy palette of flavorings, such as rose water, wine, raisins (very common), orange and lemon peel (sometimes candied), and a narrow choice of spices that included cinnamon, nutmeg, mace, and ginger. This picture scarcely changed for fifty years, awaiting the development of commercially prepared condiments.

From Mrs. Rundell, *A New System of Domestic Cookery* (London, 1806; recipe from 1811 edition): *They should be small, and with thick rinds ; rub them with a piece of flannel ; then slit them half down in four quarters, but not through to the pulp ; fill the slits with salt hard pressed in, set them upright in a pan for four or five days, until the salt melts ; turn them thrice a-day in their own liquor, until tender ; make enough pickle to cover them, of rape-vinegar, the brine of the lemons, Jamaica pepper, and ginger ; boil and skim it ; when cold, put it to the lemons, with two ounces of mustard-seed, and two cloves of garlick to six lemons. When the lemons are used, the pickle will be useful in fish or other sauces.*

Pickled Lemons

WHEN SALTED OR PRESERVED LEMONS hit the culinary scene a decade ago, I never thought to look back two hundred years. Yet here they are, in a sophisticated pickled version that is lively with vinegar, allspice, ginger, and mustard seeds. Mrs. Rundell does not need to instruct her readers on how to serve the finished recipe. In England, everyone knew that a jar of homemade pickle of some kind would be on the table with any cold meats and poultry, and often with the famous roast beef as well. As for me, I like to serve a bowl of the pickled lemon wedges with a little of their juices with hot or cold roasted chicken.

Generous amounts of juices are left with the pickles, and Mrs. Rundell suggests adding them to sauces for fish. I've substituted some for vinegar in potato and other root vegetable salads with great success. Try them, too, as the marinade for seviche. Pickling lemons is a long project, taking six weeks or more, but the results are an ample reward. Thick-skinned lemons are best, says Mrs. Rundell, easy to pick out by their bumpy skins and knobs at each end. Rapes were wild turnips, which would have added herbal flavor to vinegar. Here, I suggest substituting tarragon vinegar. Don't be put off if the pickles turn a bit cloudy. The pickle is an invigorating balance of hot, sour, and salt, a very English pick-me-up.

Pickled Lemons with Allspice, Ginger, and Mustard *Makes 2 quarts (2 liters)*

    6 lemons with thick skins
    1 cup (225 g) fine sea salt
    3 cups (750 ml) tarragon vinegar
    2 tablespoons (20 g) whole allspice

2-inch (5-cm) piece fresh ginger, peeled and thinly sliced

½ cup (60 g) mustard seeds

2 large garlic cloves, peeled

2-quart (2-liter) preserving jar

To salt the lemons: Wipe the lemons with paper towels. With the point of a small knife, score the lemon skin in quarters, cutting halfway through the peel and pith but not down to the flesh. Push salt into the slits. Wedge the lemons upright in a deep stainless-steel or glass container. Sprinkle the remaining salt on top. Cover the container and leave at room temperature until the salt dissolves to form a brine, 4 to 5 days. Turn the lemons in the liquid a few times each day.

To pickle the lemons: Put the vinegar, allspice, ginger, mustard seeds, and garlic cloves in a saucepan. Remove the lemons from the brine and pack them into the preserving jar. Add the brine to the saucepan holding the flavorings, bring to a simmer, and simmer, skimming off any froth that forms on the surface, until the ginger is tender, 10 to 15 minutes. Set aside to cool.

Pour the pickling liquid over the lemons to submerge them, and arrange the lemons and flavorings so they are evenly distributed. (You may have extra pickling liquid, so add all the flavorings to the pickling jar and save the extra liquid for another use.) Cover tightly and leave in a cool cupboard for at least 6 weeks to mellow. After 3 months, the lemons will be even better.

A Crookneck or Winter Squash Pudding

From Lucy Emerson, *The New-England Cookery* (Montpelier, VT, 1808): *Core, boil and skin a good squash, and bruize it well ; take 6 large apples, pared, cored, and stewed tender, mix together ; add 6 or 7 spoonfuls of dry bread or biscuit, rendered fine as meal, half pint milk or cream, 2 spoons of rose-water, 2 do. [ditto] wine, 5 or 6 eggs beaten and strained, nutmeg, salt and sugar to your taste, one spoon flour, beat all smartly together, bake.*

The above is a good receipt for Pompkins, Potatoes or Yams, adding more moistening or milk and rose-water, and to the latter a few black or Lisbon currants, or dry whortleberries scattered in, will make it better.

THIS HANDY RECIPE COVERS almost all seasons, calling for a soft-skinned summer squash, like zucchini or yellow squash, or a more robust winter squash with a thick skin, such as a Hubbard, acorn, or the like. "A good squash" could mean almost any size, so I've assumed that the finished volume after boiling and "bruising," or puréeing, should equal that of the six puréed apples. Mrs. Emerson's quantities produced such a massive pudding (reflecting the size of a typical household of the time) that I've halved the original recipe to serve a more modest party of six.

After boiling, any squash will purée easily, but for the apples you should look for a variety that loses its shape when cooked to dissolve easily to pulp. An heirloom apple adds authenticity, though Macintosh or Granny Smith apples do fine in a pinch. Dry bread crumbs can be made by trimming sliced white bread, baking it in a low oven until very dry, and then grinding it in a food processor. Plain crackers will do, too. This pudding can be a savory side dish, or a dessert after sugaring it to your taste. Personally, I like just a little sugar so the pudding complements pork chops, roast duck, even chicken. For dessert, try doubling the sugar and serving the pudding with vanilla ice cream.

Squash and Apple Pudding   *Serves 6 to 8*

1½ pounds (675 g) crookneck summer squashes or 1 medium winter squash
(about 3 pounds or 1.35 kg)

3 large tart apples (about 1½ pounds or 675 g)

Butter for the dish

⅓ cup (30 g) dry white bread crumbs

½ cup (125 ml) milk or light cream

1 tablespoon rose water

1 tablespoon white wine

½ teaspoon salt

1½ tablespoons (22 g) sugar, more to taste

3 tablespoons (22 g) flour

3 eggs

7-by-11-inch (18-by-28-cm) baking dish

To cook the squash: Bring a large pan of salted water to a boil. Trim the summer squashes and cut them into ¾-inch (2-cm) chunks. If using the winter squash, halve it, discard the seeds and fiber, and cut the flesh into similar-sized chunks, with the skin. Add the squash chunks to the boiling water and simmer, uncovered, until the flesh is just tender, as little as 5 to 10 minutes for young summer squashes or as long as 15 minutes for a mature winter squash.

Drain the squash well and spread the pieces on a tray to steam off moisture until they are cool enough to handle. Peel off and discard the tough skin from the winter squash; leave the more tender summer squash skin intact. Purée the squash in a food processor until smooth. If using a dense variety of winter squash, you may need to add a few spoonfuls of hot water for a smooth purée.

To cook the apples: While the squash chunks are cooking and cooling, peel, quarter, core, and thinly slice the apples. Put them in a heavy-based pan with a few spoonfuls of water, cover, and cook over medium heat, stirring often, until they soften to a purée, 15 to 20 minutes, depending on the age and variety of the apples. If the apples are very soft after cooking, leave them as they are; if they are chunky, purée them in the processor.

To assemble and bake the pudding: Heat the oven to 350°F (180°C). Butter the baking dish. In a large bowl, stir together the squash and apple purées until well mixed. Stir in the bread crumbs, milk, rose water, wine, salt, sugar, and flour. Taste and add more sugar if needed. Whisk the eggs in a separate bowl, and stir them into the pudding. Whisk the batter by hand or with a handheld mixer for 2 minutes. Pour the mixture into the prepared baking dish. Bake until the pudding is puffed and just set in the center, 55 to 65 minutes. Serve hot or warm. The pudding keeps well for a day in the refrigerator and should be warmed before serving.

Cailles au Laurier

Quail with Bay Leaf

From A. Beauvilliers, *L'art du cuisinier* (Paris, 1814): *Take seven quail, pluck them, clean them and flame them ; make a small stuffing with their livers and several chicken livers, some grated bacon fat, a very finely chopped bay leaf, and a little chopped onion chives; season with salt and coarse pepper ; stuff your quails; spear them on a spit, wrapping them with barding fat and paper; cook them on the spit, and serve them with this sauce :*

Cut two or three ham slices, and sweat them ; when they start to stick , moisten them with a glass of good white wine , two basting spoons full of consommé and the same of reduced espagnole sauce ; add a half clove of garlic and two bay leaves : bring to a boil and reduce all to the consistency of a sauce , then strain the sauce through a tamis sieve. While the quail are cooking, blanch seven large bay leaves ; when the birds are cooked, discard the barding fat; when presenting them, put one of the blanched bay leaves between each quail : add the juice of a lemon to your sauce, coarse pepper and a little butter ; strain it , whisk it until glossy, spoon the sauce over the quail, and serve.

OUR FIRST EDITION of *L'art du cuisinier* is signed with a flourish "A. Beauvilliers," triply underlined. Beauvilliers could be justly proud of his career, which began in the royal household of the comte de Provence, the title used by Louis XVIII until his accession to the throne in 1814, and ended in his own restaurant in the rue de Richelieu in central Paris. In many ways, Beauvilliers's recipe is a classic, with the little quail wrapped in barding fat (thinly sliced fresh pork fat) so they do not dry out during roasting. The liver stuffing adds body and the sauce is based on consommé and the brown sauce called espagnole, both of them standard in French professional kitchens by Beauvilliers's time. Fresh bay leaves are a must, infusing the birds with a whiff of southern France, pungent and strong. An herb garden or farmer's market is the best place to look for the fresh leaves, or you might be lucky enough to find them in the supermarket. I keep a little bay tree outside my door. The trees thrive in any temperate climate, and a few leaves are invaluable as an aromatic in soups and stews.

Bone-in quail and barding fat are available at specialty-food stores and online. Most likely the birds will come without livers, so substitute a chicken liver for every pair of quail livers. As for the classic preparations espagnole sauce and consommé (which take at least twenty-four hours to make), I find that gravy from a roast can substitute for espagnole, and well-flavored brown stock for consommé. Beauvilliers grills his birds on a spit, thus adding a touch of char, but they can also be roasted in the oven.

Spit-Roasted Quail with Bay Leaf *Serves 4 as a main course, 8 as a first course*

8 bone-in quail

SAUCE

2 to 3 slices cooked ham (about 2 ounces or 60 g)

¾ cup (175 ml) dry white wine

1 cup (250 ml) beef consommé

1 cup (250 ml) espagnole sauce

½ garlic clove

2 fresh bay leaves

1 tablespoon (15 g) cold butter, cut into small pieces

Juice of ½ lemon

STUFFING

6 ounces (170 g) barding fat

4 chicken livers

Salt and coarsely ground pepper

9 fresh bay leaves

2 green onions, green tops only, finely chopped

Grill with spit (optional), kitchen string

To make the sauce: Lay the ham slices in a saucepan and cook over medium heat until they stick and start to brown, 3 to 4 minutes. Add the wine and simmer until reduced by half, 3 to 5 minutes. Add the consommé, espagnole sauce, garlic clove, and bay leaves and continue to simmer until the sauce is reduced by about half and lightly coats a spoon, 25 to 35 minutes. Strain and set aside.

To make the stuffing: Finely chop about one-third of the barding fat. Cut the rest into 8 equal squares and set them aside. Heat the chopped fat in a frying pan over medium heat, stirring until the fat runs, about 2 minutes. Add the chicken livers and sprinkle with salt and pepper. Brown them on all sides, leaving them pink in the center, 2 to 3 minutes. Let them cool, then finely chop them, reserving the fat. Set 8 bay leaves aside for decoration and very finely chop the last one, discarding the stem. Stir together the livers, fat, chopped bay leaf, and green onion and season with salt and pepper. Taste and adjust the seasoning. If you are not cooking the quail right away, chill the stuffing.

To stuff the quail: Wipe the birds inside and out with dry paper towels, sprinkle with salt and pepper, and spoon the stuffing into the cavities. Cover the breasts with the squares of barding fat, and truss them in place with the string. If grilling the birds, thread them on the spit. If roasting the birds, set them on a rack in a roasting pan. If the stuffing has been chilled, you can refrigerate the quail for a couple of hours before roasting.

To roast the quail: If using a spit, light the grill; if using an oven, heat it to 450°F (230°C). Start the spit turning, putting it quite close to the heat, or put the roasting pan in the oven. Roast the quail until they start to brown and the meat starts to shrink from the drumsticks, 20 to 25 minutes in the oven. Cooking time on a spit will vary with the heat and its proximity to the birds. Check them after 10 to 15 minutes. If roasting in the oven, turn the birds onto their breasts halfway through cooking so they remain moist. When done, the breast meat should still be slightly pink and the legs, when wiggled, will feel loose in the sockets.

To finish: Discard the trussing string and barding fat, and arrange the quail on a platter or individual plates. Bring the sauce to a boil, take from the heat, and whisk in the butter pieces. Season the sauce with the lemon juice and pepper, and spoon it over the quail. Tuck a fresh bay leaf in each cavity for decoration (note they are too strong to be edible on their own) and serve at once.

Soufflés Parisiens aux Pommes de Reinette

Parisian Soufflés with Reinette Apples

From Antonin Carême, *Le pâtissier royal parisien* (Paris, 1815): *Cut thirty-six large reinette apples into quarters ; after peeling them, thinly slice them and cook them with a half pound of powdered sugar, the zest of a lemon, and a glass of water. When this purée is thoroughly dried, put it in a large saucepan ; then whisk eighteen egg whites until stiff, into which you mix a pound of powdered sugar, as for meringues. Then mix a quarter with the apple purée. Finally you mix all together, which makes a kind of soufflé (without butter or flour), that you turn at once into a shell [croustade] of the same volume, and prepared as in preceding recipes. Put it in an oven at medium heat, and allow a short hour of cooking. Serve with a clear glaze made with powdered sugar.*

THIS SOUFFLÉ IS IDEALLY moist and full of flavor; however, the cooking is more tricky than for other soufflés, given the extreme delicacy of its composition of only egg whites, sugar, and apple purée. The critical step is to thoroughly dry the purée, removing all moisture, so it combines closely with the egg white.

Antonin Carême was a missionary, and undoubtedly an egotist, who would write up the culinary events of the day in his diary, a kind of blog. Thus, we have detailed records of the monumental menus he constructed for the elite of Europe. Sixty different dishes was modest for him; over one hundred was not uncommon. He made the best use of the new enclosed ranges with flat cooktops, developing dishes such as sautés that call for even heat to control evaporation, plus a special wide sauté pan with shallow sides to make them. To take simple apple purée, as he does here, lighten it with meringue, and then bake it as a soufflé is typical of his imagination. In some ways, however, Carême seems old-fashioned: in 1815, he is still using pound measurements instead of the metrics mandated by Napoleon.

Soufflés were a fashionable innovation at the beginning of the century. Both Ude and Beauvilliers featured them in their cookbooks (1813 and 1814, respectively), though

Carême is often given all the credit. He describes a special portable oven heated with hot coals, the vault at least eighteen "thumbs" (inches) high to allow the soufflé space to rise. He laments the distances that food often had to be carried to the dining room from "our laboratories," but with his device he insists that a fully cooked soufflé can even wait a few minutes before serving—risky advice even in today's regulated ovens. The *croustade* he refers to in this recipe is the ancestor of our soufflé dish, a deep, straight-sided crust of pastry pleated at the sides and secured with a turned rim. Our plain white porcelain soufflé molds are an exact copy.

Be aware that the deeper the soufflé dish, the higher the mixture will rise above the rim, but the more likely it is to flop or spill. To whisk Carême's eighteen egg whites would be a major challenge, beyond any domestic electric mixer or untrained arm, so I've reduced quantities here to one-third. Likewise, I imagine our apples must be larger than Carême's because eight to ten apples make plenty of purée for six egg whites. Look for a good, flavorful sauce apple, such as MacIntosh or Jonathan, that cooks easily to form a purée. You might even be lucky enough to find the Reinette that Carême recommends in a farmer's market. This soufflé is delicious as is, but a spoonful of Calvados (apple brandy) poured into the center while hot from the oven transforms it to the sublime. Serve it at once. A soufflé cannot wait!

Apple Soufflé   *Serves 6 to 8*

> 8 to 10 medium apples (about 3 pounds or 1.35 kg total)
> 3 tablespoons (45 g) sugar, more to taste, if needed, and for glazing
> ¼ cup (60 ml) water
> Pared zest of ½ lemon
> Melted butter for the dish
>
> MERINGUE
> 6 egg whites
> ⅔ cup (140 g) sugar
>
> 6-cup (1.5-liter) soufflé dish

To make the purée: Peel, core, and thinly slice the apples and put them in a heavy-based pan with the sugar, water, and lemon. Cover and cook over medium heat, stirring often, until the apples have formed a soft, even purée, 30 to 40 minutes. The time varies with the type and ripeness of the apples. Remove the lid and cook, stirring constantly, until the purée is stiff and holds a trail for a few seconds when the spoon is lifted, 15 to 20 minutes. Discard the lemon zest. If the apples do not collapse naturally into a smooth purée, use an immersion blender or food processor to smooth them out. Taste, and if very tart, add a little sugar (more comes with the meringue). You should have nearly 3 cups (750 ml) purée. It can be stored in the refrigerator for up to 2 days.

To finish the soufflé: Heat the oven to 375°F (190°C) and put a baking sheet on a low shelf to heat. Brush the soufflé dish with melted butter, freeze it until set, and butter it again. If the apple purée is cold, heat it until hot to the touch. To make the meringue, put the egg whites in a large bowl. Using an electric mixer or by hand, whisk the egg whites until stiff. Whisk in the sugar and continue beating until the sugar dissolves enough to make a light meringue that forms a long peak when the whisk is lifted, 30 to 60 seconds. Add one-fourth of the meringue to the hot apple purée and fold until completely mixed. The heat cooks the meringue slightly so it holds better. Tip this mixture into the remaining whites and fold them together as lightly as possible.

Transfer the apple mixture to the prepared soufflé dish. The dish should be completely full. Level the surface with a metal spatula. Run your thumb around the inside of the dish to detach the mixture from the rim. Set the soufflé dish on the hot baking sheet and bake until the soufflé is risen and brown but still wobbles in the center, 15 to 20 minutes. Using a tea strainer, sprinkle the surface lightly with sugar. Continue baking until the soufflé is almost firm and the sugar melts and glazes the surface, another 5 minutes.

Transfer the dish to a plate lined with a napkin to prevent slippage and carry to the table at once. Serve the soufflé with two spoons, scooping into the center so each diner gets part of the brown outside and some of the soft center.

TOWARD THE MODERN COOKBOOK

L OOKING BACK OVER the more than four hundred years since the appearance of the first printed books about cooking, we honor and remember those that share certain characteristics. Their authors, almost all cooks by profession or occupation, seek to tempt their fellow cooks into the kitchen and encourage them to send the finest food to the table. They come from different backgrounds and write in different languages, but their passion for their subject transcends the page.

At the same time, we can see significant changes over the centuries that brought us to today's varied and sophisticated cookbooks. Fifteenth-century works were written by heads of kitchens to pay homage to their patrons by recording the splendor of their cuisine. Sixteenth-century cookbooks brought a bevy of new ideas: guides for stewards and maîtres d'hôtel of great households, insiders' books of secrets, commonplace books of useful hints including recipes, and books of medical recipes to treat the sick and maintain the healthy.

The seventeenth century witnessed the publication of specialized books devoted to pastry and confectionery, household advice books, and books addressed exclusively to women—including the first cookbook by a woman. Some eighteenth-century cookbook authors turned to science, others focused primarily on domestic skills, while one innovator, François Menon, became the first to devote an entire cookbook to *cuisine bourgeoise*, with its implication of women's cooking.

Finally, in a burst of creativity at the beginning of the nineteenth century, cookbooks by the first restaurateurs appeared, together with new forms of food writing, including restaurant reviews and guides to gourmet eating. Both in Europe and over the Atlantic, this cornucopia of books about cooking spread, and a plethora of genres flourished in the peace that was to last, with hiccups here and there, for nearly one hundred years.

Today, we reap the benefits of these developments in the myriad, often beautifully illustrated cookbooks available to the home cook. No longer are cooks restricted to one set of rules for entertaining; they can find guidance for everything from an informal

Traditional and modern dress for a cook, drawn by Antonin Carême for *Le maître d'hôtel français*, 1823 edition.

backyard barbecue to an elegant holiday party. The nineteenth-century interest in regional cooking has mushroomed to produce cookbooks for every ethnic and regional cuisine, as well as guides for fusing different traditions to explore new flavor combinations and fresh takes on familiar dishes. Earlier interest in food as medicine and the science of cooking has transformed into a rage for diet books of all types, with some diets having no more scientific foundation than had Galen's theory of the humors, while others offer us valuable instruction in how to achieve balanced meals.

The hero worship of Carême in the nineteenth century has led directly to the pantheon of famous chefs now revered by aspiring cooks, giving these chefs forums on television and in print to share their knowledge with national and sometimes international audiences. Printing technology has evolved to such a degree that publishers can offer lavish color illustrations at affordable prices, and electronic cookbooks and applications for portable devices provide a new format that no fifteenth-century chef could have envisioned. Technology in the kitchen, too, has widened the possibilities for home cooks, simplifying many cooking tasks, and bookstores now carry a range of appliance-specific cookbooks as well—for cooking in a crock pot, in a microwave, or on a grill. Clothing for today's chefs, however, has hardly changed since the early nineteenth century, as shown in Carême's sketch for *Le maître d'hôtel français*. His modern cook is wearing an embryonic toque, as well as loose sleeves that can be rolled up, a sweatband around the neck, and a knife holder and dish towel at the waist.

We owe our present rich array of cookbooks to the devoted authors whom we have met in this book. Mark and I can only imagine the contributions today's passionate chefs will make to future cookbook libraries.

COLLECTING COOKBOOKS

B ECAUSE I AM THE ONE who started us off on cookbook collecting, Anne
asked me to write a personal note about how we put together our collection
of antiquarian cookbooks. I am always happy to talk about collecting, which
in itself is a clue to the key to building a personal library: to collect old books, you have
to be a book enthusiast. A further clue is that Anne and I do not collect books as
trophies—we use them!

My first piece of advice to the new collector is, begin early. When we started collecting old cookbooks in the 1960s, we did not have much competition. Since then,
the rise of celebrity chefs and restaurateurs and the expansion and interest in the professional food world have made cookbooks much more popular, and thus increased
the prices. Second, begin cautiously, so that you can develop a good feel for what kinds
of old books capture your attention and seem worth collecting. Start with a narrow
focus on a century, topic, or nationality; for us, this has been early French and English
cookbooks. Third, be prepared to become something of a detective: you have to enjoy
the hunt. As with detective work, one contact or conversation can lead you to another,
and it pays to keep your ear to the ground.

Antiquarian, Rare, or Used?

Old books go under many names, whether antiquarian, rare, scarce, or merely used, and
the significance of these terms varies with the context. The term *antiquarian* should
present no ambiguity since a book printed after 1800 or so would never be described as
such. The older and rarer an antiquarian book and the better its condition, ideally in a
period binding, the higher the price, at which point you enter the domain of investment
rather than merely an agreeable hobby. Often collectors seek out topics relating to their
professional or avocational interests, which is what Anne and I have done in focusing
on books about cooking and food history (or that rather overblown word *gastronomy*).

Not all antiquarian cookbooks are rare, but those that are sought after can be scarce
and correspondingly expensive. The more use a book has had in the kitchen, the fewer

and rarer are the copies that survive. Until very recently, cookbooks were not a prestigious item for collectors, so they were not always guarded with particular care. The contrary is also true: a cookbook may not necessarily be old to be rare. First editions of famous titles such as *The Joy of Cooking* can be quite hard to find, and correspondingly costly, as can limited editions and certain editions with specialist art bindings. An author's signature increases the value of a book, and personal messages increase it even more. Anne is the proud possessor of a copy of the first volume of *Mastering the Art of French Cooking* with an inscription by Julia Child.

A less expensive way to enter the field of antiquarian cookbooks is to acquire a facsimile of the original edition. Thanks to modern technology, reproductions of many old and not-so-old cookbooks have been published during the last half century. The Internet makes them easy to track. The increasing availability of print on demand has broadened access to single copies of such books, and some can be viewed online at Google Books. I regard facsimiles as tools for study rather than as true collectors' items, though some are already worth more than their original price and so can be a very good place to start, particularly when the original is unobtainable or impossibly expensive to buy. Often reproductions have scholarly introductions, and possibly glossaries of obsolete terms. For example, we have long relied on the reprint of Taillevent's *Le viandier* (The Victualler) edited by Jérôme Pichon and Georges Vicaire in 1892, because the editors' annotations to this fourteenth-century manuscript make it comprehensible to the modern reader. Typically, facsimile editions come from niche publishers in various countries; they are not necessarily cheap and can become scarce, having been published in small quantities. You'll find listings of some recent facsimiles and reprints, including the 1892 *Viandier*, in the bibliography at the end of this book.

Even further from the antiquarian original are reprints of texts in which the layout and typeface are new. They too are useful for study, and some can be sought after for themselves. I think of our handsome reprint of *Le pastissier françois* (The French Pastry Cook, 1653), which appeared in a limited edition in 1921, with an introduction by the distinguished gastronome Maurice des Ombiaux. So rare was the original *Pastissier* at that time that only twenty-nine copies were known to exist, and our 1921 reprint has become worth a bit of money in its own right. Recent translations into English of rare cookbooks, often with facsimile text included, are also bringing old books to a wider audience; examples include Scappi's *Opera* (The Work by Master Bartolomeo Scappi) translated by Terence Scully (2008) and *Libre de Sent Soví* translated by Robin Vogelzang and edited by Joan Santanach (2008). The precise meaning of the book's Catalan title is still being debated.

A Book in the Hand

The weight of a book in the hand and its welcome to the eye give me as much pleasure as the thrill of the hunt. Moreover, the style of printing, craftsmanship, and binding of a new find carry interesting clues to its history. The elegant illustrated volumes of the sixteenth century were designed to grace the library of a connoisseur as well as to inform his mind. The little books of the same period, with cost a prime consideration, made less of a lasting impression; they were for use rather than for pleasure, and therefore fewer copies have survived. At the turn of the sixteenth century, the shape of books began to change. Small books grew much thicker and were more sturdily bound, often in full leather. For a sure-fire success with a title such as *The Queen's Closet Opened* (1655), the publisher might splurge on an engraved frontispiece and still manage to turn a fine profit.

By the 1650s, more and more people could read and were in search of moderately priced, durable volumes that did not cost too much money. Some of these books were destined for the kitchen, so publishers gradually worked out a standard presentation to attract buyers: a plump 4-by-6½-inch book bound in brown calfskin with a tooled gold title on the spine. A dozen or more cookbooks in several languages, particularly French, were published in this format during the next hundred years. So alike are these books on our shelves that we find it hard to distinguish one from another, especially as the embossed gold titles fade into the aging brown leather. More elaborate books may run to two volumes, and sometimes three and even five volumes were needed to maintain the compact, handy format.

The design of books' contents was equally homogeneous, featuring roman serif type, closely set in black ink with the occasional relief of an ornamental bar called a headpiece, or an ornate capital to head a chapter. In later books, an engraved frontispiece set the scene—maybe a portrait of the author or a kitchen scene. Our copy of Emy's *L'art de bien faire les glaces d'office* (The Art of Succeeding with Ices, 1768) greets the reader with an enchanting evocation of cupids making ice cream out of doors. These books are easy to use: they all feature lists of contents and recipe indexes, their recipes rarely jump tiresomely overleaf, and awkward spaces are filled with an ornamental icon. Above all, they are robust, allowing many of them to survive to the present day.

A few exceptions stand out from the brown pack. The Elzevir Press in Amsterdam published at least one cookbook, *Le pastissier françois*, in its tradition of tiny books typically measuring about 3 by 5 inches. At the other end of the scale, in our copy of *The Complete Practical Cook* (1730), Charles Carter has adopted a tall, wide format to insert a dozen pullout pages illustrating the table settings of his elaborate menus. Seventeen years later, Hannah Glasse celebrated the first appearance of *The Art of Cookery Made Plain and Easy* in a lavish format that sprawled generously across the wide-margined pages. At the opening of the nineteenth century, Grimod de la Reynière was to set another trend with his pocket-sized yearly *Almanach des gourmands*.

The nineteenth century brought new styles and different approaches to books, particularly in France. Color came to cookbook bindings, with Carême favoring Empire pine green, for example, and Beauvilliers opting for cheerful light calfskin. Half bindings with boards of decorative marbleized paper were much in vogue. If a cookbook was illustrated at all, the engravings were likely to be lavish and scattered among the pages of text. In England, the household books written mainly for women created their own economical style of cloth spines and cloth- or paper-bound boards in muted colors. As in every era, the cookbook styles reflected both fashion and the economic realities of the times.

Essential Tools for the Collector

You never know what you might find, but obviously you also have to have some idea of what you are looking for. That's why I advise every collector to start with one or more bibliographies. I am lucky in having early on acquired the 1939 Katherine Bitting *Gastronomic Bibliography* (reprinted in 2004), which I found in the Corner Bookstore, a famous New York haunt run by Eleanor Lowenstein, herself the author of the indispensable bibliography *American Cookery Books*. I used to take the Bitting bibliography to bed to read before going to sleep, one way of committing its information to memory. Katherine Bitting's advice about collecting cookbooks certainly applied to me: "Make careful selection of books according to subject matter rather than by editions; purchase only what you can afford at a time; become familiar with them by use, thus learn to appreciate them, and maybe love them."[1]

Exploring the wider world of old cookbooks, you'll come across more specialist bibliographies that focus on different languages and fields. (For a list of the most important bibliographies of European and American cookbooks, see the bibliography at the end of this book.) The irreplaceable reference for collecting French cookbooks, for instance, is the *Bibliographie gastronomique* by Georges Vicaire, published in 1890 but still the starting point for any French research. Another great source for research is the U.S. national library system; for example, Katherine Bitting's collection anchors the antiquarian cookbooks at the Library of Congress. We are lucky to live in an age when new technology is making the content of great library collections available via the Internet. Internet bibliographies are also available for some public and private libraries with important culinary collections, but often only limited explorations of their contents have been made by researchers, let alone the findings published. Gems hide in many places.

Another important resource is book dealers' catalogs, whether in print or online. Online service is especially important these days with the overall decline in the number of bookshops (though a few top antiquarian dealers refuse to post their catalogs on the Internet, preferring to rely on a strong client base rather than accept offers from unknowns in the wild blue yonder). Many antiquarian book dealers no longer have a physical storefront, and they generally specialize in a particular subject. Their regular catalogs not only provide a guide to what secondhand and antiquarian books are worth but also identify which ones are important landmarks of the genre. These catalogs can also be a terrific resource for facsimile books, which are seldom distributed in book-stores but can be tracked down online. You can also find information on facsimiles and reprints, and occasional articles and reviews of books on culinary history, in *Gastronomica,* published by University of California Press, and *Petits Propos Culinaires,* a small British journal. If a facsimile is on offer, one can surmise the book was worth copying. This tells you that finding the original would have importance, and thus value.

The best antiquarian catalogs relate a book to others in the field. The facts about each book and its author should be precise, listed together with its condition, whether pristine or shopworn. These catalogs are labors of love, crafted with all the care and pedantic accuracy that go into completing a first-class history exam or the catalog entries for a major art exhibition. Commercial as sales catalogs must be, they must also appeal to individual collectors. Book catalogs are always the first piece of the morning's mail that I open, and I am soon on the phone to pursue my inquiry.

On the Hunt

In our professional and social lives, Anne and I have traveled a great deal, spurring our urge to collect. Between 1960 and 1990, I lived in Turkey, Washington, D.C., Boston, Luxembourg, Paris, and Burgundy, and I spent a considerable amount of time in New York and London as well as various places in between. Being an adventurous spirit was a big plus. Not only do I like to visit new places, but curiosity leads me to comb used bookstores wherever I go. I have found scores of old (not necessarily valuable) cookbooks in unlikely places—in western Canada, New Zealand, and the remoter parts of the United States. For example, I came across an early copy of *The Joy of Cooking* (alas, not a first edition) in an antique mall in Lexington, Virginia. Christchurch, New Zealand, was the source for some useful nineteenth-century English books, including a fine copy of Alexis Soyer's *Pantropheon, or the History of Food* (1853). I hadn't traveled to any of these places with the intention of rooting out old books, but natural nosiness and past fruitful experiences led me to check whenever time allowed. So, you never know where you'll find a prize and must always be on the hunt.

England is the best country I have found for buying antiquarian cookbooks, at reasonable prices, if you are lucky. Thirty years ago, in one of London's antiquarian bookshops, I came across the second edition of François Marin's *Les dons de Comus* (The Gifts of Comus, 1742), a three-volume French work. It was in the form of unbound sheets. In the eighteenth century, books were often published and sold simply as sheets; binding came later, done by the book collector, who might perhaps have his coat of arms applied to the cover. I had the volumes bound by an artisan binder in Luxem-bourg—in period style, with sturdy cloth covers, marbleized endpapers, and brown leather spines embossed with the title in gold leaf. Not all finds are as exciting as this one, but modestly priced books on the shelves of a well-organized dealer can yield happy surprises. Some dealers specialize in cooking and gastronomy, and those stores are the places to begin.

There is no substitute for browsing among the books themselves, memorizing prices and titles; it is an excitement and an education in itself. As you leaf carefully from cover to cover, take note of which books appeal to you most. Picking out books you like helps define your collecting desiderata (an old-fashioned term that is still used in the trade). The bindings add great character, and with experience, you can often date a book by just a glance at its spine. Older books may contain a previous owner's bookplate or marginal notes by a long-forgotten reader, all details that add to the value. Our first edition of *Il trinciante* (The Carver, 1621) by Mattia Giegher has copious notes in a contemporary italic hand that make it unique. In later editions, these notes have been incorporated into the print. Perhaps this was an author's or a publisher's copy? We'll never know for sure, but there is great fun in imagining that we are witnessing part of the centuries-ago editing process.

Booksellers are a friendly lot, sometimes cranky but nonetheless endearing, particularly those in a specialized field. Bookshelves that are well organized by topic lend a strong clue to whether the shop will have a knowledgeable staff. In fact, one of the things I like most about collecting books is visiting the bookshops and talking to the proprietors. From these friendly, informal chats, you can learn about books in private hands or on offer at upcoming auctions. If you have knowledge or impressions to share, booksellers are happy to lend an ear. Like teachers, booksellers thrive on sharing their knowledge and imparting their advice. In one half-hour chat, you can learn more than you can glean from any bibliography or catalog.

There are several ways to track down the kind of bookseller you are looking for. In many towns, bookshops support each other, passing on information and listing other colleagues. Most booksellers are receptive to your inquiries and may even direct you to a rival bookshop that you would not otherwise find. Though I may date myself in today's digital world by suggesting that you consult the yellow pages, I still peruse the listings for secondhand bookshops or antiquarian book dealers in local phone books whenever I visit a new place.

Don't overlook the possibilities of local cookbook sales or yard sales of books in general. For example, in Los Angeles, where we now live, the Culinary Historians of Southern California holds a tantalizing sale of donated cookbooks for the benefit of the Los Angeles Public Library every year. Sadly, most used cookbooks of recent date are worth almost nothing at all, but a treasure that appeals to you personally might easily be waiting, buried in the jumble.

These days, the Internet is without question a key area to explore. Many dealers have their own websites, and some mainstream auction sites such as eBay and Amazon .com have subcategories for cookbooks that are used or "collectible"—that is, worth a bit of money. An Internet chat with a dealer specializing in cookbooks can be rewarding in itself; you'll soon come across common interests. Just trolling the Internet reveals a vast range of books, from antiquarian to simply used, and many websites are available to help sort them out, one being the electronic discussion group Exlibris. ABE (the Advance Book Exchange) is very helpful, as is WorldBookDealers.com, which is exactly what it sounds like.[2] As well as providing leads for books, the Internet is a fruitful source of ephemera—pamphlets of recipes, posters, prints, even original drawings with a culinary theme.

However, for books priced higher than, say, thirty dollars, nothing can replace a traditional relationship with a bookseller you know. To meet other cookbook collectors of like mind, you might consider joining one of the groups of culinary historians that are active in at least a dozen cities and university campuses.

In turn, live auctions and book fairs can offer rich learning opportunities. Sotheby's in London and the Salle Drouot in Paris are just two of several international auction houses that hold occasional sales specializing in cookbooks. Even if you don't end up buying a book at an auction, perusing the after-sale record listing the prices paid is an excellent way to enhance your knowledge of current book values.

To find a wide range of book dealers in one place and view books firsthand, attending a book fair can be invaluable. The annual Antiquarian Booksellers Association Book Fair in London is an excellent venue with an international scope. Los Angeles regularly hosts the Antiquarian Booksellers' Association of America, drawing a number of top sellers from around the world, and similar fairs are held in other major cities. Dealers at such fairs may be open to barter if you have some overlapping books in your collection that you want to trade. So comb the newspaper and the Internet—particularly the book review sections, websites, and book-related blogs—for notices of upcoming international gatherings. Every time I attend one of these fairs, I find something unexpected.

The Purchase: Caveat Emptor

Although the Internet is an excellent tool for tracking down elusive titles and comparing the condition and prices of books on offer, the new collector needs to be cautious in purchasing old books online. Prices can vary enormously for an almost identical item. Even more than in a bookstore, you must know what you are buying and how much it is worth. Every book has its own character, particularly a used book, and there is no substitute for holding it in your hand. I've been disappointed by Internet purchases several times. Thus, if a book predates 1900, I recommend that you take a personal look at it unless you have prior experience with the seller.

If you get hooked by the collector's craze, gradually you'll find yourself moving upmarket, increasingly tempted by books that are more and more scarce, and therefore increasingly pricey. Keep in mind that rare and antiquarian books are a province apart from merely old or secondhand books. At the top end, antiquarian books can be so expensive that you should not enter the field without the equivalent of a Wall Street investment strategy. You need a working knowledge of the bindings and appearance of books over the centuries and a sharp eye. For instance, you may not realize that an early book is missing its original, highly valuable illustrations. Check the pages: our copy of Robert May's *The Accomplisht Cook* (1660) has a single page missing, which reduces its value by about 20 percent.

Caution is also the watchword at auctions. Here you'll be bidding against dealers who know the market well, so you must, too. Logically, prices should be lower than those charged by a dealer, but bargains are unlikely. You should not rely on the auctioneers' price guidelines, as they can be way off, assigning either too high or too low a value. I am not a big fan of buying old books at auction unless you have the chance to see the book before the sale to examine its condition. It is very risky to buy an old book sight unseen, unless, of course, the title is very well known and so sought after that you are prepared to take a gamble. You can easily end up paying too much, caught in the excitement as competition from other bidders raises prices dramatically.

I HOPE THAT THIS BOOK widens your horizons about the history of food, food writing, and the creation of cookbooks and inspires you to begin or expand your own book collection. Anne and I have found that our lives are enriched by the experience of gathering, reading, and sharing the knowledge we have gained from our books. We have enjoyed every minute of searching for the books in our collection and hope that in some small way we have done our part to preserve history and impart knowledge. Why else was printing with movable type invented, and why else do people write books?

Mark Cherniavsky

NOTES

Introduction

1 Henry Notaker, *Printed Cookbooks in Europe, 1470–1700: A Bibliography of Early Modern Culinary Literature* (New Castle, DE: Oak Knoll Press, 2010), 2.

2 Bartolomeo Scappi, *Opera di M. Bartolomeo Scappi* (Venetia: Ad instantia de Giorgio Ferarij, 1596), 1.

Antiquity through the Middle Ages

1 Athenaeus, *Deipnosophists or Banquet of the Learned,* trans. C. D. Yonge (London: Henry G. Bohn, 1854), 3:1023.

2 Roy C. Strong, *Feast: A History of Grand Eating* (Orlando, FL: Harcourt, 2002), 23.

3 Apicius, *Cookery and Dining in Imperial Rome,* trans. Joseph Dommers Vehling (New York: Dover, 1977), 168.

4 Strong, *Feast,* 22.

5 Joannes Cassianus, *De institutis coenobiorum,* trans. Jean-Claude Guy (Paris: Les Editions du Cerf, 2001), 199.

6 Jérôme Pichon and Georges Vicaire, eds., *Le viandier de Guillaume Tirel dit Taillevent* (Luzarches, France: Librairie Daniel Morcrette, n.d.), xxx–xxxi.

7 Samuel Pegge, ed., *The Forme of Cury, a Roll of Ancient English Cookery* (London: J. Nichols, 1780).

8 Raphael Holinshed, *Chronicles* (London: Henry Denham, 1587).

9 The title of *Sent Soví* is a bit of a mystery, with no direct translation. The name might be a shortening of Saint Silvain, Saint Souvain in French. See *Libre de Sent Soví,* ed. Rudolph Grewe (Barcelona: Editorial Barcino, 1979), 54.

10 Hans Wegener, ed., "Einleitung," in *Küchenmeisterei* (Leipzig: Otto Harrassowitz, 1939).

11 Paul Freedman, *The History of Taste* (Berkeley: University of California Press, 2007), 148.

12 Strong, *Feast,* 79.

13 Baron Jérôme Pichon, ed., *Le ménagier de Paris* (Paris: Jérôme Pichon, 1846).

14 Eileen Power, *The Goodman of Paris* (London: George Routledge, 1928), 39.

15 Alfred Gottschalk, *Histoire de l'alimentation et de la gastronomie depuis la préhistoire jusqu'à nos jours* (Paris: Hippocrate, 1948).

16 Molly Harrison, *The Kitchen in History* (New York: Scribner's, 1972), 35–36.

The Fifteenth Century

1 Lucien Febvre and Henri-Jean Martin, *The Coming of the Book,* trans. David Gerard (London: Verso, 1976), 182. As early as 1480, 110 towns in western Europe had printing shops.

2 Gina L. Greco and Christine M. Rose, eds., *The Good Wife's Guide (Le Ménagier de Paris): A Medieval Household Book* (Ithaca, NY: Cornell University Press, 2009).

3 *Les memoires de Messire Olivier de la Marche* (Ghent: Gerard de Salenson, 1567).

4 Ibid., 418–19.

5 Platina [Bartolomeo Sacchi], *De Honesta Voluptate; the First Dated Cookery Book* [1475], trans. Elizabeth Buermann Andrews (St. Louis: Mallinckrodt Chemical Works, 1967).

6 See Barbara Santich, *The Original Mediterranean Cuisine: Medieval Recipes for Today* (Cambridge, MA: Wakefield Press, 1995), 134.

7 Luigi Ballerini, "Introduction. Maestro Martino: The Carneades of Cooks," in Martino of Como, *The Art of Cooking,* trans. Jeremy Parzen (Berkeley: University of California Press, 2005), 1.

8 Klaus Dürrschmid, *Kochbücher der Renaissance 1450–1600* (Vienna: Universität für Bodenkultur Wien, 2002).

9 Hans Wegener, ed., *Küchenmeisterei* (Leipzig: Otto Harrassowitz, 1939), 10.

10 Uta Shumacher-Voelker, "German Cookery Books, 1485–1800," *Petit Propos Culinaires* 6 (1980): 35.

11 "Nuremberg," in *Encyclopædia Britannica,* 11th ed. (New York: Encyclopædia Britannica Company, 1910), 913–14.

12 Roy C. Strong, *Feast: A History of Grand Eating* (Orlando, FL: Harcourt Publishing, 2002), 146.

13 Jérôme Pichon and Georges Vicaire, eds., *Le viandier de Guillaume Tirel dit Taillevent* (Luzarches, France: Librairie Daniel Morcrette, n.d.).

14 *Le ménagier de Paris* (Luzarches, France: Librairie Daniel Morcrette, n.d.), 2:248.

15 Jill Norman, *The Complete Book of Spices* (London: Dorling Kindersley, 1990).

16 *Boke of Cokery* (London: Richard Pynson, 1500).

17 See Bridget Ann Henisch, *Fast and Feast: Food in Medieval Society* (University Park: Pennsylvania State University Press, 1976).

18 Strong, *Feast*, 78–79.

19 Laurioux Bruno, "Introduction to Libro de Arte Coquinaria—Digital Edition," in Martino of Como (Maestro Martino), *Libro de arte coquinaria*, trans. Gillian Riley (Oakland, CA: Digital Octavo Editions, 2005), 2.

20 Philip and Mary Hyman, "Printing in the Kitchen: French Cookbooks, 1500–1800," in *Food: A Culinary History*, ed. Jean Louis Flandrin and Massimo Montanari, ed. English edition Albert Sonnenfeld (New York: Columbia University Press, 1999), 395.

The Sixteenth Century

1 Mary Hyman and Philip Hyman, "Les livres de cuisine et le commerce des recettes en France aux XV et XVI siècles," in *Du manuscrit à la table*, ed. Carol Lambert (Montreal: Les Presses de l'Université de Montréal, 1992), 149.

2 Luciano Chiappini, *La dorte estense alla metà del cinquecento: I compendi di Cristoforo di Messisbugo* (Ferrara: S.A.T.E., 1984), 51.

3 Julia Cartwright, *Isabella d'Este* (New York: E. P. Dutton, 1923), 2:292.

4 Susan Pinkard, *A Revolution in Taste: The Rise of French Cuisine* (Cambridge: Cambridge University Press, 2009), 24.

5 Ken Albala, *The Banquet* (Urbana: University of Illinois Press, 2007), 127–28.

6 Jean Bruyérin-Champier, *L'alimentation*, trans. Sigurd Amundsen (Paris: Intermédiaire des Chercheurs et Curieux, 1998), 83. Translation of 1560 *De re cibaria*.

7 Nancy Harmon Jenkins, "Two Ways of Looking at Maestro Martino," *Gastronomica* 7, no. 2 (spring 2007): 101.

8 Rudolf Grewe, "Catalan Cuisine in An Historical Perspective," in *National and Regional Styles of Cookery: Proceedings of the Oxford Symposium on Food and Cookery, 1981*, ed. Alan Davidson (London: Prospect Books, 1981), 160.

9 Jeanne Allard, "Nola: Rupture ou continuité?" in *Du manuscrit à la table*, ed. Carol Lambert (Montreal: Les Presses de l'Université de Montréal, 1992), 149–61. Nola's work was probably written before 1500, but no manuscript has been found.

10 Grewe, "Catalan Cuisine," 163.

11 Ken Albala, *Food in Early Modern Europe* (Westport, CT: Greenwood Press, 2003), 128–31.

12 Gillian Riley, *Oxford Companion to Italian Food* (Oxford: Oxford University Press, 1997), 492.

13 *Opera di M. Bartolomeo Scappi* (Venice: Ad instantia de Giorgio Ferarij, 1596), 2.

14 Lord Westbury, *Handlist of Italian Cookery Books* (Florence: Leo S. Olschki-Editore, 1963).

15 Jeanne Allard, "Diego Granado Maldonado," *Petits Propos Culinaires* 25 (1987): 35–41; Henry Notaker, "Comments on the Interpretation of Plagiarism," *Petit Propos Culinaires* 70 (2002): 58–66; Jozef Schildermnas and Hilde Sels, "A Dutch Translation of Bartolomeo Scappi's Opera," *Petit Propos Culinaires* 74 (2003): 59–70.

16 Bruyérin-Champier, *L'alimentation*, 158–59.

17 Ibid., 460.

18 Jacqueline Boucher, "L'alimentation à la cour des derniers Valois," in *Pratiques & discours alimentaires à la renaissance*, Actes du Colloque de Tours 1979, ed. J.-C. Margolin and R. Sauzet (Paris: Maisonneufe et Larose, 1982), 163.

19 Michel de Montaigne, *Essais*, ed. Pierre Michels (Paris: Librairie Générale Française, 1972), book 1, ch. 51.

20 Campbell Bonner, "Dionysiac Magic and the Greek Land of Cockaigne," in *Transactions and Proceedings of the American Philological Association* (Baltimore: Johns Hopkins University Press, 1910), 41:175–85; Elizabeth L. Eisenstein, *The Printing Revolution in Early Modern Europe*, 2nd ed. (Cambridge: Cambridge University Press, 2005), 144.

21 Agostino M. Gallo, *Le vinti giornate dell'agricoltura* (Venice: Camillo Borgominerio, 1584).

22 Albert Hauser, *Das Kochbuch des Balthasar Staindl vom Jahne* (Dietikon-Zürich: Verlag Bibliophile Druke von Josef Stocker, 1979).

23 Alix Prentki, "Repas, tables et banquets allemands," in *Tables d'hier, tables d'ailleurs*, ed. Jean-Louis Flandrin and Jane Cobbi (Paris: Odile Jacob, 1999), 151–70.

24 Lancelot de Casteau, *Ouverture de cuisine* [1604] (Antwerp: De Schutter, 1983), 8.

25 Francesco Chiericati, quoted in Cartwright, *Isabella d'Este*, 2:175–76.

26 *A Proper Newe Booke of Cokerye*, ed. Catherine Frances Frere (Cambridge: W. Heffer & Sons, 1913), 3.

27 See Paul Hentzer, *Travels in England: During the Reign of Queen Elizabeth*. Appears with *Fragmenta Regalia; Or, Observations on Queen Elizabeth's Times and Favourites*, by Sir Robert Naunton (Nuremberg, 1612; London: Cassel and Company, 1901), 47.

28 Introduction to *A Proper Newe Booke of Cokerye*, ed. Catherine Frances Frere.

29 Joan Thirsk, *Food in Early Modern England* (London: Hambledon Continuum, 2007), 5–6.

30 William Harrison, *The Description of England* [1587], ed. Georges Edelen (Toronto: Dover, 1994), 269.

31 Ibid., 265.

32 William Eamon, *Science and the Secrets of Nature: Books of Secrets in Medieval and Early Modern Culture* (Princeton, NJ: Princeton University Press, 1993), 8–10, 126–33.

33 Ibid., 33.

34 Charles Estienne and Jean Liébault, *L'agriculture et maison rustique* [1564] (Lyon: Simon Rigaud, 1654), 241.

35 *Oxford History of England*, ed. Kenneth O. Morgan (Oxford: Oxford University Press, 1988), 319; Mark Girouard, *Life in the English Country House* (New Haven, CT: Yale University Press, 1978), 104.

36 David Cressy, "Literacy in Context: Meaning and Measurement in Early Modern England," in *Consumption and the World of Goods,* ed. John Brewer and Roy Porter (New York: Routledge, 1993), 317.

37 Malcolm Thick, "A Close Look at the Composition of Sir Hugh Plat's *Delights for Ladies,*" in *The English Cookery Book: Historical Essays,* ed. Eileen White (Totnes, England: Prospect Books, 2004), 59–60.

The Seventeenth Century

1 Jean-Louis Flandrin, "From Dietetics to Gastronomy: The Liberation of the Gourmet," in *Food: A Culinary History,* ed. Jean-Louis Flandrin and Massimo Montanari, English edition ed. Albert Sonnenfeld (New York: Columbia University Press, 1999), 425.

2 G. M. [Gervase Markham], *The English Hous-wife* (London: W. Wilson for George Sawridge, 1664), 61.

3 Carole Shammas, "Changes in English and Anglo-American Consumption from 1550 to 1800," in *Consumption and the World of Goods,* ed. John Brewer and Roy Porter (London: Routledge, 1993), 182.

4 Laura Mason, *Sugar-Plums and Sherbet: The Prehistory of Sweets* (Totnes, England: Prospect Books, 2004), 22–23.

5 Samuel Hartlib, *His Legacy: or an Enlargement on the Discourse of Husbandry Used in Brabant & Flaunders* (London: R. & W. Leybourn, 1652), 6.

6 Paula Panich, "The Countess of Kent," *Gastronomica* 1, no. 3 (2001): 61.

7 Elizabeth David, *Is There a Nutmeg in the House?* (New York: Viking, 2001), 110–11.

8 See Dorothy Stimson, "Amateurs of Science in 17th Century England," *Isis* 31, no. 1 (November 1939): 32–47; Claude Lloyd, "Shadwell and the Virtuosi," *PMLA* 44, no. 2 (June 1929): 490.

9 John Murrell, *Two Books of Cookerie and Carving,* facsimile of 1638 edition (Yorkshire, England: Jacksons Ilkley, 1985), 1, title page.

10 Anne French and Giles Waterfield, *Below Stairs: 400 Years of Servants' Portraits* (London: National Portrait Gallery, 2003), 39.

11 See Brian Cowan, *The Social Life of Coffee: The Emergence of the British Coffeehouse* (New Haven, CT: Yale University Press, 2005).

12 Will Rabisha, *The whole Body of COOKERY DISSECTED* [1661] (London: E. Calvert, 1763), 4A.

13 G. M., *The English Hous-wife,* 71.

14 Gilly Lehmann, *The British Housewife: Cookery Books, Cooking and Society in Eighteenth-Century Britain* (Totnes, England: Prospect Books, 2003), 50.

15 Patricia Crawford, "Women's Published Writings 1600–1700," in *Women in English Society 1500–1800,* ed. Mary Prior (London: Routledge, 1991), 228.

16 Hannah Woolley, *The Gentlewomans Companion, or, a GUIDE to the Female Sex* [1673], facsimile edition (Totnes, England: Prospect Books, 2001), 73.

17 Joan Thirsk, *Early Modern England* (London: Hambledon Continuum), 92–93.

18 Miguel de Cervantes, *Don Quixote,* trans. Edith Grossman (New York: Harper Collins, 2005), 19.

19 Marie Gigault de Bellefonds, marquise de Villars, *Lettres de Madame de Villars à Madame de Coulange (1679–1681),* ed. Alfred D. Courtois (Paris: Plon, 1868), 105.

20 Joseph Wechsberg, *The Cooking of Vienna's Empire* (New York: Time-Life, 1968), 14.

21 Elizabeth David, *Harvest of the Cold Months: The Social History of Ice and Ices* (New York: Viking, 1995), 143.

22 Gillian Riley, *Oxford Companion to Italian Food* (Oxford: Oxford University Press, 2007), 274.

23 James R. Farr, *Hands of Honor: Artisans and Their World in Dijon, 1550–1650* (Ithaca, NY: Cornell University Press, 1988), 60–61.

24 *Journal d'un voyage à Paris en 1657–1658, publié par A. P. Faugère* (Paris: Benjamin Duprat, 1862), 65.

25 François Pierre de la Varenne, "Au lecteur," *Le cuisinier françois* (Paris: Pierre David, 1652).

26 Mary Hyman and Philip Hyman, introduction to *The French Cook, Englished by I. D. G.* (1653; repr. London: Southover Press, 2001).

27 François de la Varenne, *Le cuisinier françois* (Paris: Pierre David, 1652); *Le cuisinier françois,* textes présentés par Flandrin, Jean-Louis, Philip and Mary Hyman (Paris: Montalba, 1983), 19.

28 Susan Pinkard, *A Revolution in Taste: The Rise of French Cuisine* (Cambridge: Cambridge University Press, 2009), 66.

29 See Jean-Louis Flandrin, *L'ordre des mets* (Paris: Editions Odile Jacob, 2002).

30 Bertrand Guégan, *Le cuisinier français* (Paris: Emile-Paul, 1934), xlv.

31 On the makeup of the working population, see Annik Pardailhé-Galabrun, *The Birth of Intimacy: Privacy and Domestic Life in Early Modern Paris,* trans. Jocelyn Phelps (Philadelphia: University of Pennsylvania Press, 1991), 27.

32 Christian Jouhaud, "Des Besoins et des goûts: La Consommation d'une Famille de Notables Bordelais dans la Première Moitié du XVII Siècle," *Revue d'histoire moderne et contemporaine,* October–December 1980, 631–46. See also James R. Farr, "Consumers, Commerce, and the Craftsmen of Dijon: The Changing Social and Economic Structure of a Provincial Capital, 1450–1750," in *Cities and Social Change in Early Modern France,* ed. Phillip Benedict (London: Unwin Hyman, 1989), 158–61.

33 Farr, "Consumers, Commerce, and the Craftsmen of Dijon," 148–49.

34 Jennifer J. Davis, "Men of Taste: Gender and Authority in the French Culinary Trades, 1730–1830" (PhD diss., Pennsylvania State University, 2004), 28; Pierre de Lune, "Au lecteur," *Le nouveau cuisinier* (Paris: Pierre David, 1659).

35 François Massialot, *Le nouveau cuisinier royal et bourgeois* (Claude Prud-homme, 1729), 1:258.

36 Barbara Ketcham Wheaton, *Savoring the Past* (Philadelphia: University of Pennsylvania Press, 1983), 151–52.

37 Pardailhé-Galabrun, *Birth of Intimacy,* 60.

38 Nicolas de Blegny published the *Livre commode* under the pseudonym Abraham du Pradel.

The Eighteenth Century

1 Romney Sedgwick, "The Duke of Newcastle's Cook," *History Today* 5, no. 5 (May 1955): 312.

2 See Linda Colley's insightful study *Britons: Forging the Nation 1707–1837* (New Haven, CT: Yale University Press, 1992).

3 Lorna Weatherill, *Consumer Behavior and Material Culture in Britain 1660–1760* (London: Routledge, 1988), 138–39.

4 Charles Carter, "To the Reader," *The Complete Practical Cook: or, a New System of the Whole Art and Mystery of Cookery* (London: W. Meadows, 1730).

5 Charles Carter, *The Compleat City and Country Cook: or, Accomplish'd Housewife* (London: For A. Bettesworth and C. Hitch and C. Davis, 1736), v.

6 The three other eminent authors of the period were Henry Howard, Patrick Lamb, and Charles Carter. Other relevant authors of the day included John Nott (*The Cook's and Confectioner's Dictionary,* 1723), William Verral (*A Complete System of Cookery,* 1759), and James Jenks (*The Complete Cook,* 1768).

7 Barbara Ketcham Wheaton, *Savoring the Past* (Philadelphia: University of Pennsylvania Press, 1983), 163.

8 Shipley, quoted in Maxine Berg, *Luxury & Pleasure in Eighteenth-Century Britain* (Oxford: Oxford University Press, 2005), 95.

9 Thomas Turner, *The Diary of Thomas Turner, 1754–1765,* ed. David Vaisey (Oxford: Oxford University Press, 1984), 160.

10 James Boswell, *Boswell's Life of Johnson* [1719], ed. Charles Grosvenor Osgood (New York: Scribner's Sons, 1917), 942.

11 Ann Cook, *Professed Cookery,* 2nd ed. (Printed for the Author, and sold at Her House in the Groat-Market, Nowcastle, 1755), iv.

12 Mrs. E. Smith, *The Compleat Housewife* (London: For J. and H. Pemberton, 1742), preface, title page.

13 Sarah Harrison, *The House-Keeper's Pocket-Book, and Compleat Family Cook. Containing above Three Hundred Curious and Uncommon Recipes* (London: T. Worral, 1733), v, vii, x.

14 Fiennes, quoted in Weatherill, *Consumer Behavior and Material Culture,* 146.

15 Elizabeth Moxon, *English House-wifery* (Leeds: For George Copperthwaite, 1758), title page.

16 Richard Bradley, *The Country House-wife and Lady's Director* [1736], facsimile edition, ed. Caroline Davidson (London: Prospect Books, 1980), ix.

17 Weatherill, *Consumer Behavior and Material Culture,* 25, 41.

18 Gilly Lehmann, *The British House-wife: Cookery Books, Cooking and Society in Eighteenth-Century Britain* (Totnes, England: Prospect Books, 2003), 107.

19 Hannah Glasse, "To the Reader," *The Art of Cookery Made Plain and Easy* (London: Printed for the author and sold at Mrs. Ashburn's, 1747), iii.

20 Elizabeth Raffald, *The Experienced English Housekeeper* (Manchester: J. Harrop, 1769), ii.

21 Mrs. [Maria Eliza] Rundell, *A New System of Domestic Cookery* (London: George Ramsay, 1811), i, vii, vi.

22 Philip and Mary Hyman, "La Chapelle and Massialot: An Eighteenth Century Feud," *Petits Propos Culinaires* 2 (August 1979): 51.

23 François Marin, *Les dons de Comus, ou les délices de la table* (Paris: Chez Prault, 1739), xxxij.

24 Stephen Mennell, ed., *Lettre d'un pâtissier anglois, et autres contributions à une polémique gastronomique du XVIIIème siècle* (Exeter: University of Exeter, 1981).

25 J. Worth Estes, "The Medical Properties of Food in the Eighteenth Century," *Journal of the History of Medicine and Allied Sciences* 51 (1996): 127–54.

26 See also *Livres en bouche: Cinq siècles d'art culinaire français* (Paris: Bibliothèque nationale de France / Hermann, 2001), 210.

27 These were *Cuisine et office de santé* (1758) and *Le manuel des officiers de bouche* (1759).

28 See Jean-Claude Bonnet's analysis in "The Culinary System in the *Encyclopédie,*" trans. Elborg Forster, *Annales, E.S.C.* 32 (September–October 1977): 891–914.

29 Stephen Mennell, *All Manners of Food: Eating and Taste in England and France from the Middle Ages to the Present* (Oxford: Basil Blackwell, 1985), 82.

30 Voltaire, quoted in Wheaton, *Savoring the Past,* 213.

31 A. Beauvilliers, *L'art du cuisinier* (Paris: Pilet, 1814), 1:viii.

32 *Biographie universelle, ancienne et moderne, supplément* 73: 446.

33 M. C. D., *Dictionnaire des alimens, vin et liqueurs* (Paris: Gissey, 1750).

34 See Philippe Meyzie's extensive study, *La table du sud-ouest et l'émergence des cuisines régionales (1700–1850)* (Rennes: Presses Universitaires de Rennes, 2007).

35 Alain Girard, "Le triomphe de 'La cuisinière bourgeoise': Livres culinaires, cuisine et societé en France aux XVII et XVIII siècles," *Revue d'histoire moderne et contemporaine* 24 (October–December 1977): 504.

36 Mark Girouard, *Life in the French Country House* (London: Cassell, 2001), 257.

37 Sarah Maza, *Servants and Masters in Eighteenth-Century France* (Princeton, NJ: Princeton University Press, 1983), 276–77.

38 Antonin Carême, *L'art de la cuisine française au dix-neuvième siècle* (Paris: Au Dépot de Librairie, 1854), 1:lvij.

39 Ken Albala, *Food in Early Modern Europe* (Westport, CT: Greenwood Press, 2003), 150.

40 Elizabeth Pennell, *My Cookery Books* (Boston: Houghton Mifflin, 1903), 90.

41 Beverley, *The History,* quoted in Genevieve Yost, "The Compleat Housewife or Accomplish'd Gentlewoman's Companion: A Bibliographical Study," *William and Mary College Quarterly Historical Magazine* 18, no. 4 (October 1938): 419–35.

42 Amelia Simmons, *American Cookery* (Hartford, CT: Hudson & Goodwin, 1796), 3; Mary Tolford Wilson, "The First American Cookbook," in *American Cookery* [1796], facsimile edition, ed. Amelia Simmons (New York: Oxford University Press, 1958).

43 Amelia Simmons, preface to *American Cookery* [1796], facsimile edition (New York: Oxford University Press, 1958).

44 Nancy Siegel, "Cooking Up American Politics," *Gastronomica* 8, no. 3 (Summer 2008): 58.

45 Lucy Emerson, preface to *The New-England Cookery* (Montpelier, VT: Josiah Parks, 1808).

46 Lucien Febvre and Henri-Jean Martin, *The Coming of the Book,* trans. David Gerard (London: Verso, 1976).

47 Susan Scott Parrish, *American Curiosity: Cultures of Natural History in the Colonial British Atlantic World* (Chapel Hill: University of North Carolina Press, 2006), 94–106.

The Early Nineteenth Century

1 A. Viard, *Le cuisinier impérial* (Paris: J. N. Barba, 1806), ix.

2 Antoine Beauvilliers, *L'art du cuisinier,* vol. 1 (Paris: Pilet, 1814), x.

3 Lady Morgan, *France in 1829–30* (London: Saunders & Otley, 1830), 411.

4 Sarah Rutledge, *The Carolina Housewife* [1847] (Columbia: University of South Carolina Press, 1979), iv.

5 Catherine Beecher, preface to *Miss Beecher's Domestic Receipt Book* (New York: Harper & Brothers, 1851).

Afterword

1 Katherine Golden Bitting, *Gastronomic Bibliography* (San Francisco, 1939), ix.

2 Eric Holzenberg, "Second-hand and Antiquarian Books on the Internet," *Journal of Rare Books, Manuscripts, and Cultural Heritage* 2, no. 1 (2001): 35–46.

BIBLIOGRAPHY

PRIMARY SOURCES   This section cites the key original, facsimile, and reprint editions of the works mentioned in this book. Whenever possible, entries give the earliest known date of origin, in the case of a manuscript, or the date of the first printed edition. For entries that cite multiple editions, the first edition appears in brackets. Unless stated otherwise, the first printed edition of an early handwritten work follows the original manuscript both in content and in the language in which it was written.
Indicates books that Mark and I hold in our collection.

Antiquity through the Middle Ages

Apicius, M. Gabius. *De re coquinaria* [Rome, late 4th or early 5th century MS]. Modern edition: *Apicius: A Critical Edition.* Edited and translated by Christopher Grocock and Sally Grainger. Totnes, England: Prospect Books, 2006. Also see the translation by Joseph Dommers Vehling: *Cookery and Dining in Imperial Rome.* Mineola, NY: Dover Publications, 1977.

Athenaeus. *Athenaei dipnosophistarum* [2nd-century MS]. First printed edition: Venice, 1514, from original MS. Reprint: Basel: Apud Joannem Valderum, 1535. Modern edition: *Deipnosophists or Banquet of the Learned.* Translated by C. D. Yonge. London: Henry G. Bohn, 1854.

Bartholomaeus Anglicus [Bartholomé de Glanville]. *De proprietatibus rerum* [c. 1220–40 MS]. First printed edition: c. 1482. Abridged version printed in French as *Le grand proprietaire de toutes choses.* Translated by Jean Corbichon. Paris: Charles l'Angler, 1556.

Butlân, Ibn. *Tacuinum sanitatis* [11th-century MS]. Illustrated MS: Paris, 1474, Bibliothèque Nationale de France.

Cassianus, Joannes [John the Hermit]. *De institutis coenobiorum et de octo principalium viliorum remediis* [5th-century MS]. First printed edition: *Venice, 1491. Modern edition: Boniface Ramsey, ed. and trans. *John Cassian: The Institutes.* Mahwah, NJ: Newman Press, 2000.

Crescentius, Petrus de [Pierre de Crescens]. *Ruralia commoda* [Italy, c. 1306 MS]. First printed edition: Augsburg: Johann Schüssler, 1471. Second edition: *Le bon mesnaiger.* Paris: Charles Langellier, 1540.

Libre de Sent Soví [early 14th-century MS]. Also, Catalonia, early fifteenth-century MS. Modern edition: *Joan Santanach, ed. *The Book of Sent Soví: Medieval Recipes from Catalonia.* Translated by Robin Vogelzang. Barcelona: Barcino Tamesis, 2008. Also see *Libre de Sent Soví.* Edited by Rudolph Grewe. Barcelona: Editorial Barcino, 1979.

Master cook to King Richard II of England. *Forme of Cury* [England, 1390 MS]. Reprint: *The Forme of Cury, a Roll of Ancient English Cookery.* Edited by Samuel Pegge. London: J. Nichols, 1780.

Le ménagier de Paris [Paris, 1393 MS]. Modern edition: *Le ménagier de Paris.* Edited by Baron Jérôme Pichon. Paris: Jérôme Pichon, 1846. Also see Gina L. Greco and Christine M. Rose, eds. and trans. *The Good Wife's Guide (Le Ménagier de Paris): A Medieval Household Book.* Ithaca, NY: Cornell University Press, 2009. *Le ménagier de Paris.* Luzarches, France: Daniel Morcrette [twentieth century].

Plinius Secundus, Gaius [Pliny the Elder]. *Naturalis historia* [Rome, c. 77–79 MS]. Modern edition: *Pliny. Natural History: A Selection.* Translated and edited by John F. Healy. London: Penguin Books, 1991.

Regimen sanitatis salernitatum [11th- or 12th-century MS]. Modern edition: *Regimen Sanitatis Salernitatum: A Poem on the Preservation of Health in Rhyming Latin Verse.* English translation of 1607, etchings from sixteenth-century German edition. Edited by Sir Alexander Croke. Oxford: D. A. Talboys, 1830.

Taillevent [Guillaume Tirel]. *Le viandier* [1392 MS]. First printed edition: Paris: Caillot, c. 1486, from original MS. Modern edition: *Le viandier de Guillaume Tirel dit Taillevent.* Edited by Jérôme Pichon and Georges Vicaire. Paris: Techener, 1892. Facsimile edition: Luzarches, France: Daniel Morcrette, late twentieth century. Also see *Le viandier.* Edited by Philip and Mary Hyman. Houilles, France: Éditions Manucius, 2001.

Warraq, Ibn Sayyar al-. *Kitāb al-tabīkh* [Baghdad, 10th-century MS]. Modern edition: "A Baghdad Cookery Book." Translated by A. J. Arberry. In *Medieval Arab Cookery: Essays and Translations by Maxine Rodinson, A. J. Arberry, and Charles Perry.* Totnes, England: Prospect Books, 2001.

The Fifteenth Century

Chiquart, Amiczo. *Du fait de cuisine* [Savoy, 1420 MS]. Modern edition: *Chiquart's "On Cookery": A Fifteenth Century Savoyard Culinary Treatise.* Translated and edited by Terence Scully. New York: Peter Lang, 1986.

Curion, Jean. *De conservanda bona valetudine* [1480]. Reprint: *Frankfurt: Chr. Egenolphum, 1545.

Fifteenth Century Schoolbook: From a Manuscript in the British Museum (Ms. Arundel 849). Edited by William Nelson. Oxford: Clarendon Press, 1956.

Küchenmeisterei [1485]. Reprint: Nuremberg: Peter Wagner, 1490. Modern edition: *Hans Wegener, ed. *Küchenmeisterei.* Leipzig: Otto Harrassowitz, 1939.

La Marche, Olivier de. *Les memoires de Messire Olivier de la Marche* [late 15th-century MS]. First printed edition: 1562, from original MS. Reprint: *Ghent: Gerard de Salenson, 1567.

Maria, Infanta da, de Portugal. *Livro de cozinha* [1480]. Portugal, sixteenth-century MS, after fifteenth-century MS. Modern edition: *"Livro de cozinha," Infanta da Maria de Portugal.* Coimbra, Portugal: Universidade de Coimbra, 1967.

Martino of Como [Maestro Martino]. *Libro di arte coquinaria* [Rome, c. 1465]. Facsimile edition on CD-ROM: *Maestro Martino, Libro de arte coquinaria.* Translated by Gillian Riley. Oakland, CA: Octavo Editions, 2005. Modern edition: *Martino of Como, The Art of Cooking: The First Modern Cookery Book.* Edited by Luigi Ballerini. Translated by Jeremy Parzen. Berkeley: University of California Press, 2005.

A Noble Boke of Cookry [c. 1468 MS]. Modern edition: *A Noble Boke of Cookry,* reprint of Holkham Collection manuscript. Edited by Robina Napier. London: Elliot Stock, 1882.

Platina [Bartolomeo Sacchi]. *De honesta voluptate et valetudine* [c. 1474]. Reprint: *De ratione victus, & modo viuendi. De natura rerum & arte coquendi libri.* [Paris]: Joannis Parui, 1520. Modern edition: *Platina's On Right Pleasure and Good Health.* Translated by Mary Ella Millham. Asheville, NC: Pegasus Press, 1999.

Régime des princes [15th-century MS]. Bibliothèque de l'Arsenal, Paris.

Très riches heures du duc de Berri [France, c. 1412–89]. Illustrated by Barthélemy van Eyck and Jean Colombe Limbourg. Modern edition: *Illuminations of Heaven and Earth: The Glories of the* Très Riches Heures du Duc de Berry. Text by Raymond Cazelles and Johannes Rathofer. New York: Harry N. Abrams, 1988.

Villena [Enrique de Aragón]. *Arte cisoria* [1423 MS]. Reprint: *Madrid: Antonio Marin, 1766. Modern edition: *Don Henrique de Aragon, Marques de Villena. *Arte cisoria, ó tratado del arte del cortar del cuchillo.* Madrid: Ediciones Guillermo Blázquez, 1981.

The Sixteenth Century

A. W. *A Booke of Cookrye, Very Necessary for All Such as Delight Therin* [1584]. Reprint: London: Edward Allde, 1591.

Modern edition: *A Booke of Cookrye, with the Serving In of the Table.* Amsterdam: Theatrum Orbis Terrarum, 1976.

Badianus, Johannes, and Martinus de la Cruz. *The Badianus Manuscript* [Mexico, 1552]. Modern edition: *The Badianus Manuscript.* Edited and translated by Emily Walcott Emmart. Baltimore: Johns Hopkins Press, 1940.

Belon, Pierre. *L'histoire de la nature des oiseaux* [Paris, 1555]. Modern edition: Edited by Philippe Glardon. Geneva: Librairie Droz, 1997.

Boke of Cokery [London: Richard Pynson, 1500]. Digital facsimile edition: Early English Books Online, http://eebo.chadwyck.com.

Boke of Kervynge [London: Wynkyn de Worde, 1508]. Digital facsimile: Early English Books Online, http://eebo.chadwyck.com.

Boorde, Andrewe. *The First Boke of the Introduction of Knowledge Made by Andrewe Boorde of Physycke Doctore. A Compendyous Regyment or a Dyetary of Helth* [c. 1552]. Reprint: *London: N. Trübner, 1870.

Brunfels, Otto. *Herbarum vivae eicones.* Strasbourg: Apud Joannem Schottu, 1530 (vol. 1), 1536 (vol. 2).

Bruyérin-Champier, Jean. *De re cibaria* [Lyon: Nicolas Edoard, 1560]. Modern edition: *L'alimentation.* Translated by Sigurd Amundsen. Paris: Intermédiaire des Chercheurs et Curieux, 1998.

Castiglione, Baldassare. *Il libro cortegiano* [*1528]. Reprint: Venice: Appresso Gabriel Giolito de Ferrari e fratelli, 1552. Modern edition: *The Book of the Courtier.* Mineola, NY: Dover, 2003.

Cervio, Vincenzo. *Il trinciante* [1581]. *Venice: Appresso gli Heredi di Giovanni Varisco, c. 1593. Modern edition: *"Il trinciante." In *Arte della cucina: Dal XIV al XIX secolo,* 69–118. Milan: Edizioni el Polifilo, 1966.

Christol, Desdier, trans. *Platine en françois* [Lyon: Frâçoys fradin pres nostre dame de côfort, 1505]. Modern edition: *Le Platine en françois: d'après l'édition de 1505.* Houilles, France: Éditions Manucius, 2003.

Dawson, Thomas. *The Good Huswifes Jewell* [1585]. Reprint: London: Edward White, 1596. Modern edition: *The Good Huswifes Jewell*. Amsterdam: Theatrum Orbis Terrarum, 1977.

Della Porta, Giambattista. *Magia naturalis* [1559]. Reprint: Naples, 1589.

Estienne, Charles, and Jean Liébault. *Prædum rusticum* [1564]. Reprint: *L'agriculture et maison rustique*. Lyon: Simon Rigaud, 1654. Also published in Italian as *L'agricoltura, e casa di villa*, 1677; in German, as *XV Bücher von dem Feldbaw*, 1588; in English, as *Maison Rustique, or, The Countrey Farme*, 1600.

La fleur de toute cuisine. Paris: Alain Lotrian, 1543. Also published as *Le grand cuisinier de toute cuisine*. Paris: Jehan Bonfons, c. 1543.

Gallo, Agostino. *Le vinti giornate dell'agricoltura* [1569]. Reprint: *Venice: Camillo Borgominerio, 1584.

Gerarde, John. *The Herball or Generall Historie of Plantes* [1597]. *London: Adam Islip Joice Norton, 1633. Modern edition: *Gerard's Herbal: Selections from the 1633 Enlarged & Amended Edition*. Edited by Holly Ollivander and Huw Thomas. N.p.: Velluminous Press, 2008.

Granado, Diego [Diego Granado Maldonado]. *Libro del arte de cozina, en el qual se contiene el modo de guisar de comer en cualquier tiempo, assí de carne, como de pescado, para sanos y enfermos y convalescientes: assí de pasteles, tortas, y salsas, como de conservas a la usança Española, Italiana, y Tudesca, de nuestros tiempos* [1599]. Reprint: N.p.: Por Diego Granado, 1614. Modern edition: *Libro del arte de cozina*. Lleida, Spain: Pagès Editors, 1991.

Harrison, William. *The Description of England* [1577]. First edition part of Holinshed's *Chronicles*. Second edition: London: Henry Denham, 1587. Modern edition: *The Description of England: The Classic Contemporary Account of Tudor Social Life*. Mineola, NY: Dover, 1995.

Hill, Thomas. *The Proffitable Arte of Gardening*. London: Thomas Marshe, 1568.

Hogenberg, Nicolas, engraver. *The Procession of Pope Clement VII and the Emperor Charles V after the Coronation at Bologna* [1530]. Facsimile edition: *The Procession of Pope Clement VII and the Emperor Charles V after the Coronation at Bologna*. Edinburgh: Edmonston & Douglas, 1875.

Livre de cuysine tres utile. Paris, 1540.

Livre fort excellêt de cuysine tres utile. Lyon: Olivier Arnoullet, 1508.

Messisbugo, Cristoforo di. *Banchetti composizioni di vivande e apparecchio generale* [Ferrara: Giovanni de Buglhat, Antonio Hucher Compagni, 1549]. Modern edition: *Banchetti di Cristoforo da Messisbugo*. Venice: Neri Pozza Editore, 1960.

Nola, Ruberto de [Mestre Robert]. *Libre del coch* [Barcelona: Carles Amorós, 1520]. Later translated and republished as *Libro de cozina*. Toledo: Ramon de Petras, 1525. Modern edition: *Libro de cozina*. Valencia: Editores de Facsimiles Vicent García, 2002.

Nostredame, Michel de [Nostradamus]. Modern edition: *The Elixirs of Nostradamus: Nostradamus's Original Recipes for Elixirs, Scented Water, Beauty Potions, and Sweetmeats*. Edited by Kurt Boeser. London: Bloomsbury, 1995.

———. *Excellent et moult utile opuscule à touts nécessaire qui désirent avoir cognoissance de plusieurs exquises recettes*. Lyon: Jean Pullon de Trin, 1552. Modern edition: *La façon & maniere de faire toutes confitures liquids, tant en succre, miel, qu'en vin cuit*. Paris: Fernand Hazan, 1962.

Partridge, John. *The Treasurie of Commodious Conceits, & Hidden Secrets*. London: Richarde Jones, 1573.

———. *The Widdowes Treasure*. London: For Henry Dizle, 1582.

Pinguillon, de. *Menu de la maison de la Royne*. 1562.

Plat, Sir Hugh. *Jewel House of Art and Nature* [1594]. Reprint: N.p.: Bernard Alsop, 1653. Modern edition: *Jewel House of Art and Nature*. Amsterdam: Theatrum Orbis Terrarum, 1979.

A Proper Newe Book of Cokerye [1545]. Reprint: c. 1558. Modern edition: *A Proper Newe Book of Cokerye*. Edited by Catherine Frances Frere. Cambridge: W. Heffer & Sons, 1913.

Romoli, Domenico [Panunto/Panonto]. *La singolare dottrina di M. Domenico Romoli sopranominato Panunto*. Venice: Michele Tramezzino, 1560. Spelling changed from *Panunto* to *Panonto* for another printing of the same year.

Rosselli, Giovanne de. *Epulario* [1516]. Reprint: *Venice: Antonio Remondini, c. 1750.

Rumpolt, Marx. *Ein new Kochbuch* [1576]. Reprint: Frankfurt, 1581. Modern edition: *Ein new Kochbuch* (from 1581 edition). Hildesheim, NY: Olms Presse, 1980.

Ruscelli, Girolamo [Alexis of Piedmont]. *Secreti del reverendo donno Alessio piemontese*. Venice, 1555.

Ryff, Walther Hermann [Gualtherum Ryff]. *Wahrhaftige Unterweisung Confect zu bereiten*. Strasbourg: Balthasar Beck, 1540.

Scappi, Bartolomeo. *Opera di M. Bartolomeo Scappi* [1570]. Reprint: *Venice: Ad instantia de Giorgio Ferarij, 1596. Modern edition: *The Opera of Bartolomeo Scappi*. Translated by Terence Scully. Toronto: Toronto University Press, 2008.

Staindl, Balthasar. *Ein sehr künstlichs und nützlichs Kochbuch* [1544]. Reprint: Augsburg: Matthäus Franck, 1569. Modern edition: *Dietikon, Switzerland: Verlag Bibliophile Drucke von Joseph Stocker, 1979.

Tusser, Thomas. *Five Hundredth Pointes of Good Husbandrie*. R. Tottell, 1573.

———. *A Hundredth Good Pointes of Husbandrie*. [R. Tottell, 1557]. Modern edition: *His Good Pointes of Husbandry*. Edited by Dorothy Hartley. London: Country Life Limited, 1931.

Weckerin, Anna. *Ein köstlich new Kochbuch*. Amberg, Germany: Michael Forstern [1597]. Modern edition: Munich: Heimeran, 1977.

The Seventeenth Century

The Accomplish'd Ladies Delight [1675]. Reprint: *London: Benjamin Harris, 1683. (Often wrongly attributed to Hannah Woolley.)

Audiger, Nicolas. *La maison réglée* [Paris: Lambert Roulland, 1692]. Reprint: *Amsterdam: Paul Marret, 1700.

Barra, Pierre. *L'usage de la glace, de la neige et du froid.* Lyon: Chez Antoine Cellier fils, 1676.

Barrios, Juan de. *Libro en cual se trata del chocolate, que provechos haga, y si sea bebida saludable o no, y en particular de todas las cosas que lleva, y qué receta conviene para cada persona, y cómo se conocerá cada uno de qué compléxion sea, para que pueda beber el chocolate de suerte que no le haga mal.* Mexico, 1609.

Blegny, Nicolas de. *Le bon usage du thé du caffé et du chocolat pour la preservation & pour la guerison des maladies.* Lyon: Thomas Amaulry, 1687.

Bonnefons, Nicolas de. *Les delices de la campagne* [1654]. Reprint: *Amsterdam: Jean Blaev, 1661.

———. *Le jardinier françois* [1651]. Reprint: *Paris: Chez Anthoine Cellier, 1666.

Brieve e nuovo modo da farsi ogni sorte di sorbetti con facilità. Naples, seventeenth century.

Casteau, Lancelot de. *Ouverture de cuisine.* Liège: Leonard Streel [1604]. Modern edition: *Antwerp: De Schutter, 1983.

Castelvetro, Giacomo. *The Fruit, Herbs and Vegetables of Italy* [1614 MS]. Modern edition: *Translated by Gillian Riley. Totnes, England: Prospect Books, 2010.

Le confiturier de la cour. Published in one volume with Pierre de Lune, *Le nouveau cuisinier* and with *Le maistre d'hostel qui apprend l'ordre de bien server sur table & d'y ranger les services.* Paris: Pierre David, 1659. Possibly later published as *Confiturier françois,* 1660, often attributed to La Varenne.

Cooper, Joseph. *The Art of Cookery Refined and Augmented. Containing an Abstract of Some Rare and Rich Unpublished Receipts of COOKERY.* London: J. G., 1654.

The Court and Kitchin of Elizabeth, Commonly Called Joan Cromwel, The Wife of the Late Usurper. London: Milbourn, 1664.

Culpeper, Nicholas. *Culpeper's Complete Herbal* [1653]. Reprint: *London: Richard Evans, 1815. Modern edition: *Culpepper's Complete Herbal.* Chatham, England: Wordsworth, 1998.

D'Emery, Sieur. *Le nouveau recueil de curiositez.* Paris: Chez Pierre Vander, 1685.

Digby, Sir Kenelm. *The Closet Opened* [1669]. Reprint: *London: H. C. for H. Brome, 1677. Modern edition: *The Closet of the Eminently Learned Sir Kenelme Digbie, Kt., Opened.* Edited by Peter Davidson and Jane Stevenson. Totnes, England: Prospect Books, 1997.

Dufour, Philippe Sylvestre. *Traitez nouveaux & curieux du café, du thé et du chocolat* [1685]. Reprint: *Novi tractatus de potu caphé, de Chinensium thé et de chocolata a D. M. notis illustre.* Geneva: Cramer & Perachon, 1699.

L'ecole des ragousts. Volume includes *Le cuisinier françois et méthodique, Le pastissier françois,* and *Le confiturier françois.* Lyon: Jacques Canier et Martin Fleury, 1668.

Endter, Anna Juliana. *Vollständiges Nürnbergisches Koch-Buch* [Nuremberg: In Verlegung Wolfgang Moritz Endters, 1691]. Modern edition: *Hildesheim: Olms Presse, 1979.

L'escole parfaite des officiers de bouche [1662]. *Reprinted in a volume that includes *L'écuyer tranchant, Le cuisinier parfait,* and *Le patissier parfait.* Paris: Veuve de Pierre Ribou, 1729. English edition: *A Perfect School of Instructions for the Officers of the Mouth.* Translated by Giles Rose. London: For Bentley and Mary Magnes, 1682.

Evelyn, John. *Acetaria; A Discourse of Sallets* [London: For B. Tooke, 1699]. Modern edition: *The Rusticall and Economical Works of John Evelyn: Acetaria, a Discourse of Sallets.* Edited by Christopher Driver. Totnes, England: Prospect Books, 2005.

Giegher, Mattia. *Il trinciante di Messer Mattia Giegher* [Padua: Martini Stampator Camerale, 1621]. Reprint: Bound with *Lo scalo di M.Mattia Giegher.* Padua: Guasparri Crinellari, 1623.

Grey, Elizabeth, Countess of Kent. *A True Gentlewomans Delight* [1653]. Reprint: bound with *A Choice Manual, or Rare and Select Secrets in Physick and Chirurgery.* London: Gartrude Dawson, 1665.

Harington, Katherina Elisa. *Commonplace book. England, 1672 MS.

Hartlib, Samuel. *His Legacy: or an Enlargement on the Discourse of Husbandry Used in Brabant & Flaunders.* London: R. & W. Leybourn, 1652.

Hentzer, Paul. *Travels in England: During the Reign of Queen Elizabeth* [Nuremberg, 1612]. Reprints: Translated from German to English and printed by Horace Walpole at Strawberry Hill (London), 1797; also, London: Cassel and Company, 1901. Modern edition: Dodo Press, 2007.

Klett, Andreas. *Neu-vermehrt nützliches Trencher-Buch* [1657]. Reprint: Hamburg, c. 1700. Modern edition: *Leipzig: Edition Leipzig, 1974.

La Quintinie, Jean-Baptiste de. *Instruction pour les jardins fruitiers et potagers* [Paris, 1690]. 2 vols. Modern edition: *Arles: Actes Sud, 1999.

Larmessin (II), Nicolas de. *Les costumes grotesques et les métiers* [Paris: N. De Larmessin, 1695]. Modern edition: *Les costumes grotesques et les métiers de Nicolas de Larmessin.* Paris: Henri Veyrier, 1974.

Latini, Antonio. *Lo scalco alla moderna* [Naples: Ant. Parrino, e Michele Luigi Mutii, 1692 (vol. 1), 1694 (vol. 2)]. Modern edition: *Lodi: Bibliotheca Culinaria / Milan: Appunti di Gastronomia, 1993.

La Varenne, François Pierre de. *Le cuisinier françois* [1651]. Reprint: *Paris: Pierre David, 1652. Modern edition: *La Varenne's Cookery: The French Cook;

The French Pastry Chef; The French Confectioner. Edited and translated by Terence Scully. Totnes, England: Prospect Books, 2006. Also see *Le cuisinier françois*. Edited by Philip and Mary Hyman. Houilles, France: Éditions Manucius, 2002.

Lawson, William. *The Countrie Housewife's Garden* [London, 1617]. Reprint: London: Anne Griffin for John Harrison, 1637. Modern edition: *Milford, CT: Salt Acres, 1940. Facsimile edition: *A New Orchard and Garden with The Country Housewife's Garden.* Totnes, England: Prospect Books, 2003.

———. *New Orchard & Garden* [London, 1618]. Modern edition: *London: Cresset Press, 1927. Facsimile edition: *A New Orchard and Garden with The Country Housewife's Garden.* Totnes, England: Prospect Books, 2003.

Lichtenstein, Eleonora Maria Rosalie Fürstin zu. *Freywillig aufgesprungener Granat–Apfel des christlichen Samariters* [Vienna: L. Voight, 1697]. Reprint: Leipzig: 1709.

L. S. R. *L'art de bien traiter* [1674]. Reprint: *Lyon: Claude Bachelu, 1693.

Lune, Pierre de. *Le nouveau cuisinier* [1656]. First edition: *Le cuisinier*, 1656. *Bound with *Le maistre d'hostel qui apprend l'ordre de bien server sur table & d'y ranger les services.* Paris: Pierre David, 1659.

Le maistre d'hostel qui apprend l'ordre de bien server sur table & d'y ranger les services. Bound in Pierre de Lune, *Le nouveau cuisinier*, also with *Le confiturier de la cour.* Paris: Pierre David, 1659.

[Markham, Gervase]. *The English Hous-wife* [1615]. By "G. M." Reprint: *London: W. Wilson for George Sawridge, 1664. Modern edition: Gervase Markham, *The English Houswife.* Edited by Michael R. Best. Montreal: McGill-Queen's University Press, 1986.

Massialot, François. *Le cuisinier roial et bourgeois* [1691]. Reprints: *Paris: Charles de Sercy, 1693; *Le nouveau cuisinier royal et bourgeois.* Paris: Claude Prudhomme, 1729. *English edition: *The Court and Country Cook.*

Translated by J. K. London: W. Onley, 1702.

———. **Nouvelle instruction pour les confitures, les liqueurs, et les fruits.* Paris: Charles de Sercy, 1692.

May, Robert. *The Accomplisht Cook* [1660]. Fifth edition: *London: For Obadiah Blagrave, 1685. Modern edition: *Totnes, England: Prospect Books, 2000.

Meurdrac, Marie. *La chymie charitable et facile, en faveur des dames* [Paris, 1666]. Modern edition: *Chymie charitable et facile, en faveur des dames : 1666.* Edited by Jean Jacques. Paris: CNRS Editions, 1999.

[Montagu, Walter]. *The Queen's Closet Opened. Incomparable Secrets in Physick, Chirurgery, Preserving, Candying, and Cookery; as They Were Presented to the QUEEN by the Most Experienced Persons of Our Times* [1655]. By "W. M." Reprint: London: Nathaniel Brook, 1656.

Montiño, Francisco Martínez. *Arte de cocina, pastelería, vizcochería y conserveria* [1611]. Reprint: *Barcelona: Oficina de Juan Francisco Piferrer, c. 1750. Modern edition: Barcelona: Tusquets, 1982.

Murrell, John. *A Daily Exercise for Ladies and Gentlewomen.* London: Printed for the widow Helme, 1617.

[———]. *A New Booke of Cookerie.* By "J. M." London: John Browne, 1615. Modern edition: *John Murrell. *A New Booke of Cookerie.* Amsterdam: Theatrum Orbis Terrarum / New York: Da Capo Press, 1972.

Le pastissier françois [1653]. Reprint: *Paris: Jean Gaillard, 1657. Modern edition: *Edited by Maurice des Ombiaux. Paris: Dorbon-Aîné, 1931. (Often wrongly attributed to La Varenne.)

Pepys, Samuel. *The Diary of Samuel Pepys.* 1660–69. Modern edition: *11 vols. Edited by Robert Latham and William Matthews. Berkeley: University of California Press, 1970.

Plat, Sir Hugh. *A Closet for Ladies and Gentlewomen, or The Art of Preserving, Conserving, and Candying*

[1608]. Reprint: London: John Parker, 1630.

———. *Delightes for Ladies* [1600]. Reprint: London: H. L. and R. Y., 1628. Modern edition: *Brighton: Liz Seeber, 2002.

Pradel, Abraham du [Nicholas de Blegny]. *Le livre commode des adresses de Paris pour 1692* [Paris, 1692]. Reprint: *Paris: Paul Daffis de la Bibliothèque Elzeverienne, 1878.

Rabisha, Will. *The whole Body of COOKERY DISSECTED* [1661]. Reprint: *London: For E. Calvert, 1673. Modern edition: *The whole Body of COOKERY DISSECTED.* Totnes, England: Prospect Books, 2003.

Sandford, Francis. *The History of the Coronation.* Savoy: Thomas Newcomb, 1687.

Serres, Olivier de. *Le theatre d'agriculture et mesnage des champs* [1600]. Reprint: *Paris: Chez Abr. Savgrain, 1617.

Le thresor de la santé, ou mesnage de la vie humaine. Lyon: Estienne Servain for Jean Antoine Huguetan, 1607.

Tillinghast, Mary. *Rare and Excellent Receipts.* London, 1678.

De verstandige Kock, of sorghvuldige Huyshoudster. Amsterdam: Marcus Doornick, 1667.

Vizé, Jean Donneau de [founder]. *Le mercure galant.* Paris. First issue 1672.

Woolley, Hannah. *The Gentlewomans Companion; or, a GUIDE to the Female Sex* [1673]. Reprint: London: A. Maxwell, 1675. Modern edition: *The Gentlewomans Companion or, a Guide to the Female Sex; The Complete Text of 1675.* Totnes, England: Prospect Books, 2001.

———. *The Queen-like Closet, or Rich Cabinet: Stored with All Manner of Rare Receipts* [1670]. Fourth edition: *London: For R. Chiswel, 1681.

The Eighteenth Century

Altamiras, Juan. *Nuevo arte de cocina* [1745]. Reprint: Barcelona: Don Juan de Bezàres, 1758. Modern edition (facsimile of 1758 edition): *Borriana,

Spain: Ediciones historico Artisticas, 1986.

Borella. *The Court and Country Confectioner: or, the House-Keeper's Guide.* London: G. Riley and A Cooke, 1770.

Boswell, James. The Life of Samuel Johnson. London: Henry Baldwin for Charles Dilly, 1791. Modern edition: Edited by Christopher Hibbert. New York: Penguin Classics, 1979.

Bradley, Mrs. Martha. *The British Housewife: or, the Cook, Housekeeper's and Gardiner's Companion* [London: For S. Crowder and H. Woodgate, 1755]. Modern edition: *The British Housewife.* Edited by Gilly Lehmann. Totnes, England: Prospect Books, 1996.

Bradley, Richard. *The Country Housewife and Lady's Director* [1727]. Sixth edition: London: D. Browne, 1736. Modern edition: *Edited by Caroline Davidson. Totnes, England: Prospect Books, 1980.

Briggs, Richard. *The English Art of Cookery* [1788]. Reprints: *The New Art of Cookery.* Philadelphia: W. Spotswood, R. Campbell, and E. Johnson, 1791; and *The English Art of Cookery.* London: For C. G. and J. Robinson, 1794.

Bull, Katherina. *Commonplace book. England, 1715 MS.

Byrd, William. *Neu-gefundenes Eden* [Switzerland 1737]. Modern edition: *William Byrd's Natural History of Virginia.* Translated by Richmond C. Beatty and William J. Mulloy. Richmond, VA: Dietz Press, 1940.

Carter, Charles. *The Compleat City and Country Cook: or, Accomplish'd Housewife* [1732]. Reprint: *London: For A. Bettesworth and C. Hitch and C. Davis, 1736.

———. *The Complete Practical Cook: or, a New System of the Whole Art and Mystery of Cookery* [*London: W. Meadows, 1730]. Modern edition: Totnes, England: Prospect Books, 1984.

Carter, Susannah. *The Frugal Housewife* [1772]. Reprint: *London: For E. Newbery, n.d.

Cook, Ann. *Professed Cookery* [1754]. Second edition: *Newcastle: For the author, 1755.

Corrado, Vincenzo. *Il credenziere di buon gusto* [Naples: Raimondiana, 1778]. Modern edition: Whitefish, MT: Kessinger Publishing, 2010.

———. *Il cuoco galante* [Naples: Raimondiana, 1773]. Modern edition: *Florence: Officine Grafiche Firenze, 1970.

Diderot, Denis, and Jean le Rond d'Alembert. *Encyclopédie, ou dictionnaire raisonné des sciences, des arts et des métiers.* Paris: Briasson, David, Le Breton, Durand, 1751–80.

Duhamel du Monceau, Henri-Louis. *Art de raffiner le sucre* [1764]. Facsimile edition: in *Les arts des aliments,* along with *Description et détails des arts de meunier, du vermicelier et du boulanger* by Paul-Jacques Malouin [1767]. Modern edition: Geneva: Slatkine Editions, 1984.

Eales, Mary. *Receipts* [London: H. Meere, 1718]. Modern edition: *Mrs. Mary Eales's Receipts.* Totnes, England: Prospect Books, 1985.

Ellis, William. *The Country Housewife's Family Companion* [London: J. Hodges, 1750]. Modern edition: Totnes, England: Prospect Books, 2000.

Emy, M. *L'art de bien faire les glaces d'office.* Paris: Chez Le Clerc, 1768.

Gazetin du comestible. Paris: Gueffier, January–December 1767.

Gilliers [Joseph]. *Le cannameliste français* [1751]. Reprint: *Nancy: La veuve Leclerc, 1768.

[Glasse, Hannah]. *The Art of Cookery Made Plain and Easy* [London: Printed for the author and sold at Mrs. Ashburn's, 1747]. By "A Lady." *The fourth edition of 1751 includes her name and an advertisement as Habit-Maker to the Princess of Wales. Modern edition: *First Catch Your Hare . . . : The Art of Cookery Made Plain and Easy.* Totnes, England: Prospect Books, 1995.

———. *The Compleat Confectioner.* London: Mrs. Ashburn, 1760.

Le Grand d'Aussy. *Histoire de la vie privée des français* [1782]. Third edition: *Paris: Laurent-Beaupré, 1815.

Hapsell, Elizabeth Elenner. *Commonplace book. England, 1727 MS.

Harrison, Sarah. *The House-Keeper's Pocket-Book, and Compleat Family Cook. Containing above Three Hundred Curious and Uncommon Recipes.* London: T. Worral, 1733.

Hayton, Thomas. *Commonplace book. England, 1711 MS.

Howard, Henry. *England's Newest Way in All Sorts of Cookery, Pastry, and All Pickles That Are Fit to Be Used* [*1703]. Reprint: London: Chr. Coningsby, 1708.

Jenks, James. *The Complete Cook.* London: For E. and C. Dilly, 1768.

La Chapelle, Vincent. *The Modern Cook.* London: Nicolas Prevost, 1733. French editions: *Le cuisinier moderne,* The Hague: Antoine de Groot, 1735; *The Hague: L'Auteur, 1742. Modern edition: *Le cuisinier moderne.* Boston: Adamant Media Corporation, 2003.

Lamb, Patrick. *Royal Cookery or, The Compleat Court-Cook* [*1710]. Reprint: London: For J. Nutt, and A. Roper, 1716.

Lemery, Louis. *Traité des aliments* [1702]. Reprint: Paris: Pierre Witte, 1705. English edition: *A Treatise of Foods.* London: For Andrew Bell, 1706.

Leonardi, Francesco. *L'Apicio moderno* [1790]. Reprint: *Roma: Giunchi, 1807–8.

Lettre d'un pâtissier anglois au nouveau cuisinier françois avec un extrait du craftsman [Paris: Chez Prault, 1739]. First edition bound with François Marin, *Les dons de Comus, ou les délices de la table,* and including the anonymous *Avertissement* essay on the new cuisine. Modern edition: *Lettre d'un pâtissier anglois, et autres contributions à une polémique gastronomique du XVIIIème siècle.* Edited by Stephen Mennell. Exeter: University of Exeter Press, 1981.

Liger, Louis. *Le ménage des champs et le jardinier françois accommodez au gout du temps.* Paris: Michel David, 1711.

———. *Oeconomie générale de la campagne, ou La nouvelle maison rustique*. Paris: Charles de Sercy [1700]. Reprint: **La nouvelle maison rustique*. Paris: Durand, 1775.

Marin, François. **Les dons de Comus, ou les délices de la table* [Paris: Prault fils, 1739]. *Also bound with *Lettre d'un pâtissier anglois*. Later enlarged and published as **Suite de dons de Comus*. 3 vols. Paris: la Veuve Pissot Didot / Brunet fils, 1742.

Mata, Juan de la. *Arte de reposteria*. Madrid: Antonio Martín, 1747.

M. C. D. **Dictionnaire des alimens, vin et liqueurs*. Paris: Gissey, 1750.

Menon, François. **Cuisine et office de santé*. Paris: le Clerc, 1758.

———. *La cuisinière bourgeoise* [1746]. Reprint: **Paris: Guillyn, 1748.

———. **Le manuel des officiers de bouche*. Paris: le Clerc, 1758.

———. **Nouveau traité de la cuisine*. 3 vols. Paris: J. Saugrain, 1739–42.

———. **La science du maître d'hôtel confiseur*. Paris: Paulus-du-Mesnil, 1749.

———. **La science du maître d'hôtel cuisinier*. Paris: Paulus-du-Mesnil, 1749.

———. **Les soupers de la cour*. 4 vols. Paris: Guillyn, 1755.

Méthode pour faire la cuisine. Commonplace book. France, 1775 MS.

Moxon, Elizabeth. *English Housewifery* [1749]. Reprint: **Leeds: For George Copperthwaite, 1758.

Nott, John. **The Cook's and Confectioner's Dictionary*. London: C. Rivington, 1723.

Nutt, Frederick. *The Complete Confectioner* [1789]. Eighth edition: **London: G. Biggs, c. 1819.

Parmentier, Antoine-Augustin. *Le parfait boulanger*. Paris: De l'Imprimerie Royale, 1778. Modern edition: **Marseille: Jeanne Laffitte, 1981.

———. **Traité sur la culture et les usages des pommes de terre*. Paris: Chez Barrois, 1789.

Raffald, Elizabeth. **The Experienced English Housekeeper*. Manchester: J. Harrop, 1769.

Simmons, Amelia. *American Cookery* [Hartford, CT: Hudson & Goodwin, 1796]. Facsimile of first edition: **American Cookery*. New York: Oxford University Press, 1958.

Smith, Mrs. E. *The Compleat Housewife* [1727]. Reprint: **London: For J. and H. Pemberton, 1742.

Smollett, Tobias. *Travels through France and Italy* [1766]. Modern edition: New York: I. B. Tauris, 2010.

Turner, Thomas. *The Diary of Thomas Turner* [1754–65]. 111 vol. MS at Sterling Memorial Library, Yale University. Modern edition (abridged): *The Diary of Thomas Turner, 1754–1765*. Edited by David Vaisey. Oxford: Oxford University Press, 1984.

Verral, William. **A Complete System of Cookery*. London: For the author, 1759.

Warner, Richard. *Antiquitates Culinariae or Curious Tracts Relating to the Culinary Affairs of the Old English* [**London: R. Blamire, 1791]. Modern edition: Totnes, England: Prospect Books, 1981.

The Early Nineteenth Century

Appert, Nicolas. *L'art de conserver, pendant plusieurs années, toutes les substances animales et végétales* [Paris: Patris et Cie, 1810]. Modern edition: **Le livre de tous les ménages, ou l'art de conserver, pendant plusieurs années*. Brive: Jean Coudert, 1974.

Artusi, Pellegrino. *La scienza in cucina e l'arte di mangiar bene* [1891]. Reprint: Florence: Presso l'Autore, 1906. Modern editions: **Florence: Marzocco, 1962; and *Science in the Kitchen and the Art of Eating Well*. Translated by Murtha Baca and Stephen Sartarelli. Toronto: University of Toronto Press, 2003.

Bauvillers. **Manuel de la cuisine*. Metz: C. M. B. Antoine, 1811.

Beauvilliers, A. **L'art du cuisinier*. 2 vols. Paris: Pilet, 1814.

Beecher, Catherine. *Miss Beecher's Domestic Receipt Book* [1846]. Reprint: **New York: Harper & Brothers, 1851. Modern edition: Mineola, NY: Dover, 2001.

———. *Treatise on Domestic Economy* [1841]. New York: Harper & Brothers, 1891.

Beeton, Isabella. **The Book of Household Management* [London: S. O. Beeton, 1861]. Modern edition: *Mrs Beeton's Book of Household Management: Abridged Edition*. Edited by Nicola Humble. Oxford: Oxford University Press, 2000.

Brillat-Savarin, Jean Anthelme. *Physiologie du gout* [1826]. 2 vols. Reprint: **[Paris]: Gabriel de Gonet, c. 1848. Modern edition: *The Physiology of Taste: or Meditations on Transcendental Gastronomy*. Translated by M. F. K. Fisher. New York: Everyman's Library, 2009.

Cadet de Gassicourt, Charles Louis. *Cours gastronomique*. Paris: Capelle et Renand, 1809.

Carême, Antonin. *L'art de la cuisine française au dix-neuvième siècle* [1833–35]. 5 vols. Reprint: **Paris: Au Dépot de Librairie, 1854. Modern edition: Boston: Adamant Media Corporation, 2005.

———. *Le maître d'hôtel français* [1822]. 2 vols. Reprint: **Paris: L'imprimerie de Firmin Didot, 1823. Modern edition: Whitefish, MT: Kessinger Publishing, 2010.

———. *Le pâtissier pittoresque* [1815]. Reprint: **Paris: J. Renouard; Chez Mansut; Chez Tresse; Chez Maison, 1842. Modern edition: Paris: Mercure de France, 2003.

———. *Le pâtissier royal parisien* [1815]. Reprint: **Paris: l'Auteur, 1828. Modern edition: Marseille: Laffitte Reprints, 1980.

Child, Lydia Maria. *The Frugal Housewife* [Boston: Marsh & Capen, and Carter & Hendee, 1829]. Modern edition: **The American Frugal Housewife* (reprint of 1832 edition). Worthington: Ohio State University Libraries, 1971.

La cuisinière du Haut-Rhin [1829]. Reprint: Mulhouse: J. P. Risler, 1842. Modern edition: *Luzarches, France: Librairie Daniel Morcrette, 1981.

Durand, C. *Le cuisinier Durand.* Nimes: P. Durand-Belle, 1830.

Emerson, Lucy. *The New-England Cookery.* Montpelier, VT: Josiah Parks, 1808.

Grimod de la Reynière, Alexandre-Balthazar-Laurent. *Almanach des gourmands* [*Paris: Chez Maradan / Chez Joseph Chaumerot, 1803–12]. 8 vols. Reprint: Paris: Charles-Béchet, 1828. Modern edition: Paris: Mercure de France, 2003.

———. *Manuel des Amphitryons* [*Paris: Capelle et Renand, 1808]. Modern edition: Paris: Éditions A. M. Metailie, 1983.

Grimod de la Reynière, Alexandre-Balthazar-Laurent, and Charles-Louis Cadet de Gassicourt. *Le gastronome français, ou, l'art de bien vivre.* Paris: Charles-Béchet, 1828.

Kitchiner, William. *The Cook's Oracle* [1817]. Third edition: *London: A.

Constable / Edinburgh: Hurst, Robinson, 1821. Modern edition: Carlisle, MA: Applewood Books, 2008.

Machet, J. J. *Le confiseur moderne.* Paris: Chez Maradan, 1803.

Modern Domestic Cookery [1851]. By "A Lady." Reprint: London: John Murray, 1853.

Morgan, Lady. *France in 1829–30.* London: Saunders & Otley, 1830.

The New American Cookery. By "An American Lady." New York: D. D. Smith, 1805.

Randolph, Mrs. Mary. *The Virginia Housewife: or, Methodical Cook* [1824]. Reprint: Washington, DC: Way & Gideon, 1825. Modern edition: *The Virginia Housewife.* Richmond, VA: Avenel Books, n.d.

Rumohr, C. Fr. v. [Carl Friedrich von]. *Geist der Kochkunst.* Stuttgart: Cotta'sche Buchhandlung, 1822. Modern edition: *Carl Friedrich von Rumohr. The Essence of Cookery.* Translated by Barbara Yeomans. Totnes, England: Prospect Books, 1993.

Rundell, Mrs. [Maria Eliza]. *A New System of Domestic Cookery* [1806]. "By a Lady." Reprint: *London: George Ramsay, 1811. Modern edition: *A New System of Domestic Cookery: Formed upon Principles of Economy and Adapted to the Use of Private Families.* New York: Vantage Press, 1977.

Rutledge, Sarah. *The Carolina Housewife* [1847]. Modern edition: *Columbia: University of South Carolina Press, 1979.

Soyer, Alexis. *The Pantropheon, or the History of Food* [*London, 1853]. Reprint: New York: Paddington Press, 1977.

Ude, Louis Eustache. *The French Cook* [1813]. Reprint: *London: John Ebers, 1818.

V…Y, A. M. [Véry]. *Le cuisinier des cuisiniers.* Paris: Audin, 1825.

Viard, A. *Le cuisinier impérial* [*Paris: J. N. Barba, 1806]. Also published as *Le cuisinier royale* (1820) and as *Le cuisinier national de la ville et de la campagne* (1852). Modern edition: *Le cuisinier impérial.* Nîmes: C. Lacour, 1993.

FURTHER READING   We have found the following works of particular interest in learning about old cookbooks and compiling this book. The list excludes journal articles, online sources, and works that are obscure or peripheral to the main subject. Also of value (and amusement) in further research are the journals *Petits Propos Culinaires* (Prospect Books) and *Gastronomica* (University of California Press). Constant references for us are the *Oxford English Dictionary* (1971 Complete Edition) and the landmark 11th edition of the *Encyclopedia Britannica* (1910). *Designates books in our collection.*

Albala, Ken. *The Banquet.* Urbana: University of Illinois Press, 2007.

———. *Eating Right in the Renaissance.* Berkeley: University of California Press, 2002.

———. *Food in Early Modern Europe.* Westport, CT: Greenwood Press, 2003.

Alberini, Massimo. *4000 anni a tavola: Della bistecca preistorica al pic-nic sulla luna.* Milan: Fratelli Fabbri Editori, 1972.

American Philosophical Society. *Benjamin Franklin on the Art of Eating.* Princeton, NJ: Princeton University Press, 2004.

Aresty, Esther. *The Best Behavior: The Course of Good Manners—From Antiquity to the Present—As Seen through Courtesy and Etiquette Books.* New York: Simon and Schuster, 1970.

Arte della cucina: Libri di ricette testi sopra lo scalco il trinciante e i vini. Milan: Emilio Faccioli, Edizioni il Polifilo, 1966.

Batterberry, Michael, and Ariane Batterberry. *On the Town in New York: A History of Eating, Drinking and Entertainments from 1776 to the Present.* New York: Charles Scribner's Sons, 1973.

Beck, Leonard N. *Two "Loaf-Givers" or A Tour through the Gastronomic Libraries of Katherine Golden Bitting and Elizabeth Robins Pennell.* Washington, DC: Library of Congress, 1984.

Belozerskaya, Marina. *Rethinking the Renaissance: Burgundian Arts across Europe.* Cambridge: Cambridge University Press, 2002.

Berg, Maxine. *Luxury & Pleasure in Eighteenth-Century Britain.* Oxford: Oxford University Press, 2005.

Blake, N. F. *Caxton and His World.* London: Andre Deutsch, 1969.

Blunt, Wilfrid, and Sandra Raphael. *The Illustrated Herbal.* London: Frances Lincoln Publishers, 1979.

Boswell, James. *Boswell's Life of Johnson* [1791]. Edited by Charles Grosvenor Osgood. New York: Scribner's Sons, 1917.

Boucher, Jacqueline. "L'alimentation en milieu de cour sous les derniers Valois." In *Pratiques et discours alimentaire à la renaissance,* edited by Jean-Claude Margolin and Robert Sauzet. Paris: Maisonneuve et Larose, 1982.

Breen, T. H. *The Marketplace of Revolution: How Consumer Politics Shaped American Independence.* Oxford: Oxford University Press, 2004.

Brewer, John, and Roy Porter, eds. *Consumption and the World of Goods.* London: Routledge, 1993.

Brown, Peter, and Ivan Day. *Pleasures of the Table: Ritual and Display in the European Dining Room, 1600–1900.* York: York Civic Trust, 1997.

Calmette, Joseph. *The Golden Age of Burgundy.* London: Weidenfeld & Nicolson, 1962. First edition: *Grands ducs de Bourgogne.* Paris: A. Michel, 1949.

Campbell, Susan. *Charleston Kedding: A History of Kitchen Gardening.* London: Ebury Press, 1996.

Carson, Jane. *Colonial Virginia Cookery.* Williamsburg, VA: Colonial Williamsburg Foundation, 1985.

Cartwright, Julia. *Isabella d'Este: A Study of the Renaissance.* New York: E. P. Dutton, 1923.

Chiappini, *La corte estense alla metà del cinquecento: I compendi di Cristoforo di Messisbugo.* Ferrara, Italy: Belriguardo, 1984.

Coe, Sophie D., and Michael D. Coe. *True History of Chocolate.* London: Thames & Hudson, 1996.

Cowan, Brian. *The Social Life of Coffee: The Emergence of the British Coffeehouse.* New Haven, CT: Yale University Press, 2005.

Dalby, Andrew. *Dangerous Tastes: The Story of Spices.* Berkeley: University of California Press, 2000.

David, Elizabeth. *Harvest of the Cold Months: The Social History of Ice and Ices.* New York: Viking, 1995.

———. *Is There a Nutmeg in the House?* New York: Viking, 2001.

Davidson, Alan, ed. *National and Regional Styles of Cookery: Proceedings of the Oxford Symposium on Food and Cookery, 1981.* Totnes, England: Prospect Books, 1981.

———. *Oxford Companion to Food.* Oxford: Oxford University Press, 1999.

Davidson, Caroline. *A Woman's Work Is Never Done: A History of Housework in the British Isles 1650–1950.* London: Chatto & Windus, 1982.

Davies, Norman. *Europe: A History.* New York: Harper Collins, 1998.

Davis, Natalie Zemon. *Society and Culture in Early Modern France.* Stanford, CA: Stanford University Press, 1975.

Del Conte, Anna. *Gastronomy of Italy.* New York: Prentice Hall, 1987.

Dürrschmid, Klaus. *Kochbücher der Renaissance (1450–1600).* Vienna: Universität für Bodenkultur Wien, 2002.

Eamon, William. *Science and the Secrets of Nature: Books of Secrets in Medieval and Early Modern Culture.* Princeton, NJ: Princeton University Press, 1993.

Febvre, Lucien, and Henri-Jean Martin. *The Coming of the Book.* Translated by David Gerard. London: Verso, 1976.

Ferguson, Priscilla Parkhurst. *Accounting for Taste: The Triumph of French Cuisine.* Chicago: University of Chicago Press, 2004.

Flandrin, Jean-Louis. *L'ordre des mets.* Paris: Éditions Odile Jacob, 2002.

Flandrin, Jean-Louis, and Jane Cobbi. *Tables d'hier, tables d'ailleurs.* Paris: Éditions Odile Jacob, 1999.

Flandrin, Jean-Louis, and Massimo Montanari, eds. *Food: A Culinary History.* English edition edited by Albert Sonnenfeld. New York: Columbia University Press, 1999.

Fox, Robert, and Anthony Turner, eds. *Luxury Trades and Consumerism in Ancient Régime Paris.* Aldershot, England: Ashgate, 1998.

Franklin, Alfred. *La vie privée d'autrefois: Les repas.* Paris: Librairie Plon, 1889.

Freedman, Paul, ed. *Food: The History of Taste.* Berkeley: University of California Press, 2007.

Girouard, Mark. *Life in the English Country House.* New Haven, CT: Yale University Press, 1978.

———. *Life in the French Country House.* London: Cassell, 2001.

Goldstein, Darra, ed. *The Gastronomica Reader.* Berkeley: University of California Press, 2010.

Goldstein, Darra, and Kathrin Merkle. *Culinary Cultures of Europe: Identity, Diversity and Dialogue.* Strasbourg: Council of Europe Publishing, 2005.

Gottschalk, Alfred. *Histoire de l'alimentation et de la gastronomie depuis la préhistoire jusqu'à nos jours.* 2 vols. Paris: Hippocrate, 1948.

Guégan, Bertrand. *Le cuisinier français.* Paris: Emile-Paul, 1934.

Hammond, P. W. *Food and Feast in Medieval England.* Phoenix: History Press, 1993.

Harkness, Deborah E. *The Jewel House: Elizabethan London and the Scientific Revolution.* New Haven, CT: Yale University Press, 2007.

Hartley, Dorothy. *Food in England.* London: Macdonald, 1954.

Hauser, Albert. *Das Kochbuch des Balthasar Staindl vom Jahne.* Dietikon, Switzerland: Verlag Bibliophile Druke von Josef Stocker, 1979.

Henisch, Bridget Ann. *Fast and Feast: Food in Medieval Society.* University Park: Pennsylvania State University Press, 1976.

Hess, John L., and Karen Hess. *The Taste of America.* Columbia: University of South Carolina Press, 1989.

Hieatt, Constance B., J. Terry Nutter, and Johnna H. Holloway. *Concordance of English Recipes: Thirteenth through Fifteenth Centuries: Medieval and Renaissance Texts and Studies.* Tempe: Arizona Center for Medieval and Renaissance Studies, 2006.

Houston, R. A. *Literacy in Early Modern Europe.* New York: Longman, 2002.

Huizinga, Johan. *Waning of the Middle Ages.* Mineola, NY: Dover Publications, 1999.

Hyman, Philip, and Mary Hyman. "Printing the Kitchen: French Cookbooks, 1480–1800." In *Food: A Culinary History,* edited by Jean-Louis Flandrin and Massimo Montanari, English edition edited by Albert Sonnenfeld, 394–402. New York: Columbia University Press, 1999.

Johns, Adrian. *The Nature of the Book: Print and Knowledge in the Making.* Chicago: University of Chicago Press, 1998.

Jones, Colin. *Paris: The Biography of a City.* New York: Viking, 2005.

Keay, John. *The Spice Route: A History.* Berkeley: University of California Press, 2006.

Kiple, Kenneth F., and Kriemhild Coneè Ornelas. *The Cambridge World History of Food.* Cambridge: Cambridge University Press, 2000.

Lambert, Carol, ed. *Du manuscrit à la table.* Montreal: Les Presses de l'Université de Montréal, 1992.

Lehmann, Gilly. *The British Housewife: Cookery Books, Cooking and Society in Eighteenth-Century Britain.* Totnes, England: Prospect Books, 2003.

Livres en bouche: Cinq siècles d'art culinaire français. Paris: Bibliothèque nationale de France, Hermann, 2001.

Margolin, J. C., and R. Sauzet, eds. *Pratiques & discours alimentaires à la renaissance.* Actes du Colloque de Tours 1979. Paris: Maisonneufe et Larose, 1982.

Mason, Laura. *Sugar-Plums and Sherbet: The Prehistory of Sweets.* Totnes, England: Prospect Books, 2004.

Maza, Sarah. *Servants and Masters in Eighteenth-Century France.* Princeton, NJ: Princeton University Press, 1983.

McGee, Harold. *The Curious Cook.* San Francisco: North Point Press, 1990.

Mennell, Stephen. *All Manners of Food: Eating and Taste in England and France from the Middle Ages to the Present.* Oxford: Basil Blackwell, 1985.

Mercier, Louis-Sebastien. *Tableau de Paris.* 12 vols. Amsterdam, 1782–88.

Mintz, Sidney W. *Sweetness and Power: The Place of Sugar in Modern History.* London: Penguin, 1985.

Montanari, Massimo. *Food Is Culture.* New York: Columbia University Press, 2006.

Morgan, Kenneth O., ed. *Oxford History of England.* Oxford: Oxford University Press, 1988.

Newnham-Davis, Lieut.-Col. *The Gourmet's Guide to Europe.* 3rd ed. New York: Brentano, 1911.

Norman, Jill. *The Complete Book of Spices.* London: Dorling Kindersley, 1990.

Palmer, Arnold. *Movable Feasts.* Oxford: Oxford University Press, 1952.

Pardailhé-Galabrun, Annik. *The Birth of Intimacy: Privacy and Domestic Life in Early Modern Paris.* Translated by Jocelyn Phelps. Philadelphia: University of Pennsylvania Press, 1991.

Paston-Williams, Sara. *The Art of Dining: A History of Cooking and Eating.* London: National Trust, 1999.

Perry, Charles, ed. *A Baghdad Cookery Book.* Totnes, England: Prospect Books, 2005.

Pinkard, Susan. *A Revolution in Taste: The Rise of French Cuisine.* Cambridge: Cambridge University Press, 2009.

Power, Eileen. *The Goodman of Paris.* London: George Routledge, 1928.

Prentki, Alix. "Repas, tables, et banquets allemands." In *Tables d'hier, tables d'ailleurs,* edited by Jane Cobbi and Jean-Louis Flandrin. Paris: Éditions Odile Jacob, 1999.

Quinzio, Jeri. *Of Sugar and Snow: A History of Ice Cream Making.* Berkeley: University of California Press, 2009.

Reader, John. *Potato: A History of the Propitious Esculent.* New Haven, CT: Yale University Press, 2009.

Redon, Odile, Françoise Sabban, and Silvano Serventi. *The Medieval Kitchen: Recipes from France and Italy.* Chicago: University of Chicago Press, 1998.

Revel, Jean François. *Culture and Cuisine: A Journey through the History of Food.* New York: Doubleday, 1982.

———. *Un festin en paroles: Histoire littéraire de la sensibilité gastronomique de l'antiquité à nos jours.* Paris: Plon, 1995.

Riley, Gillian. *Oxford Companion to Italian Food.* Oxford: Oxford University Press, 2007.

Robinson, Jancis, ed. *The Oxford Companion to Wine.* 2nd ed. Oxford: Oxford University Press, 1999.

Root, Waverly. *The Food of France.* New York: Vintage, 1977.

Rubel, William. *The Magic of Fire: Hearth Cooking: One Hundred Recipes for the Fireplace or Campfire.* New York: Ten Speed Press, 2002.

Saint'Ange, Madame E. de. *Le livre de cuisine.* Paris: Larousse, 1927.

Sambrook, Pamela A., and Peter Brears, eds. *The Country House Kitchen 1650–1900.* London: Alan Sutton Publishing, 1996.

Santich, Barbara. *The Original Mediterranean Cuisine: Medieval Recipes for Today.* Cambridge, MA: Wakefield Press, 1995.

Smithsonian Institution. *Feeding Desire: Design and the Tools of the Table 1500–2005.* New York: Assouline Publishing, 2006.

Spang, Rebecca L. *The Invention of the Restaurant.* Cambridge, MA: Harvard University Press, 2000.

Spencer, Colin. *British Food: An Extraordinary Thousand Years of History.* New York: Columbia University Press, 2002.

Strong, Roy C. *Feast: A History of Grand Eating.* Orlando, FL: Harcourt Publishing, 2002.

Symons, Michael. *A History of Cooks and Cooking.* Urbana: University of Illinois Press, 1998.

Tannahill, Reay. *Food in History*. New York: Stein and Day, 1973.

Thick, Malcolm. "A Close Look at the Composition of Sir Hugh Plat's *Delightes for Ladies*." In *The English Cookery Book: Historical Essays*, edited by Eileen White, 55–71. Totnes, England: Prospect Books, 2004.

Thirsk, Joan. *Food in Early Modern England*. London: Hambledon Continuum, 2007.

Trubek, Amy B. *Haute Cuisine: How the French Invented the Culinary Profession*. Philadelphia: University of Pennsylvania Press, 2000.

Varriano, John. *Tastes and Temptations: Food and Art in Renaissance Italy*. Berkeley: University of California Press, 2009.

Visser, Margaret. *Much Depends on Dinner: The Extraordinary History and Mythology, Allure and Obsessions, Perils and Taboos of an Ordinary Meal*. New York: Grove, 1986.

Weatherill, Lorna. *Consumer Behavior and Material Culture in Britain 1660–1760*. London: Routledge, 1988.

Wechsberg, Joseph. *The Cooking of Vienna's Empire*. New York: Time-Life, 1968.

Wheaton, Barbara Ketcham. *Savoring the Past*. Philadelphia: University of Pennsylvania Press, 1983.

White, Eileen, ed. *The English Cookery Book: Historical Essays*. Totnes, England: Prospect Books, 2004.

Wilson, C. Anne. *Food & Drink in Britain: From the Stone Age to Recent Times*. London: Constable, 1973.

Wilson, Mary Tolford. "The First American Cookbook." In *American Cookery* [1796] by Amelia Simmons (facsimile). New York: Oxford University Press, 1958.

Woolgar, M. C. *Great Household in Late Medieval England*. New Haven, CT: Yale University Press, 1999.

Wright, Clifford A. *A Mediterranean Feast*. New York: Morrow, 1999.

Young, Carolin C. *Apples of Gold in Settings of Silver: Stories of Dinner as a Work of Art*. New York: Simon & Schuster, 2002.

BIBLIOGRAPHIES OF EUROPEAN AND AMERICAN COOKBOOKS When one is collecting cookbooks, specialized bibliographies are indispensable sources, and they have also been invaluable in writing this history. For European and American books, these are the most important.

Bagnasco, Orazio. *Catalogo del fondo italiano e latino delle opera di gastronomia sec. xiv–xix*. Canton Ticino: Edizione B.IN.G., 1994.

Bitting, Katherine Golden. *Gastronomic Bibliography*. San Francisco, 1939. Reprint: Mansfield, CT: Martino Publishing, 2004.

Cagle, William R. *A Matter of Taste: A Bibliographic Catalogue of the Gernon Collection of Books on Food and Drink*. New York: Garland Publishing, 1990.

Henssler, Maria Paleari. *Bibliografia latino-italiana di gastronomia*. Milan: Chimera Editore, 2001.

Lowenstein, Eleanor. *American Cookery Books 1742–1860*. Worcester, NY: American Antiquarian Society, 1972.

Maclean, Virginia. *A Short-Title Catalogue of Household and Cookery Books Published in the English Tongue, 1701–1800*. Totnes, England: Prospect Books, 1981.

Notaker, Henry. *Printed Cookbooks in Europe, 1470–1700*. New Castle, DE: Oak Knoll Books, 2010.

Oberlé, Gérard. *Les fastes de Bacchus et de Comus: ou histoire du boire et du manger en Europe, de l'antiquité a nos jours, à travers les livres*. Paris: Belfond, 1989.

Oxford, Arnold Whitaker. *English Cookery Books, to the Year 1850*. London: Holland Press, 1977.

Palmer, Carmen Simon. *Bibliografia de la gastronomia española: Notas para su realización*. Madrid: Ediciones Velazquez, 1997.

Pennell, Elizabeth. *My Cookery Books*. Boston: Houghton Mifflin, 1903. Facsimile edition: Nabu Press, 2010.

Simon, Andre L. *Bibliotheca gastronomica: A Catalogue of Books and Documents on Gastronomy*. London: Wine and Food Society, 1953.

Vicaire, Georges. *Bibliographie gastronomique* [1890]. Reprint: London: Holland Press, 1954.

Weiss, Hans U. *Gastronomia: Eine Bibliographie der deutschsprachigen Gastronomie 1485–1914*. Zürich: Bibliotheca Gastronomica, 1996.

Westbury, Lord Richard. *Handlist of Italian Cookery Books*. Florence: Leo S. Olschki-Editore, 1963.

GENERAL INDEX

RECIPE INDEX

California Studies in Food and Culture

DARRA GOLDSTEIN, EDITOR

University of California Press, one of the most distinguished university presses in the United States, enriches lives around the world by advancing scholarship in the humanities, social sciences, and natural sciences. Its activities are supported by the UC Press Foundation and by philanthropic contributions from individuals and institutions. For more information, visit www.ucpress.edu.

University of California Press
Berkeley and Los Angeles, California

University of California Press, Ltd.
London, England

Text: 10.25/14.75 Adobe Caslon
Display: Adobe Caslon; DIN
Designer: Nola Burger
Compositor: Integrated Composition Systems
Photographer: John Kiffe
Indexer: Thérèse Shere
Printer and binder: Thomson-Shore, Inc.

Library of Congress Cataloging-in-Publication Data

Willan, Anne.
 The cookbook library : four centuries of the cooks, writers, and recipes that made the modern cookbook /
Anne Willan ; with Mark Cherniavsky and Kyri Claflin.
    p.   cm. (California studies in food and culture ; v.35)
 Includes bibliographical references and index.
 ISBN 978-0-520-24400-9 (cloth : alk. paper)
  1. Cooking—History. 2. Cookbooks. I. Cherniavsky, Mark,
1937– II. Claflin, Kyri. III. Title.
  TX645.W53 2012
  641.509—dc23

                                            2011024489

Manufactured in the United States of America

21 20 19 18 17 16 15 14 13 12
10 9 8 7 6 5 4 3 2

The paper used in this publication meets the minimum requirements of ANSI/NISO z39.48–1992 (R 1997) (*Permanence of Paper*).

TITLE PAGE ILLUSTRATION: Detail from Francis Sandford, *The History of the Coronation*. Full image on page 135.

PICTURE CREDITS: Unless otherwise noted, illustrations are in the Willan/Cherniavsky collection.

p. 15 *A Princely Banquet,* 1491 (woodcut) (b/w photo) by German School (fifteenth century). Private collection/The Bridgeman Art Library. Nationality/copyright status: German/out of copyright.

p. 16 Monastery of Monte Oliveto Maggiore. Ministry of Cultural Heritage and Activities. Photo: Soprintendenza BSAE of Siena and Grosseto.

p. 22 Ms. 4182 *Theatrum sanitatis,* pl. CLX (Rome, Casanatense Library, MiBAC-Italy).

p. 28 © Editions Slatkine, Paul-Jacques Malouin, "Description et détails des arts du meunier, du vermicelier et du boulanger," 1767, in *Les Arts des Aliments,* 1984.

p. 41 © Royal Library of Belgium.

p. 42 Réunion des Musées Nationaux/Art Resource, NY.

p. 44 © Royal Library of Belgium.

p. 49 Image courtesy of Octavo Corp. and Library of Congress.

p. 51 Herzog August Bibliothek Wolfenbüttel: 276 Quod. (2).

pp. 58–59 © The British Library Board. Licence Number: ANNWIL01. All rights reserved.

p. 61 © Reading Museum Service, Reading Borough Council. All rights reserved.

p. 62 © The Metropolitan Museum of Art/Art Resource, NY.

p. 81 © Editions Slatkine, Henri-Louis Duhamel du Monceau, "Art de raffiner le sucre," 1764, in *Les Arts des Aliments,* 1984.

p. 96 Georg Olms Verlag AG: Hildesheim–Zürich–New York. Reproduced from *Ein new Kochbuch.* Hildesheim, New York: Olms Presse, 1980 reprint of 1581 edition.

pp. 101 and *102* Georg Olms Verlag AG: Hildesheim–Zürich–New York. Reproduced from *Ein new Kochbuch.* Hildesheim, New York: Olms Presse, 1980 reprint of 1581 edition.

p. 106 The Bodleian Libraries, University of Oxford (Douce W 23, fol. A2v and A3r).

p. 107 The Master and Fellows of Corpus Christi College, Cambridge.

p. 153 Reprinted from Denis Diderot and Jean Le Rond d'Alembert, *Encyclopédie, ou Dictionnaire Raisonné des Sciences, des Arts et des Métiers,* vol. II, p. 281, Pergamon Press: 1969.

p. 226 Portrait of Antoine Augustin Parmentier (1737–1813) (oil on canvas) by François Dumont (1751–1831), Faculté de Pharmacie, Paris, France/Archives Charmet/The Bridgeman Art Library. Nationality/copyright status: French / out of copyright.

p. 230 Collection American Folk Art Museum, New York.

p. 232 By permission of Oxford University Press.

p. 236 Photograph © 2012 Museum of Fine Arts, Boston.